A Topical Guide to the STRATEGIES Boxes

W9-AXR-368

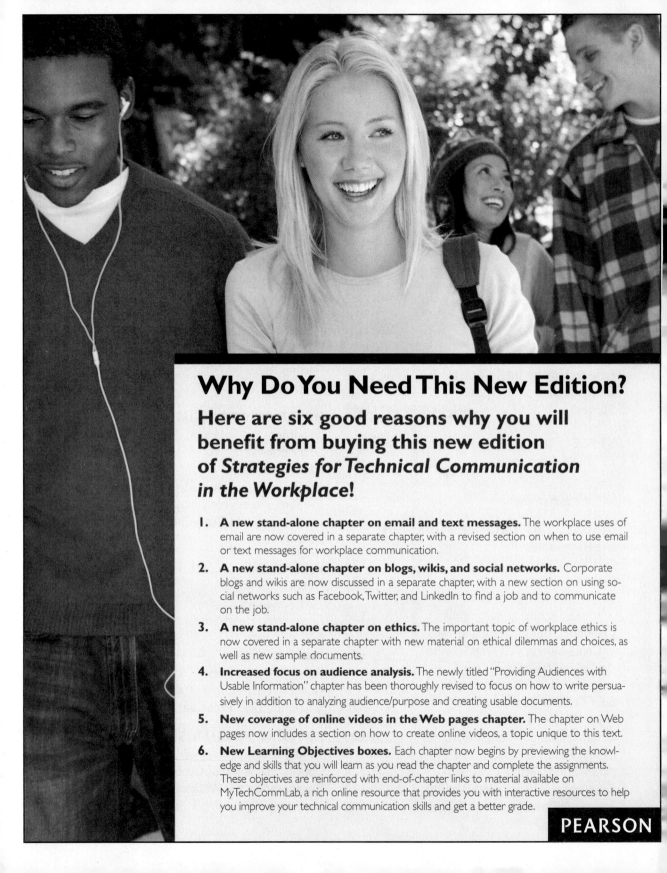

Why Do You Need This New Edition?

Here are six good reasons why you will benefit from buying this new edition of *Strategies for Technical Communication in the Workplace!*

1. **A new stand-alone chapter on email and text messages.** The workplace uses of email are now covered in a separate chapter, with a revised section on when to use email or text messages for workplace communication.

2. **A new stand-alone chapter on blogs, wikis, and social networks.** Corporate blogs and wikis are now discussed in a separate chapter, with a new section on using social networks such as Facebook, Twitter, and LinkedIn to find a job and to communicate on the job.

3. **A new stand-alone chapter on ethics.** The important topic of workplace ethics is now covered in a separate chapter with new material on ethical dilemmas and choices, as well as new sample documents.

4. **Increased focus on audience analysis.** The newly titled "Providing Audiences with Usable Information" chapter has been thoroughly revised to focus on how to write persuasively in addition to analyzing audience/purpose and creating usable documents.

5. **New coverage of online videos in the Web pages chapter.** The chapter on Web pages now includes a section on how to create online videos, a topic unique to this text.

6. **New Learning Objectives boxes.** Each chapter now begins by previewing the knowledge and skills that you will learn as you read the chapter and complete the assignments. These objectives are reinforced with end-of-chapter links to material available on MyTechCommLab, a rich online resource that provides you with interactive resources to help you improve your technical communication skills and get a better grade.

PEARSON

STRATEGIES FOR
Technical Communication in the Workplace

SECOND EDITION

Laura J. Gurak
University of Minnesota

John M. Lannon
University of Massachusetts–Dartmouth

PEARSON

Boston   Columbus   Indianapolis   New York   San Francisco   Upper Saddle River
Amsterdam   Cape Town   Dubai   London   Madrid   Milan   Munich   Paris   Montréal   Toronto
Delhi   Mexico City   São Paulo   Sydney   Hong Kong   Seoul   Singapore   Taipei   Tokyo

Executive Editor: Suzanne Phelps Chambers
Development Editor: Bruce Cantley
Executive Marketing Manager: Joyce Nilsen
Editorial Assistant: Laney Whitt
Senior Supplements Editor: Donna Campion
Executive Digital Producer: Stefanie A. Snajder
Digital Project Manager: Janell Lantana
Digital Editor: Sara Gordus

Production Manager: Ellen MacElree
Project Coordination, Text Design, and Electronic Page Makeup: Integra
Cover Designer/Manager: John Callahan
Cover Images: Denis Babenko/Shutterstock
Senior Manufacturing Buyer: Roy L. Pickering, Jr.
Printer/Binder: R. R. Donnelley & Sons, Crawfordsville
Cover Printer: Lehigh-Phoenix Color/Hagerstown

Between the time the Web site information is gathered and published, some sites may have closed. Also, the transcription of URLs can result in typographical errors. The publisher would appreciate notification where these occur so that they may be corrected in subsequent editions.

Many of the designations used by manufacturers and sellers to distinguish their products are claimed as trademarks. Where these designations appear in the book, and Pearson Education was aware of a trademark claim, the designations have been printed in initial caps.

Library of Congress Cataloging-in-Publication Data
Gurak, Laura J.
  Strategies for technical communication in the workplace / Laura J.
Gurak, John M. Lannon.
    p. cm.
  Includes bibliographical references and index.
  ISBN-13: 978-0-205-24552-9
  ISBN-10: 0-205-24552-8
  1. Business communication.   2. Communication of technical information.
  3. Technical writing.   I. Lannon, John M.   II. Title.
  HF5718.G87 2013
  658.4'5—dc23

                                                                    2011030314

For permission to use copyrighted material, grateful acknowledgment is made to the copyright holders on pp. 485–486, which are hereby made part of this copyright page.

10 9 8 7 6 5 4 3 2 1—DOC—16 15 14 13

www.pearsonhighered.com

ISBN-13: 978-0-205-24552-9
ISBN-10:   0-205-24552-8

BRIEF CONTENTS

v

DETAILED CONTENTS

3   The Research Process in Technical Communication   31

4   Providing Audiences with Usable Information   51

5 Recognizing Ethical Issues in Technical Communication   72

PART 2   Blueprints   81

6 Structuring Information for Your Readers   82

7 Writing with a Readable Style   102

8 Using Audience-Centered Visuals   120

12 Definitions   217

18 Proposals 340

PART 4 Digital Media and Presentations 363

19 Email and Text Messages 364

Appendices 426

B   A Brief Handbook

PREFACE

OVERVIEW

In today's workplace, professionals in all fields are expected to adapt to a variety of communication situations. Virtually everyone must be able to write routine workplace documents such as memos, emails, letters, and informal reports. In addition, they must create more complex forms of communication such as formal reports and proposals, instructions, definitions and descriptions, Web pages, oral presentations, video presentations, and more. All the while, these professionals must also negotiate technological innovations, communicate in a global marketplace, work in teams, write persuasively, research effectively, and understand the ethical implications of the documents they produce.

We wrote the first edition of *Strategies for Technical Communication in the Workplace* as a medium-length textbook that covers all the preceding topics thoroughly and concisely. Like the first edition, this second edition text draws on the strengths of our other two technical communication books: the best-selling *Technical Communication*, 12th edition, and *Concise Guide to Technical Communication*, 3rd edition. We hope that students and faculty alike will appreciate the new edition of this distinctive textbook.

NEW TO THE SECOND EDITION

We have targeted most of our second edition changes to Parts 1 and 4 of the book to provide more background on such topics as audience analysis and ethics (Part 1) and more about the latest technological innovations in today's workplace (Part 4). Following is a quick guide to what is new in this edition.

An Expanded Part 1 on Technical Communication Foundations

To provide more information on foundational topics in technical communication, we have split the first edition's multitopic Chapter 2 into three distinct chapters. Chapter 2 now focuses exclusively on the related topics of teamwork and global issues in technical communication. Persuasion, formerly in Chapter 2, has been moved into Chapter 4 (now titled "Providing Audiences with Usable Information"), where it allows for an increased emphasis on audience analysis. The important topic of workplace ethics, also previously included in Chapter 2, is in a new stand-alone Chapter 5 ("Recognizing Ethical Issues in Technical Communication") and has been expanded to include discussions of ethical dilemmas and types of ethical choices. This chapter also includes relevant new figures.

A Thoroughly Revised Part 4 on Digital Media and Presentations

Part 4 conforms to the latest innovations in digital workplace communication and oral presentations. Workplace uses of email are now covered in a stand-alone chapter (Chapter 19, "Email and Text Messages"), with a new up-to-the-minute section on using text messages on the job. Corporate blogs and wikis are now discussed in a stand-alone chapter (Chapter 20, "Blogs, Wikis, and Social Networks"), with a brand new section on using social networks (such as Facebook, Twitter, MySpace, and LinkedIn) to communicate on the job or to enhance one's career. The chapter on Web pages (Chapter 21, now titled "Web Pages and Online Videos") has been expanded to include coverage of online videos, increasingly a component of today's corporate Web sites. Finally, Chapter 22 ("Oral Presentations") includes new material on the various types of presentation software available.

New Learning Objectives

Learning Objectives boxes have now been added to every chapter's opening page to give students a goal-oriented preview of the skills they will be expected to learn. These Learning Objectives are followed up at chapter's end with links to topic-specific areas of Pearson's MyTechCommLab.

KEY FEATURES

To help you get a better idea how *Strategies* works as a whole, following is a point-by-point discussion of the key features of this book.

Complete but Streamlined Coverage

Strategies includes all topics essential for an undergraduate technical communication course in a compact yet thorough format. The book covers everything technical communicators need to know—from writing basic letters and memos, to writing complex proposals and formal reports, to delivering oral presentations and writing for the Web—in roughly 500 pages. In addition, *Strategies* offers innovative coverage of emerging technologies used in the workplace, including text messages, social networks, and online videos.

Emphasis on Student Practice

This book is guided by the idea of providing students with practical, accessible concepts that are easy to follow and that get students writing and designing documents immediately. One key feature, as the title suggests, is the Strategies box, which provides step-by-step advice to follow in writing and discussing a given document. In addition, chapters in Parts 3 and 4 emphasize the importance of "doing" immediately via the Let's Get Started feature; students are asked to draft their best version of each chapter's document type or communication situation before they read the chapter. Then, as they work through the chapter content, students are encouraged to review and revise their original work. Finally, every chapter, including the foundational and "blueprints" chapters in Parts 1 and 2, includes Applications exercises, grouped into general, collaborative, global, and computer/Web-based categories.

Clear Explanations and Straightforward Organization

As we wrote and organized this book, we kept in mind five essential questions students most frequently ask: "What needs to be done?", "What should it look like?", "How do I do it?", "What should be avoided?", and "How well have I done it?" The features described previously focus on these questions. Also, marginal notes summarize and reinforce main points in each chapter.

Chapter Outlines and Learning Objectives boxes at the beginning of each chapter preview what is to come, whereas the heading structure moves logically from point to point. In addition, the Strategies boxes in each chapter provide a systematic way to prepare documents or presentations.

The chapter sequence in *Strategies* proceeds from general foundational concepts and blueprints in Parts 1 and 2 to cumulatively more complex writing and communicating situations in Parts 3 and 4.

Practical Pedagogical Features

Strategies includes several practical, easy-to-access pedagogical tools. These features include

- **Chapter Outlines and Learning Objectives.** On the opening page of each chapter, the outlines provide a quick orientation to the chapter topics and sequence, whereas the learning objectives emphasize the practical skills students can expect to acquire.

- **Let's Get Started boxes.** At the beginning of each chapter in Parts 3 and 4, the Let's Get Started boxes encourage students to begin "doing" immediately by producing the type of draft document or communication product discussed in each chapter based on their prior knowledge. Then as they work through the chapter, students can refine their draft.

- **Strategies boxes.** Featured in every chapter, the "Strategies" boxes summarize key strategies discussed in the text, and provide additional pointers for approaching each communication situation.

- **Checklists.** End-of-chapter "Checklists" summarize each chapter, and more importantly, they emphasize "doing" by asking students to check off each item as they review their work.

- **Applications.** Called "applications" rather than "exercises" to emphasize applied learning, the end-of-chapter Applications fall into four categories: General Applications (for individual practice), Team Applications (for pair or group practice), Global Applications (for highlighting global issues in workplace communication), and Computer/Web-based Applications (for highlighting the use of technology in workplace communication).

Realistic and Accessible Annotated Model Documents

Model documents resemble the kinds of documents students will write in the workplace. Accessible, engaging, and easy to emulate, most of these documents are fully annotated.

Consistent Focus on Audience and Purpose

Technical communication in the workplace is more than a mere exercise in "information transfer"; it is also a social transaction involving individuals, teams, companies, and organizations that are national and international in scope. In the contemporary workplace, a one-size-fits-all approach to technical communication doesn't work. Effective communication must be tailored for different audiences and different purposes. Today's communicator must be smart about researching, summarizing, and customizing information to meet many different situations. *Strategies* has therefore been designed to provide much more than a "cookie cutter" approach to creating typical workplace documents and making presentations by focusing on key rhetorical principles of audience and purpose.

The Latest Technology and Global Issues Coverage

With the Internet and digital technology at our fingertips and with companies and teams spread across the world, communication reaches a wide audience and often is transmitted instantly. We receive or convey professional information in a variety of ways—handwritten, in word-processed documents, via email or text messaging; in video format; as a Web page; via blogs, wikis, or social networks; or as live presentations—and each medium and potential audience brings with it unique challenges about how to best present the information. *Strategies* incorporates relevant technology coverage and stresses the importance of thinking about global audiences wherever relevant.

ORGANIZATION OF THE BOOK

Strategies begins with foundational concepts, then moves to "blueprints," and finally applies the foundations and blueprints to increasingly complex documents and communication situations.

- **Part 1 ("Foundations")** introduces the underlying concepts for creating effective technical communication. This section provides a definition of technical communication (Chapter 1); discussions of teamwork and global issues (Chapter 2); coverage of research as a pivotal part of technical communication (Chapter 3); an introduction to the analysis of audience, purpose, and other factors (Chapter 4), and in-depth coverage of workplace ethics (Chapter 5).

- **Part 2 ("Blueprints")** builds upon Part 1 by discussing four basic considerations for approaching each type of workplace document or communication situation: understandable structure (Chapter 6), readable style (Chapter 7), audience-centered visuals (Chapter 8), and user-friendly design (Chapter 9).

- **Part 3 ("Documents")** applies the previous foundations and blueprints, presenting increasingly complex types of print documents. This section begins with the types of documents students need to get hired and concludes with the two most complex types of documents: formal reports and proposals. Specific documents covered in Part 3 include résumés and other employment materials (Chapter 10), memos and letters (Chapter 11), definitions (Chapter 12), descriptions (Chapter 13), instructions and procedures (Chapter 14), summaries (Chapter 15), informal reports (Chapter 16), formal reports (Chapter 17), and proposals (Chapter 18).

- **Part 4 ("Digital Media and Presentations")** provides guidance for creating documents for digital media and for giving oral presentations. Included are chapters on email and text messages (Chapter 19); blogs, wikis, and social networks (Chapter 20); Web pages and online video (Chapter 21); and oral presentations (Chapter 22).

- **Appendices A ("Documenting Sources") and B ("Grammar, Usage, and Mechanics")** offer guidance on citations and grammar. Appendix A includes guidelines for avoiding plagiarism and documenting sources completely and accurately. Appendix B provides a brief handbook of grammar, punctuation, mechanics, and usage. This appendix also includes useful advice on formatting lists and using transitions in written work.

SUPPLEMENTS TO THE BOOK

Accompanying *Strategies* is a wide array of instructor and student supplements, most of which are available packaged with this book at no additional cost.

For Instructors

- **Instructor's Manual, by Lee Scholder, University of Minnesota, and Daun Daemon, North Carolina State University.** Available both in print and online, the Instructor's Manual includes general and chapter-by-chapter teaching tips, sample syllabi, and additional chapter exercises and quizzes. In addition, the

Instructor's Manual provides guidance on using MyTechCommLab and the companion Web site as online teaching resources.

- **Companion Web site <www.pearsonhighered.com/gurak>.** The "Instructor Resources" portion of the companion Web site includes teaching strategies, PowerPoint slides, Web links, sample syllabi, and the complete text of the Instructor's Manual in downloadable PDF format.

For Students

- **Companion Web site <www.pearsonhighered.com/gurak>.** The companion Web site features self-scoring multiple choice quizzes, exercises, case studies, tutorials, key terms flashcards, and printable versions of the book's checklists and forms.

- **MyTechCommLab <www.mytechcommlab.com>.** Instructors who package MyTechCommLab with *Strategies* provide their students with a comprehensive resource that offers the best multimedia support for technical communication in one integrated, easy-to-use site. Features include a wide selection of interactive model documents; realistic case studies covering all areas of the technical communication field; and comprehensive sections on document design, writing, grammar, and research that include audio and video lessons, practice quizzes and assignments, and much more. MyTechCommLab's grammar diagnostics produce personalized study plans that help students improve their grammar skills outside of classroom time. A dynamic Composing space provides students with writing, grammar, research, and online tutoring help in one convenient place, with flexible commenting tools that make peer review projects easier to execute. For instructors, MyTechCommLab's commenting tools and gradebook help reduce the amount of time they spend grading assignments and make it easy to capture, assess, and manage student submissions and practice results. MyTechCommLab is available packaged with Strategies at no additional cost or for purchase at <www.mytechcommlab.com>.

- **Interactive Pearson eText.** A dynamic, online version of the text is available with a subscription to MyTechCommLab. Icons throughout the text link students to animations, interactive documents, case studies, and activities to create an enriched, interactive learning experience for students.

- **À la Carte Edition.** Students want choices, so we've created a line of highly portable and affordable books which gives them just that: our *à la Carte* editions. *Strategies for Technical Communication in the Workplace, à la Carte* edition features the exact same content from the traditional textbook in a convenient notebook-ready, loose-leaf version—allowing students to take only what they need to class. Best of all? Our *Books à la Carte* titles offer students a savings and typically cost less than a used textbook!

- **CourseSmart.** Students can subscribe to *Strategies* as a CourseSmart eText (at CourseSmart.com). The site includes all of the book's content in a format that enables students to search the text, bookmark passages, save their own notes, and print reading assignments that incorporate lecture notes.

- *Resources for Technical Communication,* **Second Edition (ISBN: 0-321-45081-7).** This print supplement offers a wide range of sample documents for use in technical communication courses, including letters, proposals, reports, memos, emails, résumés, abstracts, instructions, descriptions, and slide presentations.

ACKNOWLEDGMENTS

We appreciate the valuable advice from our reviewers, who helped us determine the direction of this revision: Michael Avery, Jefferson Community College; Teresa Foxworthy Cook, University of Cincinnati; Laura H. Davis, Cleveland Community College; Carolyn Kusbit Dunn, East Carolina University; Sean Flannery, Immaculata University; Terri Gordon, Lake Michigan College; Michael F. Johanyak, The University of Akron; Christine Laursen, Red Rocks Community College; Lynnette Porter, Embry-Riddle Aeronautical University; Erin M. Price, Bismarck State College; Anne Regan, California Polytechnic State University; Betty H. Stack, Rowan Cabarrus Community College; Barry Thatcher, New Mexico State University; and Candace A. Welhausen, The Georgia Institute of Technology.

In addition, we thank the reviewers who helped shape the first edition of this book: Carol Ann Britt, San Antonio College; Sherry A. Cisler, Arizona State University at the West Campus; Michael Creeden, Florida International University; Michael-John DePalma, University of New Hampshire; Leslie Janac, Blinn College-Bryan Campus; Clay Kinchen Smith, Santa Fe College; Nancy R. MacKenzie, Minnesota State University, Mankato; Lisa Meloncon, University of Cincinnati; Traci Nathans-Kelly, University of Wisconsin–Madison; Julianne Newmark, New Mexico Tech; Barbara Rau Kyle, University of Central Florida; Kelly Sassi, North Dakota State University; Carey E. Smitherman, Worcester State College; Karina Stokes, University of Houston–Downtown; Suba Subbarao, Oakland Community College; Ronald J. Tulley, The University of Findlay; and Miriam F. Williams, Texas State University.

A special thanks to our students who allowed us to reproduce versions of their work and who are named in the text. From Suzanne Phelps Chambers, Joe Opiela, Brad Potthoff, Mary Ellen Curley, Ellen MacElree, and Joyce Nilsen we received outstanding editorial guidance and support. Thank you to Lee Scholder for her work preparing the first edition of the Instructor's Manual and to Daun Daemon for her work revising the Instructor's Manual for its second edition. Many thanks to Bruce Cantley for his generous and unflagging development help and invaluable ideas and to Martha Beyerlein for expertly managing production.

—**Laura J. Gurak and John M. Lannon**

Foundations

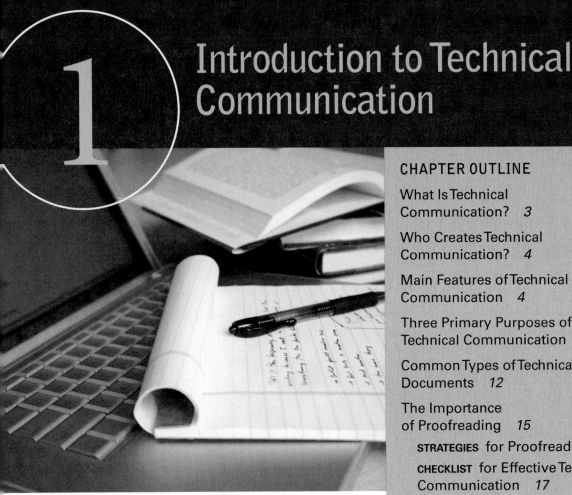

1 Introduction to Technical Communication

LEARNING OBJECTIVES FOR THIS CHAPTER

- ▶ Define technical communication
- ▶ Envision how people at work create technical communication
- ▶ Describe the key characteristics of effective technical communication
- ▶ List the primary purposes of technical documents
- ▶ Recognize typical technical documents
- ▶ Proofread effectively

WHAT IS TECHNICAL COMMUNICATION?

Technical communication is the exchange of information that helps people interact with technology, advance workplace goals, and solve complex problems.

    We live in a world in which many of our everyday actions depend on complex but usable technical information. When you purchase a cell phone, you immediately turn to the instruction manual. When you install any new device, from a DVD player to a microwave oven to a cable modem or computer, you look for the setup information as soon as you open the box. From banking systems to online courses to business negotiations, countless aspects of daily life are affected by technology. To interact with technology in so many ways, we all rely on technical information that is easy to understand and use. In our daily lives, technical communication answers questions such as these:

- How do I set up my new Web camera?
- Which button on the ATM do I press to obtain my monthly activity summary?
- How do I paste a digital photo into a text document and resize the image?

    In the workplace, we are not only consumers of technical communication but also producers. People might need information to complete a task, answer a question, solve a problem, or make a decision. Any document or presentation we prepare at work (memo, letter, report, Web page, PowerPoint presentation) should advance the goals of the intended audience. On the job, technical communication might answer questions such as these:

- What is our competition doing and how should we respond?
- What new government regulations should we address?
- What new technology should our company be thinking about?

    Technical information is also used in more specialized settings. For example, a physician performing heart surgery must have clear information about how to install a pacemaker. A government research scientist must have accurate instructions about how to write a grant or how to perform a particular experiment. An engineer must have access to the correct specifications for designing a bridge or configuring a software application. In specialized settings, technical communication answers questions such as these:

- Do the benefits of the Lyme disease vaccine outweigh its risks?
- What are the technical limits to wind energy?
- How effectively will the new heating system circulate in the top floors of the new office complex?

Definition of technical communication

Technical communication helps us interact with technology in our daily lives

Day-to-day questions

Technical communication helps advance workplace goals

Workplace questions

Technical communication helps specialists solve complex problems

Specialized questions

Technical communication differs from most academic writing

In first-year writing (freshman composition) or expository writing, the emphasis typically is on one type of document: the traditional college essay. Technical documents differ from college essays in that they are

- **Reader based:** For a technical document, you research, write, and design your message not from your own personal perspective but according to the needs of your readers. Professors read to *test* your knowledge, but colleagues, customers, and supervisors will read to *use* your knowledge.

- **Task oriented:** Technical documents are typically oriented toward completing a task, filling a need, or solving a problem, rather than supporting a personal stance, as in an academic essay.

- **Context sensitive:** Technical documents are written with the context and situation in mind (e.g., the politics of what's happening at work or government regulations that affect what the document needs to contain).

- **Design based:** Unlike college essays, which take essentially one shape (paragraphs of text), a technical document may take the form of a brochure, a memo, a report with different sections, a numbered set of instructions, a blog, or a Web site.

- **Written, visual, digital, and oral:** This book refers to "technical communication" and not "technical writing" because *communication* implies more than just words on a page. Technical communication also includes using visuals, working with digital media, and making oral presentations.

As you work on the assignments for this course, the skills you learned in previous writing classes will remain important, but the writing will often be different.

WHO CREATES TECHNICAL COMMUNICATION?

Anyone in a workplace setting can be a technical communicator

Virtually all professionals, at some point, function as technical communicators. Experts in any field are often required to present their knowledge to nonexpert audiences. For instance, the writer of instructions for uploading new software would need to be sure that a general audience could perform the task without having to call a customer service representative; a manager preparing a presentation for a client would need to create clear and concise PowerPoint slides; and a nuclear engineer testifying before Congress would need to write a report explaining nuclear science in nonscientific language to policy makers.

MAIN FEATURES OF TECHNICAL COMMUNICATION

Creating effective documents is at the core of technical communication

Despite the importance of phone calls, face-to-face conversations, and meetings, writing and producing paper and electronic documents remain at the core of technical communication. Such communication is most effective when it displays the features previewed on the following pages and covered in later chapters.

Technical Communication Focuses on the Reader Not the Writer

Unlike poetry, fiction, or essays, technical documents rarely focus on the author's personal thoughts and feelings. This doesn't mean that technical documents should have no personality (or voice), but it does mean that the needs of your readers must come first. Users of technical communication are only interested in you, the communicator, to the extent that they want to know what you have done, what you recommend, or how you speak for your company or organization. This type of communication is called "user-centered communication" (see Figure 1.1). User-centered communication requires a focus on the people who will be *using* the document. What do your readers need to know? What tasks are they trying to perform?

Produce user-centered documents

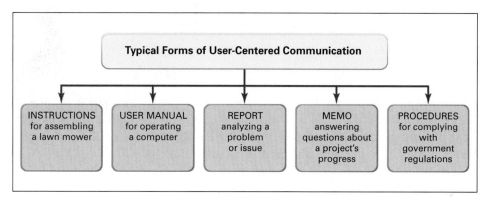

FIGURE 1.1
User-centered communication

Placing the reader's needs and interests first takes practice because many of us are taught to write from our own perspectives. For instance, assume you've been asked to create a set of instructions that explain how people in the community can bring household hazardous waste (gasoline, paint) for recycling. Assume also that you live in the neighborhood near the recycling center and often visit that location. In this instance, you could easily forget to include a map and directions to the center, unless you focus consistently on your actual readers—people who are new in town, people who don't live close to the facility, and so on.

Learn to put yourself in the reader's place

Technical Communication Is Efficient and Accessible

When technical communication is efficient and accessible, users can actually find the information they need and get their questions answered quickly. For instance, in the bioremediation document (Figure 1.3, page 9), a scientific topic is presented so that the general public can make sense of it.

Produce documents that are easy for readers to use

People using a technical document often go back and forth: instead of reading from beginning to end, they look up the information they need at a particular

Make documents easy to navigate

moment. For readers to find what they need, a document has to be easy to navigate in its layout on the page or screen.

Technical Communication Is Clear and Relevant

Write clearly

Technical communication uses clear language. For example, the instructions for using a fire extinguisher (Figure 1.4, page 10) are written for a wide range of readers. Likewise, the letter from the company's general manager to a potential client (Figure 1.5, page 13) is another example of clear communication.

Provide only relevant information

Information is relevant if the audience can apply it to the task at hand. Say, for instance, that a person is interested in learning to use Internet service provider (ISP) software to connect to the Internet: In this case, the documentation should explain how to install the software and connect to the ISP instead of digressing into a history of how the Internet developed.

Technical Communication Uses Media Effectively

Use the media that suit your purpose

Say you are writing a report for a team at work, and team members are situated in three different countries; in this situation, paper is probably not the best medium for delivering the document. Instead, a PDF version, available on the Web or via the company's intranet, would be more effective.

Use an appropriate combination of text, visuals, and sound

Effective use of media also requires an appropriate combination of words, pictures or other visuals, and sounds (as in videos and podcasts). Some documents, such as formal letters, rely heavily or solely on words; other documents, such as instructions, blend words and pictures or diagrams.

Technical Communication Is Created by Both Individuals and Teams

Learn to work with teams when preparing technical documents

Instead of being produced by a lone writer, most complex documents are created by teams of writers, Web designers, engineers or scientists, managers, and legal experts, among others. Teams may consist of people from one site or location, but increasingly, members are distributed across different job sites, time zones, and countries.

Technical Communication Targets a Global Audience

Because we are electronically linked, our global community shares social, political, and financial interests. Corporations are increasingly multinational. Research crosses national boundaries, and people transact across cultures with documents such as these (Weymouth 143):

- scientific reports and articles on AIDS, influenza, and other diseases
- studies of global pollution and industrial emissions
- specifications for hydroelectric dams and other engineering projects
- operating instructions for appliances and electronic equipment

Documents geared toward an international audience

To address diverse communities, any document needs to connect with everyone involved. Also, the message must embody respect for language differences as well as cultural differences.

Technical Communication Is Persuasive and Truthful

Persuasion means trying to influence someone's actions, opinions, or decisions. In the workplace, we rely on persuasion daily: to win coworker support, to attract clients and customers, or to request funding. But changing someone's mind is never easy, and sometimes it is impossible. Your success will depend on who you are trying to persuade, what you are requesting, and how entrenched they are in their own views.

All technical documents are persuasive, in some sense. Some documents, such as (the letter in Figure 1.5,) are explicitly persuasive, in that the writer is trying to convince the reader that the proposed project is the right choice. Other documents, such as the instructions in Figure 1.4, are mainly informative, but they are also implicitly persuasive: The writer is also trying to show readers that the fire extinguisher is easy to use and safe.

All documents are at least in part persuasive

In short, a technical communicator is a problem solver and, as such, must be aware of the best balance between providing readers with the information they need and persuading them to respond as desired, as illustrated in Figure 1.2.

Balance information and persuasion

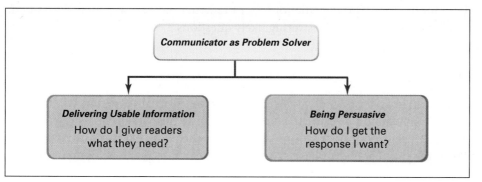

FIGURE 1.2
Balancing information and persuasion

All documents must
be ethical

Be careful though to not let your persuasive goal prevent you from writing ethically. Even when you need to be overtly persuasive, as in a sales proposal, honesty is essential. A document that is highly persuasive but in some way dishonest may influence readers in the short term but will lead to long-term problems. You will lose credibility with the client or your boss and could potentially damage a working relationship for life.

Technical Communication Is Based on Research

Base your
documents on
careful research

Watch the Video
on Characteristics
of Technical Communi-
cation at
mytechcommlab

Even routine technical documents produced on the job are based to some extent on research. For example, though a memo or email may not require extensive searching for data online or at a library, the information must be accurate. Accuracy in this case may only involve double-checking meeting notes or asking a coworker for clarification on some point, but double-checking facts is still research. For more complex documents, the research component of technical communication becomes more obvious.

THREE PRIMARY PURPOSES OF TECHNICAL COMMUNICATION

Three purposes of
technical documents:
inform, instruct, and
persuade

Most technical communication seeks to address one of three primary purposes: to anticipate and answer questions (inform), to enable people to perform a task (instruct), or to influence people's thinking (persuade). Keep in mind that these purposes often overlap (as in the following sample documents). However, most documents have one *primary* purpose: to inform, to instruct, or to persuade.

Informational Purpose

Informational
documents
anticipate and
answer questions

Figure 1.3 displays an *informational* document created by the U.S. Environmental Protection Agency. It is designed for a wide audience of readers who may know little about the topic (bioremediation), but the writer has kept audience diversity in mind by anticipating and answering likely questions.

Instructional Purpose

Instructional
documents help
people perform
a task

Figure 1.4 is an *instructional* document. As we have all experienced, effective instructions can be a pleasure to work with because they help people do what they want to do. But poor instructions can create frustration, often causing people to return the product and to have second thoughts about purchasing that brand in the future.

United States
Environmental Protection
Agency

Office of Solid Waste and
Emergency Response
(5102G)

EPA 542-F-01-001
April 2001
www.epa.gov/superfund/sites
www.cluin.org

⊕EPA

A Citizen's Guide to Bioremediation

FIGURE 1.3

An informational document

◀● The title is clear and easy to understand

The Citizen's Guide Series

EPA uses many methods to clean up pollution at Superfund and other sites. Some, like bioremediation, are considered new or innovative. Such methods can be quicker and cheaper than more common methods. If you live, work, or go to school near a Superfund site, you may want to learn more about cleanup methods. Perhaps they are being used or are proposed for use at your site. How do they work? Are they safe? This Citizen's Guide is one in a series to help answer your questions.

What is bioremediation?

◀● User-centered headings are phrased as questions that readers would need answered

Bioremediation allows natural processes to clean up harmful chemicals in the environment. Microscopic "bugs" or microbes that live in soil and groundwater like to eat certain harmful chemicals, such as those found in gasoline and oil spills. When microbes completely digest these chemicals, they change them into water and harmless gases such as carbon dioxide.

| Microbe eats oil | Microbe digests oil and changes it to water and harmless gases | Microbe releases water and harmless gases into soil or ground |

◀● Illustrations combine text and visuals

How does it work?

◀● Headings and a clean layout make this document easy for readers to navigate

In order for microbes to clean up harmful chemicals, the right temperature, nutrients (fertilizers), and amount of oxygen must be present in the soil and groundwater. These conditions allow the microbes to grow and multiply—and eat more chemicals. When conditions are not right, microbes grow too slowly or die. Or they can create more harmful chemicals. If conditions are not right at a site, EPA works to improve them. One way they improve conditions is to pump air, nutrients, or other substances (such as molasses) underground. Sometimes microbes are added if enough aren't already there.

◀● Text provides the most relevant information without being too detailed

The right conditions for bioremediation cannot always be achieved underground. At some sites, the weather is too cold or the soil is too dense. At such sites, EPA might dig up the soil to clean it above ground where heaters and soil mixing help improve conditions. After the soil is dug up, the proper nutrients are added. Oxygen also may be added by stirring the mixture or by forcing air through it. However, some microbes work better without oxygen. With the right temperature and amount of oxygen and nutrients, microbes can do their work to "bioremediate" the harmful chemicals.

Source: U.S. Environmental Protection Agency website <www.epa.gov>, April 2001

1

Title announces document's exact purpose

How to Operate a Multipurpose Dry-Chemical Fire Extinguisher

Introduction provides appropriate level of detail for first-time users

Introduction

The Occupational Safety and Health Administration (OSHA) requires that all employees know how to operate a fire extinguisher and how to recognize the hazards associated with small or developing fires.

Portable fire extinguishers in our buildings are easily found in various areas: public hallways, laboratories, mechanical rooms, break rooms, chemical storage areas, company vehicles, and other areas that contain flammable liquids. Please note the specific location of extinguishers in each of these areas.

Clearly labeled illustration helps readers understand the product

Portable fire extinguishers apply an extinguishing agent that will either cool burning fuel, displace or remove oxygen, or stop the chemical reaction so a fire cannot continue to burn. When the extinguisher handle is compressed, it opens an inner canister of high-pressure gas that forces the extinguishing agent from the main cylinder through a siphon tube and out the nozzle (Figure 1). A fire extinguisher works much like a can of hair spray.

FIGURE 1
How a fire extinguisher works

All of our fire extinguishers are *multipurpose dry-chemical extinguishers*. This type of extinguisher puts out fires by coating the fuel with a thin layer of fire-retardant powder, separating the fuel from the oxygen. The powder also works to interrupt the chemical reaction, making these extinguishers extremely effective for ordinary combustibles (such as wood or paper), flammable liquids, and electrical equipment.

Overview of major steps

These instructions cover four simple steps in operating the extinguisher safely and effectively: Pull, Aim, Squeeze, and Sweep.

FIGURE 1.4 An instructional document
Source: Text and figures from the Occupational Safety and Health Administration <www.osha.gov>.

FIGURE 1.4
(Continued)

2

> **WARNING:** At the first sign of fire, sound the alarm and call the fire department. Before approaching the fire, identify a safe evacuation path. **Never** allow the fire, heat, or smoke to come between you and your evacuation path. **If you have the slightest doubt about your ability to fight a fire . . .** EVACUATE **IMMEDIATELY!**

A prominent warning box alerts users before they take action

Using the Fire Extinguisher

Even though extinguishers come in a number of shapes and sizes, they all operate in a similar manner. Here is an easy acronym to remember for rapid and safe fire extinguisher use: PASS—Pull, Aim, Squeeze, and Sweep (Figure 2).

A short, simple title, starting with an action verb ("using") makes this instructional document efficient and easy to understand

1. **PULL** . . . Pull the pin. This will also break the tamper seal.

2. **AIM** . . . Aim low, pointing the extinguisher nozzle (or its horn or hose) at the base of the fire.

3. **SQUEEZE** . . . Squeeze the handle to release the extinguishing agent.

Numbered steps make the instructions easy to navigate and use

4. **SWEEP** . . . Sweep from side to side at the base of the fire until it appears to be out. Watch the area. If the fire reignites, repeat steps 2–4.

Conclusion

Your first concern is **safety:** Always back away from an extinguished fire in case it flames up again. Evacuate immediately if the extinguisher is empty and the fire is not out. Evacuate immediately if the fire worsens.

FIGURE 2
The PASS Technique

A simple illustration complements the information in the numbered list to help users see how the process works

Persuasive Purpose

Figure 1.5 shows a *persuasive* document, in the form of a letter from a company that distributes systems for generating electrical power from recycled steam. General Manager William Bullock writes a persuasive answer to a customer's question: "Why should I invest in the system you are proposing for my plant?" As you read the letter, note how the writer focuses on reasons that are important to the reader.

COMMON TYPES OF TECHNICAL DOCUMENTS

Many of you probably encounter the following types of documents routinely, either through work or school. You may also be asked to produce such documents for a class, an internship, or your job.

- **Memos.** Organizations use memos as the primary means of internal written communication. Unlike a conversation, a memo leaves a record for future reference. An employee might write a memo to a manager requesting a pay raise; a team of students might write a memo to an instructor explaining their progress on a term project; or an office manager might write a memo to company employees to outline the new vacation policy.

- **Emails.** In today's workplace, email messages are far more common than paper memos. People use email to communicate with clients, customers, suppliers, and associates worldwide. Email messages are generally written more informally and hastily than paper memos.

- **Letters.** Letters are the most personal form of technical communication, but they also provide written records and often serve as contracts. As a student you might write a letter to request research data or to apply for a summer internship. On the job, you might write to persuade a client to invest in a new technology or to explain the delay in a construction project.

- **Instructions.** Instructions explain the steps or course of action for completing a specific task, such as how to program a DVD player or how to install system software. Instructions come in various formats: online instructions may be built right into a computer application; brief instructions may be written on single-page reference cards; longer instructions may be assembled in magazine format to be mailed or handed out.

- **Procedures.** Procedures are similar to instructions in that they explain how to perform a task step by step; however, procedures are different in that they always deal with matters of company or organizational policy. Many companies maintain standard operating procedures (SOPs) for tasks such as how to test soil samples or how to access corporate databases.

Turbosteam LLC
161 Industrial Boulevard
Turners Falls, MA 01376
Phone: 413-863-3500
Fax: 413-863-3157
www.turbosteam.com

July 20, 20XX

Mr. Richard White, President
Southern Wood Products
Box 84
Memphis, TN 37162

Dear Mr. White:

In our meeting last week, you asked me to explain why we have such confidence in the project we are proposing. Let me outline what I think are excellent reasons.

First, you and Don Smith have given us a clear idea of your needs, and our recent discussions confirm that we fully understand these needs. For instance, our proposal specifies an air-cooled condenser rather than a water-cooled condenser for your project because water in Memphis is expensive. And besides saving money, an air-cooled condenser will be easier to operate and maintain.

Second, we have confidence in our component suppliers and they have confidence in this project. We don't manufacture the equipment; instead, we integrate and package cogeneration systems by selecting for each application the best components from leading manufacturers. For example, Alias Engineering, the turbine manufacturer, is the world's leading producer of single-stage turbines, having built more than 40,000 turbines in 70 years. Likewise, each component manufacturer leads the field and has a proven track record. We have reviewed your project with each major component supplier, and each guarantees the equipment. This guarantee is of course transferable to you and is supplemented by our own performance guarantee.

FIGURE 1.5
A persuasive document

- A nicely designed letterhead creates an effective, professional visual appeal

- The opening paragraph is written clearly and in a direct but polite manner

- Each item in the writer's list of reasons starts out with "first," "second," and "third," making the document easy to navigate

- The writer provides the relevant information without going into too much technical detail

Source: Courtesy of Turbosteam LLC. Reprinted with permission.

FIGURE 1.5
(Continued)

 Richard White, July 20, 20XX, page 2

The letter is persuasive because it offers convincing examples and facts

Third, we have confidence in the system design. We developed the CX Series specifically for applications like yours, in which there is a need for both a condensing and a backpressure turbine. In our last meeting, I pointed out the cost, maintenance, and performance benefits of the CX Series. And although the CX Series is an innovative design, all components are fully proven in many other applications, and our suppliers fully endorse this design.

Finally, and perhaps most important, you should have confidence in this project because we will stand behind it. As you know, we are eager to establish ourselves in Memphis-area industries. If we plan to succeed, this project must succeed. We have a tremendous amount at stake in keeping you happy.

If I can answer any questions, please phone me. We look forward to working with you.

Sincerely,

William Bullock

General Manager

- **Manuals.** Almost every technology product or service comes with a manual. Manuals may include instructions on how to assemble, set up, and use a product, but they also include background information, such as technical specifications or lists of materials. You have certainly used manuals to perform tasks such as connecting the components of your sound system, or setting up the voice mail on your cell phone. Most manuals are also available in electronic form: as help files, on a CD, or as PDF documents on a company's Web site.

- **Brochures.** To market goods or services, companies produce brochures. Brochures from professional organizations such as the American Medical Association may define various medical conditions, explain the causes, and describe available treatments. The government creates brochures to help with issues such as how to obtain student loans or how to start a small business.

- **Proposals.** Proposals offer solutions to problems and make specific recommendations for how to implement those solutions. A proposal's purpose is usually to persuade readers to improve conditions, accept a service or product, or otherwise support a plan of action. Proposals are often written in response to calls for proposals (CFPs) or requests for proposals (RFPs). For example, a nonprofit child-care facility may seek safer playground equipment, or a pharmaceutical company may wish to develop a new Web-based education program for its employees. These organizations would issue RFPs, and each interested vendor would prepare a proposal that examines the problem, presents a solution, and defines the process and associated fees.

- **Reports.** Reports, both short and long, are generally based on the study of a specific problem or issue. Some reports are strictly informative ("Why Laptop Computer Batteries Can Explode"); other reports recommend solutions to urgent problems ("Recommended Security Measures for Airline Safety"); and still others have an overtly persuasive goal, advocating a particular course of action ("Why Voters Should Reject the Nuclear Waste Storage Facility Proposed for Our County").

THE IMPORTANCE OF PROOFREADING

No matter how engaging and informative a document, basic errors will distract the reader and make the writer look careless. Proofreading is vital in detecting easily correctable errors such as these:

All technical documents should be proofread carefully

- Sentence errors, such as fragments, comma splices, or run-ons
- Punctuation errors, such as missing apostrophes or excessive commas

- Usage errors, such as "it's" for "its"; "lay" for "lie"; or "their" for "there"
- Mechanical errors, such as misspelled words, inaccurate dates, or incorrect abbreviations
- Formatting errors, such as missing page numbers, inconsistent spacing, or incorrect form of documenting sources
- Typographical errors (typos), such as repeated or missing words or letters, missing word endings (say, *-s* or *-ed* or *-ing*), or an omitted quotation mark

When proofreading, refer to this book's final page as well as the following Strategies.

STRATEGIES
for Proofreading

▸ **Save it for the final draft.** Proofreading previous drafts might cause writer's block and distract you from the document's rhetorical features (content, organization, style, and design).

▸ **Take a break before proofreading your final document.** Revisit your document with a fresh, rested pair of eyes.

▸ **Work from hard copy.** Research indicates that people read more perceptively (and with less fatigue) from a printed page than from a computer screen.

▸ **Keep it slow.** Read each word—don't skim. Slide a ruler under each line or move backward through the document, sentence by sentence. For a long document, read only small chunks at one time.

▸ **Be especially alert for problem areas in your writing.** Do you have trouble spelling? Do you get commas confused with semicolons? Do you make a lot of typos? Make one final pass to check on any problem areas like these.

▸ **Proofread more than once.** The more often you proofread, the more likely you will catch all errors.

▸ **Never rely only on computerized writing aids.** A synonym found in an electronic thesaurus may distort your meaning, and a computerized spell checker cannot differentiate among correctly spelled words such as "their," "they're," and "there" or "nope" versus "hope." In the end, nothing can replace your own careful proofreading.

CHECKLIST
for Effective Technical Communication

☐ Does my document focus on the reader not the writer?

☐ Is the document efficient and accessible?

☐ Is the document clear and easy to understand?

☐ Does the document give readers what they need?

☐ Have I used the appropriate media to convey my message?

☐ Have I created the document to address a global audience as needed?

☐ Am I able to work as part of a team?

☐ Is the document sufficiently persuasive to get the response I want?

☐ Is the document ethically acceptable?

☐ Is the document based on careful research?

☐ Does the document achieve its primary purpose (i.e., inform, instruct, persuade)—or a combination of purposes?

☐ Have I proofread the document carefully?

APPLICATIONS

GENERAL APPLICATIONS

1. Write an email to your boss, requesting that the company pay your tuition for this class. Explain how the class will help you be more effective on the job. Proofread your email: Is it too long or too short? Is the tone professional or demanding? Did you write from your perspective or the reader's (your boss)?

2. Find an example of an informational document or a set of instructions or a persuasive letter. Identify in your document the features of effective technical writing discussed in this chapter. Discuss your findings in class.

TEAM APPLICATION

Class members will work together often this semester. So that everyone becomes acquainted, your task is to introduce to the class the person seated next to you. (That person, in turn, will introduce you.) Follow this procedure:

a. Exchange with your neighbor whatever personal information you think the class needs: background, major, career plans, communication needs of your intended profession, and so on. Each person gets five minutes to tell her or his story.

b. Take careful notes; ask questions if you need to.

c. Take your notes home and select only what you think the class will find useful.

d. Prepare a one-page memo telling your classmates who this person is. (See pages 188 and 189 for memo elements and format.)

e. Ask your neighbor to review the memo for accuracy; revise as needed.

f. Present the class with a two-minute oral paraphrase of your memo and submit a copy of the memo to your instructor.

GLOBAL APPLICATION

Technical documents are often read by international audiences. Some companies handle this issue by translating their documentation into multiple languages; other companies use a combination of words and pictures or just pictures. Find an example of technical communication written for an international audience. You might look at the instructions that came with your computer, cell phone, unassembled bookshelves, or other products. Write a short memo explaining what techniques the writer used to make the information useful for people who may not speak English or who speak English as a second language.

COMPUTER/WEB-BASED APPLICATION

Use the Internet to research examples of technical communication that are common in your profession or major. For example, if you are studying electrical engineering, what are the typical types of reports or studies you might need to write when you get a job? Using the Checklist for Effective Technical Communication at the end of this chapter, evaluate whether a selected document appears to be effective. Write a memo to your instructor explaining your findings. Include the Web address (URL) for the document you found.

For additional technical writing resources that will help you master the chapter objectives, go to **www.mytechcommlab.com**.

2

Teamwork and Global Issues in Technical Communication

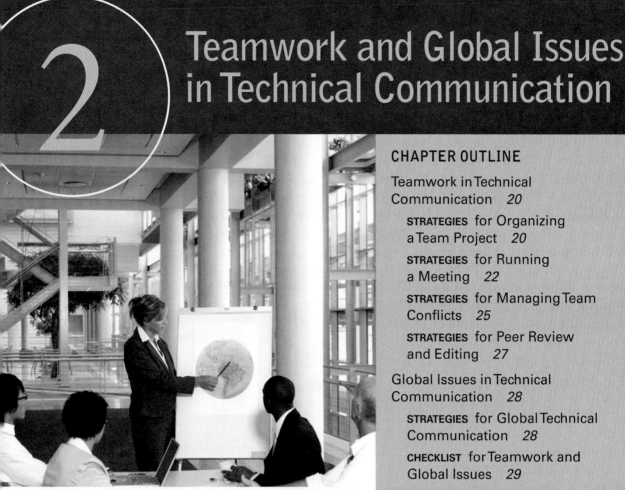

LEARNING OBJECTIVES FOR THIS CHAPTER

▶ Organize and manage a team project

▶ Run a successful meeting

▶ Identify and manage team conflicts

▶ Review and edit the work of others on a team

▶ Understand that technical communication
is used by international audiences

Two vital technical communication skills introduced in Chapter 1 receive closer examination here: working effectively in teams and recognizing global issues in technical communication.

TEAMWORK IN TECHNICAL COMMUNICATION

Teamwork is a frequent part of technical communication

As noted previously, complex documents (especially long reports, proposals, and manuals) are rarely created by one person working alone. In the workplace, such documents are typically produced by teams of writers, engineers, graphic artists, editors, reviewers, marketing personnel, lawyers, and other professionals.

Characteristics of effective in-person and virtual teams

Teams can work in person or virtually. Usually, though, teamwork involves a combination of face-to-face meetings and technology-facilitated exchanges, such as those via the phone, email, or the Web. Whether the team shares information in person or virtually, members have to find ways of openly sharing their ideas, expressing their views persuasively, giving and accepting constructive criticism, and reaching agreement with others who hold different views. Teamwork is successful only when there is strong cooperation, a recognized team structure, and clear communication. The following Strategies explain how to work on a team project systematically.

STRATEGIES
for Organizing a Team Project

- ▶ **Appoint a group manager.** The manager assigns tasks, enforces deadlines, conducts meetings, consults with supervisors, and "runs the show."
- ▶ **Define a clear and definite goal.** Compose a purpose statement that spells out the project's goal and the plan for achieving the goal. Be sure each team member understands the goal.
- ▶ **Identify the type of document required.** Is this a report, a proposal, a manual, or a brochure? Are visuals and supplements (abstract, appendices, and so on) needed? Will the document be in hard copy, digital form, or both?
- ▶ **Divide the tasks.** Who will be responsible for which parts of the document or which phases of the project? Who is best at doing what (writing, editing, layout and graphics, oral presentation)? Which tasks will be done individually and

which collectively? Spell out—in writing—clear expectations for each team member. Also keep in mind that the final version should display a consistent style throughout, as if written by one person only.

▶ **Establish a timetable.** A timetable will help the team visualize the whole project, each part of the project, and completion dates for each phase.

▶ **Decide on a meeting schedule.** How often, where, and for how long will the group meet?

▶ **Establish a procedure for responding to each other's work.** Will reviewing and editing be done in writing, face-to-face, as a group, one-on-one, or online?

▶ **Develop a file-naming system for various drafts.** Be careful about saving documents. It's too easy to save over a previous version and lose something important.

▶ **Establish procedures for dealing with interpersonal problems.** How will disputes be discussed and resolved (by vote, by the manager, or by other means)? How will irrelevant discussion be curtailed?

▶ **Select a group decision-making style.** Will decisions be made by the group manager alone, by group input, or by majority vote?

▶ **Decide how to evaluate each member's contribution.** Will the manager assess each member's performance and in turn be evaluated by each member? Will members evaluate each other? What are the criteria?

▶ **Prepare a project planning form.** Figure 2.1 shows a sample form. Distribute completed copies to members.

▶ **Submit regular progress reports.** These reports (see pages 295–298) track activities, problems, and rate of progress.

Running Successful Meetings

Despite the many digital tools available for collaboration (see page 24), face-to-face meetings provide vital personal contact. Meetings are usually scheduled for one of two purposes: to convey or exchange information or to make decisions. Informational meetings tend to run smoothly because there is less cause for disagreement. But decision-based meetings often fail to reach clear resolution because the meeting leader fails to take charge. Running a meeting doesn't mean imposing one's views or stifling opposing views, but it does mean keeping the discussion moving and centered on the issue, as explained in the Strategies on page 22.

Face-to-face meetings are either informational or decision based

FIGURE 2.1
Project planning form

 View the **Project Planning Form** at mytechcommlab

Project Planning Form

Project title:
Audience:
Project manager:
Team members:
Purpose of the project:
Type of document required:

Specific Assignments	**Due Dates**
Research:	Research due:
Planning:	Plan and outline due:
Drafting:	First draft due:
Revising:	Reviews due:
Preparing final document:	Revision due:
Presenting oral briefing:	Progress report(s) due:
	Final document due:

Work Schedule

Team meetings:	Date	Place	Time	Note-taker
#1				
#2				
#3				
etc.				
Mtgs. w/instructor				
#1				
#2				
etc.				

Miscellaneous

How will disputes and grievances be resolved?
How will performances be evaluated?
Other matters (Internet searches, email routing, online conferences, etc.)?

STRATEGIES
for Running a Meeting

▶ **Set an agenda.** Distribute copies of the agenda to participants beforehand: "Our 10 A.M. Monday meeting will cover the following items: . . . " Spell out each item, set a strict time limit for discussion of each item, and stick to this plan.

▸ **Ask each person to prepare as needed.** A meeting works best when each participant makes a specific contribution. Appoint someone to take notes or minutes, and appoint others to other roles, such as doing background research on a particular topic that will be discussed.

▸ **Appoint a different "observer" for each meeting.** This person's job is to take notes on what aspects of the meeting did or did not work well.

▸ **Begin by summarizing the minutes of the last meeting.** This process will ensure that the conversation in this meeting moves beyond what was concluded previously. (For preparing meeting minutes, see pages 304–305.)

▸ **Give all members a chance to speak.** Don't allow anyone to monopolize. At the same time, encourage quiet members to contribute.

▸ **Stick to the issue.** Curb irrelevant discussion. When the conversation strays, politely nudge members back on track.

▸ **Keep things moving.** Don't get hung up on a single issue. Work toward a consensus by highlighting points of agreement and pushing for a resolution.

▸ **Observe, guide, and listen.** As the meeting leader, don't lecture or dictate. Instead, take charge by steering the group discussion.

▸ **Summarize major points before calling for a vote.** Paraphrase what has been discussed to be sure that everyone has understood the major points and so that clarifications or corrections can be made before the vote.

▸ **End the meeting on schedule.** This is not a hard-and-fast rule. If you feel the issue is about to be resolved at the meeting's end time, continue. Understand, however, that some participants may need to leave for other appointments.

Using Technology to Help with Team Projects

Teams are increasingly distributed across different job sites, time zones, and countries. Even for a school project, you and the other team members may have very different work schedules and may need to meet virtually. The Internet—via email, streamed video, instant messaging, blogs, and other communication tools—offers the primary means for virtual teams to interact. In addition, tools such as computer-supported cooperative work (CSCW) software and project management software (such as Microsoft Project) can be helpful.

Digital technology can help virtual teams collaborate

For personal contact, face-to-face meetings are essential. But virtual collaboration may allow some people to feel more secure about saying what they really think because they eliminate public speaking fears as well as "status cues" such as age, gender, appearance, or ethnicity (Wojahn 747–48).

Advantages of virtual collaboration

Various technologies enable virtual teams to work together:

Virtual collaboration
technologies

- **Teleconferencing.** The oldest form of virtual collaboration—still very much in use—occurs when multiple callers hold a conference via the telephone.

- **Email.** The most popular tool today, email is great for keeping track of discussions among multiple recipients.

- **Instant messaging (IM).** IM is a fast and easy way to hold a real-time conversation among multiple people, as long as they are all logged in.

- **Project management software.** Most large organizations use dedicated software, such as Microsoft Project, to manage complex team projects.

- **Editing software.** Editing tools allow multiple users to see each other's edits (which are tagged by the user's initials) and to accept or reject those changes. An example is Microsoft Word's "track changes" feature.

- **Digital whiteboards.** These tools provide a large screen that allows participants to write, sketch, and erase from their own computers in real time.

- **Web conferencing.** A password-protected Web site provides the medium for this more contemporary version of teleconferencing.

- **Blogs.** Short for "Web logs," blogs allow users to create postings or add comments to previous postings as a way for teams to share and refine ideas.

- **Intranets.** Intranets are sites set up for internal company use only. Users can access files, blogs, and other information.

- **Wikis.** These Web sites can be set up to allow access only to those directly involved in the project. When a team member edits a document, a new version is created and old versions saved.

Identifying and Managing Group Conflicts

Even when all team members have good working relationships and positive attitudes, conflicts still can arise, usually because of the following differences:

Differences that may
lead to group conflict

- **Interpersonal differences.** People might clash because of differences in personality, working style, standards, or ability to take criticism. Some might disagree about exactly what or how much the group should accomplish, who should do what, or who should have the final say. Some might feel intimidated or hesitant to speak out. These interpersonal conflicts can actually worsen when the group interacts exclusively online; lack of personal contact makes it hard for trust to develop.

- **Gender differences.** Research on the ways women and men communicate in meetings indicates a definite gender gap: Women tend to be more hesitant to speak up, and when they do, they are often seen as overbearing. In contrast, men tend to speak up and sometimes dominate discussions, and when they do, they are typically considered strong and leadership oriented. People of either gender can be soft-spoken and reflective; but such traits most often are attributed to the "feminine" stereotype.

- **Cultural differences.** International business expert David A. Victor writes about cultural codes that influence interaction in group settings. According to Victor, some cultures value intuition and ambiguity more than hard evidence or data, or they prioritize politeness and personal relationships more than business relationships. Cultures also differ in their perceptions of time. Some are "all business" and like to get directly to the point; others take as long as they feel is needed to weigh the issues and come to carefully considered conclusions (233). Finally, cultures differ in their accepted methods of communication, varying in their willingness to express disagreement, question or be questioned, leave things unstated, or use nonverbal language (shaking hands, kissing, hugging, making eye contact, using facial expressions) (206).

When group conflicts do arise, deal with them directly and openly by using the following Strategies.

STRATEGIES
for Managing Team Conflicts

- **Listen actively.** Perhaps the most constructive way to manage team conflict is to avoid it by *really* listening to others. Listening actively means focusing your attention when people speak, keeping your mind open to what they say, letting them finish before you interject, using direct eye contact and body language that communicates interest, and asking for clarification when genuinely needed. In short, observe the 90/10 rule: listen 90 percent of the time, and speak only 10 percent of the time. As President Calvin Coolidge once said, "Nobody ever listened himself out of a job." Some historians would argue that "Silent Cal" listened himself right into the White House.

- **Avoid gender and cultural bias.** Respect the fact that men and women must be treated equally as team members, and understand that assertiveness and reserve are qualities of both genders. Also, do not assume that one culture's approach to business, time, or communication is better than that of another.

- **Research cultures other than your own.** Apply what you learn to situations in which you collaborate with members of multiple cultures.

- **Give everyone a chance to be heard.** Encourage quieter members to speak up and curtail dominating members from speaking excessively.

▶ **Take everyone's feelings and opinions seriously.** Don't play favorites. Every team member has something valid to contribute.

▶ **Don't be afraid to disagree.** Politely let other team members know if you don't agree with their ideas or opinions. Your point of view is as important as anyone else's.

▶ **Offer and accept constructive criticism.** Criticism focused on helping reach the team's goal, as opposed to seeming like a personal attack, creates an atmosphere of open communication.

▶ **Find points of agreement with others who hold different views.** Although you might not agree with everyone in the group, find those points on which you do agree.

▶ **When the group does make a decision, support it fully.** At some point, decisions must be made. If you are outvoted, accept the fact that a vote is binding and that you represent the group as a whole, even if you disagree with the final decision.

Reviewing and Editing the Work of Others

The process of reviewing a document

Documents produced in teams must be reviewed and edited extensively. *Reviewing* means evaluating how well a document connects with its audience and meets its purpose. When reviewing, you explain to the writer how you respond as a reader; you point out what works or doesn't work. This commentary helps the writer think about ways of revising. Reviewers typically examine a document to make sure it includes these features:

Qualities reviewers look for

- accurate, appropriate, useful, and legal content
- material organized for the reader's understanding
- clear, easy-to-read, and engaging style
- effective visuals and page design

The process of editing a document

Editing means polishing a document by making it more precise and readable at the sentence and word level. Editing may happen simultaneously with reviewing, but usually it comes after a document has been reviewed and revised—when the more global considerations of content, organization, style, and design have already been resolved and the editor can focus on more particular details. Editors typically suggest improvements such as these:

Types of "fixing" that editors do

- rephrasing or reorganizing sentences
- clarifying a topic sentence

⊙ **Watch** the **Video** on Peer Reviewing a Technical Document at **mytechcommlab**

- choosing a better word or phrase
- correcting spelling, usage, punctuation, and so on

For a team project, at work or at school, you can each take turns reviewing and editing drafts of the document by using the following Strategies.

STRATEGIES
for Peer Review and Editing

▸ **Read the entire piece at least twice before you comment.** Develop a clear sense of the document's purpose and audience. Try to visualize the document as a whole before you evaluate specific parts.

▸ **Focus first on the big picture.** Begin with the document's content and organization. Is the document appropriate for its audience and purpose? Is the supporting material relevant and convincing? Is the discussion easy to follow? Does each paragraph do its job? Do all the visuals serve a distinct and appropriate purpose? Is the design appropriate for this document?

▸ **Be honest but diplomatic.** Say what you think, but don't merely offer negative comments. Begin with something positive before moving to suggested improvements. Maintain a supportive tone.

▸ **Explain why something doesn't work.** Instead of "this paragraph is confusing," say "because this paragraph lacks a clear topic sentence, I had trouble discovering the main idea." Instead of "I don't like this visual," say "this visual doesn't work, not only because it is a little blurry, but also because it doesn't add to the discussion."

▸ **Make specific recommendations for improvements.** Write out suggestions in enough detail for the writer to know what to do. Don't just say "I think you should add a chart here." Instead offer "I think you should add a new chart here to show all the numerical information you've provided in an easy-to-understand visual way."

▸ **Don't expect everyone to agree with your suggestions.** Even professional editors can disagree. Offer your best advice but don't dictate—others may have better suggestions. If different readers offer conflicting opinions of what needs to be revised, seek your team leader's opinion or take it to a vote.

▸ **Understand the acceptable limits of editing.** Don't simply rewrite an entire document in your own words. Although changes can range from making a few suggestions and additions to closely editing every paragraph, always preserve the author's original vision and style.

▸ **Focus next on the particulars.** Once the document has been reviewed and revised for content, organization, style, and design, refine the sentences and word choice—and proofread several times.

GLOBAL ISSUES IN TECHNICAL COMMUNICATION

Why global issues are important in today's workplace

Employees who work across different continents, countries, and cultures must pay special attention to various customs and values. Key to this practice is "face saving." No one wants to be embarrassed in public, have his or her traditions or values criticized, or be treated with disrespect. All these situations represent a loss of "face." But people in different cultures have different views about what is embarrassing or insulting. For example, in some cultures a "tell it like it is" approach is considered rude, while in others, body language such as leaning back in your chair and crossing your arms signals disrespect.

Do your research on international business culture

If you are working on a team project and the team spans different countries and cultures, do some research to learn about your team members, to appreciate their frame of reference, and to establish common ground. You may find, for example, that your team members in another country value a slower, more patient approach or put a value on oral communication (by phone or video conference) rather than written communication at certain stages of the project.

Remember that any document may be transmitted globally

Any document can reach across the globe. For example, the instructions you write for a new cell phone may well end up on a Web site, where they will be used by customers worldwide. Some international readers of your instructions may be offended by commands in strongly worded imperative forms, such as "STOP: Do not insert the storage card until you reach Step 3." Or they may be baffled by icons and other visuals that have no meaning in their culture.

Explore the Concept with the Case Study on Global Research at **mytechcommlab**

Documents may originate in English but then be translated into other languages. In these cases, writers must be careful to use English that is easy to translate. Idioms, humor, and analogies are often difficult for translators. One famous example of translation difficulty is the case of the Chevrolet Nova, a car that was successful in the United States but met resistance in Latin America. When translated into Spanish, Nova means "Does Not Go"!

For more advice on global communication, see the following Strategies as well as advice throughout this book.

STRATEGIES for Global Technical Communication

▸ **Learn as much as possible about the culture and background of your team members or customers.** Use the Internet or find books that can help you understand the communication norms for the countries or cultures with which you will be working.

➡

STRATEGIES *continued*

▶ **Be respectful and considerate.** Do nothing that will cause anyone to lose face.

▶ **Avoid the use of humor, slang, and idioms.** These items are culturally specific, do not translate well, and could be misunderstood by nonnative audiences.

▶ **Avoid stereotyping.** Violating a person's cultural frame of reference is offensive, but so is reducing individual complexity to a laundry list of cultural stereotypes. Any generalization about a culture is just that—a generalization. People are still individuals and should be respected as such.

CHECKLIST
for Teamwork and Global Issues

TEAMWORK

☐ Has our team appointed a team manager?

☐ Does the team agree on the type of document required?

☐ Do we have a plan for how to divide the tasks?

☐ Have we established a timetable and decided on a meeting schedule?

☐ Do we have an agenda for our first meeting?

☐ Do we have a clear understanding of how we will share drafts of the document and how we will name the files?

☐ Have we decided what technology we should use for our collaboration (e.g., track changes; a wiki; a blog)?

☐ Are we using the project planning form (page 22) to help us get organized?

GLOBAL ISSUES

☐ Do I understand the communication customs of the international audience for my document?

☐ Is my writing clear and direct, so that it is easy to translate?

☐ Have I avoided idioms, humor, and slang?

☐ Have I avoided stereotyping of different cultures and groups of people?

☐ Does my document enable everyone to save face?

APPLICATIONS

GENERAL APPLICATION

Find an example of technical communication: a manual for your new computer, a medical or technical report from the Web, or a technical brochure. Write a brief description of places in this document where you think teamwork was important or where you think the writers considered (or ignored) the importance of writing for a global audience.

TEAM APPLICATION

Write a short memo to your instructor describing the role of teams in a company, organization, or campus group where you have worked or volunteered. Your memo should address questions such as what type of projects your team worked on, how the teams were organized, what worked, and what did not work.

GLOBAL APPLICATION

The techniques that are effective in one culture may fail in a different culture. Do a Web search on "intercultural communication" and locate a topic that is important for technical communication. For instance, you might locate information about the different ways in which certain types of visuals that are acceptable in one culture are not in another. Write a short summary of your findings, cite your sources, and present your information in class.

COMPUTER/WEB-BASED APPLICATION

The Internet has made it easy for companies to have teams that are spread out across the globe. Locate a professional who works in a technical or scientific area and interview that person about what technologies they use for their global, virtual team meetings. Ask about both the pros and the cons of global, virtual teams.

 For additional technical writing resources that will help you master the chapter objectives, go to **www.mytechcommlab.com**.

3

The Research Process in Technical Communication

LEARNING OBJECTIVES FOR THIS CHAPTER

▶ Apply critical thinking to your research

▶ Understand the difference between primary and secondary research

▶ Locate the Web-based and hard-copy secondary sources you need

▶ Consult primary sources via inquiries, informational interviews and surveys, observations, and experiments

All technical communication requires some degree of research, even if that research merely entails checking a fact or consulting a colleague before writing a memo, letter, or email. This chapter explains how to conduct more complex research for such technical documents as long reports and proposals. As you read, consider how research in technical communication often differs from research conducted in an academic setting.

THINKING CRITICALLY ABOUT RESEARCH

Research is a vital part of technical communication

Most major decisions in the workplace are based on careful research, often with the findings recorded in a written report, in a long memo, on a Web site, or in some combination of documents. The types of research you will perform as a technical communicator depend largely on your workplace assignment.

Not all findings will be of equal value. For instance, if you really want to know how well the latest invention in robotic surgery works, you need to check with sources other than the inventor (from whom you could expect an overly optimistic or insufficiently critical assessment). Likewise, if you only consult books published before 1990 and don't consult any online sources, you are not likely to get a current and balanced view. Further, if you interpret your findings inaccurately—say, by ignoring a study that contradicts your viewpoint or claim—your research will be invalid.

Why critical thinking is essential in research

Whether you work with your own findings or the findings of other researchers, you need to decide if the information is reliable. Then you need to decide what your information means. *Critical thinking* means that you test the quality of your information and the accuracy of your interpretations. Instead of accepting information at face value, you examine, evaluate, verify, analyze, and weigh alternatives during every stage of your research. You use critical thinking to examine your evidence and your reasoning to discover new connections and new possibilities and to test the soundness of your conclusions. The following Strategies provide specific guidelines.

STRATEGIES
for Thinking Critically about Research

▶ **Ask the right questions.** To get the right answers, start by asking the right questions. Instead of researching an overly general topic that will lead to an enormous variety of information, such as "genetically modified foods," ask a specific, narrowed question, such as "What are the positive and negative effects of genetically modified foods on human health?"

➡

▶ **Explore a balance of views.** Consider your research topic from a variety of angles. Don't just consult one expert because experts may disagree. Instead find out what multiple experts say and examine the points on which the experts agree and disagree.

▶ **Explore your topic in sufficient depth.** Different sources of information represent different levels of detail and dependability. At the surface layer is information from the popular press (newspapers, commercial Web sites, TV shows). This surface information may be useful and valid, but you should also go further and explore deeper levels, such as trade and business publications and Web sites or specialized literature (journals and Web sites from professional associations and government sources).

▶ **Evaluate your sources.** The information you find may be incomplete or misleading. While you can't always verify that a source is trustworthy, you can weed out unreliable sources by looking for common ground among sources, by determining if any of them are driven by an agenda, and by checking the source's credentials.

▶ **Interpret your findings objectively.** Examine what you've uncovered from multiple angles. Do your findings support only one viewpoint or are there several ways to interpret them? If your research yields indefinite findings, don't try to force a definite conclusion. A wrong conclusion is worse than an indefinite one.

PRIMARY VERSUS SECONDARY SOURCES

Primary research means getting information directly from the source by conducting interviews and surveys and by observing people, events, or processes in action. *Secondary research* means getting information second hand by reading what other researchers have compiled in books and articles in print or online. Most information found on the Internet would be considered a secondary source. Some Web-based information is more accurate than others; for instance, a Web page created by a high school student might be interesting but not overly reliable, whereas a Web site that is the equivalent of a traditional secondary source (encyclopedia, research index, newspaper, journal) would be more reliable for your research.

How primary and secondary research differ

Whenever possible, combine primary and secondary research. Typically, you would start by using secondary sources because they are readily available and can help you get a full background understanding of your topic. However, don't neglect to add your own findings to existing ones by doing primary research. Working with primary sources can help you expand on what other people have already learned and add considerable credibility to your work. For instance, assume that your boss asks you to write a report about how successfully your company's new product is

Why you should combine primary and secondary research

being received in the marketplace: you might consult sales reports and published print and online reviews of the product (secondary research); but you might also survey product users and interview some of them individually (primary research).

EXPLORING SECONDARY SOURCES

Types of secondary sources

Secondary sources include Web sites; online news outlets and magazines; blogs and wikis; books in the library; journal, magazine, and newspaper articles; government publications; and other public records. Research assignments begin more effectively when you first uncover and sort through what is already known about your topic before adding to that knowledge yourself.

Pros and cons of using hard-copy versus Web-based secondary sources

Although Internet searches are becoming the norm, thorough research often requires careful examination of hard-copy sources as well. The advantages and drawbacks of each search medium, listed in Table 3.1, provide good reason for exploring both.

TABLE 3.1
Hard-copy versus Web-based sources: benefits and drawbacks

	Benefits	Drawbacks
Hard-copy sources	• Available on library shelves, where you might also find related material	• Time-consuming and inefficient to search
	• Easy to determine author, publication date, and page number	• Offer only text and images
	• Easier to preserve and keep secure	• Hard to update
Web-based sources	• More current, efficient, and accessible	• Access to recent material only
	• Searches can be narrowed or broadened	• Not always reliable
	• Can offer material that has no hard-copy equivalent	• User might get confused by too many choices

Web-based Secondary Sources

Locate Web-based secondary sources by using subject directories and search engines

Information in virtually any format—journals, newspapers, and magazines; government documents and research reports; corporate Web sites; library databases—can be accessed on the Internet. To find various sites on the Web, we use two basic tools: *subject directories* and *search engines*.

- **Subject Directories.** Subject directories are indexes compiled by editors who sift through Web sites and sort the most useful links. Popular general subject directories include *Yahoo! Directory* <dir.yahoo.com>, *About.com* <www.about.com>, and *Librarians' Internet Index* <www.lii.org>. Specialized directories focus on a single topic such as software, health, or employment. See *Beaucoup!*, a "directory of directories," at <www.beaucoup.com> for listings of specialized directories organized by category.

- **Search Engines.** Search engines, such as *Google* <www.google.com>, *Ask* <www.ask.com>, *Yahoo! Search* <search.yahoo.com>, and *AltaVista* <www.altavista.com>, scan for Web sites containing key words. Even though search engines yield a lot more information than subject directories, much of it can be irrelevant. Some search engines, however, are more selective than others, and some focus on specialized topics.

To research on the Internet, use the following Strategies.

Subject directories are maintained by editors

● **Watch** the **Video** on Narrowing a Subject Online at **mytechcommlab**

Most search engines are maintained by computers not people

✳ **Explore** the Concept with the Case Study on Online Research at **mytechcommlab**

STRATEGIES
for Researching on the Internet

▸ **Expect limited results from any one search engine or subject directory.** No single search engine, not even a popular one like Google, can index more than a fraction of material available on the Web. No subject directory will list the same Web sites as another.

▸ **When using a search engine, select keywords or search phrases that are varied and technical rather than general.** Some search terms generate more useful hits than others. In addition to "electromagnetic radiation," for example, try "electromagnetic fields," "power lines and health," or "electrical fields." Specialized terms (say, "vertigo" versus "dizziness") offer the best access to reliable sites. However, if you are not able to locate much by using a specialized term, widen your search somewhat.

▸ **When using a subject directory, drill down to an appropriate level of specificity.** Don't rely on finding what you need at the top, or most general, topic level (e.g., "business" or "education"). The best subject directories will be organized into multiple levels of specificity. Keep digging until you either find what you want or discover that the subject directory doesn't list topics relevant to your research.

▸ **Consider the domain type (where the site originates).** Standard domain types in the United States include .com (commercial organization), .edu (educational institution),

.gov or .mil (government or military organization), .net (general usage), and .org (nonprofit organization). While a .com site or a .net site may contain reliable information, you may be better off with a .gov or .mil site that provides official government information, an .edu site that is written by discipline-specific experts, or an .org site that is written by parties who specialize in a particular area.

▶ **Identify the site's purpose and sponsor.** Is the intent merely to relay information, to sell something, or to promote an ideology or agenda? The domain type might alert you to bias or a hidden agenda. A .com site might provide accurate information but also some type of sales pitch. An .org site might reflect a political or ideological bias. Looking for a site's sponsor can also help you evaluate its postings. A Web site about the dangers of bioengineered foods sponsored by an advocacy organization may be biased toward one point of view. Figure 3.1 shows a Web site that advocates a particular agenda.

▶ **Look beyond the style of a site.** Sometimes the most reliable material resides in less attractive, text-only sites. A flashy site does not necessarily indicate reliable content.

▶ **Assess the currency of the site and its materials.** When was the material created, posted, and updated? Many sites have not been updated in months or years.

▶ **Assess the author's credentials and assertions.** Check the author's reputation, expertise, and institutional affiliation (university, company, environmental group). Do not confuse the *author* (the person who wrote the material) with the *Webmaster* (the person who created and maintains the site). Follow links to other sites that mention the author. Where, on the spectrum of expert opinion and accepted theory, does this author fall? Is each assertion supported by solid evidence? Verify any extreme claim through other sources, such as a professor or expert in the field. Consider whether your own biases might predispose you to accept certain ideas.

▶ **Use bookmarks and hotlists for quick access to favorite Web sites.** It is always frustrating when you can't find a helpful Web site that you accessed previously but didn't bookmark.

▶ **Save or print what you need before it changes or disappears.** Web sites often change their content or "go dead." Always record the Web address and your access date.

▶ **Download only what you need; use it ethically; obtain permission; and credit your sources.** Unless they are crucial to your research, omit graphics, sound, and video files. Do not use material created by others in a way that disrespects or otherwise harms the material's creator. For any type of commercial use of material from the Web, obtain written permission from the source's owner and credit the source exactly as directed by its owner. For more information on copyright, see Chapter 19 and Appendix A.

INSTITUTE FOR
RESPONSIBLE TECHNOLOGY

Your Consumer Safety Partner
www.responsibletechnology.org

search [ ] [Go]

Home | Donate | Media Center | Newsletter | Contact Us

| Campaign for Healthier Eating in America | About the Institute | About GM Foods | Health Risks | rBGH in Dairy Products | Non-GMO Shopping | Take Action | Educational Materials |

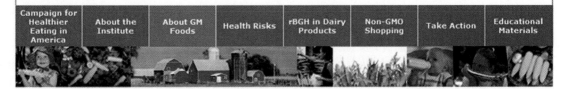

Dangers of Genetically Engineered Foods

(Footnotes refer to pages in the book *Seeds of Deception* by Jeffrey M. Smith.)

The following presents some of the dangers of genetically engineered foods and reasons why avoiding them is an important step to safeguard our health. The footnotes refer to page references in the book *Seeds of Deception*; there you can find meticulously documented evidence that leaves no doubt that GM food should never have been approved.

For a more in-depth look at 65 health risks of GM foods, excerpted from Jeffrey Smith's comprehensive new book Genetic Roulette: The Documented Health Risks of Genetically Engineered Foods, click here.

For more information, see also these articles:

- Jeffrey Smith's Testimony to the EPA - June 2007
- Genetically Modified Foods Are Inherently Unsafe
- Genetically Engineered Foods Pose Higher Risk for Children
- Case Study on Industry Research: Soy Study by Monsanto
- Inhaled GM Maize Pollen May Cause Disease
- GM Food Promoter Transfers to Rat Cells
- GM Vaccines Recombine into Unpredictable Hybrid Viruses in Human and Animal Cells
- A Deadly Epidemic and the Attempt to Hide its Link to Genetic Engineering
- 55.6% Mortality in Rats Whose Mothers Were Fed GM Soy
- Terje Traavik, PhD, responds to criticism about his studies
- Article update linking health problems in the Philippines with Bt corn

The biotech industry claims that the FDA has thoroughly evaluated GM foods and found them safe. This is untrue. Internal FDA documents made public from a lawsuit, reveal that agency scientists warned that GM foods might create toxins, allergies, nutritional problems, and new diseases that might be difficult to identify.[131-140] Although they urged their superiors to require long-term tests on each GM variety prior to approval, the political appointees at the agency, including a former attorney for Monsanto, ignored the scientists. Official policy claims that the foods are no different[130] and do NOT require safety testing. A manufacturer can introduce a GM food without even informing the government or consumers.[146] A January 2001 report from an expert panel of the Royal Society of Canada said it was

FIGURE 3.1 A Web site that advocates a particular viewpoint
Source: From the Institute for Responsible Technology website, <www.responsibletechnology.org>. Reprinted with permission.

Following are the principal categories of information sources on the Internet.

Watch the Video
on Decoding Web
sites at **mytechcommlab**

General Commercial, Organizational, and Academic Web Sites.
Search engines pull up a wide variety of hits, most of which will be commercial (.com), organizational (.org), and academic (.edu) Web sites. If the content within a commercial site looks directly relevant to your search, by all means use it, as long as you think critically about the information presented. Does the fact that the company is likely trying to sell you something affect the content? Be careful also of organizational Web sites, which are likely to be well researched but which may have a particular social or political agenda. Are the opinions expressed by the organization designed to sway you to their agenda? Academic Web sites tend to be credible. However, some academics may also have biases, so never stop thinking critically about what you find on the Web.

Government Web Sites.
Search engines will also pull up government Web sites, but your best way to access them is by going through the U.S. government's Web portal at <www.usa.gov>. Most government organizations (local, state, and federal) have a Web site and online access to research and reports. Examples include the Food and Drug Administration's Web site at <www.fda.gov>, which offers information on food recalls, clinical drug trials, and countless related items; and the Federal Bureau of Investigation's Web site at <www.fbi.gov>, which provides information about the most wanted fugitives in the United States, tips on how to avoid being the victim of a crime, and much more. State and local sites provide information on auto licenses, state tax laws, and local property and land issues. From some of these sites you can link to specific government-sponsored research projects.

Be sure to check the dates of reports or data you locate on a government Web site, and find out how often the site is updated.

Online News Outlets and Magazines.
Most major news organizations offer online versions of their broadcast and print publications. Examples include online versions of newspapers such as The *New York Times* <www.nytimes.com> and The *Wall Street Journal* <online.wsj.com>, CNN <www.cnn.com>, and National Public Radio <www.npr.org>. Major magazines, such as *Time* <www.time.com>, *Newsweek* <www.newsweek.com>, *Forbes* <www.forbes.com>, and other more specialized magazines also offer Web versions. Some news is available online only, as in the online magazines *Slate* <www.slate.com> and *Salon* <www.salon.com>.

Make sure you understand how the publication obtains and reviews information. Is it a major news site, such as CNN, or is it a smaller site run by a special-interest group? Each can be useful, but you must evaluate the source. Also keep in mind that many online magazines have a particular political bias. Is the magazine conservative or liberal in its point of view?

Blogs. *Blogs* (short for *Web logs*) are Web sites on which the blog's author posts ideas and other users reply to and discuss those postings. The postings and attached discussions are displayed in reverse chronological order, with the newest topic first, and an index of previous posts or an internal search engine leading to previous postings/discussions. Links that the owner has hand chosen also supply ways to connect to other blogs on the same or similar topics. Blogs are great for finding current information from individuals, companies, and nonprofit organizations that are knowledgeable about particular topics. You will find more blogs than you can use, so you need to evaluate the information on individual blogs carefully and decide which ones are most relevant and reliable.

Colleges and universities also host blogs as a way to support classroom teaching, provide space for student discussion, allow faculty to collaborate on research projects, and more. One excellent example is the University of Minnesota's UThink Project at <blog.lib.umn.edu>.

Keep in mind that blogs nearly always represent the particular views of the blog author (whether an individual, company, organization, or academic institution) and of those who reply to the blog postings. Check any information you find on a blog against a professionally edited or peer-reviewed source.

Wikis. *Wikis* are community encyclopedias that allow anyone to add to or edit the content of a listing. The most popular wiki is *Wikipedia* <www.wikipedia.org>. The theory of a wiki is that if the information from one posting is wrong, someone else will correct it, and over time the site will reach a high level of accuracy and reliability.

Always keep in mind that many wikis have no oversight. Aside from a few people who determine whether to delete articles based on requests from users, the content on a wiki is not checked by editors for accuracy. Always check information you find on a wiki against several other peer-reviewed or traditional sources. Remember that most of what is posted on a wiki has not been evaluated objectively.

Internet Forums and Electronic Mailing Lists. For almost any topic imaginable, you will find a Web forum, or discussion group, such as <discussions.apple.com/index.jspa> for users of Apple products. One way to locate relevant forums is to search through one of the major Internet forum providers. For instance, if you are researching a health-related issue such as stress among college students, you might want to visit *Google Groups* <groups.google.com> or *Yahoo! Groups* <groups.yahoo.com> and join a group related directly to that issue. As with blogs, you will find more Internet forums than you could ever possibly use, so choose them with care.

Electronic mailing lists, or e-lists, are essentially the same as Internet forums. Most Internet forums offer two options: either subscribing to and visiting the forum via the Web or subscribing to and receiving messages and responses from participants directly into your email inbox. Messages may be sent to the entire group, or you may reply to participants individually.

Material you find on Internet forums or receive via e-lists may be insightful but may not represent an adequate range of responses. Visit a variety of forums or subscribe to multiple e-lists to get a broad perspective on the issue. Information posted on Internet forums or sent out to e-list subscribers may or may not be moderated (approved by a reviewer prior to being posted). Unmoderated material is usually less reliable.

E-Libraries.

Entirely searchable via the Internet, e-libraries are excellent research tools. Aside from the online sites sponsored by most public libraries, the most notable e-library is the Internet Public Library at <www.ipl.org>, an online-only, noncommercial, and academically reliable virtual library founded by the University of Michigan's School of Information. Like other e-libraries, the Internet Public Library includes links to online books, magazines, and newspapers, along with online ready references (almanacs, dictionaries, encyclopedias, etc.), links to periodical databases, online exhibits, links to special collections organized by subject area, and even "live" librarians.

Although e-libraries can be extremely useful stand-ins for traditional, physical libraries, they can never entirely take the place of traditional libraries. They are limited to resources available in electronic form, which will not include current books under copyright or a wide range of magazine and newspaper articles and other resources. Supplement what you discover at an e-library with hard-copy materials from a traditional library.

Periodical Databases.

Virtually all libraries have their own Web site where, if you are a library cardholder or a student, you can access a wide variety of periodical databases. Periodical databases are electronic collections of articles from newspapers, magazines, journals, and other publications. You can search these databases by title, author, keyword, and so on.

When searching a periodical database, follow the same keyword guidelines you would use when searching the Internet (page 35); for instance, narrow your search when you get too many hits or expand your search if you don't find enough relevant material. Once you have typed in your keyword(s), you will be presented with a citation page that includes some or all of the following information: author(s), title, source, subject area, abstract (a brief summary of the article), ISSN (International Standard Serial Number—an identifier for the article much like a book's ISBN number), and DOI (or Digital Object Identifier—where the article can be found on the Web if it is available online).

Some of the most popular general periodical databases include *InfoTrac*, *NewsBank*, *ProQuest*, and *EBSCOHost*, but there are also many specialized periodical databases in a variety of subjects areas to which your library may also subscribe.

Before initiating a periodical database search, try to meet with your local reference librarian for a tour of the various databases and the instructions for searching them effectively. Also be aware that some databases may not be accessible from school or home—you may need to visit your library in person.

Hard-Copy Secondary Sources

As noted previously, traditional printed secondary research tools are still of great value. Unlike much of what you may find on the Web, most hard-copy secondary sources are carefully reviewed and edited before they are published. Although it may take more time to go to the library and look through a printed book or other hard-copy source, it's often a better way to get solid information. Also, even though the digitizing of hard-copy materials continues to grow, many of these printed sources are not available on the Web, particularly the full texts of books.

Hard-copy secondary sources can be located in your library by using the "card catalog," or, to use a more contemporary term (because cards are no longer used in most libraries), your library's online public access catalog (OPAC). This catalog can be accessed through the Internet or at terminals in the library. You can search a library's holdings by subject, author, title, or keyword in that library's OPAC. Visit the library's Web site, or ask a librarian for help. To search catalogs from libraries worldwide, go to the *Library of Congress Gateway* at <www.loc.gov/z3950> or *LibrarySpot* at <www.libraryspot.com>.

> Locate hard-copy secondary sources using your library's "card catalog," or OPAC

The following are the principal categories of hard-copy information sources found at libraries, and one type of source material (gray literature) that you will need to track down on your own.

Books and Periodicals. Most obviously, any library will be well stocked with books as well as numerous hard-copy magazines, journals, and newspapers. The smaller and more general the library you visit, the less likely you are to find highly specialized print sources, and the larger or more specialized the library, the more likely you are to find books by specialist publishers and periodicals that delve into more specific subject areas.

Although not technically in hard-copy format, you may also want to consult available CD-ROMs and microfiche. However, these technologies are now out of date and have largely migrated to a Web-based environment.

When consulting books and periodicals, be sure to check the copyright date and supplement the source with additional information from more recent sources, if necessary.

Reference Works. Reference works are general information sources that provide background and can lead to more specific information.

- **Bibliographies.** Bibliographies are lists of books or articles by subject field. To locate bibliographies in your field, begin by consulting the *Bibliographic Index Plus*, a list (by subject) of major bibliographies, which indexes over 500,000 bibliographies worldwide. You can also consult such general bibliographies as *Books in Print* or the *Reader's Guide to Periodical Literature*. Or, consult subject area bibliographies, such as *Bibliography of World War II History*, or highly focused bibliographies, such as *Health Hazards of Video Display Terminals: An Annotated Bibliography*.

- **Indexes.** Book and article bibliographies may also be referred to as indexes. However, other types of indexes collect information not likely to be found in standard bibliographies, such as indexes to conference proceedings (e.g., the *Index to Scientific and Technical Proceedings* and *Engineering Meetings*), which collect the most current information in various fields not yet published in book or periodical form; patent indexes (e.g., the *Index of Patents Issued from the United States Patent and Trademark Office* and the *World Patents Index*), which collect cutting-edge technological descriptions not yet widely available to the public; and technical report indexes (e.g., *Scientific and Technical Aerospace Reports* and the *Government Reports Announcements and Index*), which also collect highly current information unavailable elsewhere.

- **Encyclopedias.** Encyclopedias are alphabetically arranged collections of articles (written by the encyclopedia's editors and contributors). You may want to start by consulting a general encyclopedia, such as *Encyclopedia Britannica* or the *Columbia Encyclopedia*, but then consult more specific subject-focused encyclopedias, such as *Encyclopedia of Nutritional Supplements*, *American Jurisprudence*, *Encyclopedia of Business and Finance*, or *Illustrated Encyclopedia of Aircraft*.

- **Dictionaries.** Dictionaries are alphabetically arranged lists of words, including definitions, pronunciations, and word origins. If you can't locate a particular word in a general dictionary (e.g., a highly specialized term or jargon specific to a certain field), consult a specialized dictionary, such as *Dictionary of Engineering and Technology*, *Dictionary of Psychology*, or *Dictionary of Media and Communication Studies*.

- **Handbooks.** Handbooks are books that offer condensed facts (formulas, tables, advice, examples) about particular fields. Examples include the *Civil Engineering Handbook* and *The McGraw-Hill Computer Handbook*.

- **Almanacs.** Almanacs are collections of factual and statistical data, usually arranged by subject area and published annually. Examples include general almanacs, such as the *World Almanac and Book of Facts*, or subject-specific almanacs, like the *Almanac for Computers* or *Baer's Agricultural Almanac*.

- **Directories.** Directories are books that provide updated information about organizations, companies, people, products, services, or careers, often listing addresses and phone numbers. Examples include *The Career Guide: Dun's Employment Opportunities Directory* and the *Directory of American Firms Operating in Foreign Countries*. For electronic versions, ask your librarian about *Hoover's Company Capsules* (for basic information on thousands of companies) and *Hoover's Company Profiles* (for detailed information).

- **Abstracts.** Abstracts are collections of summaries of books or articles, as you might find when searching a periodical database, but collected in one place. Abstracts can save you from having to track down a journal before deciding whether to read or skip the article. Abstracts usually are titled by discipline: *Biological Abstracts, Computer Abstracts,* and so on. For some current research, you might consult abstracts of doctoral dissertations in *Dissertation Abstracts International*.

Many of the reference works mentioned here are accessible free via the Internet. Go to the Internet Public Library at <www.ipl.org>. This site provides links to many of the best available online reference works. When using a reference work, check the copyright date to make sure you are accessing the most current information available.

Gray Literature. Some useful printed information may not be available at any library. This is known as "gray literature," or materials that are unpublished or not typically catalogued. Examples include such helpful documents as pamphlets published by organizations or companies (such as medical pamphlets or company marketing materials), unpublished government documents (available under the Freedom of Information Act, with the exception of classified documents), dissertations by graduate students, papers presented at professional conferences, or self-published works.

The only way to track down gray literature is to contact organizations, companies, or individuals who may produce such literature and ask them if they have anything available in your subject area. For instance, you could contact a professional organization asking for papers on your topic delivered at their recent annual conference, or contact a specific government agency for statistics reports directly relevant to your topic. Before doing so, know your research topic well and know specifically who to contact and why, in case they should ask. Don't contact potential gray literature providers with vague, general requests for information.

Keep in mind that gray literature, like much material found on the Web, is often not carefully scrutinized for content by editors. Therefore, the material may not be reliable and should be backed up by information from other sources.

EXPLORING PRIMARY SOURCES

Types of primary sources

Analyze the Survey at **mytechcommlab**

Once you have explored your research topic in depth by finding out what others have already uncovered, supplement that knowledge with information you uncover yourself by doing primary research. Primary sources include unsolicited inquiries, informational interviews, surveys, and observations or experiments.

Unsolicited Inquiries

Unsolicited inquiries uncover basic but important information

The most basic form of primary research is making simple unsolicited inquiries. Letters, phone calls, or email inquiries to experts listed in Web pages or to people you find out about in other ways can yield information that adds to, clarifies, or supplements information you already have. When making an unsolicited inquiry, make sure you contact the right individual or individuals. Don't just contact a company or department. Also, ask exactly what you need to know, rather than vague, general questions, and be sure what you ask is not confidential or otherwise sensitive.

Note that unsolicited inquiries, especially by phone or email, can be intrusive or even offensive. Therefore, limit yourself to one or two questions that don't require extensive research or thought on the part of the person or persons you contact.

Informational Interviews

Informational interviews lead to original, unpublished material

An excellent primary source of information is the informational interview, a solicited and extended form of inquiry. Much of what an expert knows may never be published. Therefore, you can uncover highly original information by spending time with someone and asking pertinent questions. In addition, an interviewee might refer you to other experts or sources of information.

Expert opinion is not always reliable

Watch the Video on Conducting an Interview at **mytechcommlab**

Of course, an expert's opinion can be just as mistaken or biased as anyone else's. Like patients who seek second opinions about serious medical conditions, researchers seek a balanced range of expert opinions about complex problems or controversial issues—not only from a company engineer and environmentalist, for example, but also from independent and presumably more objective third parties such as a professor or journalist who has studied the issue. See the following Strategies for advice on effective interviews.

STRATEGIES
for Informational Interviews

▸ **Know exactly what you're seeking.** Write out a purpose statement. For example, "The purpose of my interview with Leslie Brown, clinical nutritionist, is to ask about her latest research on the possible links between certain genetically modified foods and childhood Attention Deficit Disorder."

▶ **Do your homework.** Learn all you can about the topic beforehand. If the interviewee has published anything relevant, read it. Be sure the information this person might provide is unavailable in print.

▶ **Request the interview at your respondent's convenience.** Ask whether the person objects to being quoted or taped. If possible, submit your questions beforehand.

▶ **Make each question clear, specific, and open-ended.** Don't ask vague or general questions, and avoid questions that can be answered with a mere *yes* or *no*. Get the benefit of the interviewee's elaboration.

▶ **Avoid loaded questions.** A loaded question invites or promotes a particular bias. For example, don't ask, "In what ways do you think the hazards of genetically modified foods have been overstated?" Ask impartial questions instead, such as "In your opinion, have the hazards associated with genetically modified food been accurately stated, overstated, or understated?"

▶ **Save the most difficult, complex, or sensitive questions for last.** Leading off with your toughest questions might annoy interviewees, making them uncooperative for the remainder of the interview.

▶ **Be polite and professional.** Arrive on time, express your gratitude, and explain why you believe the interviewee can be helpful and how you will use the information.

▶ **Let your interviewee do most of the talking.** Be a good listener. This courtesy ensures that the interviewee will provide the most information with the least interruption or leading from you.

▶ **Ask for clarification if needed, but do not put words in the respondent's mouth.** Questions such as "Could you go over that again?" or "What did you mean by that word?" are fine, but do not impose erroneous conclusions. Instead, paraphrase what the interviewee said so that she or he can verify your interpretation.

▶ **Stick to your interview plan.** If the interviewee wanders off topic, politely nudge him or her back on track (unless the information is useful).

▶ **Ask for closing comments.** Questions such as "Would you care to add anything?" or "Do you feel you've said what you wanted to say?" give the interviewee a chance to elaborate and clarify, and you may end up with useful additional information.

▶ **Ask for permission to follow up.** Additional questions may come to mind later, so find out if your interviewee would be willing to help with those new questions.

▶ **Invite the interviewee to read your version of the interview.** If the interview is to be published, this prevents possible misquotation or misinterpretation.

▶ **End on time and thank the interviewee.** Don't drag the interview on longer than the interviewee expected. Be sure to thank the interviewee for his or her time.

▶ **As soon as possible, transcribe your notes or recordings.** Get the interview down in writing before you forget important details.

Surveys

Surveys provide multiple, fresh viewpoints on a topic

 Explore the Concept with the Case Study on Surveys at mytechcommlab

Surveys help you form impressions of the concerns, preferences, attitudes, beliefs, or perceptions of a large, identifiable group (a *target population*) by studying representatives of that group (a *sample*). While interviews allow for greater clarity and depth, surveys offer an inexpensive way to get the viewpoints of a large group. Respondents can answer privately and anonymously—and often more candidly than in an interview.

The tool for conducting surveys is the questionnaire. Use the following Strategies to plan a survey and to develop a questionnaire.

STRATEGIES for Surveys

▶ **Define the survey's purpose and target population.** Ask yourself, "Why is this survey being performed?" "What, exactly, is it measuring?" "How much background research do I need?" "How will the survey findings be used?" and "Who is the exact population being studied?"

▶ **Identify the sample group.** Determine how many respondents you need. Generally, the larger the sample surveyed the more dependable the results (assuming a well-chosen and representative sample). Also determine how the sample will be chosen. Will they be randomly chosen? In the statistical sense, *random* does not mean "haphazard." A random sample means that each member of the target population stands an equal chance of being in the sample group.

▶ **Define the survey method.** Decide how the survey will be administered—by phone, by mail, or online. Each has its benefits and drawbacks. Phone surveys yield fast results and high response rates; however, they take longer than written surveys, many respondents find them annoying, and respondents tend to be less candid when speaking with someone in person. Mail surveys are less expensive than phone surveys and promote candid responses, but many people won't bother taking a trip to the mailbox or post office to return the survey, and results can be slow to arrive. Online surveys, conducted via a Web form or an email, are the least expensive and yield quick results, but computer connections can fail, and (in the case of Web surveys) you have less control over how many times the same person responds to the survey.

▶ **Decide on the types of questions.** Questions can be open-ended or closed-ended. Open-ended questions ("How much do you know about genetically modified food products?") allow respondents to answer in any way they choose. Data gathered from open-ended questions are time-consuming to measure, but they provide rich information. Closed-ended questions ("Are you concerned about genetically modified food products? Yes/No.") do not allow respondents to elaborate on their responses. Data from closed-ended questions are easily measured but more limited in value.

➡

▶ **Develop an engaging and informative introduction.** Thank the respondents; persuade them that the questionnaire relates to their concerns and that their answers matter; provide directions for completing the survey; and ensure the anonymity of respondents. For example: "Thank you for helping us with our survey. Your responses will help determine the public's view regarding genetically modified foods. Please answer each question by filling in one reply only in black ink and return the completed questionnaire in the enclosed postage paid return envelope. All responses will be kept confidential. Again, thank you for your input."

▶ **Phrase questions precisely.** Vague phrasing will only lead to inaccurate answers and findings. Avoid combining questions or asking the same basic question more than once.

▶ **Avoid loaded questions.** Do not invite or advocate a particular point of view or bias.

▶ **Make the survey brief, simple, and inviting.** Respondents don't mind giving up some time to help, but long and difficult-to-read questionnaires usually get few replies.

▶ **Have an expert review your questionnaire whenever possible.** A survey expert or an expert on the topic can help you ask just the right questions.

Observations and Experiments

Observations or experiments should be your final step because you now know exactly what to look for.

Observations are firsthand examinations of people, processes, places, and so on, using only your senses. When you make observations, have a plan in place. Know how, where, and when to look, and jot down your observations immediately. You might even take photos or draw sketches of what you observe.

Experiments are controlled forms of observations designed to verify assumptions (e.g., the role of fish oil in preventing heart disease) or to test something untried (e.g., the relationship between background music and productivity). Each field has its own guidelines for conducting experiments (e.g., you must use certain equipment, scrutinize your results in a certain way), and you must follow those guidelines to the letter when you conduct your own experiments.

Remember that observations and experiments are not foolproof. When making an observation or performing an experiment, you may be biased about what you see (focusing on the wrong events, ignoring something important). In addition, if you are observing people or experimenting using people as subjects, they may be conscious of being observed and may alter their normal behaviors.

Observations and experiments offer proof to back up assumptions about a topic

CHECKLIST
for Doing Research

- ☐ Have I maintained a high level of critical thinking while researching?
- ☐ Have I asked the right questions?
- ☐ Have I considered a balance of views?
- ☐ Have I explored my topic in sufficient depth?
- ☐ Have I evaluated each source for reliability?
- ☐ Have I interpreted my sources objectively?
- ☐ Have I effectively used search engines and subject directories to consult Web-based secondary sources?
- ☐ Have I used critical thinking to assess Web-based secondary sources?
- ☐ Have I consulted hard-copy secondary sources (including gray literature) as needed?
- ☐ Have I supplemented findings from secondary sources with primary research whenever possible?
- ☐ Have I added my own findings to existing findings whenever possible?
- ☐ Have I kept careful and precise track of each source I am using?

APPLICATIONS

GENERAL APPLICATIONS

▪▪▪▪ Analyze the **Research Report,** "Study Habits of Introverts and Extroverts," at **mytechcommlab**

1. Locate an expert in your field or your major for an upcoming project (such as a long report). Arrange to interview that person. You may wish to make your initial contact via email. Follow the Strategies on pages 44–45. Discuss your interview experiences and your findings with classmates.

▪▪▪▪ Analyze the **Research Report,** "Service Lifetimes of Mineral End Uses," at **mytechcommlab**

2. Identify two major indexes to locate research articles for your field or topic. One source should be a traditional periodical index, and the other should be an Internet search engine. Find a recent article on a specific topic (e.g., privacy laws in your state), and write a short summary.

▪▪▪▪ Analyze the **Research Report,** "Voice over Internet Protocol (VoIP): An Analysis," at **mytechcommlab**

TEAM APPLICATION

Divide into small groups, and prepare a comparative evaluation of literature search media. Each group member should select one of the resources listed here and create an individual bibliography of at least 12 recent and relevant works on a specific topic of interest selected by the group.

- Conventional print media
- Electronic catalogs
- CD-ROM services
- A commercial database service such as DIALOG
- The Internet and the World Wide Web
- An electronic consortium of libraries, if applicable

After recording the findings and keeping track of the time spent in each search, compare the ease of searching and quality of results obtained from each type of search on your group's selected topic. Which medium yielded the most current sources? Which provided abstracts and full texts as well as bibliographic data? Which consumed the most time? Which provided the most dependable sources? Which provided the most diverse or varied sources? Which cost the most to use? Finally, which yielded the greatest depth of resources? Prepare a report, and present your findings to the class.

GLOBAL APPLICATION

The International Space Station (ISS) is undoubtedly the largest and most complex international scientific project in history. Begun in 1995, the project requires the collaboration, expertise, and technological resources of 16 nations. The ISS has encountered delays and difficulties for a variety of reasons, including funding problems and the grounding of the NASA space shuttle program following the 2003 *Columbia* disaster.

Do some preliminary research on the scope and history of the project by visiting <www.shuttlepresskit.com/ISS_OVR>, and then follow the links from that site to the sites for the European, Japanese, and Canadian space agencies. How do those sites differ from the U.S.-based NASA sites? Do you find any differences in the way the mission of the ISS is described? In the ways the roles of each nation are defined?

Imagine that you have been assigned to produce a campaign to rally and reenergize public support around the world for the ISS project. What information would you use to persuade citizens of the participating nations that in today's world, it is worth their nation's time and money to support continued development of an international space station? Would you use different strategies to persuade people in different countries? Why?

Develop a one-page proposal that outlines the key features of your campaign, detailing how you would customize the style and argument of your campaign to persuade public audiences in the diverse nations involved in the ISS initiative.

COMPUTER/WEB-BASED APPLICATION

Researchers often have difficulty judging the validity of information found on a Web site. Working in small groups of three or four, do some research and develop a set of criteria that can be used when evaluating a Web site for research purposes.

Begin by visiting two to three Web sites related to a research project for this or another class. Compile a working list of criteria based on these sites; then work as a group to expand your list. For example, do you consider good design to be an indicator of credibility? What else do you look at when you are assessing the relevance, currency, and validity of information on a particular site? How do you know if a site is commercially or politically biased? Test the criteria you have developed by using a search engine to locate Web sites on a current topic (e.g., global warming, genetically modified foods, software piracy, or mp3 file downloading). Select one site and evaluate its credibility as a source for research information using your own criteria. Revise your list as needed and then format it as a document that can be shared with the rest of your class.

For additional technical writing resources that will help you master the chapter objectives, go to **www.mytechcommlab.com.**

4

Providing Audiences with Usable Information

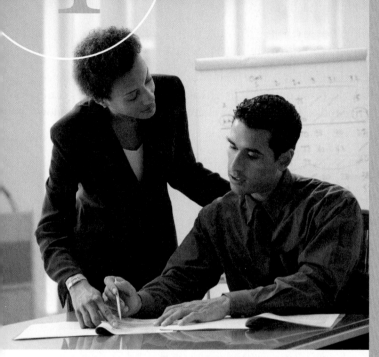

LEARNING OBJECTIVES FOR THIS CHAPTER

▶ Analyze a document's audience (primary and secondary, relationship to you, technical and cultural background)

▶ Determine a document's purpose (primary and secondary, intended use)

▶ Identify the persuasive elements involved

▶ Create a task analysis for a document (main task and subtasks)

▶ Consider a document's setting, potential problems, length, format, timing, and budget

▶ Develop an information plan for a document

▶ Understand the stages in writing, testing, and revising a document

Definition
of usability

A document's *usability* is a measure of how well that document fulfills the information needs of its audience. Whatever their specific goals and concerns in using a particular document, readers must be able to do at least three things (Coe, *Human Factors* 193; Spencer 74):

What a usable
document enables
readers to do

- Locate the information they need easily.
- Understand the information immediately.
- Use the information safely and successfully.

To assess the usability of a manual that comes with your new gas grill, for instance, you would ask: "How well do these instructions enable me to assemble, operate, and maintain the grill safely and effectively?" To prepare a usable document, follow these six steps:

Steps in preparing
a usable document

1. Analyze the document's audience.
2. Determine the document's purpose.
3. Create a task analysis for the document.
4. Consider the setting, potential problems, length, format, timing, and budget.
5. Develop an information plan for the document.
6. Write, test, and revise the document.

✳ Explore the Tutorial
on Usability
at mytechcommlab

ANALYZE THE DOCUMENT'S AUDIENCE

You cannot create an effective document until you first explore all you can about *who* will use your document. In other words, understand your audience. Ask these questions:

Questions to ask
to analyze a
document's audience

- Who is the main audience for this document?
- Who else is likely to read it?
- What is your relationship with the audience? Are there multiple types of relationships involved?
- How familiar might the audience be with technical details?
- What culture or cultures does your audience represent?

▪▪ Analyze the Fact
▪▪▪ Sheet for
audience-
friendliness at
mytechcommlab

Answer these questions by considering the suggestions in the sections that follow, and by filling in the audience portion of the Audience and Purpose Profile Sheet shown in Figure 4.1 before writing any technical documents. Also, have a look at the Strategies for Analyzing Your Audience on page 57.

Primary and Secondary Audiences

Determine the
primary and
secondary audiences

When writing a technical document, keep two audiences in mind. Most documents are geared to an immediate audience. This is your *primary audience*. For instance,

Audience

Primary audience: _____ (*name, title*)

Secondary audience(s): _____

Relationship with audience members: _____

_____ (*client, employer, other*)

Technical background of audience: _____

_____ (*layperson, expert, other*)

Cultural background of audience: _____

Purpose

Primary purpose: _____ (*inform, instruct, persuade*)

Secondary purpose(s): _____

Intended use of document: _____

_____ (*master concepts, follow directions, other*)

FIGURE 4.1
Audience and purpose profile sheet

 View the **Audience and Purpose Profile Sheet** at **mytechcommlab**

a set of instructions for installing new email software for an office might be directed primarily at the computer support staff who would be doing the installing. But most documents also have a *secondary audience* as well, those people outside the immediate circle of people who will be needing the information directly. For example, a secondary audience for software instructions might be managers, who will check to see if the instructions comply with company policy, or lawyers, who will make sure the instructions meet legal standards.

Relationship with Audience

Besides identifying the primary and secondary audiences in a general way, you also need to understand your relationship with everyone involved. In your situation, are the primary readers of your document going to be superiors, colleagues, or subordinates? Determining which will help you decide the level of formality and authority to use in the document. Are they going to be from inside or outside your organization? Answering this question will help you to decide how confidential you need to be. Do you know your readers personally? This information can help you decide if you can adopt a more informal tone. Are they likely to welcome or reject your information? Knowing the answer will help you decide how persuasive you need to be. Are they a combination of people from various levels, both inside and outside the company? This knowledge will help you to determine how evenhanded your writing needs to be. Also, how might you speak to the needs of secondary audience members, who may be interested in or affected by your document?

Determine your relationship with the audience or audiences

Audience's Technical Background

Be aware of your audience's technical background

Any message can be conveyed in numerous ways, depending on how it is written and designed for different audiences. For example, information about a new cancer treatment may appear in a medical journal for health care professionals, in a textbook for nursing or medical students, or in a newspaper article for the general public. Always keep in mind the technical background of your audience.

Consider the technical level of your general target audience

A document's technical level needs to target the intended audience. For example, an audience of medical professionals will understand technical terms readily; an audience of medical and nursing students will have some familiarity with such terms but will be in the process of learning; and the general public may not understand technical terminology at all. Thus, articles for each of these audiences will differ in language, content, organization, illustrations, and overall design.

Consider the technical level of your specific target audience

The larger the audience the more you must consider the various levels of expertise and language differences. For example, medical professionals can be divided into subgroups of specialists and general practitioners; medical and nursing students can be divided into subgroups based on years of training; and the general public can be divided into subgroups who read popular medical journals and those who have little or no familiarity with medical information.

To illustrate the importance of these audience differences, Figures 4.2 and 4.3 show two pieces of information, both about the over-the-counter medication Bayer aspirin. Both items address the same topic, but each document is designed and written for a different audience. The Web page in Figure 4.2 is designed for a general audience. It uses straightforward, nontechnical language and color visuals. Note, however, that the page is written not for just any general audience but more specifically for a subgroup: readers who have some awareness of the medical uses of aspirin (for pain; for the heart) and want to learn more. The page from the *Physicians' Desk Reference* (PDR) in Figure 4.3, on the other hand, is designed for an audience of health care professionals not patients. It uses highly technical language and a molecular diagram as its one visual. Yet it, too, targets a specific audience within the larger group: not all health care professionals, but physicians, nurses, and pharmacists who will understand the complex statistics, terminology, and visuals.

Audience's Cultural Background

Consider the audience's cultural background

Information needs and preferences often are culturally determined. German audiences, for example, often value thoroughness and complexity with detail included and explained in a businesslike tone. Japanese audiences generally prefer multiple perspectives on the material, plenty of graphics, and a friendly, encouraging tone (Hein 125–26). Western business culture generally values plain talk that gets right

FIGURE 4.2 Bayer aspirin Web page written and designed for a general audience
Source: Copyright © 2009 BayerHealthCare LLC. All rights reserved. Reproduced by permission.

to the point, but Eastern cultures consider this rude, preferring indirect, more ambiguous messages, which leave interpretation up to the reader. Consider how cultural differences might create misunderstanding in your situation, and seek an approach that bridges these differences.

The Strategies on page 57 will help you analyze your audience.

FIGURE 4.3
Bayer aspirin entry from the _Physicians' Desk Reference_, written and designed for a technical audience

Bayer HealthCare LLC

Consumer Care
36 COLUMBIA ROAD
P.O. BOX 1910
MORRISTOWN, NJ 07962-1910

Direct Inquiries to:
Consumer Relations
(800) 331-4536
www.BayerAspirin.com

BAYER® ASPIRIN   **OTC**
Comprehensive Prescribing Information

DESCRIPTION
Aspirin for Oral Administration
Regular Strength 325 mg and Low Strength 81 mg Tablets
Antiplatelet, Antiarthritic

Aspirin

COOH

CH₃

$C_9H_8O_4$
Mol. Wt.: 180.16
C 60.00 %; H 4.48 %; O 35.52%

Aspirin is an odorless, white, needle-like crystalline or powdery substance. When exposed to moisture, aspirin hydrolyzes into salicylic and acetic acids, and gives off a vinegary-odor. It is highly lipid soluble and slightly soluble in water.

CLINICAL PHARMACOLOGY
Mechanism of Action
Aspirin is a more potent inhibitor of both prostaglandin synthesis and platelet aggregation than other salicylic acid derivatives. The differences in activity between aspirin and salicylic acid are thought to be due to the acetyl group on the aspirin molecule. This acetyl group is responsible for the inactivation of cyclo-oxygenase via acetylation.

Pharmacokinetics
Absorption: In general, immediate release aspirin is well and completely absorbed from the gastrointestinal (GI) tract. Following absorption, aspirin is hydrolyzed to salicylic acid with peak plasma levels of salicylic acid occurring in 1–2 hours of dosing (see Pharmacokinetics—Metabolism). The rate of absorption from the GI tract is dependent upon the dosage form, the presence or absence of food, gastric pH (the presence or absence of GI antacids or buffering agents), and other physiologic factors. Enteric coated aspirin products are erratically absorbed from the GI tract.
Distribution: Salicylic acid is widely distributed to all tissues and fluids in the body including the central nervous system (CNS), breast milk, and fetal tissues. The highest concentrations are found in the plasma, liver, renal cortex, heart, and lungs. The protein binding of salicylate is concentration-dependent. i.e., non-linear. At low concentrations (< 100 micrograms/milliliter (mcg/mL)), approximately 90 percent of plasma salicylate is bound to albumin while at higher concentrations (>400 mcg/mL), only about 75 percent is bound. The early signs of salicylic overdose (salicylism), including tinnitus (ringing in the ears), occur at plasma concentrations approximating 200 mcg/mL. Severe toxic effects are associated with levels >400 mcg/mL. (See **ADVERSE REACTIONS** and **OVER DOSAGE.**)

Metabolism: Aspirin is rapidly hydrolyzed in the plasma to salicylic acid such that plasma levels of aspirin are essentially undetectable 1–2 hours after dosing. Salicylic acid is primarily conjugated in the liver to form salicyluric acid, a phenolic glucuronide, an acyl glucuronide, and a number of minor metabolites. Salicylic acid has a plasma half-life of approximately 6 hours. Salicylate metabolism is saturable and total body clearance decreases at higher serum concentrations due to the limited ability of the liver to form both salicyluric acid and phenolic glucuronide. Following toxic doses (10–20 grams (g)), the plasma half-life may be increased over 20 hours.

Elimination: The elimination of salicylic acid follows zero order pharmacokinetics; (i.e., the rate of drug elimination is constant in relation to plasma concentration). Renal excretion of unchanged drug depends upon urine pH. As urinary pH rises above 6.5, the renal clearance of free salicylate increases from < 5 percent to >80 percent. Alkalinization of the urine is a key concept in the management of salicylate overdose. (See **OVERDOSAGE.**) Following therapeutic doses, approximately 10 percent is found excreted in the urine as salicylic acid, 75 percent as salicyluric acid, 10 percent phenolic and 5 percent acyl glucuronides of salicylic acid.

Pharmacodynamics
Aspirin affects platelet aggregation by irreversibly inhibiting prostaglandin cyclo-oxygenase. This effect lasts for the life of the platelet and prevents the formation of the platelet aggregating factor thromboxane A2. Non-acetylated salicylates do not inhibit this enzyme and have no effect on platelet aggregation. At somewhat higher doses, aspirin reversibly inhibits the formation of prostaglandin I2 (prostacyclin), which is an arterial vasodilator and inhibits platelet aggregation. At higher doses aspirin is an effective anti-inflammatory agent, partially due to inhibition of inflammatory mediators via cyclo-oxygenase inhibition in peripheral tissues. In vitro studies suggest that other mediators of inflammation may also be suppressed by aspirin administration, although the precise mechanism of action has not been elucidated. It is this nonspecific suppression of cyclo-oxygenase activity in peripheral tissues following large doses that leads to its primary side effect of gastric irritation. (See **ADVERSE REACTIONS.**)

CLINICAL STUDIES
Ischemic Stroke and Transient Ischemic Attack (TIA):
In clinical trials of subjects with TIA's due to fibrin platelet emboli or ischemic stroke, aspirin has been shown to significantly reduce the risk of the combined endpoint of stroke or death and the combined endpoint of TIA, stroke, or death by about 13–18 percent.
Suspected Acute Myocardial Infarction (MI):
In a large, multi-center study of aspirin, streptokinase, and the combination of aspirin and streptokinase in 17,187 patients with suspected MI, aspirin treatment produced a 23-percent reduction in the risk of vascular mortality. Aspirin was also shown to have an additional benefit in patients given a thrombolytic agent.
Prevention of Recurrent MI and Unstable Angina Pectoris:
These indications are supported by the results of six large, randomized, multi-center, placebo-controlled trials of

Continued on next page

Information will be superseded by supplements and
subsequent editions.

STRATEGIES
for Analyzing Your Audience

▶ **Picture your readers and exactly what they need and expect.** Whether your audience is the company president or the person next to you in class, that person has specific concerns and information needs. Your readers may need to complete a task, solve a problem, make a decision, evaluate your performance, or take a stand on an issue.

▶ **Identify the primary and secondary audiences, your relationship to them, and their technical and cultural background.**

▶ **When you don't know exactly who will be reading your document, picture the "general reader."** General readers are impatient with abstract theories yet expect enough background to help them grasp your message. They are bored or confused by excessive detail, and frustrated by raw facts left unexplained or not interpreted. Instead of trying to show readers how smart you are, make *them* feel smart. Whoever they are, readers need enough material to understand your position and to react appropriately.

▶ **Anticipate readers' questions.** Based on their needs and concerns, readers have questions: What is it? What does it mean? What happened? Who was involved? When, where, and why did it happen? What might happen? How do I do it? How did you do it? Why is X better than Y? Can you give examples? Says who? So what? Give readers what they need to know.

▶ **Recognize that audiences are not merely passive recipients of information.** Technical communicators and their audiences should overlap and interact. Therefore, as you analyze and learn about your audience, remember that the communication process works both ways.

DETERMINE THE DOCUMENT'S PURPOSE

To create an effective technical document you need to understand *how* readers will use it. In other words, determine your purpose. Ask these questions:

- What is the main purpose of the document?
- What other purpose or purposes does the document serve?
- What will readers do with this information?

Questions to ask to determine a document's purpose

Answer these questions by considering the suggestions in the sections that follow and by filling in the purpose portion of the Audience and Purpose Profile Sheet shown in Figure 4.1 before writing any technical document.

Primary and Secondary Purposes

Decide if the primary purpose of the document is to inform, instruct, or persuade

All forms of technical communication are intended to fulfill a specific *primary purpose*. As discussed in Chapter 1, the primary purpose (to inform, to instruct, or to persuade) will affect the document's overall shape and substance.

Determine if the document serves any secondary purposes

Many documents have a primary purpose and one or more *secondary purposes*. For example, the primary purpose in most instruction manuals is to instruct, that is, to teach an audience how to assemble or use the product. But for ethical and legal reasons, companies also want people to use the product safely. A manual for a power tool or a lawnmower, for instance, typically begins with a page that spells out safety hazards, before instructing readers how to assemble and use the mechanism.

Always write a comprehensive purpose statement

In planning a document, work from a clear statement of purpose that takes into account both the primary and secondary purposes. For example, "The purpose of my document is to inform my readers of the new absentee policy, and to instruct them on how to follow the procedures properly," or "The purpose of my document is to inform my readers about the new antivirus software, as well as to instruct them on how to install the software and to persuade them of the importance of running weekly virus scans."

Intended Use of the Document

Determine how the document will be used

In addition to determining purposes of a document from your own perspective, also consider how and why it will be used by others. Answer a variety of questions: Do my readers simply want to learn facts or understand concepts? Will they use my information in making some decision? Will people act immediately on the information? Do they need step-by-step instructions? In my audience's view, what is most important about this document? In addition to asking yourself these questions, try asking members of your audience directly, so you can verify what they want to know.

KNOW HOW TO BE PERSUASIVE

In the workplace, we rely on persuasion daily: to win coworker support, to attract clients and customers, to request funding. An email, a memo, a product description, or a set of instructions can be an implicitly persuasive document. Even the most complex report, which at first glance may appear to be "all facts," can be persuasive, because the writer probably shaped the report to favor a particular interpretation of the data.

Why persuasion is difficult

Changing someone's mind is never easy—in fact, sometimes it is impossible. Your success will depend on what you are requesting, who you are trying to persuade, and how entrenched those people are in their own views.

Using Claims as a Basis for Persuasion

Explicit persuasion is required whenever you tackle an issue about which people disagree. Assume, for example, that you are Manager of Employee Relations at Softbyte, a software developer whose recent sales have plunged. To avoid layoffs, the company is trying to persuade employees to accept a temporary cut in salary. As you plan your various memos and presentations on this volatile issue, you must first identify your major claim or claims (a claim is a statement of the point you are trying to prove).

Claims set the stage for a persuasive appeal

For example, in the Softbyte case, you might first want employees to recognize and acknowledge facts about which they may have been unaware or have ignored:

> Because of the global recession, our software sales in two recent quarters have fallen nearly 30 percent, and earnings should remain flat all year.

A claim about what the facts are

Even when a fact is obvious, people often disagree about what it means or what should be done about it. And so you might want to influence their interpretation of the facts:

> Reduced earnings mean temporary layoffs for roughly 25 percent of our staff. But we could avoid layoffs entirely if each of us at Softbyte would accept a 10-percent salary cut until the market improves.

A claim about what the facts mean

And eventually you might want to ask for direct action:

> Our labor contract stipulates that such an across-the-board salary cut would require a two-thirds majority vote. Once you've had time to examine the facts, we hope you'll vote "yes" on next Tuesday's secret ballot.

A claim about what should be done

As you present your case, you will offer support for your claims before you finally ask readers to take the action you favor.

Whenever people disagree about what the facts are or what the facts mean or what should be done, you need to make the best case for your own view by presenting an argument that is not only well supported but that also connects with your audience.

Connecting with Your Audience

Determine how best to connect with your audience. Persuasive people know when to simply declare what they want (get the reader to *comply* with what you say), when to reach out and create a relationship (get the reader to *identify* with what you say), when to appeal to reason and common sense (get the reader to *internalize* what you say), and when to employ some combination of these approaches (Kipnis and Schmidt 40–46). These three approaches, respectively, can be labeled the *power connection*, the *relationship connection*, and the *rational connection*, as illustrated in Figure 4.4.

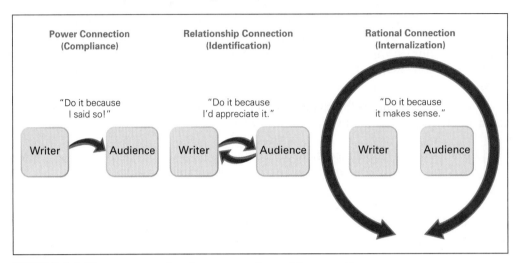

FIGURE 4.4 Three approaches for connecting with an audience

Choosing the best connection(s)

To get a better understanding of these three different approaches, consider the following scenario: Your Company, XYZ Engineering, has just developed a fitness program based on findings that healthy employees work better, take fewer sick days, and cost less to insure. This program offers clinics for smoking cessation, stress reduction, and weight loss, along with group exercise.

In your second month on the job you read this notice in your email:

> TO: Employees at XYZ.com
> FROM: GMaximus@XYZ.com
> DATE: June 6, 20xx
> SUBJECT: Physical Fitness
>
> *Power connection*
>
> On Monday, June 10, all employees will report to the company gymnasium at 8:00 A.M. for the purpose of choosing a walking or jogging group. Each group will meet for 30 minutes three times weekly during lunch time.

How would you react to the previous notice? Despite the reference to "choosing," the recipients of this memo are given no real choice. They are simply ordered to show up at the company gymnasium. Typically used by bosses and other authority figures, this type of approach does get people to comply, but it almost always alienates them as well.

Suppose, instead, that you receive this next version of the memo. How would you react in this instance?

TO: Employees at XYZ.com

FROM: GMaximus@XYZ.com

DATE: June 6, 20xx

SUBJECT: An Invitation to Physical Fitness

I realize that most of you spend lunch hour playing cards, reading, or just enjoying a bit of well-earned relaxation in the middle of a hectic day. But I'd like to invite you to join our lunchtime walking/jogging club.

We're starting this club in the hope that it will be a great way for us all to feel better. Why not give it a try?

Relationship connection

This second version conveys the sense that "we're all in this together." Instead of being commanded, readers are invited to participate in the exercise program. Someone who seems likable and considerate offers readers a real choice.

Often the biggest variable in a persuasive message is the reader's perception of the writer. Readers are more open to people they like and trust. The relationship connection often works for this reason, and it is especially vital in cross-cultural communication—as long as it does not sound too "chummy" and informal to carry any real authority.

Of course, you would be unethical using a relationship connection merely to hide the fact that you have no evidence to support your claim (R. Ross 28). People need to find the claim believable ("Exercise will help me feel better") and relevant ("I personally need this kind of exercise").

Here is a third version of the memo. As you read, think about the ways in which its approach differs from the first two examples.

TO: Employees at XYZ.com

FROM: GMaximus@XYZ.com

DATE: June 6, 20xx

SUBJECT: Invitation to Join One of Our Jogging or Walking Groups

I want to share a recent study from the *New England Journal of Medicine*, which reports that adults who walk two miles a day could increase their life expectancy by as much as three years.

Other research shows that 30 minutes of moderate aerobic exercise, at least three times weekly, has a significant and long-term effect in reducing stress, lowering blood pressure, and improving job performance.

As a first step in our exercise program, XYZ Engineering is offering a variety of daily jogging groups: The One-Milers, Three-Milers, and Five-Milers. All groups will meet at designated times on our brand new, quarter-mile, rubberized clay track.

For beginners or skeptics, we're offering daily two-mile walking groups. For the truly resistant, we offer the option of a Monday–Wednesday–Friday two-mile walk.

Rational connection

> Coffee and lunch breaks can be rearranged to accommodate whichever group you select.
>
> Why not take advantage of our hot new track? As small incentives, XYZ will reimburse anyone who signs up as much as $100 for running or walking shoes, and will even throw in an extra fifteen minutes for lunch breaks. And with a consistent turnout of 90 percent or better, our company insurer may be able to eliminate everyone's $200 yearly deductible in medical costs.

This version conveys respect for the reader's intelligence and for the relationship. With any reasonable audience, the rational connection stands the best chance of success.

For more on persuasion see the Strategies that follow.

STRATEGIES
for Persuasion

- **Identify your specific goal.** What exactly do you want readers to do: change their opinion, change their behavior, or take specific action?

- **Anticipate your audience's reaction.** Typically, when you try to change people's minds or get them to do something, they will naturally resist. Try to address their biggest objections beforehand. Will people be surprised, annoyed, or angry at your attempt? Will they agree with you in essence but want to know further details? Be careful to express your arguments ("We could do better") without making people defensive ("It's all your fault"). Also, be prepared to field negative reactions after your message is delivered and to back off if your message is rejected.

- **Don't ask for too much.** No matter how persuasive you are, if you ask for what seems like too much, your argument will fail. Ask for what your audience will consider reasonable, not outlandish. Consider what is achievable in this situation.

- **Allow for give-and-take.** Be flexible in your argument. Indicate you are able to see your argument from the recipient's point of view, and offer possible alternatives or compromises along with what you want to accomplish.

- **Recognize constraints.** For various reasons other than their personal opinions, recipients may be unable to comply with your request. For example, readers may have time constraints, organizational constraints (deadlines, budgets), legal constraints (agreements, laws), ethical constraints (when the request is legal, but not necessarily ethical), and social and psychological constraints (shyness, fear of failure, fear of disruption, fear of the unknown).

- **Consider the cultural context.** How people react to your persuasive appeals may be culturally based. Will some audience members feel that your message ignores

➡

customs? Will they be offended by too many facts and figures without a relationship connection? Will they be offended by a direct approach? Remember that cultural groups consist not only of racial and ethnic groups but also groups connected by religious or spiritual views, sexual orientation, physical ability, and so on.

▶ **Choose the right time and the right medium.** Consider how the timing of your message (just prior to a vacation, during the busy season, during a period of optimism) and the way in which it is delivered (in person, over email, in a printed memo) will affect how positively it is received.

▶ **Connect with your audience.** Using the power connection may work but it will likely alienate your audience; using the relationship connection may appeal to readers but fail to convince them. Whenever possible, use the rational connection, or even better, a rational connection combined with a relationship connection.

CREATE A TASK ANALYSIS FOR THE DOCUMENT

Most technical documents entail a series of tasks to be completed, tasks most evident in a set of instructions: if users want to change an oil filter, assemble a new gas grill, or install a new word-processing program, they clearly must follow a step-by-step procedure. Less obvious is that other documents, such as reports, memos, and brochures, also involve a series of user tasks. For instance, when reading a report, a manager may need to extract information and write a response. Similarly, a technician may need to make a persuasive argument as to why the company should purchase new equipment. In short, most technical communication is task-oriented. People come to the information wanting to *do* something, and you want to ensure that they achieve their goal; therefore, you need to think through the step-by-step nature of your document before you write it by creating a *task analysis*.

For your task analysis, you can create a worksheet similar to those shown in Figures 4.5 and 4.6. Begin by defining the main tasks. For example, in planning an instruction manual to accompany a gas grill, you might start your task analysis (Figure 4.5) by defining the main user tasks as "assemble the grill," "use the grill," and "maintain the grill," and then divide these larger tasks into several smaller tasks, or subtasks ("locate all parts," "get the required tools," "lay out parts in order," etc.). Note that both the tasks and subtasks should be listed using active verb forms (*assemble, locate, get*, and so on).

Similarly, planning a short report to management, arguing for change in a company policy, you would begin your persuasive task plan (Figure 4.6) with the main task to be accomplished ("get company dress code policy changed"), and then plan out the subtasks required to accomplish that main task.

Explore the **Concept** with the Case Study on Planning Usability Tests at **mytechcommlab**

Define main tasks, then subtasks

FIGURE 4.5
**Sample task
analysis for a
procedure**

Main task: Assemble the grill.

Subtasks   1. Locate all parts.

2. Get the required tools.

3. Lay out parts in order.

4. Assemble parts into smaller units.

5. Assemble these smaller units into large units.

Main task: Use the grill.

Subtasks   1. Attach the gas canister.

2. Turn on the main gas valve.

3. Turn on the individual burners.

4. Press button to ignite.

Main task: Maintain the grill.

Subtasks   1. Turn off the main gas valve when not in use.

2. Cover to protect from rain.

3. Clean the grate regularly.

You can determine these tasks by interviewing users and watching them perform each step to complete the project (Figure 4.5), or by just carefully thinking through the approach that will yield the results you want (Figure 4.6). In short, your document will be most useful if you know what your audience needs to *do* in order to produce the desired results.

CONSIDER OTHER RELATED USABILITY FACTORS

Think about setting, potential problems, length, format, timing, and budget

Once you've answered questions about audience (*Who?*), purpose (*Why?*), and tasks (*How?*), it's time to consider smaller but no less important factors that influence the usability of your document: setting (*Where?*), potential problems (*What are the hazards?*), length (*How much information?*), format (*How does it look?*), timing (*When?*), and budget (*How much money?*).

Setting

Determine where your document will be used

Will distractions or interruptions make it hard for users to pay attention? Will users always have the document in front of them? Will they be scanning the

Main task: Persuade management to change company dress code policy.

Subtasks
- Remind management of specifics of current company dress policy.
- Persuade management to agree to first reason for new policy: employee resentment over too-strict policy.
- Persuade management to agree to second reason for new policy: changing attitude toward office dress countrywide (e.g., acceptance of "business casual," "casual Fridays").
- Persuade management to agree to third reason for new policy: flat salaries during recession versus rising cost of business attire.
- Win management over to new policy by highlighting beneficial results: higher employee morale, less absenteeism, more respect for management.

FIGURE 4.6
Sample task analysis worksheet for a goal

document, studying it, or memorizing it? Will they read page by page or consult the document randomly?

Potential Problems

How might the document be misinterpreted or misunderstood? Are there potential "trouble spots" (material too complex for these users, hard to follow, or packed with information)? Are any important points missing? Anticipating problems is important in creating any technical document but especially in a set of instructions; therefore, when preparing instructions plan on background research. In planning the gas grill instruction manual, for example, learn all you can about the typical users (age, education, and so on). If possible, observe first-time operators using the instructions for a previous model and then ask for their feedback. Also, find out how most injuries occur; check company records for customer complaints; get feedback from dealers; and ask your legal department about prior injury claims by customers.

Anticipate what might go wrong

Length

Decide on an acceptable length

How much information is enough? This depends on what you can learn about your audience's needs. Were you asked to "keep it short" or to "be comprehensive"? Are people more interested in conclusions and recommendations, or do they want everything spelled out?

Format

Decide on your document's format

Does your audience expect a letter, a memo, a short report, or a long, formal report with supplements (title page, table of contents, appendixes, and so on—see pages 321–324)? Can visuals and page layout (charts, graphs, drawings, headings, lists) make the material more accessible?

Timing

Consider due dates and timing

Does your document have a deadline? Workplace documents almost always do. Is there a best time to submit it? Do you need to break down the deadline into a schedule of milestones? Will any of your information become out of date if you wait too long to complete the document?

Budget

Consider the financial issues

Does your document have a budget? If so, how much? Where can you save money? How much time can your company afford to allot you for creating the document? How much money can you spend obtaining permission to use materials from other sources? How much can you spend on printing, binding, and distributing your document?

DEVELOP AN INFORMATION PLAN FOR THE DOCUMENT

Write out your plan

✳ Explore the Concept with the Case Study on Designing Usability Tests at **mytechcommlab**

Once you have a clear picture of the audience, purpose, user tasks, and related factors, you can draft an *information plan:* an outline based on all the previous considerations in this chapter. Information plans can be as short as a two- to three-page memo or as long as a multipage report, depending on your project. Begin with a clearly stated purpose statement ("Users will be able to assemble a gas grill within 30 minutes") so you can measure when a task has been success-fully completed (Rubin 97). Also include information about the audience, user tasks, setting, potential problems, length, format, timing, and budget.

Figure 4.7 is a sample information plan created in a short-memo format for the gas grill instructions. Note how this plan takes into account not just audience,

FIGURE 4.7
Sample
information
plan

GrillChef Corporation

To: Technical writing design team
From: Erin Green and Geoff Brannigan, team leaders
Date: January 21, 20XX
Re: Information plan for gas grill manual

As you know, our team recently performed an analysis of user needs as we prepare to design and write the new User Manual for the new GrillChef Model 2000 double-burner grill. This memo summarizes our findings and presents a plan for proceeding.

Part One: Analysis

Audience—The audience for this manual is very broad. It consists of consumers who purchase the grill. This purchase may be their first gas grill, or they may be replacing an old grill. Some users are making a switch from charcoal to gas. Our analysis revealed that the primary users are male and female, ranging in age from 25 to 50. From a focus group, we determined that most users are afraid to assemble the grill. But all members expressed enthusiasm about using the grill. Also, according to marketing, this grill is only sold in the United States.

Purpose—The manual has several purposes:
1. Instruct the user in assembling and using the grill.
2. Provide adequate safety instructions. These are to protect the user and to make sure we have complied with our legal requirements.
3. Provide a phone number, Web address, and other contact information if users have questions or need replacement parts.

User tasks—Our task analysis revealed three main tasks this manual must address:
1. How to assemble the grill. Users need clear instructions, a list of parts, and diagrams that can assist them. Users wish to be able to assemble the grill within 30 minutes to one hour.
2. How to use the grill. Users need clear instructions for operating the grill safely. Because some users have never used gas for grilling, we need to stress safety.
3. How to maintain the grill. Users need to know how to keep the grill clean, dry, and operational.

Part Two: Design Plans

Based on our analysis, we suggest designing a manual that is simple, easy to use, and contains information users need. We will follow the layout and format of our other manuals.

Rough outline—Cover with drawing of grill, model number, company name.

Inside front cover: safety warnings (our legal department has indicated that these warnings need to go first).

First section: Exploded diagram, list of parts, drawings of parts, numbered list of instructions for assembly.

Second section: Numbered list of steps for using the grill, accompanied by diagrams.

Third section: Bulleted list of tasks users must perform to maintain the grill.

Final page: Company address, phone number, and Web address.

Production guidelines—Our budget for this project will not allow for color printing or any photographs. We suggest black ink on white paper, 8-1/2 x 11 folded in half vertically. We can use line drawings of the Model 1999 and modify these to the specifications of the Model 2000.

Schedule—The manual must be ready for shipping on April 1, 20XX. We will follow our usual production and writing schedule, briefly summarized here:

February 21: First draft of manual is complete. Manual is usability tested on sample customers.

March 1: Manual is revised based on results of usability test.

March 3: Copyediting, proofreading, and final changes. Manual goes to the printer.

March 30: Manual is back from printer and sent to the warehouse.

April 1: Product is shipped.

purpose, and tasks (each get their own section), but also all the related factors (some of which are implied):

- **Setting.** Although not spelled out, it is understood that users will be reading the instructions while assembling their grills, which the authors have accounted for via the document's simple, lightweight design.

- **Potential problems.** Although safety issues are not given their own subheaded section, the authors have considered safety measures at a number of points.

- **Length.** In the "Rough outline" section, the authors have determined that the instructions will be four pages long.

- **Format.** In the "Rough outline" section, both text and visuals have been carefully considered, page by page.

- **Timing.** In the "Schedule" section, the authors have not only accounted for the due date but also the various milestones to be reached along the way.

- **Budget.** Under the "Production guidelines" section, the authors note that the budget will not allow for color printing or photographs.

WRITE, TEST, AND REVISE THE DOCUMENT

Explore the Concept with the Activity on Assessing Usability at **mytechcommlab**

When your planning is completed, you will be ready to write, test, and revise your document. For a gas grill manual, you would write the instructions and design the graphics as you've planned, and select a medium (print, CD, Web—or some combination) for distributing the information.

Once you have a workable draft, test the document on potential users or readers, if possible. Ask people what they find useful and what they find confusing. If you have created a set of instructions, watch people use the document and measure their ability to perform the task based on what you have written. If someone trying to assemble the gas grill, for instance, could not locate a part because of unclear instructions, knowing about this would be valuable as you revise your material. Ask respondents to identify specific difficulties they encountered in reading the instructions and in performing the task:

Questions for assessing a document's usability

- **Content.** Are there any inaccuracies? Is the level of technicality appropriate to this audience? Are claims, conclusions, or recommendations supported by evidence? Are all key terms defined? Is the material free of gaps, foggy areas, or needless details?

- **Organization.** Is the structure of the document visible at a glance? Is anything out of order, hard to find or follow? Is the material "chunked" into easily digestible parts? Is the material organized in a logical sequence?

- **Style.** Is anything hard to understand, imprecise, too complex, or too wordy? Are sentences put together with enough variety? Is the tone appropriate for the situation? Are words chosen for exactness, not for camouflage?

- **Layout and visuals.** Are there adequate aids to navigation (heads, numbered lists, bullets, type styles)? Are there any excessively long paragraphs, lists, or steps? Are any visuals overly complex or misleading? Could anything be clarified by a visual? Is anything cramped and hard to read?

- **Ethical, legal, and cultural considerations.** Is there any distortion or misrepresentation of facts? Are there any potential legal problems? Does the document respect users' cultural diversity?

Finally, based on user feedback, revise your plan and your draft document. You may also want to review the Brief Handbook (Appendix B) to fix any sentence-level problems.

CHECKLIST
for Usability

☐ Have I identified my exact audience (primary and secondary)?

☐ Have I identified my relationship with this audience?

☐ Have I identified this audience's technical background?

☐ Have I identified the exact purpose of this document (primary and secondary)?

☐ Am I seeking an outcome that is achievable in this situation?

☐ Have I anticipated my audience's reaction?

☐ Have I stated my claim clearly?

☐ Have I supported my claim with convincing evidence?

☐ Have I considered the various constraints and the cultural context?

☐ Have I chosen the approach most likely to connect with my audience?

☐ Have I written a purpose statement?

☐ Do I know exactly how this information will be used?

☐ By creating a task analysis, have I identified the steps involved?

☐ Have I pinpointed the main tasks and the subtasks?

☐ Have I considered the document's setting, potential problems, length, format, timing, and budget?

☐ Have I developed an information plan that outlines all the preceding factors?

☐ After drafting the document, have I tested it with potential users or readers?

☐ Have I identified any problems in terms of content, organization, style, layout and visuals, and ethical/legal/cultural/persuasive considerations?

☐ Did I make needed revisions based on testing?

APPLICATIONS

GENERAL APPLICATIONS

1. Identify an activity that could require instructions for a novice to complete. Prepare a task analysis for this activity similar to the one in Figure 4.5. Exchange your task analysis with another student in your class, and critique each other's work. With your class, discuss the challenges of doing such an analysis and identify strategies for performing a task analysis effectively.

2. Find a set of instructions or another type of technical document that is easy to use. Identify specific characteristics of the document, including any persuasive elements, that make it usable. (Refer to the usability questions on page 68 to guide your assessment.) Then find a technical document that is hard to use. What characteristics make it unusable? In a memo to your instructor, define specific changes that you would make in revising the document. Submit both examples along with your memo.

TEAM APPLICATION

Bring in some children's connecting blocks, such as TinkerToys or Lego blocks. Form teams of four to six people, and assign two people as technical writers. The technical writers should assemble a few of the pieces into a simple design (don't use more than three or four pieces). Then the technical writers should write up a quick instruction card explaining how to assemble the pieces into the design they've created. For example, the card for Lego blocks might read like this:

1. Select two large red blocks and two small green blocks.
2. Place one red block on its side.
3. Attach one green block to the red block.

... and so on. Then present the "parts" and your instructions to team members. Watch as your team tries to assemble the blocks according to your instructions. Assess the instructions for usability. Were all tasks accounted for? Did any terms or language confuse the users? Go back and perform a task analysis, and discuss what you could do to improve the usability of your instruction card.

GLOBAL APPLICATION

Astronomy and planetary science have become truly global sciences, and space exploration is now conducted by multinational teams. Knowledge about astronomy belongs to everyone, regardless of nationality or language. Do the Web sites representing these disciplines succeed in making themselves accessible to and useful for a global audience?

Explore the Web sites listed at the end of this Application, and assess their usability for international audiences. Would non-English speakers be able to access the information on these sites? What efforts are made to inform and persuade international readers? Are language and cultural differences accounted for in the design, content, and interface?

Draw up a list of key elements and features of each site that contribute to or detract from usability for international audiences. What changes would you recommend to make each site more accessible, usable, and persuasive for non-English readers? Summarize your assessment in a brief memo, including printed copies of specific pages from each Web site that you discuss.

- <www.planetary.org>

  Planetary Society

- <www.nasa.gov/home>

  National Aeronautics and Space Administration

- <www.esa.int/esaCP/index.html>

  European Space Agency

COMPUTER/WEB-BASED APPLICATION

Locate a Web site that accommodates various users at various levels of technicality. Sites for government agencies such as those listed are good sources of both general and specialized information.

- Environmental Protection Agency (EPA) <www.epa.gov>
- Nuclear Regulatory Commission (NRC) <www.nrc.gov>
- National Institutes of Health (NIH) <www.nih.gov>
- Food and Drug Administration (FDA) <www.fda.gov>

Examine one of these sites and find one example of (a) material aimed at a general audience and (b) material on the same topic aimed at a specialized or expert audience. First, list the features that enabled you to identify each piece's level of technicality. Next, using the Audience and Purpose Profile Sheet, record assumptions about the audience made by the author of the nontechnical version. Finally, evaluate how well that piece addresses a nontechnical user's information needs. (*Hint:* Check out, for instance, the MEDLINE link at the NIH site.)

Print out the site's home page as well as key linking pages, and be prepared to discuss your evaluation in class.

For additional technical writing resources that will help you master the chapter objectives, go to **www.mytechcommlab.com**.

5 Recognizing Ethical Issues in Technical Communication

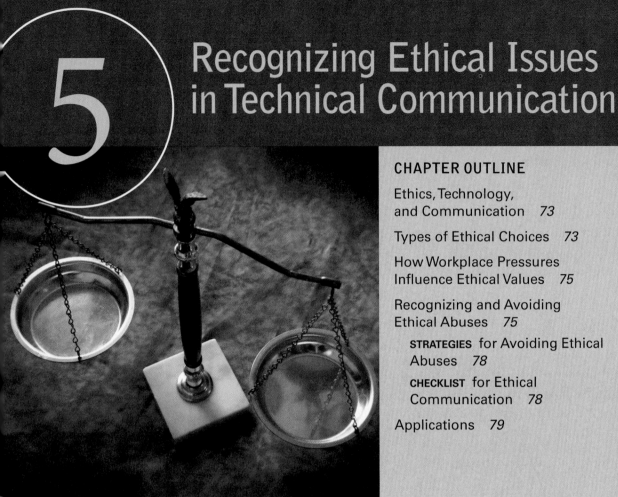

LEARNING OBJECTIVES FOR THIS CHAPTER

▸ Recognize ethical dilemmas and understand that they are not always black and white

▸ Realize how ethics are often compromised by workplace pressures

▸ Avoid various types of ethical abuses

Technical communication does not occur in a void. It happens in the world of human beings, politics, and social conditions, a world in which we regularly face ethical dilemmas that balance our sense of what is right against a decision that may be more efficient, profitable, or better for the company.

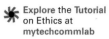

Explore the Tutorial on Ethics at mytechcommlab

ETHICS, TECHNOLOGY, AND COMMUNICATION

Ethical questions often revolve around topics related to technology. For example, a new computer chip that secretly collects personal information about a person's Web-surfing habits presents a privacy dilemma. Should users be allowed to choose whether to have out this information collected? Some people would say yes, but in the United States, few laws address personal privacy at this level. So the decision becomes less a legal one than an ethical one. The communication about this product (a press release announcing it or a user's manual that accompanies the computer) plays a central role in this ethical dilemma. Should the technical writer include this information, exclude it altogether, or deemphasize it by using a small font?

Typical ethical dilemmas

These are not simple questions. Taking an ethical stance requires a personal decision on your part as to how to weigh your ethical and moral beliefs against the realities of the job. This stance requires you to consider the effects of your decisions on the users of your product, on your company, on society at large, and on your job. Sometimes standing your ground on an ethical issue may mean losing your job or suffering retaliation from coworkers.

Ethical decisions are not always "black and white"

TYPES OF ETHICAL CHOICES

Virtually all areas of science and technology are involved in issues of communication and ethics. Here are a few examples:

- *Medical technologies,* such as genetic testing, raise questions about personal privacy and medical insurance.
- *Banking and retail operations,* which increasingly collect personal information on consumers, raise concerns about how this information is used and who has access to it.
- *Environmental pollutants,* such as pesticides or smokestack output, raise serious questions about the long-term health of the planet.

In your own communication, you will often face ethical decisions—about how much information to include, how much to leave out, how to word an issue, or how to shape the information for users and consumers. Note how the memo from David Michem in Figure 5.1 sounds completely well-reasoned and persuasive. An employee reading the memo, especially one with an existing medical condition, might go straight to the company Web site and sign up for a Medical History Card. But in his desire to make the card program a success, Michem has provided employees with no

FIGURE 5.1
An unethical document

Note the misleading omission of information about employee confidentiality.

 Andrews McNeel

MEMORANDUM

To: All Employees
From: David Michem, Health Benefits Manager *D.M.*
Date: November 10, 20XX
Subject: *Medical History Card Program*

Last week, you received a brochure about the new Medical History Cards (MHCs) available through the Human Resources Department. I encourage you to enroll in the card program for a variety of reasons:

• **MHCs ensure that all employees receive safe and efficient health care.** Whether you have a serious medical condition, take a prescription medication, have an allergy, or none of the above, MHCs instantly provide medical personnel with personalized medical data during an emergency or routine visit.

• **The cards are free to all Andrews and McNeel employees.** Any employee at Andrews and McNeel—whether full-time, part-time, or contract—may enroll in the program and receive a card free of charge.

• **Enrolling in the MHC program is easy.** Simply go to http://www.andrews-mcneel.com/hr/mhc to enroll in the program and fill out the requested personal and medical information to be uploaded to your card.

• **MHCs contain much more information than standard medical ID bracelets.** While an emergency bracelet may only provide basic information, such as the fact that a person is diabetic, MHCs hold your complete medical data, including emergency contact information, prescription information, and so on.

• **MHCs are easy to update.** If your medical information changes (for example, you are prescribed a new medication or your emergency contact information changes) simply update that information online. You will receive a replacement card within 5 business days.

Please take advantage of this program by re-reading your brochure or simply going to the Human Resources MHC Web page above to learn more. This is an excellent benefit not offered at many companies. We strongly encourage you to participate.

cc: Elizabeth Sanchirico-Edwards, Director of Human Resources

information about confidentiality in his memo. Will the company have access to personal and medical information when employees sign up via the Andrews and McNeel Web site? Will the information be password-protected? Will third parties have access to this information? By omitting this information from the memo, Michem has been misleading, as reasonable as his memo may sound. In the end, communication is never neutral but instead always carries some type of consequence.

HOW WORKPLACE PRESSURES AFFECT ETHICAL VALUES

Usually, ethical rules are broken not because people are dishonest but because they feel pressure to bend or break the rules. More than 50 percent of managers surveyed nationwide feel "pressure to compromise personal ethics for company goals" (Golen et al. 75). To save face, escape blame, or get ahead, anyone might feel obliged to say what other people want to hear or to suppress or downplay bad news. Figure 5.2 depicts how workplace pressures to "succeed at any cost" can influence ethical values.

Ethics are often compromised by outside pressure

Despite outside pressures, however, everyone must maintain ethical standards at all times on the job. Unethical decisions can harm a company's reputation and bottom line. More importantly, unethical decisions can compromise the safety and welfare of workers and customers. When an instruction manual is written and vital safety information is purposely omitted to save on the cost of printing, for example, people can be injured.

Why ethics matter

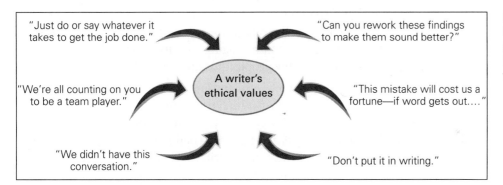

FIGURE 5.2
How workplace pressures can influence ethical values

RECOGNIZING AND AVOIDING ETHICAL ABUSES

Following are some of the major examples of unethical communication in the workplace.

- **Plagiarizing the work of others.** Technical communicators may feel pressure from upper management to produce results quickly and may be tempted to cut corners. Workplace plagiarism occurs when a person claims the work of someone else as one's own, without citing or even mentioning the original source. Plagiarism may also happen in collaborative work, as when a team leader claims all the credit for the work of team members.

- **Falsifying or fabricating information.** Outside pressure to produce results that others seek may tempt people to distort information. For example, research data

Types of ethical abuses

Watch the Video on Unethical Documents at mytechcommlab

might be manipulated or invented by a scientist seeking grant money. Developments in fields such as biotechnology often occur too rapidly to allow for adequate peer review of articles before they are published, thereby leading to the release of information that isn't verifiably correct ("Misconduct Scandal" 2).

- **Suppressing or downplaying information.** Withholding information is just as unethical as supplying false information. For example, a report author may purposely fail to mention an important study that contradicts what he or she wants to prove. Or a company may fail to inform the public about a safety hazard in one of its products—or, if the hazard is revealed, may downplay its importance.

- **Exaggerating claims.** Organizations that have a stake in a particular technology (e.g., bioengineered foods) may be especially tempted to exaggerate its benefits, potential, or safety, and to downplay its risks. If your organization depends on outside funding (e.g., defense or space industry), you might find yourself pressured to make unrealistic promises.

- **Using visual images that conceal the truth.** Pictures are generally more powerful than words and can easily distort the real meaning of a message through manipulation. For example, an individual might create a pie chart that paints a more optimistic picture than the data indicates by distorting the sizes of the pie pieces. Or a TV commercial for a prescription drug may list its drastic side effects while showing images of smiling, healthy people, thus downplaying the dangers.

- **Stealing or divulging proprietary information.** Information that originates in a specific company is the exclusive intellectual property of that company. Proprietary information includes company records, product formulas, test and experiment results, surveys financed by clients, market research, plans, specifications, and minutes of meetings (Lavin 5). In theory, such information is legally protected, but it remains vulnerable to sabotage, theft, or leaks to the press. Fierce competition among rival companies for the very latest intelligence gives rise to theft or unethical divulging of such information.

- **Misusing electronic information.** Ever-increasing amounts of personal information are stored in databases (by schools, governments, credit card companies, insurance companies, pharmacies), and all employers, of course, keep data about their employees. How we combine, use, and share all of this electronic information raises questions about privacy. If you are designing a Web site, for example, should you create a page that asks customers for their name, address, and other personal information without providing information about how your company intends to use that information? Most Web sites have links to privacy policies that allow customers to learn more about the company's approach to privacy. The lack of such a policy could be considered an ethical breach.

- **Exploiting cultural differences.** Both individuals and organizations can exploit the vulnerabilities of various cultural groups through manipulation or deception. For instance, one employee of a company might exploit another's

English-language limitations for personal gain. So too, an organization might exploit clients for whom the culture places greater emphasis on interpersonal trust than on lawyers or legal wording.

To avoid ethical abuses, follow the guidelines provided by professional organizations in your field (e.g., see the American Medical Writers Association Code of Ethics in Figure 5.3), and use the Strategies on page 78.

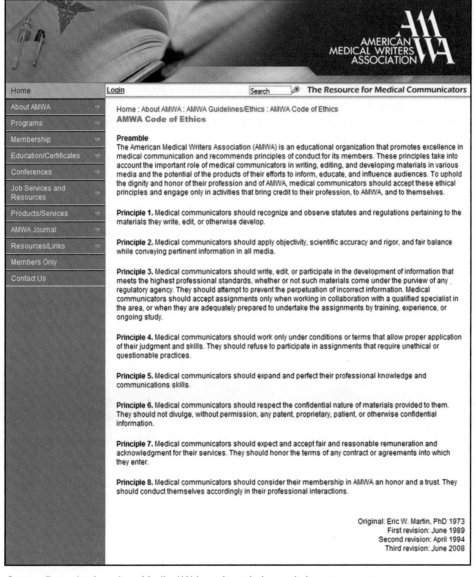

FIGURE 5.3
A code of ethics from a professional organization

STRATEGIES
for Avoiding Ethical Abuses

▶ **Always cite your sources if the information or data is not your own.** For specific advice on avoiding plagiarism and citing outside sources, see Appendix A.

▶ **Give the audience everything it needs to know.** To accurately see things as you do, people need more than just a partial view. Don't bury readers in needless details, but do make sure they get all the facts and get them straight.

▶ **Give people a clear understanding of what the information means.** Even when all the facts are known, they can be misinterpreted. Try to ensure that readers understand the facts as you do. If you are not certain about your own understanding, say so.

▶ **Never manipulate information or data in your writing or in your visuals.** If you encounter data that contradicts what you want to say, include and interpret that data honestly. Likewise, do not make your case via exaggeration, understatement, sugarcoating, or any other distortion or omission.

▶ **Use common sense or follow your company's confidentiality guidelines.** If you suspect that information may be confidential, assume that it is or ask the appropriate personnel to clarify.

▶ **Do not exploit cultural inequalities or manipulate international readers.** Try to be fair. When producing a document for an international audience, be especially careful about using simple and honest language and visuals.

▶ **Constantly ask yourself, "Would I stand behind what I have created if I were held publicly accountable for it?"** If you would not, then chances are what you have written is unethical to some degree. It may be not entirely honest, fair, confidential, or safe.

CHECKLIST
for Ethical Communication

Use this checklist for any document you prepare or for which you are responsible.

ACCURACY

☐ Have I explored all sides of the issue and all possible alternatives?

☐ Do I provide enough information and interpretation for recipients to understand the facts as I know them?

☐ Do I avoid exaggeration, understatement, sugarcoating, or any distortion or omission that leaves recipients at a disadvantage?

➡

HONESTY

☐ Do I make a clear distinction between what is certain and what is probable?

☐ Are my information sources valid, reliable, and relatively unbiased?

☐ Do I actually believe what I'm saying, instead of advancing some hidden agenda?

☐ Would I still advocate this position if I were held publicly accountable for it?

☐ Do I inform people of the consequences or risks (as I am able to predict) of what I am advocating?

☐ Do I give candid feedback or criticism, if it is warranted?

FAIRNESS

☐ Am I reasonably sure this document will not harm innocent persons or damage their reputations?

☐ Am I respecting all legitimate rights to privacy and confidentiality?

☐ Am I distributing copies of this document to every person who has the right to know about it?

☐ Do I credit all contributors and sources of ideas and information?

Sources: Brownell and Fitzgerald (1992), p. 18; Bryan (1992), p. 87; Johannesen (1983), pp. 21–22; Larson (1995), p. 39; Unger (1982), pp. 39–46; Yoos (1979), pp. 50–55.

 APPLICATIONS

GENERAL APPLICATION

Find the professional code of ethics for your major or career. Divide into groups of three or four students, each of whom has a different major. Compare your professional codes, noting similarities and differences. Discuss why each code seems appropriate for that profession.

TEAM APPLICATION

In groups of two or three, locate a piece of technical communication (or use one provided by your instructor), and evaluate its ethical stance. Is the information presented in such a way that ideas or facts are exaggerated or suppressed? Are any cultural issues exploited? Share your thoughts in class, and explain how your team would redo the information.

GLOBAL APPLICATION

Counterfeiting, sometimes known as "intellectual property piracy," has become a major point of tension between the United States and many developing nations. Counterfeit products ranging from computer chips and pharmaceuticals to cigarettes and cell phones now flood markets in Asia and South America, and many may even be found on the streets of New York and other U.S. cities.

Beginning with the Web resources listed, do some research to learn more about the problems of counterfeit products. What are the advantages and disadvantages, both economically and politically, of trying to crack down on unauthorized copycat products? Why do some countries do little to police such piracy while others, including the United States, view it as a major priority?

Write a brief report to analyze the ethical, economic, and political issues that influence the global debate on counterfeiting, and present your findings in a brief oral presentation to your class.

- <www.businessweek.com/magazine/content/05_06/b3919001_mz001.htm>

  Link to a *Business Week* cover feature on the global counterfeit business.

- <www.allianceagainstiptheft.co.uk/report_publications.html>

  The Alliance Against IP Theft, based in the United Kingdom, offers a number of reports on piracy and intellectual property theft.

COMPUTER/WEB-BASED APPLICATION

Using the material in this chapter and the Web resources listed, prepare a two-page memo as a brief guide to ethical communication. Your purpose is to explain clearly how to avoid major ethical pitfalls in corporate communication.

- <www.onlineethics.org>

  The Online Ethics Center for Engineering and Science at Case Western Reserve University. Includes extensive background on ethical issues, case studies, and sample codes of ethics from a number of disciplines.

- <ethics.tamu.edu/ethicscasestudies.htm>

  Case studies in engineering ethics, compiled by researchers at Texas A&M University.

- <www.iit.edu/departments/csep/codes/codes_index.html>

  A substantial collection of professional codes of ethics, organized by profession and discipline, compiled by the Center for the Study of Ethics in the Professions at the Illinois Institute of Technology.

For additional technical writing resources that will help you master the chapter objectives, go to **www.mytechcommlab.com**.

PART 2

Blueprints

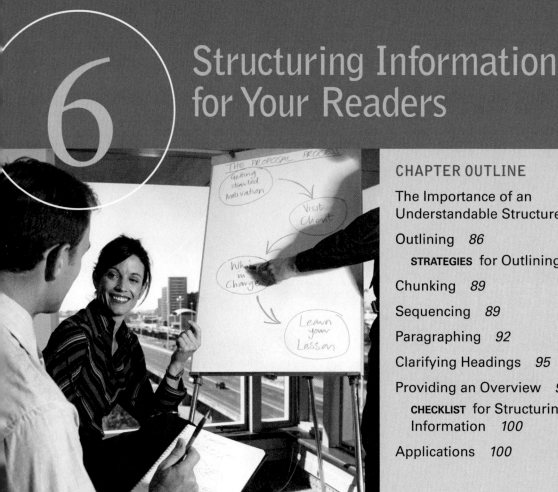

6

Structuring Information for Your Readers

LEARNING OBJECTIVES FOR THIS CHAPTER

▸ Use a standard or varied introduction/body/conclusion structure

▸ Create a brief or formal outline

▸ Chunk information into discrete units

▸ Determine the best sequence for your material

▸ Shape each paragraph for effectiveness

▸ Create clear headings

▸ Provide overviews of longer documents

To use a familiar architectural metaphor, Part I of this book has focused on the *foundations* of technical communication—the underlying supports upon which the technical communication "building" stands. To review, these foundations include: 1) a definition of technical communication; 2) teamwork, ethics, persuasion, and global issues as cornerstones; 3) research as a vital part of the technical communication process; and 4) usability as a key feature of technical communication.

Analyze the **Brochure** for structure at **mytechcommlab**

Before producing specific technical documents, you need a set of *blueprints*. This section, Part II, discusses the four components of technical communication blueprints: an understandable *structure* (Chapter 6), a readable *style* (Chapter 7), audience-centered *visuals* (Chapter 8), and a user-friendly *design* (Chapter 9).

Structure, style, visuals, and design as technical communication blueprints

This chapter focuses on the first of these blueprint components, structure.

THE IMPORTANCE OF AN UNDERSTANDABLE STRUCTURE

Structure your information in a way that readers can easily grasp. To follow your thinking, readers need a clear path from point *a* to point *b*. This path needs to be obvious as readers scan through your document, looking for its overall structure.

Your audience comes first

Unfortunately, information rarely materializes—and thinking rarely occurs—in neat, predictable sequences. As you look over your collected information, and begin to think about how you will structure it for your readers, you will face questions such as these:

- What relationships do the collected data suggest?
- What should I emphasize?
- In which sequence will users approach this material?
- What belongs where?
- What do I say first? Why?
- What comes next?
- How do I end?

Getting started: questions to ask yourself when structuring for readers

Although a great deal of thinking goes into the process of answering these types of questions, the result will be worth the effort, as Figures 6.1 and 6.2 illustrate.

The end result: two examples of well-organized writing

Figure 6.1 depicts the standard structure of a technical document, one that readers will instantly recognize: introduction, body, and conclusion. The introduction attracts the reader's attention, announces the writer's viewpoint, and previews what will follow. The body delivers on the promise implied in the introduction. The body explains and supports the writer's viewpoint, achieving *unity* by remaining focused on that viewpoint and *coherence* by carrying a line of thought from sentence to sentence in a logical order. Finally, the conclusion has various

Standard introduction/body/conclusion structure

purposes: it might reemphasize key points, take a position, predict an outcome, offer a solution, or suggest further study. Good conclusions give readers a clear perspective on what they have just read.

FIGURE 6.1
Document with a standard introduction/ body/conclusion structure

Introduction announces the topic and provides an overview of what is to follow

Body provides the evidence and data to support the claims made in the introduction

Conclusion summarizes by taking a position and making recommendations

Powell   Rabkin

MEMORANDUM

To: Department Managers
From: Jill McCreary, General Manager *J.M.*
Date: December 8, 20XX
Subject: *Diversity training initiative*

As part of our ongoing efforts to highlight the company's commitment to diversity, we recently conducted two surveys—one directed to company employees and one to our retail buyers. We have just received the survey results from our outside analysts. The employee survey indicates that the members of all departments appreciate our efforts to create a diverse and comfortable work environment. The customer survey indicates that our company is well regarded for marketing products in ways that appeal to diverse buyers. However, both surveys also illuminate areas in which we could do even better. As a result, we will be initiating a new series of diversity training workshops early next year. Let me explain the survey findings that have led to this initiative.

First, the employee survey indicates that our workforce is rated "highly diverse" in terms of gender, with nearly equal representation of male and female employees in both managerial and nonmanagerial positions; however, we could do better in terms of minority representation at the managerial level. Meanwhile, the customer survey demonstrates that our customers are "very satisfied" with the diversity of our marketing materials, but that we fail to provide enough materials for our native Spanish-speaking buyers.

Those are the survey highlights—see the attached analysis for a more detailed picture. Again, we are doing well, but could do better. We feel that the best solution to address our weaker areas is to conduct a second series of diversity training workshops in the upcoming 12 months. We hope that these workshops—which are often illuminating to both new employees and those who have attended diversity trainings earlier—will help keep the word "diversity" at the forefront of everyone's thoughts when hiring and mentoring employees and creating marketing materials. More information will follow, but for now, please emphasize to your department employees the importance and value of these workshops.

A nonstandard structure that also clarifies data for readers

There are, however, many ways of adapting this standard structure: For example, Figure 6.2 provides visual features (columns, colors), headings, and an engaging layout. Although organized differently from the previous document, Figure 6.2 does provide an introduction, a body, and a conclusion: The heading "What is arsenic?" represents a form of introduction. The next several headings answer the question posed in the introduction, forming in essence

FIGURE 6.2
Document with a nonstandard, but well-organized structure

JUST THE FACTS FOR CONSUMERS

ARSENIC IN YOUR DRINKING WATER

What is arsenic?

Arsenic is a toxic chemical element that is unevenly distributed in the Earth's crust in soil, rocks, and minerals.

Use of visuals, color, and columns makes the organization clear

"What is arsenic?" paragraph is placed above subsequent sections, indicating that it is the introduction

Three lengthier sections—all of equal importance— are balanced in the middle of the page to indicate the body

How does arsenic get into my drinking water?

Arsenic occurs naturally in the environment and as a by-product of some agricultural and industrial activities. It can enter drinking water through the ground or as runoff into surface water sources.

How is arsenic in drinking water regulated?

In 1974, Congress passed the Safe Drinking Water Act. This law directs EPA to issue non-enforceable health goals and enforceable drinking water regulations for contaminants that may cause health problems. The goals, which reflect the level at which no adverse health effects are expected, are called maximum contaminant level goals (MCLGs). The MCLG for arsenic is 0 parts per billion (ppb).

The enforceable standard for arsenic is a maximum contaminant level (MCL). MCLs are set as close to the health goals as possible, considering cost, benefits, and the ability of public water systems to detect and remove contaminants using suitable treatment technologies.

Why should I be concerned about arsenic in my drinking water?

Although short-term exposures to high doses (about a thousand times higher than the drinking water standard) cause adverse effects in people, such exposures do not occur from public water supplies in the U.S. that comply with the arsenic MCL.

Some people who drink water containing arsenic in excess of EPA's standard over many years could experience skin damage or problems with their circulatory system, and may have an increased risk of getting cancer. Health effects might include:

- Thickening and discoloration of the skin, stomach pain, nausea, vomiting, diarrhea, and liver effects;

- Cardiovascular, pulmonary, immunological, neurological (e.g., numbness and partial paralysis), reproductive, and endocrine (e.g., diabetes) effects;

- Cancer of the bladder, lungs, skin, kidney, nasal passages, liver, and prostate.

What is EPA's standard for arsenic in drinking water?

To protect consumers served by public water systems from the health risks of long-term (chronic) arsenic exposure, EPA recently lowered the arsenic MCL from 50 ppb to 10 ppb.

"What is EPA's standard" section is placed at the bottom of the page, indicating that it is a conclusion

Source: U. S. Environmental Protection Agency <www.epa.gov>

the body of the document. The final heading, asking about EPA standards, represents a form of conclusion, moving beyond data and description to the topic of policy and use.

Beyond the introduction/body/conclusion structure and its variations, there are other ways to structure information, as discussed below.

Additional ways of structuring information

OUTLINING

Outlining is essential

Watch the Video on Creating an Outline at **mytechcommlab**

Even basic documents require at least an introduction-body-conclusion outline done in your head and/or a few ideas jotted down in list form. Longer documents require a more detailed outline so that you can visualize your document overall and ensure that ideas flow logically from point to point.

Start by searching through the information you have gathered and creating a random list of key topics your document should include. For instance, in preparing the arsenic document in Figure 6.2, you might start by simply listing all the information you think readers need or expect:

Start by creating a list of essential information

- explain what the EPA is doing about arsenic in drinking water
- define what arsenic is
- explain how arsenic gets into drinking water
- list some of the effects of arsenic (stomach, heart, cancer)
- include specific data
- mention/explain the Safe Water Drinking Act
- refer to/define MCLGs

Now you can reorganize this list.

A simple list like the one above usually suffices for organizing a short document like the memo in Figure 6.1. However, for a more complex document, transform your list into a deliberate map that will guide readers from point to point. Create an introduction, body, and conclusion and then decide how you will divide each of these parts into subtopics. An outline for Figure 6.2 might look like this:

Then organize the information into an outline

I. INTRODUCTION—Define arsenic.

II. BODY

    A. Explain how arsenic gets into drinking water.

    B. Explain how it is regulated (1974 Safe Drinking Water Act/MCLGs; Maximum Contaminant Levels).

    C. List some of the health effects of arsenic (visible effects; diseases, cancers).

III. CONCLUSION—Describe the EPA's standards.

For a long, complex document, you will want a formal outline to keep you organized as you write (Figure 6.3).

FIGURE 6.3
A formal outline using alphanumeric notation

Converting ABCD's Office Building from Oil to Gas Heating: A Feasibility Analysis

I. INTRODUCTION
   A. Background
   B. Purpose of the Report
   C. Intended Audience (usually for in-school reports only)
   D. Information Sources
   E. Limitations of the Report
   F. Scope (list of major topics)

II. DATA (BODY)
   A. Description of Our Present Heating System
      1. Physical condition
      2. Required yearly maintenance
      3. Fuel supply problems
         a. Overworked distributor
         b. Varying local supply
      4. Cost of operation
   B. Removal of the Oil Burner and Tank
      1. Data from the oil company
      2. Data from the salvage company
         a. Procedure
         b. Cost
      3. Possibility of private sale
   C. Installation of a Gas Pipe from the Street to the Building
      1. Procedure
      2. Cost of installation
      3. Cost of landscaping

III. CONCLUSION
   A. Summary of Findings
   B. Comprehensive Interpretation of Findings
   C. Recommendations

Notice a few key characteristics of formal outlines:

- Roman numerals indicate the three main sections (introduction/body/ conclusion).
- The first level of subtopics under each main section is indented and preceded by capital letters; the next level is further indented and preceded by Arabic numerals; and the third level is again indented three spaces and preceded by lowercase letters. This is known as *alphanumeric notation*.

An alternate system, *decimal notation*, appears in Figure 6.4. The decimal outline makes it easier to refer readers to various sections in your final document. But both systems achieve the same organizing objective.

- Each level of division must yield at least two subtopics—if you cannot divide a larger topic into at least two subtopics, retain only your larger topic.

- A formal outline typically undergoes changes as you write. Expect to adjust it as needed. When the document is complete you can use the formal outline to create a table of contents for the document.

See also the Strategies (below) for more advice.

FIGURE 6.4
Part of a formal outline using decimal notation

```
2.0 Data (Body)
    2.1 Description of Our Present Heating System
        2.1.1 Physical condition
        2.1.2 Required yearly maintenance
        2.1.3 Fuel supply problems
            2.1.3.1 Overworked distributor
            2.1.3.2 Varying local supply
        2.1.4 Cost of operation
    2.2 Removal of the Oil Burner and Tank
        2.2.1 Data from the oil company
        2.2.2 (and so on)
```

STRATEGIES
for Outlining

▸ **List key topics and subtopics to be included in your document.** Gather your information, determine what information is important to include, decide what information is superfluous, and make a list of the topics to be included.

▸ **Set up a standard outline.** Start with a typical introduction, body, and conclusion structure, even if you plan to vary the structure later.

▸ **Place key topics and subtopics where they fit within your standard outline.** Keep your introduction brief, using it to set the stage for the rest of your document. Include your specific data in the body section, to back up what you promised in your introduction. Do not introduce new data in the conclusion.

▸ **Use alphanumeric or decimal notation consistently throughout the outline.**

▸ **Avoid excessive subtopics.** If you find that your outline is getting into multiple levels of detail too often, think of ways to combine information. Do not go to another level unless there are at least two distinct subtopics at that level.

▸ **Refine your outline as you write your document.** Continue revising your outline until you complete your document.

CHUNKING

Outlining helps to illustrate the importance of *chunking*: breaking information down into discrete, digestible units, based on the readers' needs and the document's purpose. When you chunk information into smaller portions, you help readers to see which pieces of information belong together and how the various pieces are connected.

Chunking requires careful decisions about exactly how much information is enough for each portion and what constitutes sensible proportions among the parts. For example, note how in the outline in Figure 6.3 the writer plans to break up the information for readers in a variety of ways. First, the planned report is divided into three general sections, or chunks: introduction, data section (body), and conclusion. Then each of those sections is broken into as many smaller chunks as appropriate to help the reader see how this discussion breaks into parts and yet each of these parts fits together to form a whole.

Chunking information is handled differently on the Web than on the printed page. On Web sites, readers expect information in very short chunks because they don't like reading large portions of text on a computer screen and they want the option of zeroing in on various parts of the page, and moving from link to link. In printed documents, however, readers expect longer passages of text, because the printed page is easier on the eyes and because the expectation of reading a printed page is to read sequentially rather than jump from section to section.

[margin note: Breaking information down into smaller units]

[margin note: Chunking on the Web versus chunking on a printed page]

SEQUENCING

In addition to chunking information, you also need to show readers the logical progression of information. The specific information sequence will depend on the type of document. For instance, a mechanism description usually follows a *spatial sequence* (What are the parts and how do they fit together?); a progress report or set of instructions usually follows a *chronological sequence* (In what order have things happened/should things happen?); a feasibility, recommendation, or justification report would follow a *problem-solution sequence* (What was/is the problem or goal and how was it/can it be fixed or achieved?); and an analytical report describing an incident and the reasons for the incident would follow a *cause and effect sequence* (What caused something to happen or what were the effects of something?). Below are descriptions of each of these common sequences.

[margin note: Sequencing: ordering information to follow a logical progression]

Spatial Sequence

A spatial sequence begins at one location and ends at another, and it is usually used to describe a physical object or a mechanism. You might describe the parts in the same sequence that readers would follow if they were actually looking at the item. Or you might follow the sequence in which each part of the item functions

[margin note: Spatial sequence: What are the parts and how do they fit together?]

(left to right, inside to outside, top to bottom). The following brief description of a hypodermic needle illustrates spatial sequencing, proceeding from the needle's base (hub) to its point. (A longer descriptive document, such as one of the longer technical descriptions in Chapter 13, would also use spatial sequencing.)

> A hypodermic needle is a slender, hollow steel instrument used to introduce medication into the body (usually through a vein or muscle). It is a single piece composed of three parts, all considered sterile: the hub, the cannula, and the point. The hub is the lower, larger part of the needle that attaches to the neck-like opening on the syringe barrel. Next is the cannula (stem), the smooth and slender central portion. Last is the point, which consists of a beveled (slanted) opening, ending in a sharp tip. The diameter of a needle's cannula is indicated by a gauge number; commonly, a 24–25 gauge needle is used for subcutaneous injections. Needle lengths are varied to suit individual needs. Common lengths used for subcutaneous injections are 3/8, 1/2, 5/8, and 3/4 inch. Regardless of length and diameter, all needles have the same functional design.

Chronological Sequence

Chronological sequence: In what order have things happened/should things happen?

A chronological sequence follows an actual sequence of events, either something that already happened or something that needs to follow a certain sequence in order to be completed. Explanations of how something happened or how to do something usually follow a strict time sequence: first step, second step, and so on. Chronologically sequenced documents that take the form of instructions are often numbered and usually use visual elements (photos, drawings) to further guide readers. The following brief instructions are an example of chronological sequencing, showing the steps involved in using proper form when jogging. A full set of instructions, such as one of the longer sets of instructions in Chapter 14, or a progress report, such as in Chapter 15, would also use chronological sequencing.

> Instead of breaking into a jog too quickly and risking injury, take a relaxed and deliberate approach. Before taking a step, spend at least ten minutes stretching and warming up, using any exercises you find comfortable. (After your first week, consult a jogging book for specialized exercises.) When you've completed your warmup, set a brisk pace walking. Exaggerate the distance between steps, taking long strides and swinging your arms briskly and loosely. After roughly one hundred yards at this brisk pace, you should feel ready to jog. Immediately break into a very slow trot: lean your torso forward and let one foot fall in front of the other (one foot barely leaving the ground while the other is on the pavement). Maintain the slowest pace possible, just above a walk. Do not bolt out like a sprinter! The biggest mistake is to start fast and injure yourself. While jogging, relax your

body. Keep your shoulders straight and your head up, and enjoy the scenery—after all, that is one of the most basic joys of jogging. Keep your arms low and slightly bent at your sides. Move your legs freely from the hips in an action that is easy, not forced. Make your feet perform a heel-to-toe action: land on the heel; rock forward; take off from the toe.

Problem-Solution Sequence

The problem-solution sequence proceeds from a description of the problem, through diagnosis, to a solution. The following short analysis is an example of problem-solution sequencing, describing the issue and how it was resolved. (A longer report, such as the feasibility, recommendation, or justification reports in Chapter 16, would also use problem-solution sequencing.)

> Problem-solution sequence: What was/is the problem or goal and how was it/can it be fixed or achieved?

> On all waterfront buildings, the unpainted wood exteriors had been severely damaged by the high winds and sandstorms of the previous winter. After repairing the damage, we took protective steps against further storms. First, all joints, edges, and sashes were treated with water-repellent preservative to protect against water damage. Next, three coats of nonporous primer were applied to all exterior surfaces to prevent paint from blistering and peeling. Finally, two coats of wood-quality latex paint were applied over the nonporous primer. To keep coats of paint from future separation, the first coat was applied within two weeks of the priming coats, and the second within two weeks of the first. Two weeks after completion, no blistering, peeling, or separation has occurred.

Cause and Effect Sequence

A cause and effect sequence either describes an incident and then traces its causes (effect-to-cause) or it works in reverse, following an action to its results (cause-to-effect). The following examples illustrate effect-to-cause and cause-to-effect sequencing, respectively. (In addition, the analytical report in Chapter 15 uses cause and effect sequencing.)

> Cause and effect sequence: What caused something to happen or will cause something to happen?

> Effect to cause

> Modern whaling techniques nearly brought the whale population to the threshold of extinction. In the nineteenth century, the invention of the steamboat increased hunters' speed and mobility. Shortly afterward, the grenade harpoon was invented so that whales could be killed quickly and easily from the ship's deck. In 1904, a whaling station opened on Georgia Island in South America. This station became the gateway to Antarctic whaling for world nations. In 1924, factory ships were designed that enabled round-the-clock whale tracking and processing. These ships could reduce a ninety-foot whale to its by-products in roughly thirty minutes. After World War II, more powerful boats with remote sensing devices gave a final boost to

the whaling industry. Numbers of kills had now increased far beyond the whales' capacity to reproduce.

Cause to effect

Some of the most serious accidents involving gas water heaters occur when a flammable liquid is used in the vicinity. The heavier-than-air vapors of a flammable liquid such as gasoline can flow along the floor—even the length of a basement—and be explosively ignited by the flame of the water heater's pilot light or burner. Because the victim's clothing frequently ignites, the resulting burn injuries are commonly serious and extremely painful. They may require long hospitalization, and can result in disfigurement or death. Never, under any circumstances, use a flammable liquid near a gas heater or any other open flame. (Consumer Product Safety Commission)

PARAGRAPHING

Paragraphing: the process of shaping information within paragraphs

The preceding three strategies for structuring information (outlining, chunking, and sequencing) enable you and your readers to see the "big picture" of the document. Once you have thought through the document's larger structure you need to consider how smaller-scale but no less important strategies will help readers follow your message. The first of these strategies, *paragraphing*, is the process of shaping your information within paragraphs.

Why paragraphing is important

In most documents, different types of paragraphs have different shapes and purposes. For example, introductory paragraphs set the stage for the discussion that follows; transitional paragraphs (usually brief) help hold the discussion together; concluding paragraphs wrap up the discussion. But the focus here is on standard *support paragraphs*, typically found in the document's body section. Each support paragraph advances one aspect of the main point made in the document's introduction, and each usually can stand alone in meaning.

Readers look for structures they can recognize both in the document as a whole and within individual paragraphs. Just as the document as a whole needs to have an introduction-body-conclusion structure, so must each paragraph. Most of the standard support paragraphs in a technical document begin with a clear *topic sentence*, stating a generalization. Details in the body section support that generalization. These paragraphs also display *unity* (each sentence in the paragraph's body section must relate to and expand upon the topic sentence). Finally, these paragraphs display *coherence* (all sentences form a connected line of thought, leading from the topic sentence to the conclusion).

ts   ## The Topic Sentence

Readers look to a paragraph's opening sentences for the main idea. Unless you have good reason to place it elsewhere, the topic sentence should appear first (or at least early) in the paragraph; it should focus and forecast what will come in the remainder of the paragraph. In some instances the main idea may require a "topic statement" consisting of two or more sentences, but usually a single sentence will do, as in the following example:

> Solar power offers the most efficient, economical, and safe solution to the Northeast's energy problems.

An effective topic sentence

Note that key words in the topic sentence signal that the paragraph's next sentences (the body section) will describe how solar energy is *efficient, economical,* and *safe.*

Paragraph Unity

un

The body of the paragraph must deliver on the topic sentence's promise. A paragraph is unified when all its material belongs there—when each and every sentence directly expands on the topic sentence. Here, for example, is the complete version of the solar energy paragraph, fully unified:

> *Solar power offers an efficient, economical, and safe solution to the Northeast's energy problems.* To begin with, solar power is highly efficient. Solar collectors installed on fewer than 30 percent of roofs in the Northeast would provide more than 70 percent of the area's heating and air-conditioning needs. Moreover, solar heat collectors are economical, operating for up to twenty years with little or no maintenance. These savings recoup the initial cost of installation within only ten years. Most important, solar power is safe. It can be transformed into electricity through photovoltaic cells (a type of storage battery) in a noiseless process that produces no air pollution—unlike coal, oil, and wood combustion. In contrast to its nuclear counterpart, solar power produces no toxic waste and poses no catastrophic danger of meltdown. Thus, massive conversion to solar power would ensure abundant energy and a safe, clean environment for future generations.

A unified paragraph

Note how the body of the previous paragraph tackles each of the benefits of solar energy introduced in the topic sentence, sometimes devoting two or more sentences to each benefit, but nonetheless staying on track. One way to damage unity in the paragraph above would be to veer from the focus on the key words *efficient, economical,* and *safe* into a discussion about the differences between active and passive solar heating or the advantages of solar power over wind power, neither of which was introduced in the topic sentence.

coh   ## Paragraph Coherence

The body of the paragraph must deliver on the promise of the topic sentence through paragraph unity and also lead to a conclusion via a connected line of thought, like links in a chain. This feature is called paragraph coherence. Paragraph coherence can be damaged by 1) sentences in the wrong order; 2) insufficient transitions and connectors for linking related ideas; or 3) an inaccessible line of reasoning and lack of conclusion. Here is how the solar energy paragraph might become incoherent:

An incoherent paragraph

> Solar power offers an efficient, economical, and safe solution to the Northeast's energy problems. Unlike nuclear power, solar power produces no toxic waste and poses no danger of meltdown. Solar power is efficient. Solar collectors could be installed on fewer than 30 percent of roofs in the Northeast. These collectors would provide more than 70 percent of the area's heating and air-conditioning needs. Solar power is safe. It can be transformed into electricity. This transformation is made possible by photovoltaic cells (a type of storage battery). Solar heat collectors are economical. The photovoltaic process produces no air pollution.

In the above paragraph, the second sentence, about safety, belongs near the end, because it was introduced as the third of the three benefits of solar energy. Also, because of insufficient links between ideas, the paragraph reads more like a list than like a flowing discussion. Finally, a concluding sentence is needed to complete the chain of reasoning and to give readers a clear perspective on what they've just read.

Here, in contrast, is the original, coherent paragraph with sentences numbered for later discussion and with transitions and connectors shown in boldface. Notice how this version reveals a clear line of thought:

A coherent paragraph

> [1] Solar power offers an efficient, economical, and safe solution to the Northeast's energy problems. [2] **To begin with,** solar power is highly efficient. [3] Solar collectors installed on fewer than 30 percent of roofs in the Northeast would provide more than 70 percent of the area's heating and air-conditioning needs. [4] **Moreover,** solar heat collectors are economical, operating for up to twenty years with little or no maintenance. [5] **These savings** recoup the initial cost of installation within only ten years. [6] **Most important,** solar power is safe. [7] It can be transformed into electricity through photovoltaic cells (a type of storage battery) in a noiseless process that produces no air pollution—unlike coal, oil, and wood combustion. [8] **In contrast** to its nuclear counterpart, solar power produces no toxic waste and poses no danger of catastrophic meltdown. [9] **Thus,** massive conversion to solar power would ensure abundant energy and a safe, clean environment for future generations.

We can easily trace the sequence of thoughts in the previous paragraph:

Sentence 1.	The topic sentence establishes a clear direction.
Sentences 2–3.	The first reason is given and then explained.
Sentences 4–5.	The second reason is given and explained.
Sentences 6–8.	The third and major reason is given and explained.
Sentence 9.	The conclusion reemphasizes the main point.

To reinforce the logical sequence, related ideas are combined in individual sentences, and transitions and connectors signal clear relationships between ideas. The whole paragraph sticks together.

CLARIFYING HEADINGS

One of the final steps in structuring information is to make sure you have used clear headings. Use your outline as a guide. Headings may not be appropriate for all documents, such as short documents (e.g., the memo in Figure 6.1), but most technical material relies on some use of headings as a way to break up long passages of text and give readers guideposts throughout the document.

Create headings as one of the final steps in the structuring process

Headings often follow standard formats, such as "Introduction," "Methods," "Findings," "Conclusion," and so forth. In certain cases, the type of document (a scientific paper; a report for a company that always follows the same format) will dictate the headings you need to use.

Heading format and purpose

You may use single words, phrases, brief statements, or questions as headings, as long as the headings signal to readers exactly what to expect in the section that falls under the heading's umbrella.

When used consistently, questions are often the most helpful way to construct headings. In effect, the question in the heading is answered by the material that falls under that heading. The author of Figure 6.2 has taken this user-friendly approach, anticipating reader questions ("What is arsenic?" "How does arsenic get into my drinking water?" "How is arsenic in drinking water regulated?" "Why should I be concerned about arsenic in my drinking water?" and "What is the EPA's standard for arsenic in drinking water?") and answering each in turn.

Figure 6.5 is an example of a short report that uses clear, concise, and accurate headings to break up the material into logical sections. Because it is a progress report, the introductory heading gets right to the point of progress and the concluding heading gets directly to the topic of work remaining. Meanwhile, the headings in the middle section directly signal the key topics the reader needs to know about.

For more on the use of headings, see pages 151–152.

Four headings
divide the report
into distinct, logical
sections

Information in each
headed section is
brief and does not
stray from the
heading topic

Progress Report: Equipment for New Operations Building

Work Completed

Our training group has met twice since our May 12 report. In our first
meeting, we identified the types of training we anticipate.

Types of Training Anticipated

- Loan Officer Work Experience
- Divisional Systems Training
- Divisional Clerical Training (Continuing)
- Divisional Clerical Training (New Employees)
- Divisional Management Training (Seminars)
- Special/New Equipment Training

In our second meeting, we considered various areas for the training room.

Training Room Assignment and Equipment

The frequency of training requires us to have a training room available daily.
The large training room in the Corporate Education area (10th floor) would
be ideal. Before submitting our next report, we need your confirmation that
this room can be assigned to us.

To support the training programs, we purchased this equipment:

- Audioviewer
- LCD monitor
- Videocassette recorder and monitor
- Software for computer-assisted instruction
- Tape recorder

This equipment will allow us to administer training in a variety of modes,
ranging from programmed and learner-controlled instruction to group
seminars and workshops.

FIGURE 6.5 A short report with clear headings

Work Remaining

To support the training, we need to furnish the room appropriately. Because the types of training will vary, the furniture should provide a flexible environment. Outlined here are our anticipated furnishing needs.

- Tables and chairs that can be set up in many configurations. These would allow for individual or group training and large seminars.
- Portable room dividers. These would provide study space for training with programmed instruction and allow for simultaneous training.
- Built-in storage space for audiovisual equipment and training supplies. Ideally, this storage space should be multipurpose, providing work or display surfaces.
- A flexible lighting system for audiovisual presentations and individualized study.

The project is on schedule. As soon as we receive your approval of these specifications, we will send out bids for room dividers and have plans drawn for the built-in storage.

cc. R. S. Pike, SVP

Final heading clearly signals that this section is the conclusion

PROVIDING AN OVERVIEW

Provide an overview as the last step in the structuring process

The last step in structuring information for your readers is providing an overview. An overview may not be necessary for all technical documents, particularly short documents and reports. However, if you are writing a longer, more complex document, help your readers by providing a brief (usually paragraph-length) preview of what they can expect. This will help readers get the most out of the document by answering several key questions at the outset:

- What is the purpose of this document?
- Why should I read it?
- What information can I expect to find here?

Think about it this way: if you were taking a long trip, you would probably use MapQuest or a GPS system to get the big picture of your journey and to know exactly where you were headed. Overviews provide a similar type of road map.

An overview should be placed at the beginning of a document, but you may also want to provide section overviews at the beginning of each section in a long document. The following is an example of an overview paragraph that comes at the beginning of a long report on groundwater contamination.

About This Report

A report overview

This report contains five sections. The first section describes the scope and scale of groundwater contamination in Jackson county. The second section offers background on previous legislation related to groundwater. Section Three shows the most recent data from the Jackson County Groundwater Project, and Section Four compares that data to national averages. Section Five offers recommendations and ideas for next steps.

In addition to helping readers negotiate longer reports, overviews are also extremely helpful in longer instruction and user manuals so that readers will know immediately what to expect in the longer document.

Figure 6.6 is an example of an overview page from a user guide designed to help people find and apply for federal grants. This overview (titled as "Introduction" in this document) provides a short, simple introductory paragraph explaining the context for this user guide. Additional paragraphs describe what is contained in the guide, and a bulleted list provides a streamlined, easy-to-read visual overview of what is contained in the rest of this 60-page document.

Introduction

Grants.gov has been designed to make it easier for organizations to find and apply for more than $500 billion in federal grants. With electronic access to more than 1,000 grant programs offered by all federal grant-making agencies, Grants.gov leverages the power of the Web to streamline your grant acquisition process.

This user guide has been developed to help you navigate the Grants.gov environment more easily. In it, you'll find detailed instructions for every step of the process – whether you're an applicant or grant-making agency.

From getting started and registration to viewing and tracking completed applications, this user guide offers clarification throughout the entire process.

Provided information in this user guide:
- How To Register Your Organization
- How To Register As An Authorized Organization Representative
- How To Register As An Individual
- Find and Search Grant Opportunities
- Download Application Packages
- Apply For Grants
- Track Your Application
- And How To Stay Connected

Heading lets readers know that this page will give them an overview of the user guide

Introductory paragraph provides background information in brief format

Second paragraph explains the purpose of the user guide

Bulleted list outlines the major sections in the user guide

FIGURE 6.6 Overview page from a user guide summarizes the contents of the full document

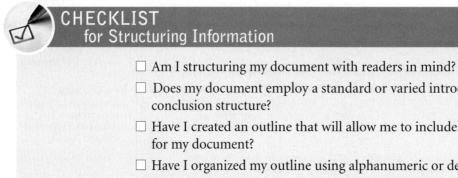

CHECKLIST
for Structuring Information

☐ Am I structuring my document with readers in mind?

☐ Does my document employ a standard or varied introduction/body/conclusion structure?

☐ Have I created an outline that will allow me to include all the necessary data for my document?

☐ Have I organized my outline using alphanumeric or decimal notation?

☐ Have I chunked my information into discrete, digestible units and for the proper medium (print or Web)?

☐ Am I using the right sequence?

- spatial: to describe a physical item or mechanism
- chronological: to describe a sequence of events
- problem-solution: to describe and diagnose a problem and offer a solution
- cause and effect: to describe an incident and trace its causes or follow an action to its results

☐ Does each of my paragraphs include these features?

- Topic sentence (introduction)
- Unity (body that supports the topic sentence)
- Coherence (connected line of thought leading to a conclusion)

☐ Have I used headings that are clear and address the sections or questions readers expect?

☐ If appropriate, does my document include an overview, helping readers understand what will follow?

APPLICATIONS

GENERAL APPLICATION

Locate a set of instructions for something you have purchased. Identify specific features of how this material is organized and written. Are the paragraphs chunked into discrete units? Are headings used, and if so are they in question format? Is the material sequenced in a standard way? Do all of the paragraphs include topic sentences and are they unified and coherent? Write a brief memo explaining why you think the technical writers who wrote the instructions made the decisions they did.

TEAM APPLICATION

With a team of 2–3 other students, consider the following documents and discuss the most logical sequence. (For instance, a description of a proposed podcasting computer lab would follow a spatial sequence).

- a set of instructions for operating a power tool
- a campaign report describing your progress in political fund-raising
- a report analyzing the desirability of a proposed oil refinery in your area
- a detailed breakdown of your monthly budget to trim excess spending
- a report investigating the reasons for student apathy on your campus
- a proposal for a no-grade policy at your college

GLOBAL APPLICATION

Find a document that presents the same information in several languages (assembly instructions, for example). Even without being able to understand all of the languages used, see if you can spot any changes made in the use of headings, the length of paragraphs, or the extent to which information is chunked. Interview a language professor on campus to find out why these choices may have been made.

COMPUTER/WEB-BASED APPLICATION

Locate a Web page and a print document (brochure, booklet, user guide) about the same product. Compare these, looking for the different ways in which material is written and chunked on the Web versus in print. Compare the use of headings, looking for any differences. In class, give a short presentation on these differences.

For additional technical writing resources that will help you master the chapter objectives, go to **www.mytechcommlab.com.**

7 Writing with a Readable Style

LEARNING OBJECTIVES FOR THIS CHAPTER

▸ Recognize that style places your audience's
  needs first

▸ Appreciate the importance of style
  in any document

▸ Use various strategies to write clearly, concisely,
  fluently, and personably

While *structure* has to do with the reader's ability to understand the document as a whole, including paragraphs, *style* has to do with readability at the sentence and word level.

Definition of style

THE IMPORTANCE OF A READABLE STYLE

No matter how technical your document, your audience won't understand the content unless your sentences are easy to understand and your words are chosen precisely. Your style is a blend of these elements:

Style emphasizes the audience's needs first

- the way in which you construct each sentence
- the length of your sentences
- the way in which you connect sentences
- the words and phrases you choose
- the tone you convey

What determines your style

Readable style, of course, also requires correct grammar, usage, mechanics, and spelling. But correctness alone is no guarantee of readability. For example, the following response to a job application follows the rules of grammar, usage, mechanics, and spelling, but it is hard to read:

Style is more than correct grammar, usage, mechanics, and spelling

> We are in receipt of your recent correspondence indicating your interest in securing the advertised position. Your correspondence has been duly forwarded for consideration by the personnel office, which has employment candidate selection responsibility. You may expect to hear from us relative to your application as the selection process progresses. Your interest in the position is appreciated.

Inefficient style

Notice as a reader how hard you have to work to extract information from the previous paragraph. This information could be expressed clearly and concisely, as in the following paragraph:

> Your application for the advertised position has been forwarded to our personnel office. As the selection process moves forward, we will be in touch. Thank you for your interest.

Readable style

Inefficient style makes readers work harder than they should. Style can be inefficient for many reasons but especially when it does the following:

- makes the writing impossible to interpret
- takes too long to make the point

Ways in which style goes wrong

- reads like a story from primary school
- sounds stuffy and impersonal

Inefficient style can
be uninformative,
unpersuasive, and
even unethical

Regardless of the cause, inefficient style results in writing that is less informative and less persuasive than it should be. Also, inefficient style can be unethical when it confuses or misleads the audience, whether intentionally or unintentionally. Therefore, take the time to write with a readable style, using the strategies described in the following sections: writing clearly, writing concisely, writing fluently, and writing personably. For advice regarding correct grammar, usage, and mechanics, see Appendix B.

WRITING CLEARLY

Why writing clearly
is important

Clear writing enables people to read each sentence only once in order to fully grasp its meaning. Strategies for writing clearly include avoiding ambiguous pronoun references, avoiding ambiguous modifiers, using active voice whenever possible, using passive voice selectively, avoiding nominalizations, unstacking nouns, and avoiding unnecessary jargon.

ref Avoiding Ambiguous Pronoun References

● **Watch** the Video
on Pronoun
Reference at
mytechcommlab

Pronouns (*he*, *she*, *it*, *their*, and so on) must clearly refer to the noun they replace; otherwise, the sentence will be ambiguous and readers will puzzle over your intended meaning. For example, consider the following sentence, in which the reader is unable to discern whether Jack *or* his assistant is competitive:

Unclear referent

| Jack resents his assistant because he is competitive.

Depending on whether the referent for "he" is Jack or his assistant, the sentence can be clarified:

Clear referent

| Because his assistant is competitive, Jack resents him.
| *or*
| Because Jack is competitive, he resents his assistant.

 EXERCISE 1

Edit each sentence below to eliminate ambiguities in pronoun reference.

- **a.** Bill told Darius that he was working too hard.
- **b.** Janice dislikes working with Magdalena because she's impatient.

    c. Our patients enjoy the warm days while they last.
    d. They couldn't start their cars because they were too cold.
    e. Celia can't talk to Betsy, because she's still too angry.

Avoiding Ambiguous Modifiers

A *modifier* is a word (usually an adjective or adverb) or a group of words (usually a phrase or clause) that provides information about other words or groups of words. If a modifier is too far from the words it modifies, the message can be ambiguous. For instance, in the following sentence, the reader cannot discern whether "only" modifies "press" or "emergency":

mod

Watch the Video
on Ambiguous
Modifiers at
mytechcommlab

| Only press the red button in an emergency.

Ambiguous modifier

If, however, the writer repositions the modifier, the sentence becomes clear:

| Press only the red button in an emergency.

Clear modifier

or

| Press the red button in an emergency only.

Position modifiers to reflect your meaning.

EXERCISE 2

Edit each sentence below to clarify ambiguous modifiers.

    a. Just place the dishes back in the cabinets after 8 P.M.
    b. He purchased a ticket for his wife from Carnegie Hall.
    c. I almost sat there waiting for Gino for 45 minutes.
    d. Before she passed away, Philippa told her mother she admired her.
    e. Only use this phone in a red alert.

Using Active Voice Whenever Possible

In general, readers understand the meaning more quickly and clearly when the writer uses active voice ("I did it") rather than the passive voice ("It was done by me"). In active voice sentences, a clear agent performs a clear action on a recipient, as in the following example:

av

| Felix lost your report

Active voice

Passive voice, by contrast, reverses this pattern, placing the recipient of the action (i.e., *report,* in the previous example) in the subject slot, as in the following sentence:

Passive voice

| Your report was lost by Felix.

Note that passive voice adds a form of the verb "be" ("was") next to the actual verb.

Some writers mistakenly rely on passive voice because they think it sounds more objective and important. But passive voice makes sentences wordier and harder to understand.

In addition, passive voice sometimes obscures the subject of the sentence, as in the following example:

Inappropriate use of passive voice (no subject identified)

| Your report was lost.

Passive voice is unethical if it obscures the person or other agent who performed the action when the person or agent responsible should be identified. In the above example, "Your report was lost" leaves out the responsible party. (Who lost the report?) For these reasons, favor the active voice in most writing situations.

EXERCISE 3

Convert these passive voice sentences to concise, forceful, and direct expressions in the active voice.

    a. The evaluation was performed by us.
    b. Unless you pay me within three days, my lawyer will be contacted.
    c. Hard hats should be worn at all times.
    d. The due date was delayed.
    e. Our test results will be sent to you as soon as verification is completed.

pv

Using Passive Voice Selectively

Watch the Video on Active vs. Passive Voice at mytechcommlab

There are times when the passive voice is appropriate: for instance, when the subject is not known or when the object is more important than the subject. For example, if a group of scientists performed an experiment and wanted to explain the results, they might write the following:

Appropriate use of passive voice

| The data were analyzed, and the findings were discussed.

Even here, active voice ("We analyzed the data . . .") would be preferable. But if it is clear who analyzed the data or truly not important who did the work, passive voice might be acceptable.

Passive voice can also ease the blow a direct sentence might deliver:

| You have not paid your bill.

To be indirect and less offensive, the writer may choose passive voice instead:

| Your bill has not been paid.

Consider this technique when you want to avoid a blunt or hostile tone. But in general, to convey clear, readable technical information, use active voice.

 EXERCISE 4

The sentences below represent blunt uses of active voice. Convert each to passive voice.

a. Joe's company fired him.
b. Cecelia's coworkers accused her of being lazy.
c. You are paying inadequate attention to worker safety.
d. You are checking temperatures too infrequently.
e. You did a poor job editing this report.

Avoiding Nominalizations

A nominalization is a noun that would be easier to understand as a verb. Verbs are generally easier to read because they signal action that can be visualized. You can usually spot a nominalization in two ways. First, look for words with *-tion* endings. Second, look for sentences in which the "[noun] of [noun]" formula appears. Following is an example of each type of nominalization:

nom

| My recommendation is for a larger budget.

| The managing of this project is up to me.

To fix the *-tion* problem, strike the ending to find the root verb ("recommend") and rewrite the sentence in a more direct form. To fix the "[noun] of [noun]" problem, identify the root verb form ("manage"), and create a more accessible sentence. Following are improved versions of the above sentences:

| I recommend a larger budget.

| I manage this project.

EXERCISE 5

Make these sentences clearer by eliminating nominalizations.

    a. Our acceptance of the offer is a necessity.
    b. Your assertion is that we spend too much time in meetings.
    c. We ask for the cooperation of all employees.
    d. My validation of the report is required.
    e. Please provide a description of the problem.

st mod ## Unstack Modifying Nouns

Too many nouns in a row can create confusion for readers. One noun can modify another (as in "software development"). But when two or more nouns modify a noun, the string of words becomes "stacked"—in other words, hard to read and ambiguous. For example:

Ambiguous use of stacked nouns

> Be sure to leave enough time for today's training session participant evaluation.

In the previous sentence, the reader is left unsure whether evaluation is of the session or of the participants. With no articles, prepositions, or verbs to unstack the nouns, readers cannot sort out the relationships among the nouns. To fix the problem, separate the stacked nouns by changing some nouns into verb forms where appropriate, as in the following example:

Clear sentence with nouns unstacked

> Be sure to leave enough time for participants to evaluate today's training session.
>
> *or*
>
> Be sure to leave enough time to evaluate the participants in today's training session.

EXERCISE 6

Make these sentences clearer by unstacking the nouns.

    a. They developed online editing system documentation.
    b. I recommend these management performance improvement incentives.
    c. Sarah's job involves fault analysis systems troubleshooting handbook preparation.
    d. Constantine read through the strategic implementation status guidelines.
    e. You should think about providing employees with memory recall stimulus devices.

Avoiding Unnecessary Jargon

Every profession has its own shorthand and accepted phrases and terms. Among specialists, these terms are an economical way to communicate. For example, "stat" (from the Latin *statim*, "immediately") is medical jargon for "drop everything and deal with this emergency." Jargon can be useful in communications among specialists. However, to avoid confusion, use jargon only when you know your audience will understand it, and not simply to sound important or pretentious. Consider the following sentence:

jarg

| We will bilaterally optimize our efforts on this project.

Needless jargon

Clearly that writer meant to sound important, but to most readers, the sentence is simultaneously meaningless and pretentious.

Following is a clear and simple version:

| We will cooperate on this project.

Jargon-free version

EXERCISE 7

Edit these sentences to eliminate useless jargon.

  a. To optimize your financial return, prioritize your investment goals.
  b. The use of this product engenders a 50-percent repeat consumer encounter.
  c. Unless all parties interface synchronously within given parameters, the project will fail.
  d. Acoustically attenuate our company's food consumption area.
  e. We need to formulate a workable paradigm for this project.

WRITING CONCISELY

Concise writing provides readers with all of the information they need but without any needless filler. Strategies for writing concisely include avoiding wordiness as well as eliminating redundancy and repetition.

Why writing concisely is important

Avoiding Wordiness

Wordiness is often unavoidable in a first draft, when a writer is simply trying to get thoughts down on the page. For your readers, however, wordiness is distracting and detracts from a writer's credibility. When you edit your document, go through each sentence and work to eliminate excess words.

w

 Watch the Video on Wordiness and Redundancy at mytechcommlab

Wordiness has multiple causes: First, some writers habitually use needless phrases that can be reduced to one word:

Wordy phrases and their one-word substitutes

at a rapid rate = rapidly

due to the fact that = because

aware of the fact that = know

in close proximity to = near

the majority of = most

Second, many writers tend to start sentences with "there is," "there are," and "it is," which can often be eliminated:

Needless "there is," "there are," and "it is" sentence openers and their corrections

There is a danger of explosion in Number 2 mineshaft. = Number 2 mineshaft is in danger of exploding.

It is necessary to complete both sides of the form. = Please complete both sides of the form.

Third, writers often gravitate to weak verbs, such as all forms of the verb "to be" ("am," "are," "is," etc.), "give," "make," "come," and "take." These verbs need to be combined with other words to express fuller meaning, but they can easily be replaced with stronger verbs that can stand on their own:

Weak verbs and their replacements

has the ability to = can

make an assumption = assume

come to the conclusion that = conclude

give a summary of = summarize

take action = act

Fourth, writers often overuse prepositional phrases, which can easily be reduced to one or two words:

Prepositional phrases and their replacements

with the exception of = except for

in the near future = soon

at the present time = now

in the course of = during

in the process of = during (*or* in)

Finally, many writers pad their writing by using clutter words (such as "very," "quite," "somewhat," "really," "actually"), needless qualifiers ("I think," "in my opinion," "it seems"), and unnecessary prefaces ("As far as I am concerned," "the purpose of this is") that add no meaning to a sentence. Of course, if you are expressing a tentative position on a complex issue, do use a qualifier ("I think," "it seems") as appropriate.

EXERCISE 8

Eliminate wordiness from the following sentences.

a. Our lateness was due to the fact that we ran into traffic.
b. I have come to the realization that I was mistaken.
c. It seems as if I have just wrecked the company car.
d. It is essential that we act immediately.
e. A malfunction occurred during the process of rebooting.

Eliminating Redundancy and Repetition

red

rep

A redundant expression says the same thing twice, in different words, whereas a repetition says the same thing twice or more in the same words. Following are examples of each, which can be fixed simply through cutting out the bracketed words.

[completely] eliminate	[mental] awareness	Redundant phrases
[end] result	[utter] devastation	
enter [into]	[mutual] cooperation	
consensus [of opinion]	[fellow] colleagues	

Techniques of artificial respiration include mouth-to-mouth [respiration] and mouth-to-nose [respiration].

Needlessly repetitious sentence

EXERCISE 9

Make these sentences more concise by eliminating redundancy and repetition.

a. Igor's fellow colleagues are ambitious.
b. We ask for everyone's mutual cooperation during this busy time.
c. This report is the most informative report on the project.
d. The consensus of opinion is that we agree with Tanisha's idea.
e. Sam agrees, Tanya agrees, and Soon-ye agrees too.

WRITING FLUENTLY

When you write fluently, you will hold your readers' interest and attention by making clear connections between ideas and by reducing monotony. Strategies for

Why writing fluently is important

writing fluently include combining related ideas, varying sentence construction and length, and using parallel structure.

comb   Combining Related Ideas

Readers who are forced to trudge through a series of short, choppy sentences will not only lose interest but will also fail to see how ideas are meant to be related or which ideas should receive emphasis. For example, the following string of five short sentences makes for dull reading. In addition, it forces readers to invent transitions between ideas and decide which points are most important:

Disconnected series of ideas

> Jogging can be healthful. You need the right equipment. Well-fitting shoes are important. You take the chance of injuring your legs. Your knees are especially prone to injury.

In contrast, the following two-sentence revision reads more smoothly and places a stronger emphasis on the importance of having the right jogging shoes:

Fluent combination of ideas

> Jogging can be healthful if you have the right equipment. Shoes that fit well are particularly important, because they prevent injury to your legs, especially your knees.

 EXERCISE 10

Combine the following sentences three times, each time creating one fluent sentence that places emphasis in a different place. For the first combination, emphasize the negative aspects of the job. For the second combination, emphasize the positive aspects. For the third combination, emphasize the salary.

> The job offers an attractive salary. It demands long work hours. It can be stressful. Promotions are rapid.

var   Varying Sentence Construction and Length

Watch the Video on Varying Sentence Structure at **mytechcommlab**

While you should combine short, choppy sentences into longer, more fluid versions, you don't want to create a string of unvaried longer sentences. Readers will find these just as monotonous, and they will also have a hard time determining which points are meant to receive emphasis. For example, the following two longer sentences are unvaried and dull, and at the same time the reader is forced to decide which of the five points made is the most important:

> Two drawbacks of diesel engines are that they are difficult to
> start in cold weather and cause sulfur dioxide pollution. In addition,
> they give off noise, emit an unpleasant odor, and cause vibrations.

In contrast, the following two-sentence revision reads less monotonously and incorporates one short sentence to place special emphasis on sulfur dioxide pollution:

> Diesel engines have a number of drawbacks, including cold weather
> starting difficulties, noisiness, odor, and vibrations. More seriously, they
> also cause sulfur dioxide pollution.

EXERCISE 11

Add variety to the following string of similar sentences.

> Because people are busy these days, television DVRs are unsurprisingly popular. Because you can record while you are at work, you don't have to worry about missing your favorite programs. In addition, because you can record programs that show late at night, you don't have to stay up late to catch your favorite programs. Finally, in case you are on vacation, you can set the DVR to record your favorite shows automatically every week.

Using Parallel Structure

Parallel structure is a fancy way of saying that similar items should be expressed in similar grammatical form. Without parallelism, readers will lose attention, being mentally forced to "fix" the grammatical fluency of your sentence. For example, the structure of the following sentence is not parallel:

> She likes many outdoor activities, including running, kayaking, and to
> design new hiking trails.

par

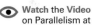 **Watch** the Video
on Parallelism at
mytechcommlab

Not parallel

This sentence is essentially a list of items. The first two items, "running" and "kayaking," are expressed as gerunds (verbs converted into nouns by using -ing endings). The third item, "to design," is not a gerund but a verb followed by an object. To make this sentence parallel and increase its fluency you would revise as follows:

> She likes many outdoor activities, including running, kayaking, and
> designing new hiking trails.

Parallel

EXERCISE 12

Make these sentences clearer by eliminating faulty parallelism.

    a. The weather today is going to be cold, rainy, and without much sun.
    b. My television picture is cloudy and I can see pixellation.
    c. My car needs a tune up, an oil change, and the tires should be replaced.
    d. The new tutor is enthusiastic, skilled, and you can depend on her.
    e. In his new job, Ramon felt lonely and without a friend.

WRITING PERSONABLY

Why writing personably is important

When you write in a personable manner, you connect directly with your readers and avoid inadvertently offending them. Strategies for writing personably include adjusting your tone and avoiding sexist and biased language.

tone

Adjusting Your Tone

Your tone is your personal stamp—the personality that takes shape between the lines. The tone you create depends on (1) the distance you impose between yourself and the reader, and (2) the attitude you show toward the subject. To increase the likelihood of bringing readers over to your side, see the Strategies that follow.

STRATEGIES
for Deciding about Tone

▸ **Determine if you want a formal, semiformal, or informal tone.** You may prefer a formal tone when writing to superiors, professionals, or academics (depending on what you think they expect), a semiformal tone for colleagues and subordinates (depending on how close you feel to your readers), or an informal tone when you want your writing to be conversational.

▸ **Remain consistent.** Once you've determined the appropriate overall tone of the document, stay with it throughout.

▸ **Address readers directly.** Prefer the personal pronouns "you" and "your" to connect with readers.

▸ **Use "I" and "we" when appropriate.** Instead of disappearing behind your writing, use "I" and "we" to connect with your readers.

▸ **Prefer the active voice.** Show confidence and directness by using active rather than passive voice.

▸ **Emphasize the positive.** Avoid a negative tone when conveying unpleasant information.

                                                   ➡

STRATEGIES *continued*

▶ **Always avoid an overly informal tone.** Achieving a conversational tone does not mean relying on substandard usage ("He ain't got none"), profanity ("This idea sucks"), and colloquialisms ("OK," "a lot," "snooze").

EXERCISE 13

Adjust the tone of the following sentences to improve the connection between the writer and the reader.

   a. The writer of this letter would like a refund.
   b. The requested report will be sent next week.
   c. Students at this college will find the faculty always willing to help.
   d. No way am I going to approve this dog of a proposal.
   e. Because of your division's lagging productivity, a management review may be needed.

Avoiding Sexist and Biased Language

sexist

bias

Language that is offensive or makes unwarranted assumptions will alienate readers. Women, for example, who receive a letter addressed to "Dear Sir" will probably discard the letter without ever reading it. Also, our communication should respect all people regardless of cultural, racial, or national background, sexual or religious orientation, age, or physical condition. See the following Strategies.

STRATEGIES
for Nonsexist Usage

▶ **Use gender-neutral expressions.** Use "chair" or "chairperson" rather than "chairman" and "postal worker" rather than "postman."

▶ **Don't mention gender if it is not relevant.** Don't use "the female police officer" unless you are talking about police officers in the context of gender.

▶ **Avoid sexist pronouns.** You can avoid using a sexist pronoun by revising the sentence ("A writer who revises will succeed" rather than "A writer will succeed if he revises"), by using a plural form ("Writers will succeed if they revise"), or by occasionally using paired pronouns ("A writer will succeed if he or she revises").

▶ **Drop condescending diminutive endings.** Avoid words such as "poetess" and "majorette" and simply use "poet" and "major" instead.

▶ **Use "Ms."** Unless you know that a person prefers a traditional title, avoid "Mrs." and "Miss." Males are not identified by marital status, nor should females have to be.

STRATEGIES
for Unbiased Usage

▶ **Be specific when referring to a person's cultural/national identity.** Instead of "Asian" or "Hispanic," for example, prefer "Korean" or "Cuban American." Use the cultural/national designation preferred by people in that group (e.g., "Native American" rather than "Indian," or "Senegalese" rather than "African").

▶ **Avoid potentially judgmental expressions.** Instead of "Third World" or "under-developed" use "newly industrialized" or "developing," and instead of "nonwhite" use "people of color."

▶ **Never use demeaning expressions.** Avoid expressions such as "lame excuse," "the blind leading the blind," or "that's queer."

▶ **Use person-first language for people with disabilities or medical conditions.** Avoid terms that place the disability over the person or that suggest pity. Use "person with a disability" rather than "disabled person," or "person with AIDS" rather than "AIDS victim."

▶ **Use age-appropriate designations.** A "girl" or a "boy" is age 14 or under: a "young person," "young adult," "young woman," or "young man" is of high school age: and a "man" or a "woman" is college-aged or older. Avoid "old" or "elderly" and use "older person" or "senior" instead, if age is relevant.

EXERCISE 14

The sentences below suffer from sexist or biased expressions. Adjust the tone.

    a. The group's spokesman demanded salary increases.
    b. The explosion left me blind as a bat for nearly two hours.
    c. While the girls played football, the men waved pom-poms to cheer them on.
    d. The Latino mechanic fixed the problem in under an hour.
    e. Lame excuses for late papers will not be tolerated.

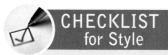

CHECKLIST
for Style

CLARITY
☐ Have I ensured that each pronoun clearly refers to the noun it replaces?
☐ Have I placed each modifier close enough to the word(s) it explains?

☐ Have I used active rather than passive voice (unless the agent is immaterial)?

☐ Have I restored nominalizations to their verb forms?

☐ Have I unstacked modifying nouns?

☐ Have I avoided needless jargon?

CONCISENESS

☐ Have I avoided needless sentence openers?

☐ Have I traded weak verbs for verbs that express a definite action?

☐ Have I avoided needless prepositional phrases?

☐ Have I avoided clutter words and needless qualifiers?

☐ Have I eliminated redundancy and needless repetition?

FLUENCY

☐ Have I combined related ideas appropriately?

☐ Have I varied sentence construction and length?

☐ Have I used parallel structure?

☐ Have I used short sentences for special emphasis?

TONE

☐ Is my tone appropriate and consistent for the situation and audience?

☐ Is the level of formality what the intended audience would expect?

☐ Is my writing free of implied bias or offensive language?

☐ Does the piece display sensitivity to cultural differences?

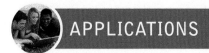 APPLICATIONS

GENERAL APPLICATION

Using the Checklist for Style, revise the following selections. (Hint: use the example on page 103 as a model for revision.) If available, use the "track changes" or "editing" function on your computer to record your suggested revisions and to identify the specific style problems in the original selection.

a. Letter to a local newspaper

In the absence of definitive studies regarding the optimum length of the school day, I can only state my personal opinion based upon observations made by me and upon teacher observations that have been conveyed to me. Considering the length of the present school day, it is my opinion that the day is excessive length-wise for most elementary pupils, certainly for almost all of the primary children.

To find the answer to the problem requires consideration of two ways in which the problem may be viewed. One way focuses upon the needs of the children, while the other focuses upon logistics, transportation, scheduling, and other limits imposed by the educational system. If it is necessary to prioritize these two ideas, it would seem most reasonable to give the first consideration to the primary reason for the very existence of the system, i.e., to meet the educational needs of the children the system is trying to serve.

b. Memo to employees

We are presently awaiting an on-site inspection of the designated professional library location by corporate representatives relative to electrical adaptations necessary for the computer installation. Meanwhile, all staff members are asked to respect the off-limits designation of the aforementioned location, as requested, due to the liability insurance provisions in regard to the computer.

TEAM APPLICATION

Locate a poorly written document. In groups of four, look for problems of style and readability. Each person in the group should be assigned to improve a different stylistic area in the document: the first person should improve clarity; the second, conciseness; the third fluency; and the fourth should make the document more personable. Keep track of the improvements each team member makes, and present your edits and final version to the class. Note how each group will have revised the document differently.

GLOBAL APPLICATION

The style guidelines in this chapter apply specifically to Standard English in North America, but technical communication is a global process. Practices and preferences differ widely. For example, some cultures prefer long sentences and elaborate language, to convey an idea's full complexity. Others expect lengthy introductions and expressions of politeness and praise rather than clarity or directness. Certain documents may originate in English but then be translated into other languages or read by audiences for whom English is a second language. In such cases, writers must be careful to use language that is easy to translate. Idioms ("cutthroat competition," "over the top," etc.), cultural references ("the Bronx Bomber," "the Deep

South") and humor ("heads I win; tails you lose") are often difficult to translate. Some words may carry insulting connotations, as in cultures in which when the terms "male" and "female" refer only to animals.

Your assignment is to search the Internet using the keywords "international business culture" to learn about the style preferences of one particular culture. Then, in a one-page memo to your instructor and classmates, describe the style preferences of that culture, and give examples of how these preferences differ from the style guidelines (i.e., for North American English) in this chapter.

COMPUTER/WEB-BASED APPLICATION

Do a Web search to find an online style guide that expands on advice offered in this chapter. Consider the following sites, but do not limit yourself to them.

- Paradigm Online Writing Assistant: <www.powa.org>
- Capital Community College Guide to Grammar and Writing: <grammar.ccc.commnet.edu/grammar>
- Purdue University Online Writing Lab: <owl.english.purdue.edu>

Prepare a one-page presentation for the class, in your own words and with examples about how that Web site describes writing style in ways that differ from this chapter. Why might that be the case? Attach a copy of the relevant Web page(s) to your presentation. Be sure to credit each source of information (Appendix A).

For additional technical writing resources that will help you master the chapter objectives, go to **www.mytechcommlab.com**.

8 Using Audience-Centered Visuals

LEARNING OBJECTIVES FOR THIS CHAPTER

- ▶ Appreciate the role of visuals
  in technical communications
- ▶ Decide when to use visuals on their
  own or with text
- ▶ Distinguish between different types of visuals
- ▶ Understand how to choose visuals appropriately
  for your audience and purpose
- ▶ Place, cross-reference, and present visuals
  appropriately for your readers
- ▶ Use color in your visuals
- ▶ Appreciate the importance of using visuals
  in an ethical manner

I n addition to structure and style, the use of audience-centered visuals is one of the four essential elements in technical communication.

Analyze the Document for effective use of visuals at mytechcommlab

THE IMPORTANCE OF USING AUDIENCE-CENTERED VISUALS

Visuals are important in print or digital documents, in oral presentations, and in multimedia programs for several reasons: they help readers interpret and remember complex information; they show how items look or work; and they show how items are organized or actions are performed.

Because they focus and organize complex information into more simplified form, visuals make data easier for readers to interpret and remember. Visuals work because readers want more than just raw information: they want the information presented so they can understand it at a glance. Consider, for example, how the following passage might be better presented using a visual:

Visuals help readers interpret and remember complex information

> The time required for the global population to grow from 5 to 6 billion was shorter than the interval between any of the previous billions. It took just 12 years for this to occur, just slightly less than the 13 years between the fourth and fifth billion and the 15 years between the third and fourth billion, but much less time than the 118 years between the first and second billion. . . .

Technical data in prose form can be hard to interpret

Now consider this same information presented as a graph in Figure 8.1.

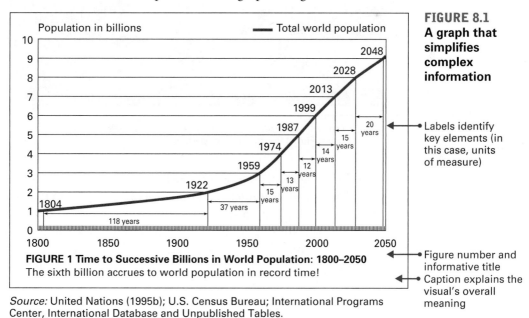

FIGURE 8.1
A graph that simplifies complex information

Labels identify key elements (in this case, units of measure)

FIGURE 1 Time to Successive Billions in World Population: 1800–2050
The sixth billion accrues to world population in record time!

Figure number and informative title
Caption explains the visual's overall meaning

Source: United Nations (1995b); U.S. Census Bureau; International Programs Center, International Database and Unpublished Tables.

Notice how Figure 8.1 makes it easier to understand and remember the upward population trend and the numerous facts and figures described in the paragraph that precedes it.

Not all visuals are designed to convey numeric or other data. A second reason visuals are important is that they can show readers at a glance what something looks like and/or how it works—as opposed to lengthy descriptions in prose form.

Visuals show readers how items look or work

Visuals that show how items look include illustrations and photographs, while visuals that show how items work include diagrams. For example, the diagram in Figure 8.2 illustrates how fireworks operate.

**FIGURE 8.2
A cutaway diagram that shows how something works**

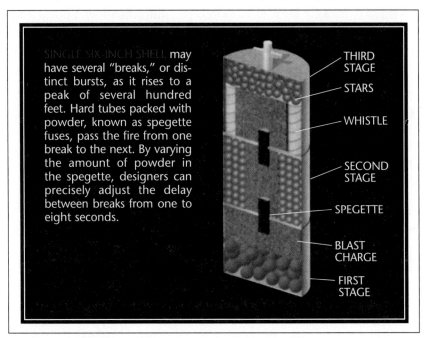

SINGLE SIX-INCH SHELL may have several "breaks," or distinct bursts, as it rises to a peak of several hundred feet. Hard tubes packed with powder, known as spegette fuses, pass the fire from one break to the next. By varying the amount of powder in the spegette, designers can precisely adjust the delay between breaks from one to eight seconds.

THIRD STAGE
STARS
WHISTLE
SECOND STAGE
SPEGETTE
BLAST CHARGE
FIRST STAGE

Source: G.R. Zambelli, Sr. from *Scientific American,* July 1999, Volume 108. Illustration by Slim Films. Reprinted with permission.

Notice how Figure 8.2 uses a cutaway illustration, annotations, color, and text to give readers an easy-to-understand snapshot of a mechanism that would be very hard to describe using text only.

Visuals show readers how items are organized or actions are performed

Finally, visuals are important because they can quickly and efficiently show how items are organized or actions are performed, without resorting to long and difficult-to-follow textual explanations. Such visuals include organizational charts and flowcharts. For example, imagine the dense and wordy paragraph that would be needed to describe the process for helping an adult choking victim, as shown in the flowchart in Figure 8.3:

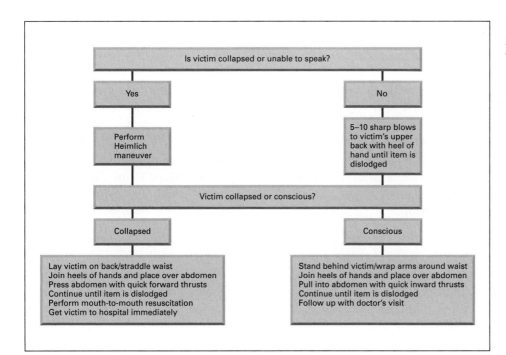

FIGURE 8.3
A flowchart that shows how an action is performed

WHEN TO USE VISUALS

Visuals should be used to enhance your document, not just to decorate it. There may also be organizational reasons for using visuals; for example, some companies may always expect photographs, charts, and graphs as part of an annual report. Certain industries, such as the financial sector, routinely use visuals (such as a line graph showing recent fluctuations in the Dow Jones Industrial Average).

Use visuals to enhance, not decorate

Explore the Concept with the Case Study on Visuals at mytechcommlab

As discussed below, you may choose to use visuals to support the text of your document, or you may choose to use visuals on their own.

Using Visuals to Support Text

In many cases, visuals are an excellent way to support, but not replace, essential discussion in the actual text. For example, you may be writing about an important financial trend, describing features about the world economy, and making a case for financial reforms. A series of graphs or charts would augment, not substitute for, the text. In a situation like that, visuals would add to your discussion.

Use supporting visuals when you want to add to important textual discussion

Be sure to refer to each visual by number ("see Figure 1") in the text. Explain what the visual means; supply a caption for it; and place the visual as close as possible to the text it supports.

Using Visuals on Their Own

In some cases, visuals may work well on their own, as when they make your point more clearly than text can. In situations like these, merely refer to the visuals that show readers what they need to see. For instance, to show how customers who have purchased your company's new plasma televisions break out by age group, don't list the percentages in a lengthy paragraph. Simply supply a chart or graph that conveys this data visually.

When you use stand-alone visuals, make sure they tell the whole story you want readers to understand and that you introduce them clearly. If you need to explain how the visual should be interpreted, do so briefly in the figure's caption.

TYPES OF VISUALS

The most commonly used types of visuals are tables, graphs, charts, illustrations, diagrams, photographs, videos, symbols, and icons. The following sections describe each type.

Tables

Tables display organized data or information across columns and rows for easy comparison. Tables can be used to display quantitative information (*numeric tables*) or qualitative information (*textual tables*), or sometimes both. For specific advice on creating tables, see the annotations to Tables 8.1 and 8.2 and the Strategies on page 126.

Numeric Tables. Numeric tables simplify complex quantitative information. Although text may be used in headings to organize the table, the primary purpose of the table is to show numbers and their relationships. Note in Table 8.1 how the data are compared in a variety of ways and how a tally of the numbers and an explanatory caption further help readers understand and interpret the data.

Textual Tables. Textual tables simplify complex qualitative information. Numbers may be used to help organize the textual information, but the primary purpose of the textual table is to show written information and relationships. Note how Table 8.2 simplifies written information that would be difficult to explain in paragraph form and uses a footnote to explain a nuance to the reader.

TABLE 8.1 A numeric table

Death Rates for Heart Disease and Cancer 1970–2006					→ Title explains the table's purpose
	Number of Deaths (per 100,000)				
	Heart Disease		Cancer		→ Each column has a clear heading
Year	Male	Female	Male	Female	
1970	419	309	248	163	
1980	369	305	272	167	
1990	298	282	280	176	→ Numbers are aligned properly for ease of reading
2000	256	260	257	206	
2006	235	236	233	161	
% change, 1970–2006	−43.9	−23.6	−6.0	−1.2	→ Where helpful, data are tallied

Both male and female death rates from heart disease decreased between 1970 and 2006, but males had nearly twice the rate of decrease. After increasing between 1970 and 1990, cancer death rates for both groups decreased to slightly below their 1970 levels. → A caption explains the numerical relationships

Source: Tables 113 and 115 from *Statistical Abstract of the United States,* 2007, 126th Edition by the U.S. Census Bureau.

TABLE 8.2 A textual table

Radon Risk if You Smoke				→ Title explains the table's purpose
Radon level	If 1,000 people who smoked were exposed to this level over a lifetime ...	The risk of cancer from radon exposure compares to ...	WHAT TO DO: Stop smoking and ...	→ Each column has a clear heading that leads readers into the information
20 pCi/L[a]	About 135 people could get lung cancer	←100 times the risk of drowning	Fix your home	
10 pCi/L	About 71 people could get lung cancer	←100 times the risk of dying in a home fire	Fix your home	
8 pCi/L	About 57 people could get lung cancer		Fix your home	→ Phrases are brief and aligned for ease of reading
4 pCi/L	About 29 people could get lung cancer	←100 times the risk of dying in an airplane crash	Fix your home	→ Numbers enhance the verbal information
2 pCi/L	About 15 people could get lung cancer	←2 times the risk of dying in a car crash	Consider fixing between 2 and 4 pCi/L	
1.3 pCi/L	About 9 people could get lung cancer	(Average indoor radon level)	(Reducing radon levels below 2 pCi/L is difficult)	
0.4 pCi/L	About 3 people could get lung cancer	(Average outdoor radon level)		

Note: If you are a former smoker, your risk may be lower.
[a]picocuries per liter → A footnote provides more detail

Source: Home Buyer's and Seller's Guide to Radon, 1993, by the U.S. Environmental Protection Agency.

STRATEGIES
for Creating Tables

- **Don't include too much information in a single table.** Overly complex tables are confusing. Limit your table to two or three areas of comparison. Or use multiple tables.

- **Provide a brief but descriptive title.** Announce exactly what is being compared.

- **Label the rows and columns.**

- **Line up data and information clearly.** Use neat columns and rows and plenty of white space between items.

- **Keep qualitative information and quantitative data brief.** When including high numbers (more than three digits), abbreviate the numbers and indicate "in thousands," "in millions," and so on. When using text in a table, limit the number of words.

- **Provide additional information, if necessary.** Add footnotes or a caption at the bottom of the table to explain anything readers may not understand at first glance.

- **Credit your sources.** Unless you collected the data or information yourself, always credit the source (see page 428 for advice on avoiding plagiarism).

Graphs

Graphs translate numbers into shapes, shades, and patterns. At a glance, graphs display the approximate values, the point being made about those values, and the relationship being emphasized. Typically, a graph's horizontal axis shows categories to be compared, such as time periods, while the vertical axis shows the range of values, such as numbers. The most common types of graphs are *bar graphs* (simple or multiple) and *line graphs* (simple or multiple). For specific advice on creating graphs, see the annotations to Figures 8.4 through 8.7 and the Strategies on page 128.

Bar graphs depict changes over time, patterns, and trends

Bar Graphs. Bar graphs present data using colored (or shaded) bars, usually lined up along the horizontal axis. Simple bar graphs depict changes over time, patterns, or trends for a single category. For instance, the simple bar graph in Figure 8.4 shows one trend extracted from Table 8.1, male deaths from heart disease between 1970 and 2006.

Multiple bar graphs, meanwhile, compare two or more categories. For example, the multiple bar graph in Figure 8.5 (also extracted from Table 8.1) shows not only a trend in male deaths from heart disease between 1970 and 2006 but also from cancer during that same period.

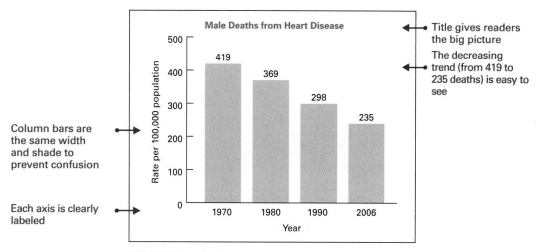

FIGURE 8.4 **A simple bar graph**

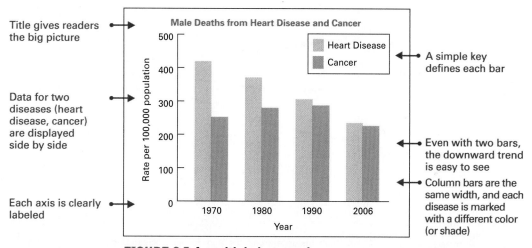

FIGURE 8.5 **A multiple bar graph**

Line Graphs. Line graphs present data using colored (or shaded) lines, marked at regular intervals so that the data points line up with the items on the horizontal axis. A line graph can accommodate and display more data points than a bar graph. Simple line graphs show changes, patterns, or trends for a single category. In Figure 8.6 the single line tracks the number of building permits issued during the year, showing how permit requests are more common between May and October.

Multiple line graphs display several relationships simultaneously, as in Figure 8.7.

Line graphs can synthesize large quantities of data

Title gives readers the big picture

The trend (up, then down) is easy to see

Data points are marked with a square shape

Each axis is clearly labeled

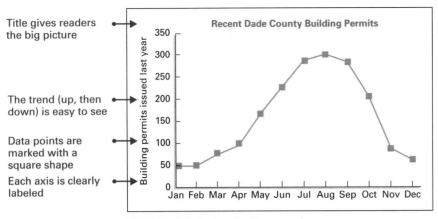

FIGURE 8.6 A simple line graph

Title gives readers the big picture

The overall trend (moving closer together) is easy to see

Each axis is clearly labeled

A short caption helps explain the relationship that the writer wants readers to notice

Data points are marked with a square shape

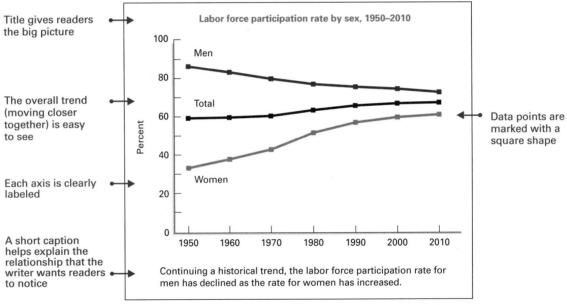

FIGURE 8.7 A multiple line graph
Source: U. S. Bureau of Labor Statistics.

STRATEGIES
for Creating Graphs

▶ **Use a graph only to compare values that are noticeably different.** A bar graph in which all bars are about the same height or a line graph depicting a single straight line (or overlapping multiple lines) serves no purpose.

▶ **Provide a clear title.** Announce exactly what is being displayed.

STRATEGIES *continued*

▸ **Label both the purpose and divisions of each axis.** Use numbers or gradations that are evenly divided (e.g., multiples of 10, spans of 5 years, months of the year), and add tick marks next to each number/gradation.

▸ **Keep the graph simple and easy to read.** Use no more than three bars (bar graph) or three to four lines (line graph) per graph. Avoid needless details; readers should understand the graph at a glance.

▸ **Make each bar or line distinct.** In multiple bar or line charts, use different colors or shades for each bar or line. Provide a key or label that indicates what each bar or line represents.

▸ **Use consistent format for bars and lines.** In a bar graph, bars should all be of the same width. In a line graph, lines should all be of the same thickness and all data points (those points at which a line intersects with gradations on the horizontal axis) should be marked.

▸ **Credit your sources.** As always, avoid plagiarism by citing the sources of your information or data.

Charts

Charts depict relationships via shapes, arrows, lines, and other design elements. The terms "chart" and "graph" are often used interchangeably; technically, however, a chart displays relationships (quantitative or cause-and-effect) that are not plotted on vertical and horizontal axes. Commonly used charts include *flowcharts*, *pie charts*, and *organization charts*. For more specific advice on creating charts, see the annotations to Figures 8.8 through 8.10 and the Strategies on page 131.

Watch the Video on Creating Graphs and Charts at **mytechcommlab**

Flowcharts. A flowchart traces a process or procedure from beginning to end, moving from top to bottom or from left to right and using connector bars to show relationships, as in Figure 8.8.

Flowcharts show processes and procedures

Pie Charts. Easy for almost anyone to understand, pie charts are circular diagrams that display the status of each "piece" of the "pie"—the percentage of the whole pie (which totals 100%) that each piece represents. Readers can compare the differently colored (or shaded) pieces to each other as well as to the whole. Figure 8.9 shows a basic pie chart comparing major food sources of trans fat for American adults.

Pie charts show proportions among the segments

Organization Charts. An organization chart shows the hierarchy and relationships between different departments and other units in an organization, using a top-down series of boxes connected by arrows, as in Figure 8.10.

Organization charts show relationships between departments or units

Title explains the big picture

Connecting lines show relationships between stages in the process

Individual boxes are of same or similar size and shape

Wording within each cell is simple and clear

Stages in the Textbook Electronic Production Process

Final manuscript including disks to production department

Director of art and design obtains art castoffs and estimates

Manuscript assigned to project editor

Production manager obtains text castoffs and estimates

Director of art and design assigns designers and art studio

Project editor reviews manuscript for design needs and gives sample manuscript pages to designer

Project editor reviews manuscript for editorial needs and gives text and art manuscripts to copyeditor

Production manager assigns compositor and printer

Designer prepares design specifications and template

Author and project editor review copyedited manuscript

Sample design pages received

Front matter released for composition

Text manuscript and disks released to compositor for copyediting updates and page makeup

Art manuscript sent to art studio for rendering

Author and project editor review art proofs

Author and project editor review front matter pages

Author and project editor review page proofs

Final art released for scanning

Author involvement at these stages

Index prepared

Pages released to compositor for correction and final proof stage

Author and project editor review index pages

In-house check of final proof stage

Final files or film released to printer

In-house check of blues

Books printed, bound, and shipped to warehouse

FIGURE 8.8 A flowchart

Source: Adapted from Harper & Row *Author's Guide*. New York: Harper & Row, 1990: 93.

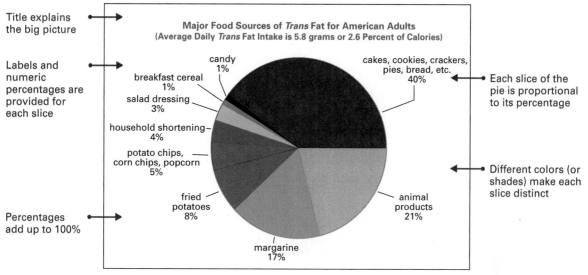

Title explains the big picture

Labels and numeric percentages are provided for each slice

Percentages add up to 100%

Each slice of the pie is proportional to its percentage

Different colors (or shades) make each slice distinct

FIGURE 8.9 A pie chart
Source: U.S. Food and Drug Administration.

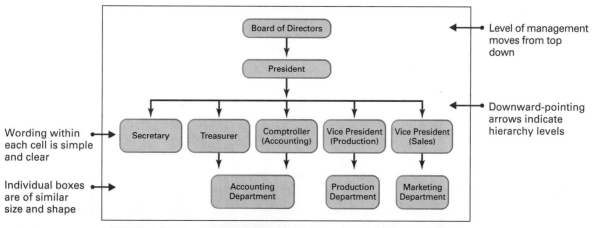

Level of management moves from top down

Downward-pointing arrows indicate hierarchy levels

Wording within each cell is simple and clear

Individual boxes are of similar size and shape

FIGURE 8.10 An organization chart

STRATEGIES for Creating Charts

(For all types of charts, provide a clear title and credit your sources.)

▶ **Flowcharts**

• **Move from top to bottom or left to right.** The process must start at the top (top-to-bottom chart) or left (left-to-right chart).

- **Use connector lines.** Show relationships between parts of the process.
- **Keep boxes uniform and text brief.** See the tips for organization charts below.

▶ **Pie charts**
- **Make sure the parts of the pie add up to 100%.**
- **Differentiate and label each slice clearly.** Use different colors or shades for each slice, and label the category and percentage of each slice.
- **Keep all labels horizontal.** Make the chart easy to read.
- **Combine very small pie slices.** Group categories with very small percentages under "other."

▶ **Organization charts**
- **Move from top to bottom or left to right.** Place the highest level of hierarchy at the top (top-to-bottom chart) or at the left (left-to-right chart).
- **Use downward- or rightward-pointing arrows.** Arrows show the flow of hierarchy from highest to lowest.
- **Keep boxes uniform and text brief.** Shape may vary slightly according to how much text is in each box. Maintain a uniform look. Avoid too much text in any box.

Illustrations and Diagrams

Illustrations and diagrams rely on drawings and sketches rather than data or words, though some words may be needed to point out names, parts, or purposes. In some cases, even if you attempt the most accurate prose description, only an illustration or diagram can show what it is you are trying to explain. Technical illustrations accomplish what text alone cannot.

Illustrations and diagrams are especially valuable when you need to convey spatial relationships or help readers visualize what an item or process actually looks like. For specific advice on creating illustrations and diagrams, see the annotations to Figures 8.11 and 8.12 and the Strategies on page 136.

Illustrations show what something looks like

Illustrations. An illustration shows with accuracy what something looks like. Impressive-looking visuals are easy to create by using electronic drawing programs or by locating clip art and other images on the Internet. However, more complex illustrations or those suited to your exact needs generally require the services of graphic artists or technical illustrators. See, for example, how the illustration in

FIGURE 8.11 An illustration

Source: U.S. Environmental Protection Agency, April 2001. Information available at <www.epa.gov/superfund/sites> or <www.cluin.org>.

Figure 8.11 (taken from the document in Figure 1.3) provides a clear visual picture of the bioremediation process.

If you are unable to locate an illustration that points out just the parts of a product, process, or other item you want to display, you may need a professional illustrator. However, the variety of illustrations available online grows every day.

Diagrams. Unlike illustrations, which simply show what something looks like, diagrams show how parts of an object fit together or how mechanisms operate. For example, the diagram of a safety belt locking mechanism in Figure 8.12 portrays the mechanism in operation by juxtaposing "normal conditions" and "emergency conditions."

Among the many types of diagrams, three of the most common are *exploded diagrams* (which separate parts of an object while showing how the parts fit together), *cutaway diagrams* (which show the interior of an object by "cutting away" the shell, as in Figure 8.2), and *maps*.

Diagrams show how parts fit or operate

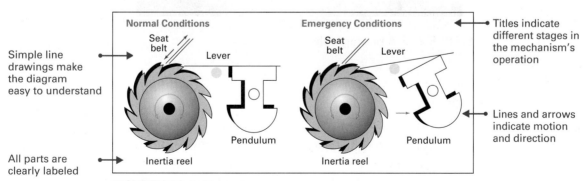

FIGURE 8.12 A diagram

Source: U.S. Department of Transportation.

Photographs

Photographs show
an ultra-realistic view

Although photographs are obviously more realistic than illustrations and diagrams (which often highlight certain parts of an object), photographs can provide *too much* detail or fail to emphasize the parts you want viewers to focus on.

Many people take their own digital photographs and then use software to crop the image for proper emphasis. For basic documents circulated to a small group inside a department or organization, this can be fine. But for important documents circulated to high-level audiences inside or outside an organization, use professionally taken photographs.

If you locate photographs on the Internet, be sure to credit your sources. You also need to request permission if your document will be printed and circulated. For more advice on taking and altering photographs, see the annotations to Figure 8.13 and the Strategies on page 136.

Photograph shows
both the object and
the person using it,
for a sense of scale

Photo is taken from
an angle that
simulates the
operator's angle of
vision

Photo has likely
been cropped to
remove needless
detail

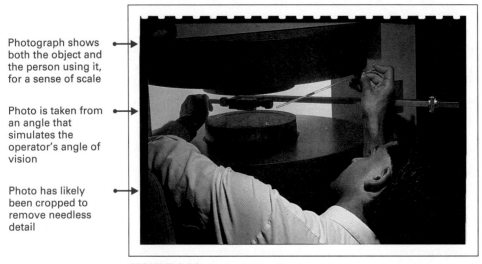

FIGURE 8.13 A photograph
Source: SuperStock.

Videos

Videos show a
full-motion view

Until recently, workplace videos were typically used for training and safety purposes only and were filmed by outside professionals. Today, with the advent of YouTube and similar sites, as well as the ease of filming by using a small video camera or even a cell phone, organizations are using videos to supplement traditional documents

FIGURE 8.14 A video frame

Source: From "Dust-Aid: DSLR Camera Sensor Cleaning Video" by Ross Wordhouse from www.youtube.com. Reproduced by permission.

such as user manuals. For instance, the video frame captured in Figure 8.14 is from a set of video instructions for a product called Dust-Aid (used to clean dust from the camera sensor of a digital SLR camera). The principles for using videos are similar to those for photographs, except that videos are altered via editing rather than cropping. For more advice, see the annotations to Figure 8.14, the Strategies on page 136, and Chapter 21.

Icons and Symbols

Icons and symbols use simple illustrations that reduce a concept or item to its most basic, understandable level. The words *icon* and *symbol* are often used interchangeably. But icons resemble the items they represent (for instance, an icon of a file folder on your computer that looks like a real file folder), whereas symbols get the meaning across without resembling the items they represent (for example, a skull-and-crossbones warning symbol that looks like "death" but gets the "do not ingest/poison" message across, or a cross that symbolizes not "cross" but "medical help"). Because these types of illustrations generally do not rely on text, they are more easily understood by international audiences, children, and people who have difficulty reading. For specific advice on using icons and symbols, see the annotations to Figure 8.15 and the Strategies on page 136.

Icons are simple concrete illustrations; symbols are simple abstract illustrations

Simplicity of the drawings reduces any chance for confusion

The first three images are icons (representative); the last two are symbols (abstract)

FIGURE 8.15 **Internationally recognized icons and symbols**

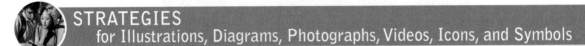

STRATEGIES
for Illustrations, Diagrams, Photographs, Videos, Icons, and Symbols

(For all such visuals, always credit the source if not self-created, and seek permission if reproduced and circulated.)

▶ **Illustrations**

- **Use illustrations that are easy to interpret.** Avoid illustrations that distort an object's actual appearances.
- **Show only those parts that your viewers need to see.**
- **Label each important part.**

▶ **Diagrams**

- **Provide clear explanations.** Explain how diagram parts fit together or operate.
- **Use lines and arrows to indicate direction and motion.** For diagrams that show action, directional markers help viewers understand the action.
- **Keep diagram illustrations simple.** Merely show viewers what they need to see.
- **Label each important part.**

▶ **Photographs**

- **Provide a sense of scale.** Try to show the object and a person using it, a ruler, or a hand.
- **Simulate the viewer's angle of vision.** Consider how your readers would need to view the item.
- **Crop out needless details.**
- **Label key parts.** A simple photograph may not need labels, but a more complicated photograph should have essential parts labeled.

▶ **Videos**

- **Provide a sense of scale.** Try to show the object and a person using it (or a ruler or a hand).

➡

- **Show only what the viewer needs to see.** For example, in a video of a long procedure, focus on just the part of the procedure that's most relevant.
- **Edit out needless detail.** If you have editing software, shorten the video to include only the essentials.
- **Avoid excess outside or office noise when recording sound.**
- ▶ **Icons and Symbols**
- **Use icons and symbols sparingly.** Use them only when directly appropriate, say, to supplement textual warnings or instructions.
- **Use internationally recognized icons and symbols.** Some icons and symbols may not convey your intended meaning in other cultures.

SPECIAL CONSIDERATIONS WHEN USING VISUALS

Once you are aware of the variety of visuals at your disposal, select those most appropriate for your audience and purpose, and consider how to integrate them within your document.

✴ **Explore** the **Concept** with the Activity on Analyzing Newsletter Visuals at **mytechcommlab**

Selecting Appropriate Visuals

When selecting visuals for any document, first ask yourself this question: Who is my audience and what do they need to know?

Generally speaking, expert audiences tend to prefer numerical tables, complex graphs and charts, and diagrams that they can interpret for themselves. Nonexpert audiences tend to prefer basic tables, graphs, and charts, uncomplicated illustrations and diagrams, and other visuals that direct their focus and interpret key points for them. If your audience is a combination of experts and nonexperts, you should err on the side of the nonexperts.

Special audience considerations

✴ **Explore** the **Concept** with the Activity on Global Visuals at **mytechcommlab**

Also be aware that your audience may include international readers or North American readers from different cultural backgrounds. When choosing icons or symbols, use those that are internationally recognized (when in doubt, check the International Organization for Standardization's Web site at <www.iso.org>). Also keep your visuals (including text within visuals) simple and basic and avoid images and colors that might unintentionally offend people from other cultures. If you are knowingly writing to members of a particular culture or nationality, search the Internet for more background on that audience.

Consider how each visual advances your purpose. For example, don't decide to use a bar chart just because you like its professional appearance; make sure the information or data you want to present is best served via a bar chart. Following are additional suggestions for fitting a visual to its purpose:

Consider
the purpose
of each visual

- To simplify complex numerical data or textual information, use a table.
- To get your audience to draw conclusions from facts and figures, use a graph or a chart that shows comparisons.
- To show how parts make up the whole, use a pie chart.
- To show hierarchy and relationships in an organization, use an organization chart.
- To show steps in a process from beginning to end, use a flowchart.
- To show what something looks like, use an illustration or photograph.
- To show how parts fit together or operate, use a diagram or a photograph depicting a process.

Placing, Cross-Referencing, and Presenting Visuals

Place visuals close to
their related topic in
the text

Place your visuals where they best serve the needs of your readers: as close as possible to the related discussion if they are central to that discussion or in an appendix if they are peripheral to your discussion. Introduce your visuals within the text by referring to them by number (Figure 1, Table 4, etc.), and explaining what they mean (e.g., "As Figure 3.4 shows . . ."), making sure that the Figure and Table numbers match the cross-references in the text. Make your visuals user-friendly in their presentation by framing them with plenty of white space, eliminating visual "noise" (excessive lines, bars, numbers, and inessential information), and sizing each visual for the right proportion and emphasis on the page.

Using Color in Visuals

Color helps focus
your reader's
attention

Color focuses reader attention and helps readers identify various elements of a visual. Most of the software you will use to create visuals (e.g., Excel, PowerPoint) automatically adds color to charts and graphs. In an illustration or diagram you can highlight particular areas by using color against a more subdued background. When color is not available, try using grayscale shades. In some visuals, however, grayscale may not be effective: for example in a pie chart with numerous "slices" (see Figure 8.9), using slight gradations of gray may cause the slices to blend too closely. Likewise, in a multiple bar chart or multiple line chart (see Figures 8.5 and 8.7) you will want to sharply differentiate bars and lines. For more information on using color, see Chapter 9.

Using Visuals Ethically

Although you are perfectly justified in presenting data in its best light, you are responsible for avoiding misrepresentation. The golden rule of using visuals ethically is to always present the real and complete picture.

Following are some of the ways in which visuals can be distorted: using inaccurately sized slices in a pie chart misrepresents the true percentages; leaving out essential information from a table, chart, or graph doesn't give readers the true picture of what's happening; inflating or reducing the size of illustrations or photographs can make items appear more or less important than they actually are. When creating visuals, take care to convey and explain information accurately.

Always present the real and complete picture

Some ways in which visuals can be distorted

Explore the Concept with the Case Study on Ethical Visuals at mytechcommlab

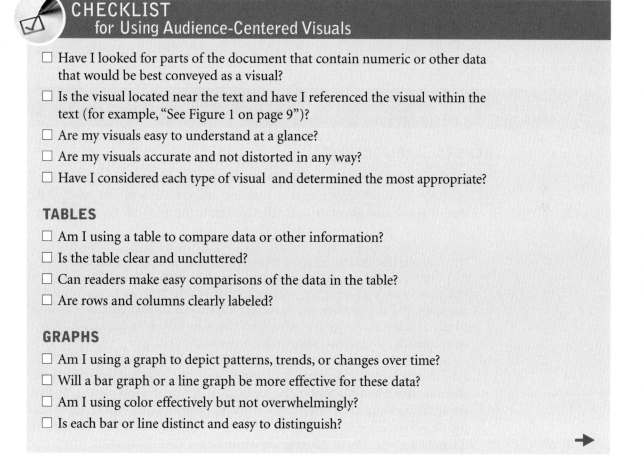

CHECKLIST
for Using Audience-Centered Visuals

☐ Have I looked for parts of the document that contain numeric or other data that would be best conveyed as a visual?

☐ Is the visual located near the text and have I referenced the visual within the text (for example, "See Figure 1 on page 9")?

☐ Are my visuals easy to understand at a glance?

☐ Are my visuals accurate and not distorted in any way?

☐ Have I considered each type of visual and determined the most appropriate?

TABLES

☐ Am I using a table to compare data or other information?

☐ Is the table clear and uncluttered?

☐ Can readers make easy comparisons of the data in the table?

☐ Are rows and columns clearly labeled?

GRAPHS

☐ Am I using a graph to depict patterns, trends, or changes over time?

☐ Will a bar graph or a line graph be more effective for these data?

☐ Am I using color effectively but not overwhelmingly?

☐ Is each bar or line distinct and easy to distinguish?

CHARTS

☐ Am I using a chart to illustrate relationships of parts to a larger whole?

☐ In a flowchart is the flow easy to follow and are all boxes connected?

☐ In an organization chart are the titles/names clear and easy to read?

☐ In a pie chart do the slices of the pie add up to 100%?

ILLUSTRATIONS, DIAGRAMS, AND PHOTOGRAPHS

☐ Are the illustrations sufficiently clear without being too detailed?

☐ Do all illustrations and diagrams have a title or explanation?

☐ Is the quality of my photographs sufficient for viewers to see what I am trying to illustrate?

☐ Am I using any symbols or icons sparingly?

APPLICATIONS

GENERAL APPLICATIONS

1. Display the following information in the visual format most appropriate for a particular audience. Describe that audience and explain why you selected the type of visual as most effective for that audience. Include with the visual a caption that interprets and explains the data.

   Data: Assume that the Department of Energy breaks down energy consumption in the United States (by source) into these percentages: In 1970, coal, 18.5; natural gas, 32.8; hydro and geothermal, 3.1; nuclear, 1.2; oil, 44.4. In 1980, coal, 20.3; natural gas, 26.9; hydro and geothermal, 3.8; nuclear, 4.0; oil, 45.0. In 1990, coal, 23.5; natural gas, 23.8; hydro and geothermal, 7.3; nuclear, 4.1; oil, 41.3. In 2000, coal, 20.3; natural gas, 25.2; hydro and geothermal, 9.6; nuclear, 6.3; oil, 38.6.

2. Find an article in a newspaper, in a journal, or on the Web that lacks the visuals necessary to support the purpose of the article or the needs of its readers. Analyze the article and identify where visuals would be helpful. Make a list of the visuals you would recommend. Pick one visual from your list and create it. Does the article contain all the data or information you need to create the visual?

3. Devise a pie chart to depict your yearly expenses. Title the chart and be prepared to discuss it in class.

TEAM APPLICATIONS

1. As a team, obtain enrollment figures at your college for the past five years by gender, age, race, or any other pertinent category. Construct a bar graph to illustrate one of these relationships over the five years.

2. As a team, decide what would be the most appropriate visual for illustrating this relationship: a comparison of three top brands of skis, according to cost, weight, durability, and edge control. In groups of two, create this visual, then compare approaches. Why did one group choose one type of visual over another?

GLOBAL APPLICATION

The International Organization for Standardization (ISO) is a group devoted to standardizing a range of material, including technical specifications and visual information. If you've ever been in an airport and seen the many international signs directing travelers to the restroom or informing them not to smoke, you have seen ISO signs. Go to the ISO Web site at <www.iso.org> to learn about ISO icons and symbols. Show some of the icons and symbols, and explain why these work for international audiences.

COMPUTER/WEB-BASED APPLICATION

Compile a list of six Web sites that offer graphics support by way of advice, image banks, design ideas, artwork catalogs, and the like. Provide the address for each site, along with a description of the resources offered and their approximate cost. Report your findings in the format stipulated by your instructor.

For additional technical writing resources that will help you master the chapter objectives, go to **www.mytechcommlab.com**.

9 Designing User-Friendly Documents

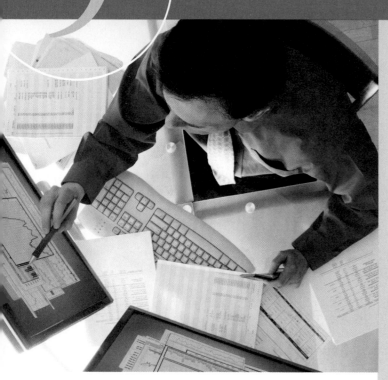

LEARNING OBJECTIVES FOR THIS CHAPTER

▸ Understand the importance of document design

▸ Identify and create well-designed documents

▸ Use design elements for consistency and coherence

▸ Use design elements for navigation and emphasis

Design, the layout of words and graphics, determines the look of a document. Well-designed pages invite readers in, guide them through the material, and help them understand and remember the information.

Explore the Tutorial on Document Design at mytechcommlab

THE IMPORTANCE OF USER-FRIENDLY DOCUMENT DESIGN

Like all decisions about technical communication, document design consists of a series of informed choices. You need to decide about fonts, typography, white space, and other visual elements, based on the document's audience and purpose. These decisions affect the usability of the document.

Design affects a document's usability

Explore the Concept with the Activity on Textbook Design at mytechcommlab

Imagine that you are asked to produce a heart surgery brochure for a hospital. The brochure's intended audience consists of patients who have a particular heart condition and may need to undergo a specific type of heart surgery. The brochure's purpose is to explain the procedure, answer frequently asked questions, and review the risks—while reassuring patients.

Before you would even begin to think about what to write or how to design the document, you would need to do an audience and purpose analysis (see Chapter 4). If the brochure also needed to include a list of tasks, such as a checklist of actions patients must take, you might also conduct a task analysis (explained in Chapter 4). Your analysis would yield much important information. For example, you are likely to determine the following as the most important outcomes for the document:

Begin by analyzing your audience and purpose

Determine your document's usability requirements by doing a task analysis

1. To reassure fearful patients that the surgery is safe and that the recovery rate is quicker than that of many other types of heart surgery.

2. To ensure that readers are able to understand what they need to do before, during, and after the surgery.

3. To make certain that older patients—who make up the largest population of candidates for this surgery, and who sometimes have poor eyesight—are able to read the document.

To reassure fearful patients, you could choose a comforting typeface, a warm color scheme, and plenty of white space to give the brochure an unimposing look. To ensure that patients understand the steps involved you could use numbered and bulleted lists to break up and simplify the various procedures. To make the document more readable for older patients, you could use a large font size.

Design the document to meet reader needs

Document design, like all aspects of technical communication, puts audience and purpose first.

CHARACTERISTICS OF WELL-DESIGNED DOCUMENTS

Readers appreciate documents that are well designed because such documents make it easy and pleasant for people to access and use the information they need. Well-designed documents typically have four characteristics: they are inviting and accessible; they flow well as a single, cohesive unit; they provide a visual hierarchy, displaying information in the right order; they address a diversity of readers. Figure 9.1 does not meet those requirements, while Figure 9.2 (a revision of the same document) does.

People generally read technical documents only because they have to. They may pick up a document because they need information, as in the heart surgery brochure described above, or they may be presented with a document they are

Four audience expectations of a document's design

Readers expect an inviting and accessible design

Document is untitled and provides no visual hierarchy: everything looks equal

Small margins make the document look crowded

Unbroken paragraph looks dense and intimidating

Inadequate white space makes this version hard on the eye

Mold is a public health problem. Molds are simple organisms that are found virtually everywhere, indoors and outdoors. The potential health effects of indoor mold are a growing concern. Mold can cause or worsen certain illnesses (e.g., some allergic and occupation-related diseases and infections in health care settings). There is not conclusive evidence, however, about whether indoor mold is associated with a multitude of other health problems, such as pulmonary hemorrhage, memory loss, and lack of energy.

The Centers for Disease Control has accomplished much on the problem. The CDC has a mold Web site (http://www.cdc.gov/nceh/airpollution/mold) that provides information on molds and health and links to resources. In conjunction with the Council of State and Territorial Epidemiologists, the CDC has created an inventory of state indoor air quality programs which is available at http://www.cdc.gov/nceh.airpollution/indoor_air.htm. The CDC assists states in responding to mold-related issues, including offering technical assistance with assessment, cleanup efforts, and prevention of further mold growth and unnecessary exposure. The CDC is strengthening state, local and tribal capacity to respond to mold-related issues, including: determining the extent to which state programs establish coordinated responses to indoor mold exposures, working with federal and other organizations to coordinate plans related to indoor air and mold, developing a coordinated public response strategy, and identifying resources for developing and implementing responses. The CDC is also developing an agenda for research, service, and education related to mold. As a first step, the CDC contracted with the Institute of Medicine (IOM) to conduct a study on the relationship between damp or moldy indoor environments and the manifestation of adverse health effects and to provide recommendations for future research. The CDC's mold-related agenda is expected to address subjects such as the following: characterizing environmental conditions that allow mold growth indoors and the association between indoor mold and disease or illness; improving the capacity of state, local, and tribal health departments to prevent, investigate, and control mold exposures; and conducting and supporting research to define the association between damp or moldy indoor environments and harmful health effects.

The next steps the CDC will take include assisting states and others in responding to mold issues and developing an agenda for research, service, and education related to mold as described above. For more information, visit http://www.cdc.gov/nceh/airpollution/mold.

May 2004

FIGURE 9.1 Ineffective page design

PROGRAM IN BRIEF

Mold

WHAT IS THE PUBLIC HEALTH PROBLEM?

Molds are simple organisms that are found virtually everywhere, indoors and outdoors. The potential health effects of indoor mold are a growing concern. Mold can cause or worsen certain illnesses (e.g., some allergic and occupation-related diseases and infections in health care settings). There is not conclusive evidence, however, about whether indoor mold is associated with a multitude of other health problems, such as pulmonary hemorrhage, memory loss, and lack of energy.

WHAT HAS CDC ACCOMPLISHED?

- CDC's Mold Web site (http://www.cdc.gov/mold) provides information on molds and health and links to resources. In conjunction with the Council of State and Territorial Epidemiologists, CDC has created an inventory of state indoor air quality programs, which is available at http://www.cdc.gov/nceh/airpollution/indoor_air.htm.
- CDC assists states in responding to mold-related issues, including offering technical assistance with assessment, cleanup efforts, and prevention of further mold growth and unnecessary exposure.
- CDC is strengthening state, local, and tribal capacity to respond to mold-related issues, including (1) determining the extent to which state programs establish coordinated responses to indoor mold exposures; (2) working with federal and other organizations to coordinate plans related to indoor air and mold; (3) developing a coordinated public response strategy; and (4) identifying resources for developing and implementing responses.
- CDC is developing an agenda for research, service, and education related to mold. As a first step, CDC contracted with the Institute of Medicine (IOM) to conduct a study on the relationship between damp or moldy indoor environments and the manifestation of adverse health effects and to provide recommendations for future research. CDC's mold-related agenda is expected to address subjects such as the following:
    - o Characterizing environmental conditions that allow mold growth indoors and the association between indoor mold and disease or illness;
    - o Improving the capacity of state, local, and tribal health departments to prevent, investigate, and control mold exposures;
    - o Conducting and supporting research to define the association between damp or moldy indoor environments and harmful health effects.

WHAT ARE THE NEXT STEPS?

CDC will continue to assist states and others in responding to mold issues and develop an agenda for research, service, and education related to *mold* as described above.

For more information, visit http://www.cdc.gov/mold.   *May 2004*

DEPARTMENT OF HEALTH AND HUMAN SERVICES
CENTERS FOR DISEASE CONTROL AND PREVENTION
SAFER · HEALTHIER · PEOPLE

Annotations (right margin):

- Even from a distance, readers can see the document as a cohesive, single unit
- Title, headings, and bullets provide a visual hierarchy
- Ample margins and white space give the document an open, accessible look
- Bulleted list breaks up dense paragraph
- Simple use of two colors for (Web address and headings) helps readers focus on essential information

---

FIGURE 9.2 Effective redesign of Figure 9.1

Source: Centers for Disease Control and Prevention, May 2004.

required to read for work. Either way, readers will resist a document that is intimidating or hard to read and will try to get the information in some other way (e.g., going to the Internet to find a more straightforward presentation or asking a colleague or the writer for clarification).

Various types of software can help with document design, but all the software in the world won't help unless writers understand basic principles of visual appeal and accessibility.

Notice how Figure 9.1 presents a barrage of information with absolutely no design elements, making the information needlessly intimidating, unappealing, and hard to grasp. In contrast, Figure 9.2 uses a clear title, margins, white space, bullets, headings, and color to present the same information in a much more open, inviting, and accessible manner.

Readers appreciate a design that works as a single, cohesive unit

Generally, readers view a document first as a whole unit, scanning the page quickly to get a sense of the overall layout. Even from a distance, without being able to read the text, readers should be able to answer the question "How is this document structured?" Design elements help readers answer that question.

Consider how Figure 9.1 tells readers nothing about how the document works as a unit—it is simply a page full of text. Figure 9.2, on the other hand, has a purpose (as indicated by a title), moves from point A to point B (as indicated by the headings), and presents a list of specific facts (as indicated by the bullets).

Readers appreciate a design that forms a visual hierarchy

Readers also expect the document to highlight the most important information. In other words, they expect the document's design to help them determine the *visual hierarchy* of the information, displayed primarily through the level and design of the headings, and the inclusion of numbered or bulleted lists.

Notice how Figure 9.1 provides no visual hierarchy. It simply offers a series of paragraphs, each seemingly offering information of equal importance. In contrast, Figure 9.2 offers a clear hierarchy of information. All three headed sections are of equal importance, and so the headers are designed identically (same font, font size, and color). The bulleted items fall into two levels of detail: general and specific (the more specific bulleted items are indented further in a different style of bullet).

Readers appreciate a design that takes a wide range of people into account

A document's design can also affect its multicultural appeal. For instance, a certain color might be interpreted differently by different readers. As a rule, use subtle and varied colors, standard fonts and font sizes, and appropriate white space.

SPECIFIC DESIGN ELEMENTS

✳ **Explore the Concept** with the Case Study on Document Design at **mytechcommlab**

The elements of document design comprise two categories: those that give a document a consistent and cohesive look and those that aid navigation and add emphasis. No design elements should be merely decorative; all should enhance the reader's orientation and understanding.

Designing for Consistency and Cohesiveness

Elements that provide consistency and cohesiveness include grid patterns, margins, paragraphs, justification, white space, line spacing and indentation, font style, and font size. Each element is described below and summarized in the Strategies on page 150.

Grid Patterns. Grid patterns help readers make sense of a document as a single unit because they create an underlying structure throughout the document. Figure 9.3 shows a sampling of grid patterns. Most documents follow a standard horizontal grid pattern, as, for example, a memo or letter. A vertical grid is commonly used in manuals, brochures, or newsletters. In rare cases, you may want to use a combined grid pattern.

Vertical Grid
(2 columns)   Horizontal Grid   Combined Grid

FIGURE 9.3 Grid patterns

Margins. Consistent margins give the document a unified appearance. Margins must not only be the same width throughout a document but also wide enough. Narrow margins crowd the page and make the material look harder than it probably is. On your 8½-by-11-inch page, provide margins of at least 1 or 1½ inches on each side, as well as at the top and bottom, of every page. If the manuscript is to be bound in a cover, increase the left (inside) margin to 2 inches.

Paragraphs. Whereas ordering information within paragraphs (as discussed in Chapter 6) affects a document's overall structure, the shape of each paragraph serves a design function. Use a long paragraph (but try to keep it to 15 lines or less) for clustering material that is closely related or best understood in one block; use short paragraphs for making complex material more digestible (as in step-by-step instructions or for emphasizing vital information). At the same time, try to vary the lengths of your paragraphs. Readers are likely to resist a document that consists primarily of long or short paragraphs only. Also, avoid "orphans" (one line of a paragraph at the bottom of a page) and "widows" (one line of a paragraph at the top of a page).

Justification. Text is always automatically flush left (lined up evenly along the left margin). However, along the right margin, you have a choice between *justified* text (even right margins) or *unjustified* text (uneven or "ragged" right margins). Each arrangement creates its own feel.

In justified text, blocks of text look clean and even on either side, but spacing varies between words and letters on a line, and you may need to frequently hyphenate words. Justified text is generally used in books, annual reports, and other formal materials. In unjustified text, text is ragged on the right side of text blocks, but spacing between words and letters on a line is even, and you can avoid overuse of hyphenation. Unjustified text is appropriate for more personal forms of communication, such as letters, memos, and in-house reports. Whichever justification you choose be consistent throughout the document. Figure 9.4 illustrates justified and unjustified text.

Right and left justified text (from a formal report)

> According to the chart in Figure 3, the population of Queens County, New York, remains the most diverse in the United States. Historically, particular populations have been concentrated in particular areas. For example, Long Island has long been known as a largely Latino area, Woodside as mostly Asian and Middle eastern, and Jamaica as primarily African and Caribbean. However, over the last 15 years, these concentrations have become less cogent.

Left-only justified text (from a memo)

> In order for this new initiative to be a success, we ask for the support and participation of every employee of the company. Please take a moment to review the enclosed list of training sessions, which will begin on August 24th. We strongly suggest that you sign up for at least one session during the first month to get an overview of the initiative, then take intermediate and advanced sessions in the upcoming months.

FIGURE 9.4 Justified and unjustified text

White Space. Sometimes, it's what's *not* on the page that makes a difference. Whereas margins are the empty spaces along the left, right, top, and bottom of a document, white space is any empty space surrounding figures and tables, between columns, and between paragraphs. Areas of text or visuals surrounded by appropriate white space draw the reader's eye to those areas. Well-designed white space is used evenly throughout an entire document, orienting users by keeping related elements together, isolating and emphasizing important elements, and providing breathing room between blocks of information, as in Figure 9.5.

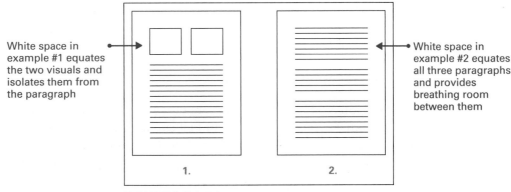

FIGURE 9.5 White space

White space in example #1 equates the two visuals and isolates them from the paragraph

White space in example #2 equates all three paragraphs and provides breathing room between them

1.

2.

Line Spacing and Indentation. Always be consistent about line spacing. In most technical documents, use double spacing for ease of reading. When inserting a long quotation, indent the quotation, use single spacing within the quotation only, then return to double spacing for regular text. Also be consistent about indentation. As a general rule, indent each paragraph unless you insert an extra line space between paragraphs.

Font Style. Font style refers to the typeface used and the personality that each typeface conveys. Fonts fall into several categories: *Serif* fonts (such as Times New Roman and Palatino) include serifs, or fine lines that extend horizontally from the main strokes of a letter. Serif fonts are generally considered more formal. *Sans-serif* fonts (such as Helvetica and Arial) do not include these fine lines ("sans" is French for "without"). They tend to look professional without being quite as formal as serif fonts and are appropriate for most other types of technical documents. Decorative fonts are often used in advertising and marketing but should be avoided in technical documents. Figure 8.6 shows the differences between these font styles. Pick an appropriate font and stick with it throughout a document. For headings, you might select a different font (and a larger size), but use those heading fonts consistently as well.

Times New Roman is a serif font.

Arial is a sans-serif font.

𝕺𝖑𝖉 𝕰𝖓𝖌𝖑𝖎𝖘𝖍 𝖎𝖘 𝖆 𝖉𝖊𝖈𝖔𝖗𝖆𝖙𝖎𝖛𝖊 𝖋𝖔𝖓𝖙.

Use serif and sans-serif fonts

Avoid decorative fonts

FIGURE 9.6 Sample font styles

Italics, **boldface**, and ALL CAPS are another element of font style you need to consider. Sometimes people use italics much as they would use a highlighter or marker, to set words apart and draw attention to these words. But excessive use of italics can make it hard for your audience to decide which information is truly important. The same is true for boldface: too much bold will lose its appeal. Bold is good for headings, subheadings, or terms or concepts in a sentence that you want to emphasize. Within text, use bold selectively. Use all-capital letters for a few words only or when creating short headings. Long strings of capital (uppercase) letters and words are hard to read.

Font Size.   Use font sizes that are easy to read. Standard guidelines suggest using between a 10-point and 12-point font size for the text of most documents (usually erring to the side of 12-point). Use a 2-point larger font for each level of headings (see page 151). Most important, be consistent throughout the document.

STRATEGIES
for Designing: Consistency and Cohesiveness

GRID PATTERNS

▸ **Select an appropriate grid pattern.** Use a horizontal grid pattern for most basic documents (memos, letters, reports). Use a vertical grid pattern for specialized documents (manuals, brochures, and newsletters). Use a combined pattern rarely.

▸ **Use the same grid pattern throughout the document.**

MARGINS

▸ **Use adequate margins.** Use a 1-inch to 1½-inch margin along the top, bottom, left, and right of the page. For bound documents, use a 2-inch inside margin.

▸ **Use the same margins throughout the document.**

PARAGRAPHS

▸ **Vary the length of paragraphs.** Use long and short paragraphs as appropriate to keep blocks of related text together.

▸ **Avoid orphans and widows.** Add extra space to bump orphans to the next page, and reduce space (or shorten paragraph content) to pull widows to the previous page.

JUSTIFICATION

▸ **Determine if your text will be justified on one or both margins.** Use justified left and right for formal documents, and use left-only justified (ragged right margin) for less formal documents (memos, letters, in-house reports, and so on).

▸ **Use the same justification throughout the document.**

WHITE SPACE

▸ **Use plenty of white space.** Use white space between paragraphs and/or columns, and around visuals, when appropriate.

➡

▸ **Use white space consistently.** If you include white space between paragraphs or columns, use the same amount throughout the document. Include the same amount of white space around each visual in the document.

LINE SPACING AND INDENTATION

▸ **Decide how you want to use line spacing and indentation.** Use single, double, or other (for instance, 1½) line spacing. Indent all paragraphs or none.

▸ **Stick with your original plan.** Don't vary the line spacing or paragraph indentation. Be consistent.

FONT STYLE

▸ **Use either a serif or sans-serif font.** Prefer a serif font for formal reports, and a sans-serif font for most other documents.

▸ **Decide which serif or sans-serif font to use.** Some of the most popular serif fonts are Times New Roman and Times. The most popular sans-serif font is Helvetica.

▸ **Stay with the same font throughout.** You might choose a different font for any headings in your document.

▸ **Use italics, boldface, and ALL CAPS selectively and sparingly.**

FONT SIZE

▸ **Use a standard font size.** Generally, a 10-point to 12-point size (depending on the font style) should be used for text, and a slightly larger size for each level of heading.

▸ **Use a consistent font size.** Stay with the font size you've chosen for each element (text, headings, notes) throughout the document.

Designing for Navigation and Emphasis

Elements that aid navigation and add emphasis include headings; color, shading, boldface, italic, and underlining; bulleted and numbered lists; running heads and feet; and tables of contents and indexes.

Headings. Headings not only help chunk information into easily digestible parts (structure, see Chapter 6) but also guide readers through a page and signal the relative importance of topics. Readers often will move back and forth in a document, searching for the sections that seem most relevant, or they will scan only the main headings, skipping the lower-level headings. To help readers navigate, design your headings consistently.

Levels and design
of headings

Headings generally break down into A-level (major headings), B-level (secondary headings, which always fall beneath A-level headings), and C-level (minor headings, which always fall beneath B-level headings). Each higher level of heading should encompass at least two heads at the next lower level, as in Figure 9.7. Lower levels of headings (D-level, etc.) make a document appear hard to navigate. Use bulleted or numbered lists instead.

Always use the same font style, size, and color at each level. Avoid orphans (headings that stand alone at the bottom of a page without any text beneath them). Figure 9.7 illustrates three levels of headings.

A-level heading
uses all caps,
boldface, and rests
above the
paragraph

B-level heading
uses initial caps,
boldface, and rests
above the
paragraph

C-level heading
uses initial caps,
boldface, and runs
into the paragraph

CURRENT MEDICATIONS AND THEIR HISTORY

Currently, several medications are popular xxxxxxxxxxxxxxxxxxxxxxxxxxxxxxxxxxxxxxxx xxxxxxxxxxxxxxxxxxxxxxxxxxxxxxxxxxxxxxxxxxxxxxx.

Medications Before the 1980s

Several medications were used prior to the 1980s when xxxxxxxxxxxxxxxxxxxxxxxxxxxxx xxxxxxxxxxxxxxxxxxxxxxxxxxxxxxxxxxxxxxxxxxxxxxxxxxxxxxxxxxxxxxxxxxxxxxxxxxxxxxxxxx.

Selective Serotonin Reuptake Inhibitors (SSRIs)

The increased research around the importance of serotonin xxxxxxxxxxxxxxxxxxxxxxxxxx xxxxxxxxxxxxxxxxxxxxxxxxxxxxxxxxxxxxxxxxxxxxxxxxxxxxxxxxxxxxxxxxxxxxxxxxxxx

    Prozac—The increased research around the importance of serotonin xxxxxxxxxxxxxxxxxxxxxxxxxxxxxxxxxxxxxxxxxxxxxxxxxxxxxxxxxxxxxxxxxxxxxxxxxxxx xxxxxxxxxxxxxxxxxxxxxxxxxxxxxxxxxx

    Effexor—The increased research around the importance of serotonin xxxxxxxxxxxxx xxxxxxxxxxxxxxxxxxxxxxxxxxxxxxxx

RECENT RESEARCH INTO NEW MEDICATIONS

New research indicates that xxxxxxxxxxxxxxxxxxxxxxxxxxxxxxxxxxxxxxxxxxxxxxxxxxxxxx xxxxxxxxxxxxxxxxxxxxxxxxxxxxxxxxxxxxxxxxxxxxxxxxx

Refining the SSRI Approach

The increased research around the importance of serotonin xxxxxxxxxxxxxxxxxxxxxxxxx

FIGURE 9.7 Headings

Explore the
Concept with the
Activity on Document
Design and Color at
mytechcommlab

Color, Shading, Boldface, Italic, and Underlining. Color can help readers move through the text and can draw attention to particular areas. For example, you can use color for headings, tabs, sidebars, callouts (labels that identify parts of a figure), and leader lines (dotted, dashed, or solid lines that connect labels with their objects), as in Figure 9.8. To highlight important information, you can use color for screens, horizontal and vertical rules, type, cross-references, and ruled boxes, as in Figure 9.9.

FIGURE 9.8 **Using color for navigation**

FIGURE 9.9 **Using color for emphasis**

Use color sparingly and use colors that aren't overly bright, that don't obscure the text they cover, and that contrast well with black print. You may also use shading, bold, italic, or underlining.

Bulleted and Numbered Lists. Whenever you include a series of similar or step-by-step items within a sentence or paragraph, consider using a bulleted or numbered list. Bulleted and numbered lists help readers navigate through dense information and emphasize the information by separating it from the text. However, don't overuse; don't use fancy icons when a plain round dot will do; and don't confuse the functions of bulleted and numbered lists. Bullets separate and highlight equally weighted items. Numbers enumerate the fixed sequence of steps in a process. Figure 9.10 compares in-text lists to bulleted and numbered lists. (For more on using lists see Appendix B.)

To organize and highlight similar items, use a bulleted list

To enumerate a fixed sequence of steps, use a numbered list

Text	Bulleted list
The fire ant has now spread to three regions: the Galapagos Islands, the South Pacific, and Africa.	The fire ant has now spread to three regions: • The Galapagos Islands • The South Pacific • Africa

Text	Numbered list
There are three steps to installing your graphics card: Open the computer case, insert the graphics card in the slot, and close the case.	Installing your graphics card: 1. Open the computer case. 2. Insert the graphics card in the slot. 3. Close the case.

FIGURE 9.10 Bulleted versus numbered lists

Running Headers and Footers. Running heads and feet in longer printed documents help readers find material. They also help readers stay oriented to their location in the document. Typically a running head includes section- or chapter-specific information (as in this book) and running feet are reserved for book titles. However, page numbers may be included either in a running head or running foot. In a document with single-sided pages, running heads or feet should be placed consistently, typically flush right. In a document with double-sided pages, the running heads or feet should appear flush left on left-hand pages and flush right on right-hand pages, as in Figure 9.11.

Tables of Contents and Indexes. In a longer print document a table of contents and an index help readers find the information they need. In addition, the table of contents signals the relationship between topics and subtopics. Make sure your table of contents matches the heading structure of your document exactly.

For single-sided pages, place running headers and footers flush right

For double-sided pages, place running headers and footers flush left on left-hand pages and flush right on right-hand pages

Running head   Running foot
(Single-sided Pages)

(Two-sided Pages)

FIGURE 9.11 Running heads and feet

Most of us have had the frustrating experience of trying to look something up in an index and discovering that the term we use is not the term the index uses. A successful index depends on knowing what categories, terms, and topics your readers are likely to look up when searching for what they need. For longer, more complex documents, consider hiring a professional indexer.

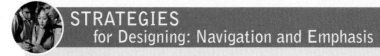

STRATEGIES
for Designing: Navigation and Emphasis

HEADINGS

▶ **Design headings consistently.** Always use the same font style, size, and color for the same level of headings. A-level headings are typically in all caps, boldface, and rest above paragraphs; B-level headings are usually in initial caps, boldface, and rest above paragraphs; and C-level heads are typically in initial caps, boldface, and run into paragraphs (whether or not the paragraphs are indented).

▶ **Divide headings logically.** Make each higher level head yield at least two heads at the next level. B-level headings always fall within A-level headed sections, and C-level headings always fall within B-level headed sections.

▶ **Avoid excessive headings.** Try to avoid D-level headings and never move to a level beyond that.

▶ **Avoid orphans.** If a heading stands alone at the bottom of a page, without at least two lines of text beneath, add more space to bump the heading to the next page.

COLOR, SHADING, BOLDFACE, ITALIC, AND UNDERLINING

▶ **Use color as needed.** Use color headings, tabs, sidebars, callouts, and leader lines (page 152) for navigation. Use color screens, horizontal/vertical rules, type, cross-references, and ruled boxes for emphasis.

▶ **Use color sparingly.** Color should not overpower the document and should complement, not obstruct, the text.

▶ **Use shading, bold, italic, and underlining.** If color is unavailable or you prefer to aid navigation and provide emphasis in other ways, use these design options.

BULLETED AND NUMBERED LISTS

▶ **Use bulleted and numbered lists appropriately.** Bulleted lists show a series of similar items, while numbered lists show a sequence of step-by-step items.

▶ **Don't overuse lists.** Otherwise, your document might look like a shopping list.

RUNNING HEADS AND FEET

▶ **Decide if running feet are necessary.** Usually, running feet are used only for full-length books, though you may use them in documents to place page numbers.

▶ **Always include page numbers.** Whether you put them in running heads or running feet, page numbers are essential. For a long document, count your title page as page i, without numbering it, and number all front matter pages, including the table of contents and abstract, with lowercase roman numerals (ii, iii, iv). Number the first and subsequent text pages with arabic numerals (1, 2, 3).

▶ **Include section- or chapter-specific information in running heads.**

▶ **Format running heads and feet correctly.** See Figure 9.11.

TABLES OF CONTENTS AND INDEXES

▶ **Use tables of contents and indexes for longer documents.**

▶ **Make sure tables of contents match document headers exactly.**

▶ **Use standard index categories and topics.** Try to accurately anticipate which terms readers will look up in searching for what they need.

CHECKLIST
for Document Design

CONSISTENCY AND COHESIVENESS

- ☐ Does my grid structure provide a consistent visual theme?
- ☐ Are margins ample?
- ☐ Is each paragraph tailored to suit its purpose?
- ☐ Is the document's right margin unjustified?
- ☐ Does the white space create areas of emphasis?
- ☐ Is the document's line spacing and indentation effective?
- ☐ Have I chosen readable and appropriate font sizes and styles?
- ☐ In general, have I used versions of a single typeface throughout?
- ☐ If different typefaces *are* used, are they used consistently?
- ☐ Have I used *italics*, **boldface**, and ALL CAPS sparingly?

NAVIGATION AND EMPHASIS

- ☐ Do headings clearly announce the document's large and small segments?
- ☐ Are headings sized to reflect their specific level in the document?
- ☐ Are headings visually consistent and grammatically parallel?
- ☐ Have I formatted a series of parallel items as a list (numbered or bulleted, as appropriate)?
- ☐ Do running headers and footers announce sections of the document?
- ☐ Have I used page numbers appropriately?
- ☐ Are the table of contents and the index complete and easy to navigate?

APPLICATIONS

GENERAL APPLICATION

With a partner, find two printed documents: one that demonstrates good use of design elements and another that demonstrates confusing or inconsistent use. Imagine that you and your partner are a team of technical communication consultants. Write a memo to the manager of the organization that produced the effective document, explaining its positive features. Write a memo to the manager of the organization that produced the confusing document, making suggestions for improvement.

TEAM APPLICATION

Working in teams of three or four people, find a document that is intended to answer a question—a patient brochure about an illness or medical procedure, a reference guide for new students on campus, or a personnel document from your company, for example. Your team's goal is to redesign the document so that it uses an appropriate grid design, makes effective use of white space, and uses formatting, fonts, headings, and other page design elements consistently and clearly.

Appoint one member of your group to serve as editor. The editor is responsible for making sure the design elements are used consistently throughout the redesigned document. Ask each team member to work on one section of the document. Assemble all the redesigned sections, and ask your editor to review the materials. The editor should check your work against the Checklist for Document Design.

GLOBAL APPLICATION

Find a document that presents the same information in several languages (assembly instructions for various products are often written in two or three languages, for example). Evaluate the design decisions made in these documents. For example, are the different languages presented side by side or in different sections? Write a memo to classmates and your instructor evaluating the document and making recommendations for improvement.

COMPUTER/WEB-BASED APPLICATION

Many of today's technical documents are designed so they can be displayed on the computer and also printed and used in hard copy. The format of choice for this approach is to create the document in the Portable Document Format, or PDF. Users then use Adobe Acrobat Reader, Apple Preview, or a Web interface to read the document online. When printed, the document retains the proper formatting. Find a government Web site, such as the Centers for Disease Control <www.cdc.gov> or the Environmental Protection Agency <www.epa.gov> and compare documents that are created as Web pages versus documents that are created as PDFs. Write a short memo to your instructor analyzing each document and explaining why you think the choice was made to use a Web versus a PDF format.

For additional technical writing resources that will help you master the chapter objectives, go to **www.mytechcommlab.com**.

PART 3

Documents

10

Résumés and Other Employment Materials

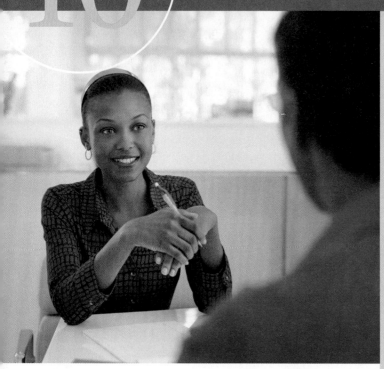

LEARNING OBJECTIVES FOR THIS CHAPTER

▶ Research jobs and narrow your job search

▶ Create hard-copy and electronic résumés

▶ Write a persuasive job application letter

▶ Compile a dossier and a portfolio (or webfolio)

▶ Prepare for job interviews

▶ Write an appropriate thank you letter

▶ Write an appropriate acceptance or refusal letter

LET'S GET STARTED
Résumés and Application Letters

Your friend has told you about a paid internship at a local company, and you would really like to get an interview because you are hoping to get a job related to your college major when you graduate. Also, the location is close to your apartment, so you could walk to and from the internship. Without reading this chapter, create a résumé and write an application letter that is targeted at getting this internship.

Questions to ask about the résumé and application letter you wrote, as you review the material in this chapter:

▸ Did you research the company?

▸ Is your résumé brief and to the point?

▸ Is the material in your résumé described and arranged in the order that makes sense for the company to which you are applying?

▸ Does your application letter contain the three basic paragraphs (introduction, body, conclusion)?

▸ Does your application letter get right to the point?

▸ Does your application letter help highlight specific and relevant items from your résumé?

At the end of this chapter, review your initial Let's Get Started résumé and application with a group of students, and compare what you wrote with what you learned from this chapter. Make a plan to revise or modify your original materials based on what you have learned from the chapter and in class.

This chapter comes first in the documents section of this book for two reasons: to highlight the importance of using the skills you have learned thus far to get hired, and to encourage you to create a portfolio of sample documents as you work through the remainder of the book.

Review the basics
of effective
communication

Enhance your job search by relying on key principles from earlier chapters. For example, research each specific position for which you apply (see Chapter 3). Show that you communicate persuasively, that you present yourself honestly, and that you understand teamwork (see Chapters 2, 4, and 5). Also, prepare all application materials with a clear sense of audience and purpose (see Chapter 4).

In today's job market, many applicants compete for few openings. Whether you are applying for your first professional job or changing careers, you need to market your skills effectively. At each stage of the job search, you must stand out among the competition.

ASSESSING YOUR SKILLS AND APTITUDES

Identify your assets

Begin your job search by assessing those qualities and skills you can offer a potential employer:

- Do I communicate well and am I also a good listener?
- Do I work well in groups and with people from different backgrounds?
- Do I have experience or aptitude for a leadership role?
- Can I solve problems and get things done?
- Can I perform well under pressure?
- Can I work independently, with minimal supervision?
- Do I have any special skills (public speaking, working with people, computer or other technical skills, aptitude with words, analytical skills, second or third languages, artistic/musical talent, mathematical aptitude)?

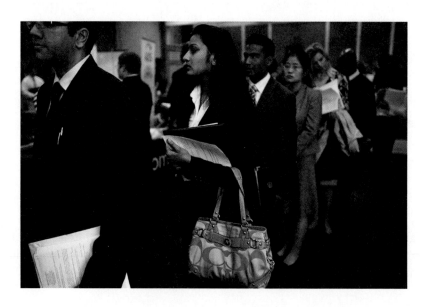

- Do I have any hobbies that could improve my job prospects?
- Would I prefer to work at a large company or a small one, or at a for-profit or a nonprofit organization?
- Do I like to travel, or would I prefer working in a single location?

Besides helping you focus your job search, your answers to these questions will come in handy when you write your résumé and prepare for job interviews.

RESEARCHING THE JOB MARKET

Narrowing your search does not mean limiting yourself to one or two types of job, but instead giving yourself a measure of realistic focus. Try to stick to those fields that interest you most and fit you best.

Begin your research well in advance of the time you need to have a job lined up. If you've never done job research, the question "Where do I start?" can be daunting: "Do I go to a career counselor first?" "Should I talk with friends and family members?" "Do I go straight to the Help Wanted section—in print or online?" "Should I buy a book on how to find a job?" "Which Web sites are the best?" More than ever, seemingly endless sources of information are available to job seekers. Try to proceed in a step-by-step, logical way—rather than going straight to the Internet and trying to navigate random Web sites.

The human connection is always the best way to start looking for a job. Once you've narrowed down your job search, go to your campus job placement office and meet with a career counselor (either at your school or outside), who will know the job search process inside and out. Also, speak with a reference librarian (in person or online), who can point you to the right library resource. Network with acquaintances who may know someone else you can speak with.

Before you apply for specific jobs, learn more about the industry. There are a number of ways to do this: Consult reference materials (books, magazines, professional journals, Web sites) specific to the industry. Join a professional group related to your industry and either attend meetings or speak with professionals online through sponsored chat groups. Learn about the key companies in your industry of choice—find out who they are, make a list, and research those particular companies. Finally, set up an informational interview with someone at a company in your field. Even busy professionals are often willing to speak with interested job seekers not applying for a specific job. These people can offer general advice about the industry as a whole and about their own company.

Job postings can be located in a variety of places: Use nationwide job portals (such as *Monster.com, Careerbuilder.com, Riley Guide,* and many others) to find jobs across the country or specific to your location; consult the print or online Help Wanted sections of your local newspapers; locate industry-specific jobs on

Search within a reasonable range

Don't just dive in; work step by step

✴ **Explore** the **Concept** with the Case Study on Job Searching at **mytechcommlab**

Start by talking to job experts, librarians, friends, and family

Next, consult industry-specific resources

✴ **Explore** the **Concept** with the Case Study on Networking at **mytechcommlab**

Finally, look for specific job postings or send out unsolicited application letters professional organization Web sites; or find jobs advertised only on human resources Web sites of particular companies. You don't have to limit your search options to advertised jobs, however. Another approach is to send an unsolicited application letter to a company that interests you (for more on unsolicited application letters, see page 172).

RÉSUMÉS

Definition and function of a résumé

👁 **Watch** the Video on Creating a Résumé at **mytechcommlab**

Of course, before applying for any job, you should create an effective résumé. A *résumé* is essentially an applicant's personal advertisement for employment. It lists, (in a standard format) education and employment history, along with other relevant information, providing a snapshot of the person's qualifications.

A résumé is designed to give an employer an instant overview. In fact, employers initially spend only 15 to 45 seconds looking at a résumé; during this scan, they are looking for a persuasive answer to the bottom-line question: "What can you do for us?"

Employers are impressed by a résumé that looks good, reads easily, appears honest, and provides only the relevant information an employer needs to determine if the applicant should be interviewed. Résumés that are mechanically flawed, cluttered, sketchy, hard to follow, or seemingly dishonest simply get discarded.

Parts of a Résumé

What to include— and not include—in a résumé

All résumés contain standard parts. Every résumé must include contact information, career objectives, education, work experience, personal data and interests, and references. A résumé is not the place to include such items as your desired salary and benefits or your requirements for time off. In addition, do not include irrelevant personal information, your photograph, or information that employers are not allowed to legally ask (such as your race, age, or marital status). As you read through this section, refer to Figure 10.1, which includes all the required parts.

Contact Information. Tell prospective employers where they can reach you. If you are between addresses, provide both addresses and check each contact point regularly. Be sure that your email address and phone number are accurate. If you use an answering machine or voice mail, record an outgoing message that sounds friendly and professional. If you have your own Web site (professional, not personal, in content), include the Web address. Remember that employers may access your Facebook or MySpace pages, so be sure to keep those pages professional in tone and content.

Career Objectives. Spell out the job you want. Avoid vague statements such as "A position in which I can apply my education and experience." Instead, be specific: "An intensive-care nursing position in a teaching hospital, with the eventual goal of supervising and instructing." Tailor your career objective statement as you apply for different jobs, in order to match yourself with each position.

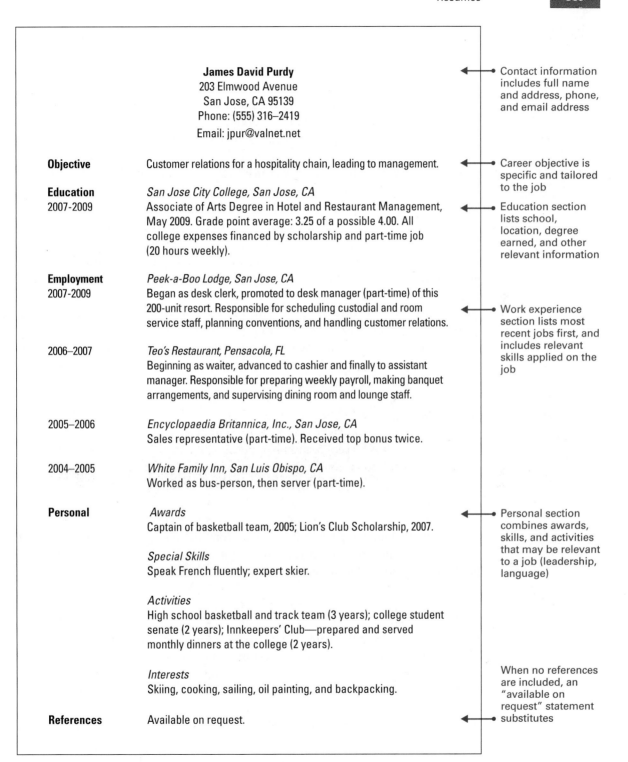

James David Purdy
203 Elmwood Avenue
San Jose, CA 95139
Phone: (555) 316–2419
Email: jpur@valnet.net

Contact information includes full name and address, phone, and email address

Objective	Customer relations for a hospitality chain, leading to management.	Career objective is specific and tailored to the job

Education
2007-2009

San Jose City College, San Jose, CA
Associate of Arts Degree in Hotel and Restaurant Management, May 2009. Grade point average: 3.25 of a possible 4.00. All college expenses financed by scholarship and part-time job (20 hours weekly).

Education section lists school, location, degree earned, and other relevant information

Employment
2007-2009

Peek-a-Boo Lodge, San Jose, CA
Began as desk clerk, promoted to desk manager (part-time) of this 200-unit resort. Responsible for scheduling custodial and room service staff, planning conventions, and handling customer relations.

Work experience section lists most recent jobs first, and includes relevant skills applied on the job

2006–2007

Teo's Restaurant, Pensacola, FL
Beginning as waiter, advanced to cashier and finally to assistant manager. Responsible for preparing weekly payroll, making banquet arrangements, and supervising dining room and lounge staff.

2005–2006

Encyclopaedia Britannica, Inc., San Jose, CA
Sales representative (part-time). Received top bonus twice.

2004–2005

White Family Inn, San Luis Obispo, CA
Worked as bus-person, then server (part-time).

Personal

Awards
Captain of basketball team, 2005; Lion's Club Scholarship, 2007.

Personal section combines awards, skills, and activities that may be relevant to a job (leadership, language)

Special Skills
Speak French fluently; expert skier.

Activities
High school basketball and track team (3 years); college student senate (2 years); Innkeepers' Club—prepared and served monthly dinners at the college (2 years).

Interests
Skiing, cooking, sailing, oil painting, and backpacking.

When no references are included, an "available on request" statement substitutes

References   Available on request.

FIGURE 10.1 A standard résumé

View the
Chronological
Résumé at
mytechcommlab

Education. Begin with your most recent schooling and work backward. Include the name of the school, degree completed, year completed, and your major and minor. Omit high school, unless the high school's prestige or your achievements there warrant its inclusion. List courses that have directly prepared you for the job you seek. If your class rank or grade point average is favorable, list it. Include specialized training during military service. If you finance your education by working, say so, indicating the percentage of your contribution.

View the Functional
Résumé at
mytechcommlab

Work Experience. If your experience relates to the job, list it before your education. List the most recent job and then earlier jobs. Include employers' names and dates of employment. Indicate whether a job was full-time, part-time (hours weekly), or seasonal. Describe your exact duties for each job, indicating promotions. If it is to your advantage, state why you left each job. Include military experience and relevant volunteer work. If you lack paid experience, emphasize your education, including internships and special projects.

Personal Data and Interests. By law, you are not required to include a photograph or reveal your sex, religion, race, age, national origin, disability, or marital status. List any awards, skills, activities, and interests that are *relevant* to the given position: say, memberships, demonstrations of leadership, languages, special skills, and hobbies that may be of interest to the employer.

Explore the Concept
with the Activity
on Requesting a
Reference at
mytechcommlab

References. List three to five people who have agreed to provide strong assessments of your qualifications and who can speak on your behalf. Never list as references people who haven't first given you express permission. Your references should not be family members or non-work-related friends; instead, list former employers, professors, and community figures who know you well. If saving space is important, simply state at the end of your résumé, "References available upon request," to help keep the résumé to one page. But if the résumé already takes up more than one page, you probably should include your references. If you don't list references, prepare a separate reference sheet that you can provide on request. Include each person's job title, company address, and contact information.

Organizing Your Résumé

Analyze the
Functional
Résumé at
mytechcommlab

Organize your résumé to convey the strongest impression of your qualifications, skills, and experience. A standard résumé, like the one in Figure 10.1, is also known as a *reverse chronological résumé*, listing the most recent school and job first. If you have limited experience or education, gaps in your work history (e.g., due to illness, raising children), or if you have frequently switched career paths, create a *functional résumé* (Figure 10.2) to highlight skills relevant to a particular job.

FIGURE 10.2
**A functional
résumé**

Carol R. Chasone
642 Eagle Lane
Eugene, OR 97405
(503-314-5555)
crchasone@eor.edu

OBJECTIVE   Position in marketing/communications with opportunity for advancement

← Includes contact
information and
objective

SALES/
MARKETING
SKILLS
- Wrote recruiting letter currently used by the Eugene Chamber of Commerce
- Designed posters for promotion of industrial development in Central Oregon
- Assisted Chamber President in promoting the organization's activities
- Recruited 7 speakers for Chamber meetings
- Wrote 3 public-relations pieces about a local hospital, for area newspapers

COMMUNICATION
AND DOCUMENT
DESIGN SKILLS
- Conducted demographic study of small businesses in Southwestern OR
- Presented study findings to Eugene Chamber of Commerce
- Wrote 15-page report on results of demographic study
- Designed and wrote two brochures to promote the Small Business Institute
- Designed 5 issues of *Patient Care*, 16-page in-house hospital newsletter
- Wrote 8 articles and conducted 3 interviews for the newsletter
- Designed 6 posters for in-service hospital programs

← Emphasizes three
skills areas
appropriate to the
job, with specific
accomplishments in
bulleted-list format

ORGANIZATIONAL/
MANAGEMENT
SKILLS
- Coordinated all weekly Chamber meetings for Feb., March, April, and May
- Attended 2 seminars (Houston, Seattle) for hospital public relations
- Trained and supervised 3 new interns at the Small Business Institute
- Scheduled and chaired weekly intern meetings

EDUCATION   Eastern Oregon University
B.S. in Marketing; Graphic Design minor—May 2008
GPA: 3.3/4.0; Dean's List, 5 semesters
Contract Learning: Eugene Chamber of Commerce, Fall 2007
Internships: EOU's Small Business Institute, Spring 2007; Mercy Hospital, Fall 2007

← Includes but
deemphasizes
education

EMPLOYMENT   Personal trainer (part-time and summers 2005–2007)—Acme Gym, Eugene
Caddy and Pro Shop salesperson—Eugene Golf Club, summers, 2002–2004

INTERESTS   Golf, fitness, modern dance, oil painting, photography

REFERENCES   Available on request

STRATEGIES
for Hard-Copy Résumés

- **Begin your résumé well before your job search.**

- **Tailor your résumé for each job.** Read the advertised job requirements, and adjust your career objective accordingly. Tailor your work experience, personal data, and personal interests to emphasize certain areas for certain jobs.

- **Try to limit the résumé to a single page.** However, if your résumé looks cramped, you might need to go to a second page—in which case you could have room to list your references (with their permission).

- **Stick to experience relevant to the job.** Don't list everything you've ever done.

- **Use action verbs and key words.** Action verbs (*supervised, developed, built, taught, installed, managed, trained, solved, planned, directed*) stress your ability to produce results. If your résumé is likely to be scanned electronically or if you post it online, list key words as nouns (*leadership skills, software development, data processing, editing*) below your contact information and your statement of objective (see Figure 9.3).

- **Use bold, italic, underlining, colors, fonts, bullets, and other devices thoughtfully, for emphasis.** Do not use these features to be artsy.

- **Never invent or distort credentials.** Make yourself look as good as the *facts* allow. Companies routinely investigate claims made in résumés, and people who lie will certainly not be hired.

- **Use quality paper and envelopes.** Use white paper.

- **Proofread, proofread, proofread.** Don't rely on a computer spell checker. Famous résumé mistakes include winning a "bogus award" instead of a "bonus award" and "ruining" rather than "running" a business.

Electronic Résumés

Today's résumés are often submitted electronically

Expect to submit your résumé electronically as well as (or instead of) in hard copy. Even if you are only asked to submit a hard-copy résumé, prospective employers may want to scan the hard copy into their computer systems, which requires special formatting. Many employers ask that résumés be submitted as email attachments, and you may want to post your resume online, either on your own Web site or on a job search database (such as *Monster.com* or *Yahoo! HotJobs*). As you read through this section, refer to the sample résumé in Figure 10.3.

KAREN P. GRANGER
P.O. Box 6772
New Bedford, MA 02720
Phone: (555) 864-9318
Email: kgrang@swis.net

OBJECTIVE
A summer internship in software documentation.

QUALIFICATIONS
Software and hardware documentation. Editing. Desktop publishing. Usability testing. Computer science. Internet research. Web collaboration. Networking technology. Instructor-led training. DEC 20 mainframe and VAX 11/780 systems. Adobe *Framemaker, RoboHelp, Webworks Publisher, PowerPoint, Excel,* and *Lotus* software. Logo, Pascal, HTML, and C++ program languages.

EDUCATION
University of Massachusetts at Dartmouth (UMD): B.A. expected January 2010. English and communications major. Computer science minor. GPA 3.54. Class rank top 7 percent.

EXPERIENCE
Conway Communications, Inc., Marlboro, MA: Intern technical writer. LAN technology. Writing, designing, and testing hardware upgrade manuals. Designing and publishing of installation and maintenance manual. Specifying art and illustrations. Designing a fully linked home page and online help for the company intranet. Summers 2007 and 2008.

Writing and Reading Center, UMD: Tutor. Individual and group instruction in writing and word processing. Training new tutors. Newsletter editing. Scriptwriting and acting in a training video. Designing home page. Fall 2006–present.

The Torch, UMD weekly newspaper: Managing editor. Conducting staff meetings. Generating story ideas. Writing editorials and articles. Supervising page layout, paste-up, and copyediting. Fall 2007–present.

ACHIEVEMENTS AND AWARDS
Writing samples published in Dr. John M. Lannon's Technical Communication, 11th ed. (Pearson/Longman, 2008).

Massachusetts State Honors Scholarship, 2006–2008.

Dean's list each semester.

ACTIVITIES
Student member, Society for Technical Communication and American Society for Training and Development.

Student representative, College Curriculum Committee.

UMD Literary Society.

REFERENCES AND WRITING PORTFOLIO
Available on request.

Annotations (right margin):

- To facilitate online confidentiality, a P.O. box, rather than a street address, is used
- Uses ALL CAPS for emphasis, rather than boldface, italics, etc.
- Uses nouns instead of verb forms
- Chooses a standard, not fancy, font
- All text is flush to the left margin

FIGURE 10.3 A résumé that can be scanned, emailed, or posted online

Scannable résumés

Scannable and Emailed Résumés. Electronic storage of hard-copy résumés enables employers to screen applicants, to compile a database of applicants (for later openings), and to evaluate all applicants fairly. An optical scanner feeds in the printed page, stores it as a file, and searches the file for keywords associated with the job opening. Resumes containing the most keywords ("hits") make the final cut.

Emailed resumes

You might also submit your résumé as an email attachment, in which case you need to format it so that it is compatible with different computers (Mac, PC) and word processing programs.

To design a résumé that can be scanned or sent as an email attachment use the following Strategies.

STRATEGIES
for Scannable and Emailed Résumés

▸ **Use a simple font.** Stick with those fonts that are the easiest to scan, such as Courier, Times, and Helvetica (Arial).

▸ **Use simple formatting.** Avoid boldface, shading, italics, underlining, tabs, and centering. Place all text flush to the left margin. For emphasis, use ALL CAPS instead of boldface, italics, shading, or underlining.

▸ **Save your résumé in "text only" or "rich text" format.** This will ensure that all fancy fonts and formats are removed and allow for smooth scanning and emailing.

▸ **Proofread your résumé.** Make sure it is free of errors and emphasizes your most important skills and qualifications.

▸ **Do not staple or fold pages.**

Online Résumés. You may also want to place your résumé online, either on your own Web site (which might include a *webfolio*, see page 175) or on an employment Web site. For an employment Web site, follow the site's posting guidelines. For your own site or social networking page (such as LinkedIn or Facebook) use the following Strategies.

STRATEGIES
for Online Résumés

▸ **Use keywords.** Use words that are likely to get hits in keyword searches. You may want to create a "qualifications" section at the top of your résumé. Include

➡

keywords for general skills (conflict management, report and proposal writing), specialized skills (graphic design, XTML), credentials (B.S. in electrical engineering, Phi Beta Kappa), and job titles (manager, technician, intern). Use nouns for keywords.

▶ **Add hyperlinks, if desired.** If you post your résumé on your own Web site, consider adding hyperlinks so that readers can link to specific documents elsewhere on your page, such as scanned samples from your portfolio (see Figure 10.5).

▶ **Avoid personal information.** Do not expose yourself or your references to identity theft by posting photographs, home addresses (use a P.O. box or simply your city and email address), or birth dates. Also avoid frivolous personal information. Post only on sites that offer privacy options, such as *Zoominfo*, *LinkedIn*, or *Ziggs.com*; at these sites you can check, update, and correct your profile at any time.

APPLICATION LETTERS

An *application letter*, also known as a *cover letter*, complements your résumé when you apply for a job. The letter's main purpose is to explain how your credentials fit the particular job and to convey a sufficiently informed, professional, and likable persona for the prospective employer to decide that you should be interviewed. Another purpose of the letter is to highlight specific qualifications or skills; for example, you might have listed "C++ programming" on your résumé, but for one particular job application you may wish to call attention to this item in your cover letter:

Definition and function of an application letter

> My résumé notes that I am experienced with C++ programming. In fact, I also tutor C++ programming students in our school's learning center.

Sometimes you will apply for positions advertised in print or by word of mouth (*solicited applications*). At other times you will write prospecting letters to organizations that have not advertised an opening but that might need someone like you (*unsolicited applications*). In either case, tailor your letter to the situation.

Solicited and unsolicited application letters

Solicited Application Letters

An application letter—whether solicited or unsolicited—consists of an introduction, body, and conclusion as in Figure 10.4.

 Analyze the Solicited Application Letter at mytechcommlab

Use the introduction
to get right to the
point

In your brief introduction (generally, five lines or fewer), do these things: Name the job you're applying for and where you have seen it advertised; identify yourself and your background; and, if possible, establish a connection by naming a mutual acquaintance who encouraged you to apply—but only if that person has given you permission.

Use the body to
demonstrate your
qualifications

In the body, spell out your case. Without merely repeating your résumé, relate your qualifications specifically to this job. Also, be specific. Instead of referring to "much experience" or "increased sales," stipulate "three years of experience" or "a 35 percent increase in sales between June and October 2009." Support all claims with evidence. Instead of saying, "I have leadership skills," say, "I served as student senate president during my senior year and was captain of the lacrosse team."

Use the conclusion
to restate interest

In the conclusion, restate your interest and emphasize your willingness to retrain or relocate if necessary. If the job is nearby, request an interview; otherwise, request a phone call, suggesting a time you can be reached.

Unsolicited Application Letters

Analyze the
Unsolicited
Application
Letter at
mytechcommlab

Do not limit your job search to advertised openings. In fact, fewer than 20 percent of all job openings are advertised. Unsolicited application letters are a good way to uncover possibilities. They do have drawbacks, however: You may waste time writing to organizations that have no openings, and you cannot tailor your letter to advertised requirements. But there are also advantages: Even employers with no openings often welcome and file impressive unsolicited applications or pass them on to another employer who has an opening.

Use the introduction
to spark reader
interest

Because an unsolicited letter arrives unexpectedly, you need to get the reader's immediate attention. Don't begin, "I am writing to inquire about the possibility of obtaining a position with your company." Instead, open forcefully by establishing a connection with a mutual acquaintance, or by making a strong statement or asking a persuasive question as in the following example:

A forceful opening

> Does your hotel chain have a place for a junior manager with a college degree in hospitality management, a proven commitment to quality service, and customer relations experience that extends far beyond textbooks? If so, please consider my application for a position.

Address your letter to the person most likely in charge of hiring. Consult company Web sites for names of company officers. Then call the company to verify the person's name and title.

203 Elmwood Avenue
San Jose, CA 10462
April 22, 20XX

Sara Costanza
Personnel Director
Liberty International, Inc.
Lansdowne, PA 24153

Dear Ms. Costanza:

Please consider my application for a junior management position at your Lake Geneva resort, as advertised in the April 19 *Philadephia Inquirer.* I will graduate from San Jose City College on May 30 with an Associate of Arts degree in hotel and restaurant management. Dr. H. V. Garlid, my nutrition professor, described his experience as a consultant for Liberty International and encouraged me to apply. | ← Writer identifies self and purpose

← Establishes a connection

As you can see from my enclosed résumé, for two years I worked as a part-time desk clerk, and I was promoted to manager, at a 200-unit resort. This experience, combined with earlier customer relations work in a variety of situations, has given me a clear and practical understanding of customers' needs and expectations. | ← Relates specific qualifications from his résumé to the job opening

As an amateur chef, I'm well aware of the effort, attention, and patience required to prepare fine food. Moreover, my skiing and sailing background might be assets to your resort's recreation program. | ← Applies relevant personal interests to the job

I have worked hard to hone my hospitality management skills. My experience, education, and personality have prepared me to work well with others and to respond creatively to challenges, crises, and added responsibilities. | ← Expresses confidence and enthusiasm throughout

If my background meets your needs, please phone me any weekday after 4:00 p.m. at (555) 316-2419. | ← Makes follow-up easy for the reader

Sincerely,

James D. Purdy

James D. Purdy

FIGURE 10.4 A solicited application letter

STRATEGIES
for Application Letters

▸ **Use caution when adapting sample application letters.** There are plenty of free, online sample letters that provide ideas for your own situation. But never borrow them whole. Most employers can spot a "canned" letter immediately.

▸ **Create a dynamic tone with active voice.** Instead of saying, "More and more management responsibilities were steadily given to me," say, "I steadily assumed ever-greater management responsibilities."

▸ **Never be vague.** Paint a clear picture for employers who may not be familiar with what you describe. Instead of saying, "I am familiar with the 1022 interactive database system and RUNOFF processing system," say, "As a lab grader, I kept grading records on the 1022 database management system and composed lab procedures on the RUNOFF text processing system."

▸ **Avoid being overly informal or overly stiff.** Avoid informal terms that sound unprofessional ("Your company sounds like a cool place to work") as well as stuffy language ("Hitherto, I request the honor of your acquaintance").

▸ **Never settle for a first draft—or even a second or third.** The application letter is your one chance to introduce yourself to a prospective employer. Make it perfect by trimming excess wording, double-checking the tone, and making sure that you have connected your qualifications directly to the job. After you are satisfied with the content, proofread repeatedly to spot any factual errors or typos.

DOSSIERS, PORTFOLIOS, AND WEBFOLIOS

Definitions and purposes of dossiers and portfolios

An employer impressed by your résumé and application letter will likely have questions about your credentials and your past work. These questions will be answered, respectively, by your dossier and your portfolio (or Webfolio).

Dossiers

What a dossier contains

Your dossier contains your credentials: college transcript, recommendation letters, and other items (such as a scholarship award or commendation letter) that document your achievements. Prospective employers who decide to follow up on your application will request your dossier. By collecting recommendations in one folder, you spare your references from writing the same letter repeatedly.

Your college placement office will keep the dossier (or placement folder) on file and send copies to employers. Always keep your own copy as well, including any nonconfidential recommendation letters. Then, if an employer requests your dossier, you can photocopy and mail it, advising your recipient that the official placement copy is on the way, as sometimes dossiers may not be mailed immediately.

Portfolios and Webfolios

Your portfolio (or Webfolio, Figure 10.5) contains an introduction or mission statement explaining what you've included in your portfolio and why. Among the included items are your résumé, uploaded or scanned examples of your work, and anything else pertinent to your job search (such as copies of documents from your dossier). Omit anything not related directly to your qualifications. An organized, professional-looking portfolio or Webfolio shows that you can apply your skills and makes you stand out as a candidate. It also gives you concrete material to discuss during job interviews.

What a portfolio contains

✴ **Explore** the **Concept** with the Case Study on Writing Application Packets at **mytechcommlab**

As you create your portfolio or Webfolio seek advice and feedback from professors in your major and from other people in the field. If you have a portfolio indicate this on your résumé, followed by "Available on request." If you have created a Webfolio provide the Web address on your résumé, but also bring printed copies of its contents to your interview.

STRATEGIES
for Dossiers, Portfolios, and Webfolios

▸ **Always provide an introduction or mission statement.** Place this page at the beginning, to introduce and explain the contents.

▸ **Collect relevant materials.** Gather documents or graphics you've prepared in school or on the job, presentations you've given, and projects or experiments you've worked on. Possible items: campus newspaper articles, reports on course projects, papers that earned an "A," examples of persuasive argument, documents from an internship, or visuals you've designed for an oral presentation.

▸ **Include copies of dossier materials.** Although they won't be official unless they go directly from your campus placement office to your prospective employer, have copies of your college transcript and recommendations on hand to give to employers during the waiting period and/or to post on your Webfolio.

▸ **Assemble your items.** Place your résumé first (after your introduction/mission statement), and use divider pages to separate groups of items. Follow the same structure for a Webfolio. Position your résumé file immediately below the introduction/mission statement file, and group similar items into appropriate files. In either case, aim for a professional look.

➡

▶ **Omit irrelevant items.** Personal photographs and other items more appropriate for a MySpace or Facebook page do not belong in portfolio or webfolio.

▶ **Omit your street address or phone number from your webfolio.** Post only your email address to avoid identity theft. If you post your references, include only their names and comments, not their contact information.

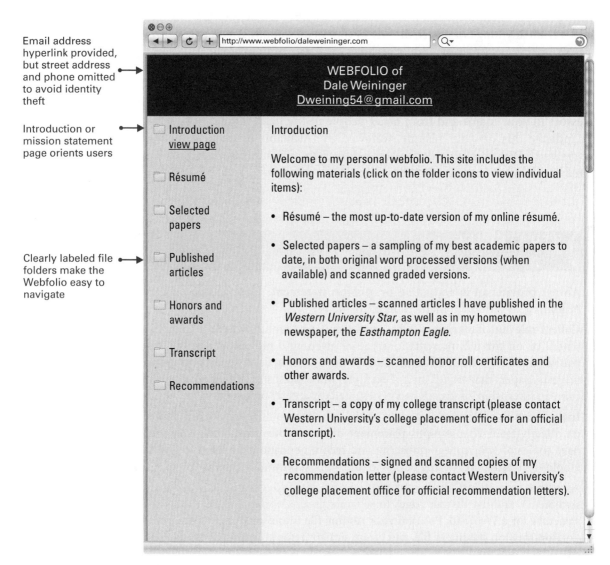

Email address hyperlink provided, but street address and phone omitted to avoid identity theft

Introduction or mission statement page orients users

Clearly labeled file folders make the Webfolio easy to navigate

http://www.webfolio/daleweininger.com

WEBFOLIO of
Dale Weininger
Dweining54@gmail.com

Introduction
view page

Résumé

Selected papers

Published articles

Honors and awards

Transcript

Recommendations

Introduction

Welcome to my personal webfolio. This site includes the following materials (click on the folder icons to view individual items):

• Résumé – the most up-to-date version of my online résumé.

• Selected papers – a sampling of my best academic papers to date, in both original word processed versions (when available) and scanned graded versions.

• Published articles – scanned articles I have published in the *Western University Star*, as well as in my hometown newspaper, the *Easthampton Eagle*.

• Honors and awards – scanned honor roll certificates and other awards.

• Transcript – a copy of my college transcript (please contact Western University's college placement office for an official transcript).

• Recommendations – signed and scanned copies of my recommendation letter (please contact Western University's college placement office for official recommendation letters).

FIGURE 10.5 A Webfolio

INTERVIEWS AND FOLLOW-UP LETTERS

All of your preparation leads to the last stages of the hiring process: the interview and follow-up to the interview.

Interviews

An employer who is impressed by your credentials will arrange an interview. The interview's purpose is to confirm the employer's impressions from your application letter, résumé, references, and dossier. You will likely be asked to present your portfolio (if you have one) at the interview, rather than beforehand. In addition to your original portfolio or the Web address for your Webfolio, bring copies/printouts of all relevant documents contained therein. Offer to leave these copies with the interviewer.

Purpose of interviews

Interviews come in various shapes and sizes. They can be face-to-face or via telephone or video conference. You might meet with a single interviewer, a hiring committee, or several committees in succession. You might be interviewed alone or as part of a group of candidates. Interviews can last an hour or less, a full day, or several days. The interview can range from a pleasant chat to a grueling interrogation. Some interviewers may antagonize you deliberately to observe your reaction.

Types of interview situations

Careful preparation is the key to a productive interview. If you haven't already done so, learn what you can about the company from trade journals, industrial indexes, business magazines (like *Forbes*, *Fortune*, and *Business Week*), and other resources. Request company literature, including the must recent annual report. Speak with people who know about the company, or (well in advance) arrange an informational interview with someone at the company. In addition, visit the company's Web site. Once you've done all this, ask yourself, "Does this job seem like a good fit?"

The importance of preparing for an interview

In addition to knowing about the company, be prepared in other ways. Dress and present yourself appropriately. Be psychologically prepared and confident (but not arrogant). Follow the rules of business etiquette. Unprepared interviewees make mistakes such as the following:

- They know little about the company or what role they would play as an employee in this particular division or department.

How people fail job interviews

- They have inflated ideas about their own worth.
- They have little idea of how their education prepares them for work.
- They dress inappropriately.
- They exhibit little or no self-confidence.
- They have only vague ideas of how they could benefit the employer.
- They inquire only about salary and benefits.
- They speak negatively of former employers or coworkers.

Practice answering
interview questions

Perhaps the most important way to prepare for an interview is to practice answering typical questions. Think about how you would answer the following:

Questions to expect
during a job
interview

- Why does this job appeal to you?

- What do you know about our company? About this division or unit?

- What do you know about our core values (for example, informal management structure, commitment to diversity, or to the environment)?

- What do you know about the expectations and demands of this job?

- What are the major issues affecting this industry?

- How would you describe yourself as an employee?

- What do you see as your biggest weakness? Biggest strength?

- Can you describe an instance in which you came up with a new and better way of doing something?

- What are your short-term and long-term career goals?

Prepare your own
questions, too

Don't forget to prepare your own list of well-researched questions about the job and the organization. You will be invited to ask questions, and what you ask can be as revealing as any answers you give.

Be truthful

Finally, tell the truth during the interview—doing so is both ethical and smart. Companies routinely verify an applicant's claims about education, prior employment, positions held, salary, and personal background. Perhaps you have some past infraction (such as a bad credit rating or a brush with the law), or some pressing personal commitment (such as caring for an elderly parent or a disabled child). Experts suggest that it's better to air these issues up front—before the employer finds out from other sources. The employer will appreciate your honesty, and you will know exactly where you stand before accepting the job (Fisher 292).

Follow-Up Letters

There are two types of follow-up letters: thank you letters, and if you are offered the job, acceptance or refusal letters.

Purpose and content
of thank you letters

Thank You Letters. Within a day or so after the interview, send a thank you letter (not an email, which will seem lazy) to the person who interviewed you. If you were interviewed by multiple people, send each one an individual thank you letter. Not only is this courteous, but it also reinforces a positive impression. Keep your letter brief, but try to personalize your connection with the reader (Crosby 20).

■■■ **Analyze** the **Thank**
■■■ **You Letter** at
■ mytechcommlab

Open by thanking the interviewer and reemphasizing your interest in the position. Then refer to some details from the interview or some aspect of your visit that would help the interviewer reconnect with the interview experience. If you forgot to mention something important during the interview, include it here—briefly. Finally, close with genuine enthusiasm, and provide your contact information again to make it easy for the interviewer to respond. Following is the text of an effective thank you letter from James Purdy, the entry-level candidate in hotel-restaurant management, whose résumé and cover letter appeared earlier:

> Thank you for your hospitality during my Tuesday visit to Greenwoods resort. I am very interested in the restaurant-management position and was intrigued by our discussion about developing an eclectic regional cuisine.
>
> Everything about my tour was enjoyable, but I was especially impressed by the friendliness and professionalism of the resort staff. People seem to love working here, and it's not hard to see why.
>
> I'm convinced I would be a productive employee at Greenwood and would welcome the chance to prove my abilities. If you need additional information, please call me at (214) 316-5555.

Acceptance or Refusal Letters. You may receive a job offer by phone or letter. If by phone, request a written offer and respond with a formal letter of acceptance. This letter may serve as part of your contract; spell out the terms you are accepting. Remember also to accept a job offer with enthusiasm. Here is James Purdy's letter of acceptance:

Content and approach of acceptance letters

> I am delighted to accept your offer of a position as assistant recreation supervisor at Liberty International's Lake Geneva Resort, with a starting salary of $44,500.
>
> As you requested, I will phone Bambi Druid in your Personnel Office for instructions on reporting date, physical exam, and employee orientation.
>
> I look forward to a long and satisfying career with Liberty International.

You may also have to refuse a job offer, for example if you receive a preferable offer or decide that the position is not the right fit for you. Even if you refuse by phone, write a prompt and cordial letter of refusal, explaining your reasons, and allowing for future possibilities. Remember to be diplomatic when refusing a job. A courteous refusal and explanation can let the employer know why you have chosen a competing employer or why you have decided against taking the job for other reasons. Purdy handled one job refusal this way:

Content and approach of refusal letters

> Although I thoroughly enjoyed my visit to your company's headquarters, I have to decline your offer of a position as assistant desk manager of your London hotel.

I've decided to accept a position with Liberty International because the company has offered me the chance to participate in its manager-trainee program. Also, Liberty will provide tuition for courses in completing my B.S. degree in hospitality management.

If any future openings should materialize at your Aspen resort, however, I would appreciate your considering me again as a candidate.

Thank you for your confidence in me.

STRATEGIES
for Interviews and Follow-up Letters

▸ **Confirm the interview's exact time and location.** Arrive early but no more than 10 minutes.

▸ **Don't show up empty-handed.** Bring a briefcase, pen, and notepad. Have your own questions written out. Bring extra copies of your résumé (unfolded) and a portfolio (if appropriate).

▸ **Make a positive first impression.** Come dressed as if you already work for the company. Learn the name of your interviewer beforehand, so you can greet this person by name—but never by first name unless invited. Extend a firm handshake, smile, and look the interviewer in the eye. Wait to be asked to take a chair. Maintain eye contact much of the time, but don't stare.

▸ **Don't worry about having all the answers.** When you don't know the answer to a question, say so, and relax. Interviewers typically do most of the talking.

▸ **Avoid abrupt yes or no answers—as well as life stories.** Just saying yes or no doesn't leave any impression—elaborate on your answers, but also keep them short and to the point.

▸ **Don't answer questions by merely repeating the material on your résumé.** Instead, explain how specific skills and types of experience could be assets to this particular employer.

▸ **Remember to smile often and to be friendly and attentive throughout.** Qualifications are not the only reason a person gets hired. People often hire the candidate they *like* best.

▸ **Never criticize a previous employer.** Above all, interviewers like positive attitudes. Complaining about a former employer, whether or not your criticisms are legitimate, only makes you look negative.

▸ **Prepare to ask intelligent questions.** When questions are invited, focus on the nature of the job: travel involved, specific responsibilities, typical job assignments, opportunities for further training, types of clients, and so on. Avoid questions that could easily have been answered by your own prior research.

➡

▸ **Take a hint.** When your interviewer hints that the meeting is ending (perhaps by checking a watch), restate your interest, ask when a hiring decision is likely to be made, thank the interviewer, and leave.

▸ **Follow up as soon as possible.** Send a thank you note to each person with whom you interviewed. Be sure to get the spelling right for each person's name.

CHECKLIST
for Résumés

- ☐ Does my résumé's organization (reverse chronological or functional) emphasize my best characteristics?
- ☐ Is my contact information accurate?
- ☐ Does my statement of objective show a clear sense of purpose?
- ☐ Have I included a summary of skills or qualifications, as needed?
- ☐ Is my educational background clear and complete?
- ☐ Have I accurately but briefly described my previous jobs?
- ☐ Have I presented education versus experience in the appropriate sequence?
- ☐ Have I included personal data and interests, as appropriate?
- ☐ Have I listed references or offered to provide them?
- ☐ Have I offered to provide a portfolio, as appropriate?
- ☐ Have I used action verbs and key words?
- ☐ Have I limited the résumé to a single page, if possible?
- ☐ Is the résumé uncluttered and tasteful?
- ☐ Have I used quality (white) paper?
- ☐ If I have a scannable résumé, does it use key words and effective formatting?
- ☐ Am I being scrupulously honest?
- ☐ Have I proofread exhaustively?

CHECKLIST
for Job Application Letters

- ☐ Is my letter addressed to a specifically named person?
- ☐ If my letter is *solicited*, do I indicate how I heard about the job?

➔

CHECKLIST *continued*

☐ If my letter is *unsolicited*, does it have a forceful opening?

☐ Does my introduction get directly to the point?

☐ Does the body section paint a clear picture of qualifications sketched in the résumé?

☐ Does the conclusion restate my interest and encourage specific action?

☐ Have I made my case without merely repeating the résumé?

☐ Is my letter free of "canned" expressions?

☐ Is my tone confident without being arrogant?

☐ Have I avoided a tone that is overly formal or overly stiff?

☐ Have I avoided flattery and exaggeration?

☐ Have I proofread exhaustively?

☐ Am I being scrupulously honest?

CHECKLIST
for Supporting Materials

☐ Is my dossier complete, with letters of recommendation and other supporting materials?

☐ Is my portfolio or Webfolio (if applicable) up-to-date?

☐ If my portfolio has hyperlinks, are they all functioning?

☐ Have I prepared for interviews?

☐ Have I sent the appropriate follow-up correspondence?

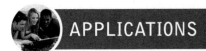

APPLICATIONS

GENERAL APPLICATIONS

1. If you have not already prepared a standard hard-copy résumé, prepare one following the guidelines in this chapter. If you already have a résumé, revise it not only to follow this chapter's guidelines but also to update your work experience, educational background, and other details. Remember to include persuasive action verbs, to design the résumé in an efficient but attractive way, and to include all relevant experience.

2. Write an application letter applying for a part-time or summer job in response to a specific ad and tailor your résumé for the job. Choose an organization related to your career goals. Identify the exact hours and calendar period during which you are free to work. Submit a copy of the ad along with your letter and résumé.

3. Make your résumé scannable and ready for sending via email or posting online. Be sure to use an easily scannable font; remove headers, boldface, underlining, bullets, tabs, and other formatting; and proofread it after you've converted it to "text only" or "rich text" format.

4. A friend has asked you for help with the following application letter. Read it carefully, evaluate its effectiveness, and rewrite it as needed.

> Dear Ms. Brown,
>
> Please consider my application for the position of assistant in the Engineering Department. I am a second-year student majoring in electrical engineering technology. I am presently an apprentice with your company and would like to continue my employment in the Engineering Department.
>
> I have six years' experience in electronics, including two years of engineering studies. I am confident my background will enable me to assist the engineers, and I would appreciate the chance to improve my skills through their knowledge and experience.
>
> I would appreciate the opportunity to discuss the possibilities and benefits of a position in the Engineering Department at Concord Electric. Please phone me any weekday after 3:00 p.m. at (555) 568-9867. I hope to hear from you soon.
>
> Sincerely,

5. Write an unsolicited application letter to the human resources director of a company that interests you. Go to the company's Web site to research the various positions for which you may be qualified. Select one, and name that position in your letter. Also learn the name of the human resources director and address your letter to that person. Be sure to grab the reader's attention, to remain persuasive throughout, and to conclude with a call to action.

TEAM APPLICATION

Divide into groups and prepare a listing of five Web sites that job seekers should visit for advice about cover letters and résumés, including online postings. Include a one-paragraph summary of the material found on each site. Compare the findings of your group with others in your class. In addition to sites mentioned in this chapter, here are other sources where you might begin (but expand your search beyond these sites):

<www.jobstar.org/tools/resume>

<www.eresumes.com>

GLOBAL APPLICATION

Assume that you and other students in your major would like to work in a particular country after graduation. Select a country and do some research on the economy, culture, and travel issues. Write a short memo that tells prospective students what they need to know about finding employment abroad.

COMPUTER/WEB-BASED APPLICATION

Online you can find many employment sites. Look at one or both of the following: <careerbuilders.com> and/or <monster.com>. Learn more about how you would go about preparing a résumé to upload to one of these sites. If the site provides sample résumés, look at a few and compare these to the strategies provided in this chapter. Create a draft résumé for one of these sites and review it with your instructor.

For additional technical writing resources that will help you master the chapter objectives, go to **www.mytechcommlab.com**.

11 Memos and Letters

LEARNING OBJECTIVES FOR THIS CHAPTER

▸ Identify the parts and format of a workplace memo or letter

▸ Achieve the right tone in a memo or letter

▸ Determine when to take a direct or indirect approach in a memo or letter

▸ Write an effective memo

▸ Write an effective inquiry, claim, sales, or adjustment letter

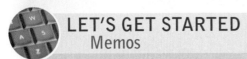

LET'S GET STARTED
Memos

You need to write a memo to your supervisor or professor requesting an extension for a project you are working on. You have decided to use a memo rather than email because a memo is more formal and indicates your professionalism and seriousness. Without reading this chapter, write such a memo. Or, if you have a different situation going on at work or school, write a memo for that situation.

Questions to ask about the memo you wrote as you review the material in this chapter:

- ▶ Does the memo contain all of the typical parts?
- ▶ Is the memo direct and to the point?
- ▶ In the memo professional and respectful in tone?
- ▶ Is the memo too long? Too short?

At the end of this chapter, review the memo you wrote for this Let's Get Started exercise. Compare what you wrote with what you learned from this chapter. Revise or modify your memo based on what you have learned from the chapter and what you learn from class. Bring your original and your revision for class, and discuss these with a small group of 2–3 students.

LET'S GET STARTED
Letters

You have been asked to write a report for a science, history, English, or other class. You would like to request information from a local company, nonprofit, or other organization. Without reading this chapter, write a letter about the topic you are investigating for your report or research assignment. In your letter you might request brochures, pamphlets, or other informative literature, or you might ask specific questions.

Questions to ask about the letter you wrote as you review the material in this chapter:

▶ What type of letter are you writing?

▶ What kind of tone or style did you use (professional, formal, informal)?

▶ How is the content of your letter organized (did you make your request first or provide introductory information first)?

▶ How long is your letter?

▶ What format and layout did you use?

▶ What revisions would you make, based on the material in this chapter and your class discussions?

At the end of this chapter, review the letter you wrote for this Let's Get Started exercise. Compare what you wrote with what you learned from this chapter. In particular, pay attention to the style and tone of your request. Revise or modify your letter based on what you have learned from the chapter and what you learn in class. Bring your original and your revision for class, and discuss these with a small group of 2–3 students.

Three common types of written communication in the workplace are memos, letters, and emails. Email will be covered in Chapter 19, as part of the digital media unit. This chapter considers two more traditional types of workplace correspondence: memos and letters.

MEMO BASICS

The most traditional form of everyday workplace correspondence is the memo, or memorandum. The word "memorandum" is derived from the same Latin roots as the words "memorize," "remember," and "remind." Accordingly, memos give directives, provide instructions, relay information, and make requests. They are typically distributed to employees within an organization only, not to people outside the company. Memos are important in the workplace because they are easy to post in a workstation or office, and they provide a paper trail.

Definition and importance of memos

✳ **Explore** the **Concept** with the Case Study on Writing Memos at mytechcommlab

Despite its explosive growth, email has not entirely taken the place of paper memos. (Memos are often turned into PDF files and attached to emails, or emails themselves can function like memos.) Although email leaves a digital trail, it is considered less formal than a memo. Also, an email message may be

Memos versus email

ignored when received in crowded in-boxes and may be inadvertently forwarded to the wrong parties. Organizations have different preferences about when memos should be used in place of emails.

MEMO PARTS AND FORMAT

Standard parts
of a memo

■ ■ ■   Analyze the
■■ ■■   Memo at
■   ■   mytechcommlab

A standard memo has the word "Memo" or "Memorandum" centered at the top of the page and includes a heading guide (flush to the left margin) identifying the recipient(s), sender (and sender's initials), date, and subject. At the bottom of the memo, include a copy notation if copies are sent to anyone not listed in the "To" line (usually managers who simply need to know that the memo was sent). Because memos are often read rapidly by busy recipients, they must follow this consistent, predictable format. Figure 11.1 shows a standard memo with all parts labeled.

Memo format:
introduction, body,
conclusion

The body copy (main text portion) of a memo should focus on one topic. Content should be complete yet compact, providing all the information readers need but not going into unnecessary detail. Organize the body of your memo by starting with a short introduction, then writing a paragraph or two to address the main issue, then concluding by suggesting a course of action or asking your readers to follow up.

MEMO TONE

The importance of
memo tone

Memos are typically distributed in-house and circulated among colleagues, subordinates, and superiors. Memo topics often involve evaluations or recommendations about policies, procedures, and, ultimately, the people with whom you work. Because people are sensitive to criticism (even when it is merely implied) and often resistant to change, an ill-conceived memo tone can create problems. So, be particularly careful about your tone.

Achieving the
right tone

Achieving the right tone in your memos involves using some common sense. Put yourself in the shoes of your recipients and write accordingly. Be polite and avoid sounding bossy, condescending, and aggressive, or deferential and passive. Don't criticize, judge, or blame any individual or department. Don't resort to griping, complaining, and other negative commentary. Try to emphasize the positive. Finally, approach difficult situations reasonably. Instead of taking an extreme stance, or suggesting ideas that will never work, be practical and realistic.

Being direct
or indirect

The tone of a memo also comes across in the sequence in which you deliver the information. Depending on the sensitivity of your memo's subject matter, you may want to take a direct or indirect approach. A direct approach (as in Figure 11.1), begins with the "bottom line" in the first sentence (as well as in the subject line) and

MEMORANDUM

To: All Marketing Assistants, Cincinnati Office Web Marketing Group
From: Marilyn Zito, Purchasing <m.zito@adco.com>*MZ*
Date: October 25, 20XX
Subject: *Your choices for new high-capacity copier*

As you requested at our October 12 meeting, I have gathered all the manufacturer information needed to order a new high-capacity photocopier to replace the inefficient one in your area. As you know, since the MAs typically make the most use of the copy machines, I would appreciate your input as to which copiers from the attached options seem most suitable for your purposes.

Please note that I was required to select from options under $8,500 in order to stay within your department's 20XX purchasing budget, a substantial portion of which was used to purchase your new high-speed fax machine in March. However, I think you will find that the copiers selected are state-of-the art and should more than meet your needs in terms of capacity, speed, quality, precision, and durability—all of which you indicated were important attributes.

Please take a careful look at the models attached, consider your impressions of each model, pick your top three preferences, and email me your lists individually by November 5. I will tabulate your votes, contact you with the results, and order accordingly.

Thank you very much for taking the time to help me make an informed decision that meets your genuine needs.

Copies: J. Herrera, Director of Marketing
           M. Ziolkowki, Vice President, Purchasing

Annotations:
- "Memo" or "Memorandum" is centered at the top of the page
- Heading guide includes "To" "From" "Date" and "Subject" lines
- Opening paragraph gets right to the point
- Provides necessary background details
- Outlines specific course of action in the conclusion
- Copy notation appears at the bottom

FIGURE 11.1 A properly formatted memo

then presents the details or analysis that support your case. An indirect approach lays out the details of the case over several sentences (and leaves the subject line vague) before delivering the bottom line later in the paragraph.

Readers generally prefer the direct approach because they want to know the bottom line without being told in advance how to feel about it. Assume, for example, that a company Payroll Manager has to announce to employees that their paychecks will be delayed by two days: this manager should take a direct approach, announcing the unpopular news in the subject line and in the opening sentence and then explaining the causes of the problem:

MEMO

To: All employees

From: Meredith Rocteau, Payroll Manager *MR*

Date: May 19, 20XX

Direct approach: Subject line gets right to the main point

Subject: *Delay in paychecks*

Opening paragraph starts with the bottom line

I regret to inform you that those employees paid by direct deposit will experience a two-day delay in receiving their paychecks.

This delay is due to a virus that infiltrated the primary computer server for our payroll system. Although we hired virus consultants to identify the virus and clean out the server, the process took nearly 48 hours.

We apologize for the inconvenience.

However, when you need to convey exceedingly bad news or make an unpopular request or recommendation (as in announcing a strict new policy or employee layoffs), you might consider an indirect approach; this way you can present your case and encourage readers to understand your position before announcing the unpopular bottom line. The danger of the indirect approach, though, is that you may come across as evasive.

MEMO

To: All employees

From: J. Travis Southfield, Director of Human Resources *JTS*

Date: September 19, 20XX

Indirect approach: Subject line is not specific about bottom line

Subject: *Difficult economic times*

Each employee of the AutoWorld family is a valued member, and each of you has played an important role in our company's expansion over the past 10 years.

Yet as you all know, times are difficult right now for the automobile industry. Sales are down; financing is hard to obtain; and consumers are holding back on major purchases.

Opening paragraph starts with an explanation before delivering the bottom line

In order to keep the company solvent, we must consider all options. Therefore, I have been informed by our company president, John Creaswell, that we must downsize. We will begin with options for retirement packages, but please be prepared for the possibility that lay-offs may follow.

The bottom line

We will have more information for you at an all-hands meeting tomorrow.

Finally, a memo's tone comes across in the way you handle its distribution. Use the appropriate delivery medium. If your topic is very short, timely, not overly formal, and needs to reach everyone quickly, consider sending the memo as an email or email attachment. But if your topic is more formal and more detailed, send out a traditional paper memo. Also, be careful about who receives your memo. Don't send a memo to everyone at work when the content is only appropriate for a few, and don't leave vital people off your distribution list.

Delivering memos in the right medium to the right people

TYPES OF MEMOS

Memo format can also be used for distributing short reports, discussed in Chapter 16. However, for the purposes of this introductory chapter, consider the following common and more basic types of memos.

Transmittal Memo

A transmittal memo accompanies a package of materials, such as a long report, a manuscript, or a proposal. Its purpose is to signal that the information is being sent from one place to another (providing a paper trail), to introduce the material, and to explain what is enclosed. A transmittal memo may be as simple as a sentence or a paragraph with a bulleted list describing the package, as in Figure 11.2.

Analyze the Transmittal Memo at mytechcommlab

Summary or Follow-up Memo

A summary or follow-up memo provides a written record of a meeting or conversation, or just a topic during the meeting or conversation that was not resolved at the time. In addition to providing documentation that the meeting or conversation took place, summary and follow-up memos also insure that each recipient has

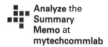
Analyze the Summary Memo at mytechcommlab

MEMORANDUM

To: D. Spring, Director of Human Resources
From: M. Noll, Head, Biology Division, *M.N.*
Date: January 16, 20XX
Subject: *Hiring of new laboratory manager*

As you know, each unit manager has been asked to prepare a hiring plan
for the coming year. Attached to this memo please find a brief report
outlining the biology division's need for a new laboratory manager.

The attached report includes

• an overview of needs

• a job description

• a budget

Please let me know if you require any additional information. I look
forward to hearing from you.

FIGURE 11.2 A transmittal memo

the same understanding of what was decided. Figure 11.3 shows a memo that
performs both a summary and follow-up function.

Informational Memo

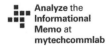

Analyze the
Informational
Memo at
mytechcommlab

Informational memos typically contain some type of announcement or update.
For instance, you may receive a memo announcing the closure of a parking
ramp over the holidays for repair, or an upcoming awards ceremony on Friday.
Such memos are increasingly sent via email, since email is quick and inexpensive
and has wide reach. But if the memo has a more formal purpose, a traditional
paper version may be preferable, as in Figure 11.4, which reiterates an important
company policy.

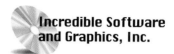

**Incredible Software
and Graphics, Inc.**

MEMO

To: Elaine Lamer and Mitchell Dramson, Software Development Team
From: Christopher Felts, Manager *C.F.*
Date: June 19, 20XX
Subject: *Follow up to today's meeting*

Thank you for meeting today to discuss next steps to complete the next version of our animation software package.

As you noted, the original release date of October 1 is probably too optimistic given the latest hiring freeze. Yet, as I mentioned, we can't afford to go beyond a date of October 15 if we are to make our fourth quarter sales goals. So, let's agree on October 15 as the new due date.

Please communicate this information to the other members of your team.

cc: E. Hearly, Division Chief

FIGURE 11.3 A summary or follow-up memo

Morris and Sutton, LLC

MEMORANDUM

To: All employees
From: Jorge Gonsalves, Human Resources *J.G.*
Date: January 12, 20XX
Subject: *401K Matching Policy*

As the new year begins, we in Human Resources would like to remind you about the company's generous 401K matching policy. We will match your 401K contributions 100% when you roll up to 10% of your salary into your 401K.

Many companies will match only up to 5% of an employee's salary, and usually not at a 100% rate, so please take advantage of this program by enrolling now. Enrollment is only open until March 1st and will not be open again until next January.

Please drop by the Human Resources office on the 6th floor to get a handout that provides more detailed information or to speak with an HR representative in person.

Thanks.

cc: Alison Sheffield, Manager, Human Resources

FIGURE 11.4 An informational memo

STRATEGIES
for Memos

- **Focus on one topic.** If you need to address more than one topic, consider a format other than a memo (for instance, a report).
- **Be brief.** People expect memos that are short and to the point.
- **Use the appropriate organizational format (direct or indirect).** Prefer the direct format when you need people to get the point quickly and the indirect format when you have something hard to say that needs to be softened.
- **Follow the standard format illustrated throughout this chapter.**
- **Use white space, headings, and bullets.** These features provide visual structure to your memo.
- **Distribute to the right people.** Do not "spam" people with your memo. Whether you are sending the memo via email or on paper, be sure it reaches only those who need the information. At the same time, don't leave out anyone who needs to read your message.

LETTER BASICS

A well-crafted workplace letter conveys a formal, professional impression. It presents a reasoned, carefully constructed case and represents not only you but also your company or organization. Letters also serve as an official notice or record. Your signature on a letter certifies your approval of the message. Letters often serve as legal documents, and so precision is crucial.

Importance of letters

LETTER PARTS AND FORMATS

All letters contain various parts (date line, return address, signature line), which are formatted in a standard way.

Parts of a Letter

The parts of a letter include the sender's address/heading, date, inside address, salutation, body text, complimentary closing, and signature. In addition a letter may include such optional parts as a company logo, typist's initials, enclosure notation, and/or copy notation. Figure 11.5 shows a workplace letter with the standard parts (as well as optional typist's initials and enclosure notation) labeled.

Standard and optional parts of a letter

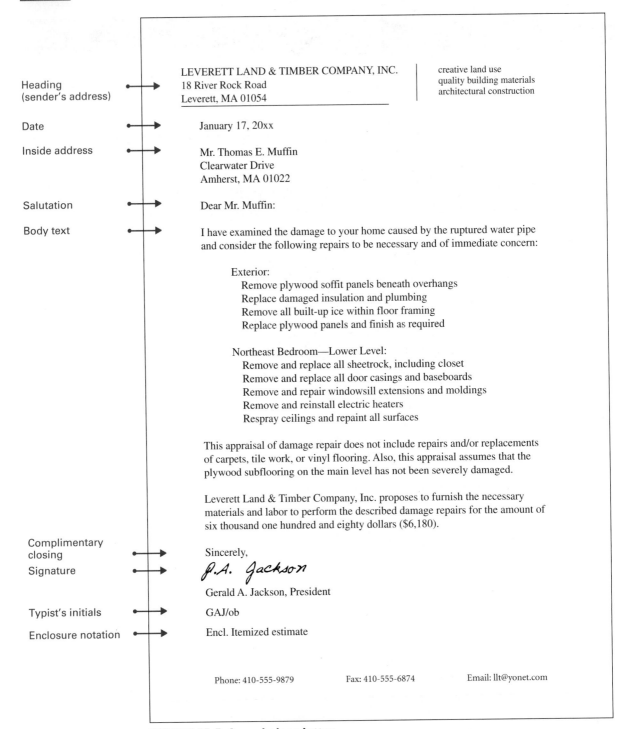

Heading (sender's address) →

LEVERETT LAND & TIMBER COMPANY, INC.
18 River Rock Road
Leverett, MA 01054

creative land use
quality building materials
architectural construction

Date →

January 17, 20xx

Inside address →

Mr. Thomas E. Muffin
Clearwater Drive
Amherst, MA 01022

Salutation →

Dear Mr. Muffin:

Body text →

I have examined the damage to your home caused by the ruptured water pipe and consider the following repairs to be necessary and of immediate concern:

 Exterior:
  Remove plywood soffit panels beneath overhangs
  Replace damaged insulation and plumbing
  Remove all built-up ice within floor framing
  Replace plywood panels and finish as required

 Northeast Bedroom—Lower Level:
  Remove and replace all sheetrock, including closet
  Remove and replace all door casings and baseboards
  Remove and repair windowsill extensions and moldings
  Remove and reinstall electric heaters
  Respray ceilings and repaint all surfaces

This appraisal of damage repair does not include repairs and/or replacements of carpets, tile work, or vinyl flooring. Also, this appraisal assumes that the plywood subflooring on the main level has not been severely damaged.

Leverett Land & Timber Company, Inc. proposes to furnish the necessary materials and labor to perform the described damage repairs for the amount of six thousand one hundred and eighty dollars ($6,180).

Complimentary closing →

Sincerely,

Signature →

P.A. Jackson

Gerald A. Jackson, President

Typist's initials →

GAJ/ob

Enclosure notation →

Encl. Itemized estimate

Phone: 410-555-9879   Fax: 410-555-6874   Email: llt@yonet.com

FIGURE 11.5 A workplace letter

Sender's Address. The sender's address appears at the top of the letter in the form of either a company letterhead or the sender's mailing address. When you use your personal address, omit your name because that will appear below your signature at letter's end. On the first line, include the full street address, and on the next line, include the city, state (abbreviated), country (if applicable), and postal code (zip code or other postal code).

Date. The date always appears immediately below the sender's address. Spell out the month completely.

Inside Address. Double space between the date and the inside address (the address of the recipient). Include the courtesy title ("Mr.," "Ms.," "Dr.") and the full name of the recipient on the first line; the person's job title (if applicable) on the second line; the name of the company (if applicable) on the next line; the full street address on the next line; and the city, state, country (if applicable), and postal code on the last line.

Salutation. Double space between the inside address and the salutation. The salutation includes a greeting (usually "Dear"), followed by a courtesy title and the recipient's last name. If you don't know the person's gender, use the full name ("Dear Sandy Martin:"). In a business letter, always use a colon at the end of the salutation, not a comma.

Use an *attention line* when you write to an organization and do not know your recipient's name but are directing the letter to a specific department or position. Place the attention line flush with the left margin two line spaces (returns) below the inside address ("ATTENTION: Director of Research and Development").

Typically, *subject lines* are used with memos, but if the recipient is not expecting your letter, a subject line can be a good way of catching a busy reader's attention ("SUBJECT: *New patent for hybrid wheat crop*"). Place the subject line below the inside address or attention line. You can italicize the subject to make it more prominent.

Body Text. Double space between the salutation and the body text. The introductory paragraph should get right to the point. The middle paragraph(s) should support the introduction without straying off topic. The concluding paragraph should summarize and call for further action.

Complimentary Closing. Double space between the body text and the complimentary closing. Use a standard, businesslike closing such as "Sincerely," "Respectfully," or "Best regards."

Signature. Type your name four lines beneath the complimentary closing and sign in the space between the complimentary closing and typed name.

Optional Parts. Most company letters will feature a preprinted logo at the very top of the page, providing the name and address of the company along with contact information. You may also need a *typist notation*: If not typed by the author, place the author's capitalized initials first, followed by a slash and the typist's lower case initials. If anything was sent in the same envelope provide an *enclosure notation*: use the abbreviation "Encl." and briefly describe the contents. If anyone is copied on the letter, provide a *copy notation*. Use the abbreviation "cc" followed by a colon and the name of each recipient. Multiple notations would appear in this order: typist, enclosures, and then copy.

Formats for Letters

Block format versus modified block format

The two standard letter formats are *block format* and *modified block format*. Figure 11.6 sketches a block format: all parts of the letter are flush to the left margin. Figure 11.7 sketches a modified block format: all parts of the letter are flush to the left margin except the date, return address, complimentary closing, and signature lines, which align at page center. Many organizations have their own formats. Depending on where you work, some of these parts may appear at different locations on the page.

LETTER TONE

The importance of a letter's tone

✳ **Explore** the **Concept** with the Case Study on Writing Diplomatic Letters at **mytechcommlab**

When you speak with someone face-to-face, you unconsciously modify your statements and facial expressions as you read and listen to the listener's signals: a smile, a frown, a raised eyebrow, a nod, a short vocal expression of agreement or disagreement. In a phone conversation, the person's voice can signal approval, dismay, anger, or confusion. Those cues allow you to modify your comments and vocal tone.

When writing a letter, however, you can easily forget that a flesh-and-blood person will be reacting to what you say—or seem to say. You will receive no visual or auditory clues to alter what you write before you send the letter. As a result, the tone of a letter, like that of a memo, is especially important to get right.

To achieve an appropriate tone, consider the factors discussed below that affect the relationship between sender and recipient. As you read through this section, refer to Figure 11.8, which maintains an appropriate tone in conveying bad news.

Establishing and Maintaining a "You" Perspective

Prioritize the readers' needs, wants, and feelings

A letter displaying a "you" perspective puts the reader's interest and feelings first. To convey a "you" perspective, put yourself in the place of the person who will read your correspondence, and ask yourself how this recipient will react to what you have written. Even a single word or sentence, carelessly chosen or phrased, can offend. Consider the following sentence in a letter to a customer:

| Our record keeping is very efficient and we have looked into it, so this is obviously your error. | Offensive |

This self-centered tone might be appropriate after numerous investigations into the customer's complaint and failed attempts to communicate your company's perspective to the customer, but in your initial correspondence it would be offensive. Page 200 shows a more considerate version. Instead of expressing only the writer's point of view, this second version conveys respect for the reader's viewpoint.

Watch the **Video** on Writing an Audience-Centered Letter at mytechcommlab

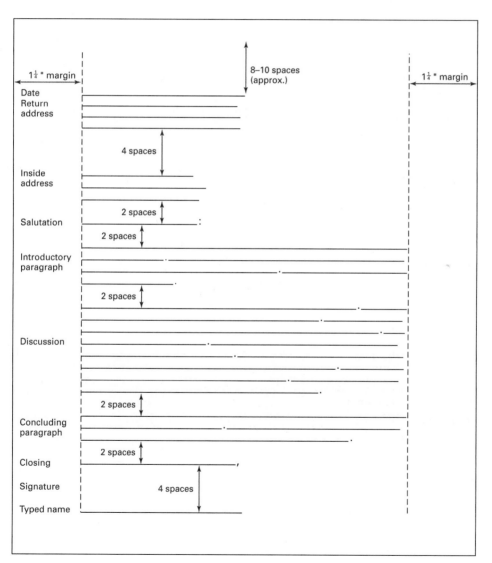

FIGURE 11.6 Block format

Considerate and respectful

> Although my paperwork shows that you were charged correctly, I will investigate this matter immediately by checking my files against our computer records.

The "you" perspective is appropriate not only at the beginning of a letter but also throughout. Do not sign and mail the letter until you are certain that the needs, wants, and feelings of your reader consistently get top billing, even when you simultaneously must assert your own perspective.

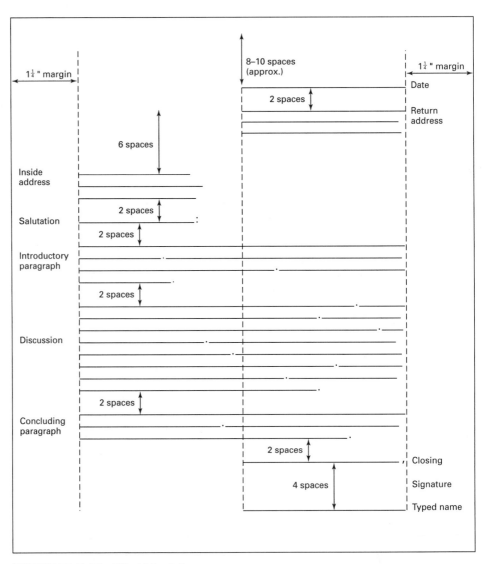

FIGURE 11.7 Modified block format

LEVERETT LAND & TIMBER COMPANY, INC.   creative land use
18 River Rock Road   quality building materials
Leverett, MA 01054   architectural construction

January 17, 20XX

Mr. Thomas E. Shaler
19 Clearwater Drive
Amherst, MA 01022

Dear Mr. Shaler:

Thank you for bringing the matter of the ruptured water pipe to my attention. I was
pleased to hear from you again these months after our firm completed construction
of your living room addition, though I was of course sorry to hear about the water
damage not only to the new construction but to the living room as a whole.

Naturally, I understand your desire to receive compensation for your home's damage,
especially taking into account how recently the extension was completed. In
reviewing the blueprints for the extension, however, I find that the pipes were
state-of-the-art and were fully insulated. In fact, it is the practice of Leverett Land
& Timber not only to use the best materials available but also to exceed piping
insulation requirements by as much as 50 percent. For this reason, we cannot fulfill
your request to replace the piping at no cost and repair the water-damaged areas.

Undoubtedly, your insurance will cover the damage. I suspect that the rupture
was caused by insufficient heating of the living room area during this unusually
cold winter, but homeowner's insurance will cover damages resulting from
cold-ruptured pipes 95 percent of the time.

Our policy is to make repairs at a 20 percent discount in situations like this.
Though the pipe rupture was not our fault, we feel personally close to every
project we do and to every client we serve. Please get in touch if you would like
to discuss this matter further. I would also be happy to speak with your insurance
company if you wish.

Sincerely,

G.A. Jackson

Gerald A. Jackson

Annotations (right margin):
- Establishes "you" perspective immediately
- Takes an indirect approach to bad news by easing into it, and saving the bad news until end of second paragraph
- Speaks clearly and directly to the reader
- Remains polite and tactful, despite delivery of bad news
- Maintains the "you" perspective through to the end

FIGURE 11.8 Appropriate tone in conveying bad news

Being Polite and Tactful

Be courteous and emphasize good will

If you must express criticism, do so in a way that conveys good will and trust in the recipient. Avoid the following type of expression:

Tactless

> I am shocked that your company lacks the standards to design and manufacture an alarm clock that actually works.

Although a company representative would be required to write a polite and thoughtful response to the above complaint, he or she might be inclined to look closely at the clock's warranty, offer only the most basic reimbursement, and not seek the customer's future business via an incentive.

In contrast, a polite and thoughtful letter might yield a full refund, a brand new replacement, or an attractive incentive:

Polite

> Although your clock worked reliably for several months, one of the internal mechanisms recently malfunctioned. I would appreciate your contacting me about an exchange or refund.

Using Plain English

Be professional without being stuffy

Avoid the stuffy, puffed-up phrases some writers think they need to make their communications sound important. Even though a letter is more formal than a memo or an email, plain English can still get your point across. For example, consider the following closing section to an inquiry letter asking for help:

Stuffy

> Humbly thanking you in anticipation of your kind assistance, I remain
>
> Faithfully yours,

The reader of this letter might feel spoken down to, and decide not to respond. However, in this revised version, the reader would likely perceive the writer as a straight-talking equal and be more inclined to follow up:

Clear and direct

> I would greatly appreciate any help you could offer me.
>
> Best wishes,

Here are a few stuffy phrasings, with clearer, more direct translations:

Stuffy, unclear	Clear and direct
As per your request	As you requested
Contingent upon receipt of	As soon as we receive
Due to the fact that	Because

Be natural. Write as you would speak in a classroom or office: professionally and respectfully but clearly and directly.

Considering the Needs of International Readers

In the increasingly global marketplace, you will often find that you need to communicate with readers outside the United States, many who do not speak English as a first language. To insure that your letter is appropriate for an international reader, avoid being overly informal, use plain English, and avoid idiomatic expressions such as "in the ball park" or "under the weather."

Any letter might be read by international readers

Being Direct or Indirect

During your career you will have to write letters that convey bad or unwelcome news. For example, you may have to say no to customers, employees, and job applicants. You may have to make difficult requests, such as asking employees to accept higher medical insurance premiums or seeking an interview with a beleaguered official. You may have to notify consumers or shareholders about accidents or product recalls. You may have to apologize for errors—and so on. In each instance, you will have to decide whether to build your case first (indirect approach) or get right to the point (direct approach).

Determine if the direct or indirect approach is preferable

✳ **Explore the Concept** with the Case Study on Writing Bad News Letters at mytechcommlab

Try to anticipate your readers' reaction. Generally speaking, when you have good news use the direct approach; readers will appreciate your getting right to the point. When presenting bad news you may prefer the indirect approach; by presenting your rationale beforehand you give readers the chance to adjust to the bad news.

When to be direct or indirect

STRATEGIES
for Letters in General

- ▶ **Determine whether the situation calls for a letter, memo, or email.** Use a letter to communicate formally with a client or customer (someone not in your organization).

- ▶ **Use proper letter format and include all the required parts.** Unless your organization has its own guidelines, use block or modified block format and the parts discussed earlier.

- ▶ **Place the reader's needs first.** Always write from the "you" perspective, putting yourself in your reader's place.

- ▶ **Decide on the direct or indirect approach.** Generally speaking, take the direct approach for good news and the indirect approach for bad news.

➡

▶ **Maintain a courteous, professional tone.** A professional tone creates goodwill and is more effective in the long run.

▶ **Avoid stuffy language.** Use plain English, no matter how formal or important the letter. Stuffy language only comes across as phony.

▶ **Keep international readers in mind.** Don't assume that every letter you write is directed at a recipient whose first language is English.

TYPES OF LETTERS

There are many types of business letters. Among the most common types you can expect to write on the job are inquiry letters, claim letters, sales letters, and adjustment letters.

Inquiry Letters

Solicited and unsolicited inquiry letters

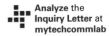 **Analyze** the **Inquiry Letter** at **mytechcommlab**

Inquiry letters ask questions and request a reply. They may be solicited (in response to an advertisement or announcement) or unsolicited (spontaneously written to request some type of information you need for your job). For example, a manager at a computer repair company might write a solicited inquiry to a computer manufacturer that offers free troubleshooting guides for repair specialists. If there has been no such advertised offer, the manager might write an unsolicited inquiry to the same company asking if any troubleshooting information is available.

In a solicited inquiry, be brief and to the point and be sure to reference the advertisement or announcement that prompted you to write. In an unsolicited inquiry, you are asking a busy person to spend the time to read your letter, consider your request, collect the information, and write a response. Therefore, keep your request reasonable and state the purpose clearly and concisely. Apologize for any imposition and express your appreciation. Avoid long, involved inquiries that are unlikely to be answered.

Figure 11.9 is an example of an unsolicited letter requesting information. Research consultant Alan Greene is preparing a report on the feasibility of harnessing solar energy for home heating in Alaska. After learning that a nonprofit research group has been experimenting with solar applications, Alan decides to write for details. Notice how Greene tries to make the respondent's task as easy as possible.

If your questions are too numerous or complex to be answered in print, you might alternately request an interview (assuming the respondent is nearby).

Solar Solutions, Inc.
234 Western Road
Fargo, ND 27116
March 10, 20XX

Rachel Cowans
Director of Energy Systems
The Earth Research Institute
Persham, ME 04619

Dear Ms. Cowans:

As a Research Consultant at Solar Solutions, Inc., I am preparing a report (April 15 deadline) on the feasibility of solar energy for home heating in Arctic regions. ◀━━● States the purpose

While gathering data on home solar heating, I encountered references (in *Scientific American* and elsewhere) to your group's pioneering work in solar energy systems. Would you please allow me to benefit from your experience? Your answers to the following questions would be a great help. ◀━━● Makes a reasonable and courteous request

1. At this stage of development, do you consider active or passive heating more practical? (Please explain briefly.) ◀━━● Presents a list of specific questions

2. Do you expect to surpass the 60 percent limit of heating needs supplied by the active system? If so, at what level of efficiency and how soon?

3. What is the cost of materials for building your active system, per cubic foot of living space?
◀━━● Leaves space for response to each question

4. What metal do you use in collectors, to obtain the highest thermal conductivity at the lowest maintenance costs?

Please record your answers in the spaces provided and return in the enclosed envelope. If an alternative medium is more suitable, here is my contact information: phone: 555-986-6578; fax: 555-986-5432; email: agreene@solarsolutions.com ◀━━● Provides complete contact information

I would be glad to send you a copy of the final document. Thank you in advance for your help. ◀━━● Offers to share findings

Sincerely,

Alan Greene

Alan Greene
Research Consultant

FIGURE 11.9 An unsolicited inquiry letter

STRATEGIES
for Inquiry Letters

▶ **Don't wait until the last minute.** Provide ample time for a response.

▶ **Whenever possible, write to a specific person.** If you need the name, call the organization and ask to whom you should address your inquiry.

▶ **Do your homework to ask the right questions.** A vague request such as "Please send me your data on . . ." is likely to be ignored. Don't ask questions for which the answers are readily available elsewhere.

▶ **Explain who you are and how the information will be used.** If you appear to be from a competing company, your request will likely be ignored. But in other situations, you still need to explain what you plan to do with the requested data.

▶ **Write specific questions that are easy to understand and answer.** If you have multiple questions, put them in a numbered list to increase your chances of getting all the information you want. Consider leaving space for responses below each question.

▶ **Provide contact information.** If you can be reached via phone, email, and fax, provide all your numbers/addresses.

▶ **Include a stamped, self-addressed envelope.** This courteous gesture will increase the likelihood of a response.

▶ **Say thank you and offer to follow up.** Even if you said it at the beginning, say thank you again at the end. Offer to send a copy of the document in which you plan to use the information, if appropriate.

Claim Letters

Routine and arguable claim letters

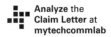 **Analyze** the **Claim Letter** at mytechcommlab

In the workplace, things do not always run smoothly. Sometimes people make mistakes, systems break down, or companies make promises that can't be kept. Claim (or complaint) letters request adjustments for defective goods or poor services, or they complain about unfair treatment or the like. Such letters fall into two categories: *routine claims* and *arguable claims*. Each calls for a different approach. Routine claims typically take a direct approach because the customer's claim is not debatable. Arguable claims present more of a persuasive challenge because they convey unwelcome news and are open to interpretation; arguable claims, therefore, typically take an indirect approach.

Figure 11.10 shows a routine claim letter. Writer Jeffrey Ryder does not ask whether the firm will honor his claim; he assumes that it will, and asks directly how to return his defective skis for repair. Notice that, in place of a salutation, an attention line directs the claim to the appropriate department, while a subject line (and its reemphasis in the first sentence) makes clear the nature of the claim.

Ryder's Ski Shop
Box 2641-A
Pocatello, Idaho 83201
April 13, 20XX

Star Ski Manufacturing Company
P.O. Box 3049
St. Paul, MN 55165

Attention: <u>Consumer Affairs Department</u>

Subject: <u>Delaminated Skis</u>

This winter, four of the pairs of Tornado skis I purchased for rental at my ski shop began to delaminate. I want to take advantage of your lifetime guarantee to have them relaminated. ◄— • States problem and action desired

I purchased the skis via your St. Paul Sales Representative in November 1989. Although I no longer have the sales slip, the registration numbers are P9906, P9961, P9965, and P9978. ◄— • Provides details

I'm aware that you no longer make metal skis, but as I recall, your lifetime guarantee on the skis I bought was a major selling point. Only your company and one other were backing their skis so strongly. ◄— • Explains basis for claim

Would you please let me know how to go about returning my delaminated skis for repair? ◄— • Courteously states desired action

Yours truly,

Jeffrey Ryder

Jeffrey Ryder

FIGURE 11.10 A routine claim letter

Figure 11.11 shows an arguable claim letter. Because the reply may not necessarily be in her favor, writer Sandra Alvarez uses a tactful and reasonable tone and an indirect approach to present her argument. Although she is courteous, she is also somewhat forceful, to reflect her insistence on an acceptable adjustment. For example, the attention line creates an immediate businesslike tone.

Office Systems, Inc.
657 High Street
Tulsa, OK 74120

Fax (302) 655-5551 Phone (302) 655-5550 Email osys@sys.com

January 23, 20XX

Consumer Affairs Department
Hightone Office Supplies
93 Cattle Drive
Houston, Texas 77028

ATTENTION: Ms. Dionne Dubree

Establishes early agreement	Your company has an established reputation as a reliable wholesaler of office supplies. For eight years we have counted on that reliability, but a recent episode has left us annoyed and disappointed.
	On January 29, we ordered 5 cartons of 700 MB "hp" CDs (#A74-866) and 13 cartons of Epson MX 70/80 black cartridges (#A19-556).
Presents facts to support claim	On February 5, the order arrived. But instead of the 700 MB "hp" CDs ordered, we received 650 MB Everlast CDs. And the Epson ribbons were blue, not the black we had ordered. We returned the order the same day.
Offers more support	Also on the 5th, we called John Fitzsimmons at your company to explain our problem. He promised delivery of a corrected order by the 12th. Finally, on the 22nd, we did receive an order—the original incorrect one—with a note claiming that the packages had been water damaged while in our possession.
Includes all relevant information	Our warehouse manager insists the packages were in perfect condition when he released them to the shipper. Because we had the packages only five hours and had
Sticks to the facts	no rain on the 5th, we are certain the damage did not occur here.
Requests a specific adjustment	Responsibility for damages therefore rests with either the shipper or your warehouse staff. What bothers us is our outstanding bill from Hightone ($2,049.50) for the faulty shipment. We insist that the bill be canceled and that we receive a corrected statement. Until this misunderstanding, our transactions with your company were excellent. We hope they can be again.
Stipulates a reasonable response time	We would appreciate having this matter resolved before the end of this month.

Yours truly,

Sandra Alvarez

Sandra Alvarez
Manager, Accounting

FIGURE 11.11 An arguable claim letter

STRATEGIES
for Claim Letters

▶ **Routine claim letters**

- **Use a direct approach.** Describe the request or problem; explain the problem clearly; close courteously, restating the action you request.

- **Be polite and reasonable.** Your goal is not to sound off but to achieve results: a refund, a replacement, or an apology. Press your claim objectively yet firmly by explaining it clearly and by stipulating the reasonable action that will satisfy you. Do not insult the reader or revile the company.

- **Provide enough detail to clarify the basis for your claim.** Explain the specific defect. Identify the faulty item clearly, giving serial and model numbers, and date and place of purchase.

- **Conclude by expressing goodwill and confidence in the company's integrity.** Do not make threats or create animosity.

▶ **Arguable claim letters**

- **Use an indirect approach.** People are more likely to respond favorably *after* reading your explanation. Begin with a neutral statement both parties can agree to—but that also serves as the basis for your request.

- **Once you've established agreement, explain and support your claim.** Include enough information for a fair evaluation: date and place of purchase, order number, dates of previous letters or calls, and background.

- **Conclude by requesting a specific action.** Be polite but assertive in how you make your request.

Sales Letters

Sales letters are written to persuade a current or potential customer to buy a company's product or try its services. Because people are bombarded by sales messages—in magazines, on billboards, on television, on the Internet—your letter must be genuinely persuasive and must get to the point quickly. First, engage the reader immediately with an attention-grabbing statement or an intriguing question. Next, describe clearly and concisely the product or service you offer and explain its appeal. Finally, conclude by requesting immediate action.

In the letter in Figure 11.12, restaurant owner Jimmy Lekkas opens with an attention-grabbing question that is hard to ignore and has universal appeal: good food, for free, right in the neighborhood. He then makes his case by explaining the history of his restaurant (which provides immediate credibility) and offering vivid descriptions of the food. He closes by asking readers to take action by a specific date.

Purpose and format of sales letters

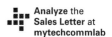 **Analyze** the **Sales Letter** at **mytechcommlab**

Jimmy's Greek Kitchen
24-52 28th Street
Astoria, NY 11102
Phone: (555) 274-5672
Fax: (555) 274-5671
Email: Jimmysgreek@comcast.net
Web site: <www.jimmysgreekkitchen.com>

July 16, 20XX

Adriana Nikolaidis
26-22 30th Street #5
Astoria, NY 11102

Dear Ms. Nikolaidis:

Opens with an attention-grabbing question → Are you in the mood to sample the best Greek food in the neighborhood absolutely free of charge? We at the newly opened Jimmy's Greek Kitchen would like to say "Thank you for having us in your neighborhood" by inviting you to sample a variety of our authentic Greek specialties.

Describes the long history and appeal of the restaurant → If you've heard of or visited the famous Jimmy's in Chicago, you know that our fare has been pleasing Chicago diners for over 40 years. At long last, we have opened a companion restaurant in Astoria, and we are proud to offer you the same high-quality appetizers, entrees, and desserts, prepared to perfection. In fact, I trained our Astoria chef myself.

Further maintains appeal by describing the menu → Ranging from charbroiled meats and grilled seafoods to vegetarian specialties and Greek favorites like tzatziki, pastitsio, and moussaka, Jimmy's is truly the best in town. Please have a look at the enclosed menu to see the full range of tasty foods we offer.

Ends by asking the reader to take action → Please take advantage of this special offer while it lasts. From now until August 31, just bring this letter to Jimmy's and lunch or dinner is on the house. You may choose any appetizer, entree, side order, beverage, and dessert on the menu—all free of charge. We hope that you will not only enjoy the dining experience but will tell others and come back to see us frequently.

Thank you,

Jimmy Lekkas

Jimmy Lekkas

FIGURE 11.12 A sales letter

STRATEGIES
for Sales Letters

- **Begin with a question or other attention-grabbing statement.**

- **Get to the point.** People resist reading long opening passages, especially if the message is unsolicited.

- **Spell out the benefits for the recipients.** Answer this implied question: "What do I stand to gain from this?"

- **Persuade with facts and with appeals to the senses.** Facts (such as the history of your company) appeal to logic. Graphic descriptions (such as the colors of your new cars or the types of food you offer) appeal to a different part of the brain—the emotions. Use both.

- **Tell the truth.** Despite your desire to sell something, it is unethical to lie, distort, exaggerate, or underestimate to make the sale.

- **Close by asking readers to take action.** Either ask for some reasonable action (such as "go to our Web site"), or offer an incentive (such as a free sample) to encourage follow-up.

Adjustment Letters

Adjustment letters are written in response to a claim letter from a customer. Even though most people never make formal complaints or follow up on warranties or product guarantees, companies generally will make a requested adjustment that seems reasonable.

Rather than quibbling over questionable claims, companies usually honor the request and show how much they appreciate the customer, as in Figure 11.13. In this example, writer Jane Duval apologizes graciously for a mistake. She omits an explanation because the error is obvious: someone sent the wrong software. Once the reader has the information and apology, Duval shifts attention to a positive feature: the gift certificate. Note the "you" perspective and friendly tone.

Of course, if a claim is unreasonable or unjustified, the recepient usually will refuse the request. In refusing to grant a refund for a 10-speed bicycle, company representative Anna Jenkins faces a delicate balance (Figure 11.14). On the one hand, she must explain why she cannot grant the customer's request; on the other hand, she must be diplomatic in how she asserts that the customer is mistaken. Although Mrs. Gower may not be pleased by the explanation, it is thorough and reasonable.

Positive and negative adjustment letters

 Analyze the **Positive Adjustment Letter** at mytechcommlab

 Analyze the **Negative Adjustment Letter** at mytechcommlab

**FIGURE 11.13
A positive
adjustment
letter**

**Software Unlimited
421 Fairview Road
Tulsa, Oklahoma 74321**

May 2, 20xx

Mr. James Morris
P.O. Box 176
Little Rock AR 54701

Dear Mr. Morris:

Apologizes
immediately

Your software should arrive by May 15. Sorry for the mixup. We don't make a practice of sending Apple software to PC owners, but we do slip up once in a while.

Offers
compensation

In appreciation for your patience and understanding, I've enclosed a $50 gift certificate. You can give it to a friend or apply it toward your next order. If you order by phone, just give the certificate number, and the operator will credit your account.

Looks toward the
future

Keep your certificate handy because you will be getting our new catalog soon. It features 15 new business and utility programs that you might find useful.

Sincerely,

Jane Duval

Jane Duval
Sales Manager

Encl. Gift Certificate

STRATEGIES
for Adjustment Letters

▶ **If you need to apologize, do so immediately and in active voice.** Don't say "An error was made . . ."; instead, say "We are sorry we made an error . . ."

▶ **Be polite and professional.** Even if you must say no to a request, you can do so respectfully.

▶ **Use passive voice if you want to avoid sounding accusatory.** If your customer made a mistake in assembling the device, you could say "The wrong bolts were used" rather than "You used the wrong bolts."

▶ **If appropriate, offer an incentive.** You can create a lot of goodwill if you reach out with even a small gift certificate or in-store credit.

▶ **Close on a positive note.** Thank the person for writing and for being a customer.

People Power, Inc.

101 Salem Street, Springfield, Illinois 32456

March 8, 20xx

Mrs. Alma Gower
32 Wood Street
Lewiston, IL 32432

Dear Mrs. Gower:

When we advertise the Windspirit as the toughest, most durable ten-speed, we stress it's a racing or cruising bike built to withstand the long, grueling miles of intense competition. The bike is built of the strongest, yet lightest, alloys available, and each part is calibrated to within 1/1000 of an inch. That's why we guarantee the Windspirit against defects resulting from the strain of competitive racing.

The Windspirit, though, is not built to withstand the impact of ramp jumps such as those attempted by your son. The rims and front fork would have to be made from a much thicker gauge alloy, thereby increasing weight and decreasing speed. Since we build racing bikes, such a compromise is unacceptable.

To ensure that buyers are familiar with the Windspirit's limits, in the owner's manual we stress that the bike should be carried over curbings and similar drops because even an eight-inch drop could damage the front rim. Damage from such drops is not considered normal wear and so is not covered by our guarantee.

Since your son appears to be more interested in a bike capable of withstanding the impact of high jumps, you could recoup a large part of the Windspirit's price by advertising it in your local newspaper. Many novice racers would welcome the chance to buy one at a reduced price. Or, if you prefer having it repaired, you could take it to Jamie's Bike Shop, the dealer closest to you.

Yours truly,

Anna Jenkins

Anna Jenkins
Manager, Customer Services

- • Introduction starts off with the facts
- • Writer doesn't accuse; she explains in a friendly tone
- • Refusal is professional, direct, and reasonable
- • Closing is helpful

FIGURE 11.14 A negative adjustment letter

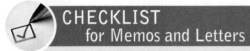

CHECKLIST
for Memos and Letters

MEMO

☐ Does my memo contain all the necessary parts (To, From, Date, Subject, body copy)?

☐ Is the text of my memo clear and direct?

☐ Does my memo follow a standard format, beginning with an introductory paragraph, explaining my points in the body of the memo, then ending with a short conclusion?

☐ Is the tone of my memo professional and polite?

☐ Have I considered whether to take a direct or an indirect approach?

☐ Does my memo focus on one topic?

☐ Is my memo directed at the right people?

LETTER

☐ Does my letter contain all the necessary parts (sender's address, date, inside address, salutation/attention line, body text, closing signature)?

☐ Am I using the block format OR the modified block format?

☐ Is the tone of my letter professional, polite, and appropriately formal?

☐ Have a considered whether to take a direct or an indirect approach?

☐ Have I put my reader's interests first (the "you" perspective)?

☐ If making a difficult request, am I being tactful yet clear about what I want?

☐ Am I writing in clear language?

APPLICATIONS

GENERAL APPLICATIONS

1. Write a memo as the sales director of a company to in-house sales department employees and to sales representatives. Announce and outline a new dress code policy and diplomatically explain why the policy is more strict for the sales reps. Remember to keep an informal but professional tone, format the memo properly, and keep it brief but complete.

2. Write and mail an unsolicited inquiry about the topic you are investigating for an analytical report or research assignment. In your letter you might request brochures, pamphlets, or other informative literature, or you might ask specific questions. Submit a copy of your letter, and the response, to your instructor.

TEAM APPLICATIONS

1. In groups of 2–3, assume that you are co-owners of a condominium complex that has been invaded by carpenter ants. Have a meeting to discuss your plans to find a way that the ants can be eliminated, using an insecticide that is proven to be non-toxic to humans. Ask each team member to write a follow-up memo that summarizes the meeting and recommends next steps for each team member to take. Compare memos and discuss the decisions each person made for how to organize and structure the memo.

2. Working in groups, respond to the following scenario. Appoint one group member to present the letter in class.

> Luke Harrington wants a $1200 refund for four Douglas fir trees that have died since your workers planted them in his yard two years ago. Because you guarantee your transplants for three years, he wants his money returned. After checking Harrington's contract, you recall his problem: you wouldn't guarantee the five Douglas firs he ordered because he wanted them planted in a wet, marshy area, and Douglas firs need well-drained soil. A check of Harrington's lot confirms that four trees planted in the wet area have died of root rot. Write to him, reminding him of the contract and refusing the adjustment. As you did two years ago, suggest that he plant balsam firs in the wet area. Although balsam needles are slightly darker than the Douglas firs', both trees have the shape he wants. The balsams would retain the symmetry of his tree line. Harrington's address: 921 Daisy Lane, Churchill, MO 61516.

GLOBAL APPLICATIONS

1. Is the standard memo format discussed in this chapter a U.S. standard or an international standard? What sorts of memos are typically written in other countries? Interview someone who works in an international business, and write a short memo to your instructor explaining what you learned about memo writing in other countries.

2. Interview a person whose work takes him or her to one or more countries outside the United States. Ask that person to describe the way letters are used for international communication, and whether any special issues involving grammar, forms of address, direct or indirect organizational patterns, or other features make letter writing different when addressing international audiences.

COMPUTER/WEB-BASED APPLICATIONS

1. Word processing programs such as Microsoft Word or Apple Pages offer users a series of templates for writing letters. (Templates are preformatted layouts that can be used to create résumés, memos, letters, and other documents.) Templates can help you get started with the writing; templates can also be a problem, however, because instead of thinking for yourself about the audience, purpose, and appropriate organizational pattern and language usage, you may end up letting the template do the thinking. Look at the various templates available in your word processing program, and make a list of ways in which the template may or may not work for your purposes.

2. Does the shape and layout of a memo influence how it is written? Conduct this small experiment. In teams of 3–4 people, consider a dangerous or inconvenient area or situation on campus (endless cafeteria lines; a poorly lit intersection; slippery stairs; a poorly timed traffic light). Select one of these situations (one that everyone is familiar with), and write a short memo to a decision maker (campus chief of police, head of food service, and so on). Each person should write his or her memo using one of the memo templates from Microsoft Word. Compare the differences.

For additional technical writing resources that will help you master the chapter objectives, go to **www.mytechcommlab.com**.

12 Definitions

LEARNING OBJECTIVES FOR THIS CHAPTER

▸ Research and write clear definitions

▸ Understand the legal, ethical, and societal
  implications of definitions

▸ Use the three types of definitions

▸ Use various methods to expand a definition,
  as the situation requires

▸ Place definitions in your document

LET'S GET STARTED
Definitions

In your college major, you become familiar with technical or specialized terms that don't mean much to people outside the field. Think about a group of readers who don't know much about what you are studying. Without reading this chapter, make a list of five specialized terms or phrases used in your major, and write definitions of these terms or phrases that would be understandable to the readers you have selected. (Do not consult dictionaries or other sources in preparing these definitions.)

Questions to ask about the definitions you wrote as you review the material in this chapter:

▶ Do the definitions all answer the question "What is it?" or "What does it entail?" in a way that will make sense for these readers?

▶ Do the definitions use metaphors, references to history, or other devices that will make it easy for these readers to understand?

▶ Would the definitions benefit from the use of visuals?

At the end of this chapter, read through the definitions you wrote for this Let's Get Started exercise. Compare what you wrote to some of the types of definitions described in this chapter. Share your definitions with a student in class who is not in your major field of study. Revise your definitions based on what your student reader tells you and what you learned in this chapter.

Meaning and importance of definitions

Explore the Concept with the Case Study on Writing Persuasive Definitions at **mytechcommlab**

Definitions explain terms or concepts that are specialized and may be unfamiliar to people who don't have expertise in a particular field. In many cases, a term may have more than one meaning or it may have different meanings in different fields. Consider a word such as *atmosphere*: To a meteorologist, it would refer to the envelope of gases that surrounds a planet ("the Earth's atmosphere"); to a politician or office manager it would typically mean the mood of the country or the workplace ("an atmosphere of high hopes"); to a geologist it would have to do with the weather conditions in a particular area ("the atmosphere of the Hawaiian forests is lush and volcanic"); to a physicist it would stand for a unit of pressure ("a standard atmosphere is 101,325 pascal"); and to a novelist it would be associated with the mood of a novel ("a gothic atmosphere").

As you can see, precision is important, especially in specialized fields, in which field-specific terminology is common and undefined terms may prevent the overall meaning of a technical document from making sense. Engineers talk about *elasticity* or *ductility*; bankers discuss *amortization* or *fiduciary relationships*. In a technical document, these terms must be defined if people both inside and outside of those fields are to understand the meaning of the document as a whole. Imagine if a doctor continually used the words *myocardial infarction* in a patient brochure without ever defining the term. The fact that a myocardial infarction is the medical name for one form of *heart attack* would be lost on patients who might benefit from a clear understanding of the brochure.

Explore the Concept with the Case Study on Writing Simplified Definitions at **mytechcommlab**

AUDIENCE AND PURPOSE OF DEFINITIONS

Definitions make a document usable for an audience by answering one of two questions: "What, exactly, does it entail?" or "What, exactly, is it?" The first question spells out for your audience how they are affected by the item defined. For example, a person buying a new computer needs to understand exactly what "manufacturer's guarantee" or "expandable memory" means in the context of that purchase. The second question spells out for your audience what makes an item, concept, or process unique. For example, an engineering student needs to understand the distinction between *elasticity* and *ductility*. Inside or outside any field, people have to grasp precisely what "makes a thing what it is and distinguishes that thing from all other things" (Corbett 38).

Audience considerations

Explore the Concept with the Activity on Definition Audience at **mytechcommlab**

Consider the purpose of using particular terms in your document by answering the question "Why does my audience need to know it?" The level of technicality you use must match the audience's background and experience. For a group of mechanical engineering students, your definition of a *solenoid*, for example, can be brief and to the point, and you can use highly technical language:

Purpose considerations

> A solenoid is an inductance coil that serves as a tractive electromagnet.

A highly technical version

For general audiences, your definition will require language they can understand:

> A solenoid is a metal coil that converts electrical energy to magnetic energy capable of performing mechanical functions.

A nontechnical version

Unless you are certain that your audience can grasp the exact meaning, always define a term the first time you use it.

LEGAL, ETHICAL, AND SOCIETAL IMPLICATIONS OF DEFINITIONS

Definitions have legal implications

Precise definition is essential, because you (or the organization, if you write a technical document on its behalf) are legally responsible for that document. The more clear and precise your definitions, the more confident both you and your readers can be that they share a mutual understanding of the document's meaning. For example, contracts are detailed (and legally binding) definitions of the specific terms of an agreement. If you lease an apartment or a car, the printed contract will define both the *lessee's* and *lessor's* specific responsibilities. Likewise, an employment contract or employee handbook will spell out responsibilities for both employer and employee. In preparing an employee handbook for your company, you would need to define such terms as *acceptable job performance*, *confidentiality*, *sexual harassment*, and *equal opportunity*.

Definitions have ethical implications

Definitions have ethical requirements, too. For example, the term *acceptable risk* had an ethical impact on January 28, 1986, when the space shuttle *Challenger* exploded 73 seconds after launch, killing all seven crew members aboard. (Two rubber O-ring seals in a booster rocket had failed, allowing hot exhaust gases to escape and igniting the adjacent fuel tank.) Hours earlier—despite vehement objections from the engineers—management had decided that going ahead with the launch was a risk worth taking, under the understood meaning of *acceptable risk*. This definition of *acceptable risk* was based not on the engineering facts but rather on bureaucratic pressure to launch on schedule. In this case, a faulty definition was not only ethically questionable but also cost lives. Agreeing on meaning in such cases rarely is easy, but you are ethically bound to convey an accurate interpretation of the facts as you understand them.

Definitions have societal implications

Clear and accurate definitions help the public understand and evaluate complex technical and social issues. For example, as a first step in understanding the debate over the term *genetic engineering*, we need at least the following basic definition:

> Genetic engineering refers to [an experimental] technique through which genes can be isolated in a laboratory, manipulated, and then inserted stably into another organism. Gene insertion can be accomplished mechanically, chemically, or by using biological vectors such as viruses. (Office of Technology Assessment 20)

Of course, to follow the debate, we would need increasingly detailed information (about specific procedures, risks, benefits, and so on). But the above definition gets us started on the course to a healthy debate, by enabling us to visualize the basic concept and mutually agree on the basic meaning of the term.

TYPES OF DEFINITIONS

Definitions fall into three distinct categories: *parenthetical*, *sentence*, and *expanded* definitions. When you define terms within a document, decide how much detail your audience actually requires in order to grasp your exact meaning: do you need to quickly define a word in parenthesis or in a sentence, or do you need to go into significant detail explaining a complex concept?

Three categories of definitions

Parenthetical Definitions

Often, you can clarify the meaning of a word by using a more familiar synonym or a clarifying phrase in parenthesis immediately after the word. This is known as a parenthetical definition and is used when a definition is relatively simple and doesn't need detailed elaboration, as in these two examples:

When to use parenthetical definitions

> The *leaching field* (sievelike drainage area) requires crushed stone.
>
> The trees on the site are mostly *deciduous* (shedding foliage at season's end).

Parenthetical definitions

On a Web page or online help system, parenthetical definitions can be linked to the main word or phrase rather than placed in parenthesis after the word. A user who clicks on *leaching field*, say, would be taken to a window containing a brief definition.

Sentence Definitions

A slightly longer way to define a phrase is to use the "term-class-features" method to form a sentence definition. Begin by stating the term. Then indicate the broader class to which this item belongs, followed by the features that distinguish it from other items in that general grouping. Use a sentence definition when a concept requires further elaboration than a parenthetical definition could offer. Here are some examples:

When to use sentence definitions

Term	Class	Features
A carburetor	is a mixing device	in gasoline engines that blends air and fuel into a vapor for combustion within the cylinders.
Diabetes	is a metabolic disease	caused by a disorder of the pituitary gland or pancreas and characterized by excessive urination, persistent thirst, and inability to metabolize sugar.
Stress	is an applied force	that strains or deforms a body.

Sentence definitions (term-class-features)

The previous elements may be combined into one or more complete sentences:

A complete sentence definition

> Diabetes is a metabolic disease caused by a disorder of the pituitary gland or pancreas. This disease is characterized by excessive urination, persistent thirst, and inability to metabolize sugar.

Sentence definitions are especially useful if you plan to use a term frequently and need to establish a working definition that you will not need to repeat throughout the document:

A working definition

> Throughout this report, the term *disadvantaged student* will refer to all students who lack adequate funds to pay for on-campus housing, food services, and medical care, but who are able to pay for their coursework and books through scholarships and part time work.

Expanded Definitions

When to use expanded definitions

■ Analyze an Extended Definition at mytechcommlab

Brief definitions such as parenthetical and sentence definitions are fine when your audience requires only a general understanding of a term, or when a term is not particularly complex to define. For example, the parenthetical definition of *leaching field* on page 221 might be enough to prevent reader confusion without providing excessive detail, or the above sentence definition of *disadvantaged student* might be enough to get a simple concept across. However, a document that requires more detail (such as a public health report on groundwater contamination from leaching fields), or a highly complex term, would call for an expanded definition.

Depending on audience and purpose, an expanded definition may be a short paragraph or may extend to several pages. For example, if a device, such as a digital dosimeter (used for measuring radiation exposure), is being introduced for the first time to an audience that needs to understand how this instrument works, your definition would require at least several paragraphs, if not pages.

METHODS FOR EXPANDING DEFINITIONS

◉ Watch the Video on Creating an Expanded Definition at mytechcommlab

An expanded definition can be created in any number of ways as described below. The method or methods you decide to use will depend on the questions you expect the audience will want answered, as illustrated in Figure 12.1.

As you read through the following sections, refer to the following sentence definition of the word *laser*, and consider how each expansion method provides further detail in a different way:

Sentence definition

> A laser is an electronic device that emits a highly concentrated beam of light.

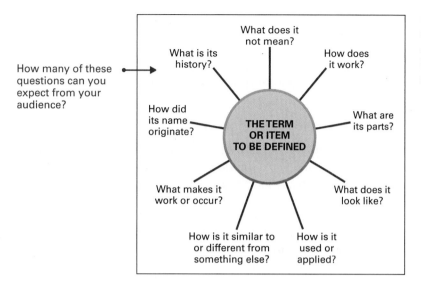

FIGURE 12.1
**Questions to
determine the
best expansion
approach**

FIGURE 12.1 Questions to determine the best expansion approach

Etymology

Sometimes, a word's origin (its development and changing meanings), also known as the word's etymology, can help clarify its meaning. For example, *biometrics* (the statistical analysis of biological data) is a word derived from the Greek *bio*, meaning life, and *metron*, meaning measure. You can use a dictionary to learn the origins of most words. Not all words develop from Greek, Latin, or other roots, however. For example, some terms are acronyms, derived from the first letters or parts of several words. Such is the case with the word *laser* (derived from *light amplification by stimulated emission of radiation*); therefore, to expand the sentence definition of *laser* on page 222, you might phrase your definition as follows:

> The word *laser* is an acronym for *light amplification by stimulated emission of radiation*, and is the name for an electronic device that emits a highly concentrated beam of light.

"How did its name originate?"

History

In some cases, the history of a term, concept, or procedure can be useful in expanding a definition. Specialized dictionaries and encyclopedias are good background sources. You might expand the definition of a laser by describing how the laser was invented:

> The early researchers in fiber optic communications were hampered by two principal difficulties—the lack of a sufficiently intense source of light and the absence of a medium which could transmit this light free from

"What is its history?"

interference and with a minimum signal loss. Lasers emit a narrow beam
of intense light, so their invention in 1960 solved the first problem. The
development of a means to convey this signal was longer in coming, but
scientists succeeded in developing the first communications-grade
optical fiber of almost pure silica glass in 1970. (Stanton 28)

Negation

"What does it not mean?"

Some definitions can be clarified by explaining what the term *does not* mean. For example, the following definition of a laser eliminates any misconceptions an audience might already have about lasers:

A laser is an electronic device that emits a highly concentrated beam
of light. It is used for many beneficial purposes (including corrective
eye and other surgeries), not—as science fiction might tell you—as
a transport medium to other dimensions.

Operating Principle

"How does it work?"

The following example not only defines what a laser is but also shows the operating principle behind it:

Basically, a laser [uses electrical energy to produce] coherent light: light
in which all the waves are in phase with each other, making the light
hotter and more intense. (Gartaganis 23)

Analysis of Parts

"What are its parts?"

Be sure to list all of the parts to create a complete picture; and, if necessary, define the individual parts as well, as in the following expanded definition of a laser:

A laser is an electronic device that emits a highly concentrated beam
of light. To get a better idea of how a laser works, consider its three
main parts:

1. [Lasers require] a source of energy, [such as] electric currents or even
   other lasers.

2. A resonant circuit . . . contains the lasing medium and has one fully
   reflecting end and one partially reflecting end. The medium—which can
   be a solid, liquid, or gas—absorbs the energy and releases it as
   a stream of photons [electromagnetic particles that emit light]. The
   photons . . . vibrate between the fully and partially reflecting ends of
   the resonant circuit, constantly accumulating energy—that is, they are
   amplified. After attaining a prescribed level of energy, the photons can

pass through the partially reflecting surface as a beam of coherent light and encounter the optical elements.

3. Optical elements—lenses, prisms, and mirrors—modify size, shape, and other characteristics of the laser beam and direct it to its target. (Gartaganis 23)

Visuals

Make sure any visual you use is well-labeled. Always introduce and explain your visual and place the visual near your discussion. If the visual is borrowed, credit the source. The following visual accompanies the previous analysis of parts:

"What does it look like?"

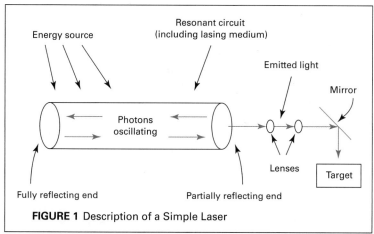

FIGURE 1 Description of a Simple Laser

Source: Gartaganis, Arthur. "Lasers." Occupational Outlook Quarterly Winter 1984: 23.

Comparison and Contrast

By comparing (showing similarities) or contrasting (showing differences) between new information and information your audience already understands, you help build a bridge between what people already know and what they don't. The following example uses both comparison and contrast to expand upon a more basic definition of a laser:

"How is it similar to or different from something else?"

Fiber optics technology results from the superior capacity of light waves to carry a communications signal. Sounds waves, radio waves, and light waves can all carry signals; their capacity increases with their frequency. Voice frequencies carried by telephone operate at 1000 cycles per second, or hertz. Television signals transmit at about 50 million hertz. Light waves, however, operate at frequencies in the hundreds of trillions of hertz. (Stanton 28)

Required Conditions

"What makes it work
or occur?"

In the following example, additional information on optics adds to the definition
of a laser:

> In order to emit a highly concentrated beam of light, the laser must
> absorb energy through the reflecting end of a resonant circuit, amplify
> the photons produced between the reflecting and partially reflecting
> end of the resonant circuit, and release the photons as a beam of light
> via a set of lenses, prisms, and mirrors.

Examples

"How is it
used or applied?"

The following expansion using an example shows how laser light is used in medical treatment:

> Lasers are increasingly used to treat health problems. Thousands
> of eye operations involving cataracts and detached retinas are
> performed every year by ophthalmologists. . . . Dermatologists
> treat skin problems. . . . Gynecologists treat problems of the
> reproductive system, and neurosurgeons even perform brain
> surgery—all using lasers transmitted through optical fibers.
> (Gartaganis 24–25)

USING MULTIPLE EXPANSION METHODS

Use as many
expansion methods
as needed

✳ **Explore** the
Concept with the
Activity on Expanded
Definition Writing
at **mytechcommlab**

Depending on the complexity of what you need to define, you may need to combine multiple expansion methods, as in Figure 12.2.

Like a good essay, this multiparagraph definition is unified and coherent: Each
paragraph is developed around one main idea and logically connected to other
paragraphs. Transitions emphasize the connection between ideas. The level of
technicality connects with the intended audience.

Because this definition deals with a vital community issue, the author uses
multiple methods to ensure that readers have a solid basis for understanding the
situation: A water reservoir is threatened by chemical seepage and depleted by
drought. This definition forms part of the introduction to a report that analyzes
the severity of the problems and explores possible solutions.

To understand the problems, readers first need to know what a water table is,
how it is formed, what conditions affect its level and quality, and how it figures
into town planning decisions. The concepts of *recharge* and *permeability* are vital
to understanding the problem, so these terms are defined parenthetically. This
audience has no interest in geological or hydrological (study of water resources)
theory. They simply need the broadest possible picture.

FIGURE 12.2
An expanded definition

EXPANDED DEFINITION: WATER TABLE

The water table is the level below the earth's surface at which the ground is saturated with water. Figure 1 shows a typical water table that might be found in the East. Wells driven into such a formation will have a water level identical to that of the water table.

→● Sentence definition
→● Example

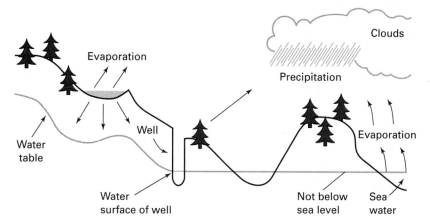

FIGURE 1 A Typical Water Table (Eastern United States)

The world's freshwater supply comes almost entirely as precipitation that originates with the evaporation of sea and lake water. This precipitation falls to earth and follows one of three courses: it may fall directly onto bodies of water, such as rivers or lakes, where it is directly used by humans; it may fall onto land, and either evaporate or run over the ground to the rivers or other bodies of water; or it may fall onto land, be contained, and seep into the earth. The latter precipitation makes up the water table.

● Operating principle

Similar in contour to the earth's surface above it, the water table generally has a level that reflects such features as hills and valleys. Where the water table intersects the ground surface, a stream or pond results.

● Comparison

A water table's level, however, will vary, depending on the rate of recharge (replacement of water). The recharge rate is affected by rainfall or soil permeability (the ease with which water flows through the soil). A water table therefore is never static; rather, it is the surface of a body of water striving to maintain a balance between the forces which deplete it and those which replenish it. In areas of Florida and some western states where the water table is depleted, the earth caves in, leaving sinkholes.

● Operating principle

● Example

The water table's depth below ground is vital in water resources engineering and planning. It determines an area's suitability for wastewater disposal, or a building lot's ability to handle sewage. A high water table could become contaminated by a septic system. Also, bacteria and chemicals seeping into a water table can pollute an entire town's water supply. Another consideration in water table depth is the cost of drilling wells. These conditions obviously affect an industry's or homeowner's decision on where to locate.

● Special conditions and examples

The rising and falling of the water table give an indication of the pumping rate's effect on a water supply (drawn from wells) and of the sufficiency of the recharge rate in meeting demand. This kind of information helps water resources planners decide when new sources of water must be made available.

● Special conditions

PLACEMENT OF DEFINITIONS

Placing printed definitions

Each time readers encounter an unfamiliar term or concept, that item should be defined in the same area on the page or screen. In a printed text, you can place brief definitions in parentheses or in the document's margin, aligned with the terms being defined. Sentence definitions should be part of the running text. Place an expanded definition either near the beginning of a long document or in an appendix (see page 324)—depending on whether the definition is essential to understanding the whole document or serves merely as a reference.

Using hyperlinked definitions

On a Web site, you would use a hypertext link for expanded definitions. Hypertext and the Web are perhaps the best answer yet to making definitions accessible, because readers can click on the item, read about it, and return to their original place on the page. Figure 12.3 demonstrates the effective use of hyperlinked definitions.

FIGURE 12.3
A hyperlinked expanded definition

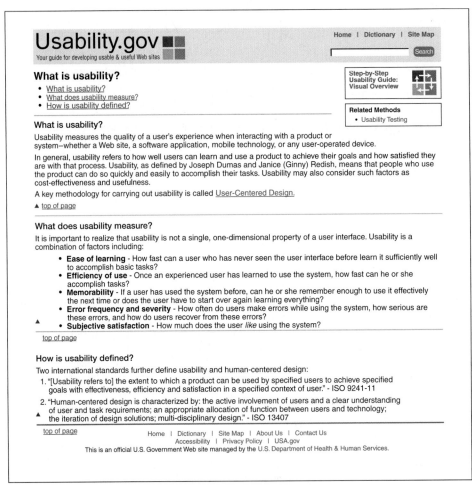

Source: From <usability.gov>

The previous Web page provides a thorough definition of "usability," but the "user-centered designed" material is at a deeper level of detail; rather than disrupting the discussion of "usability," the hyperlink allows readers to jump to it if they wish.

STRATEGIES
for Definitions

▶ **Decide on the level of detail you need.** Definitions vary greatly in length and detail, from a few words in parentheses to a multipage document. How much does this audience need in order to follow your explanation or grasp your point?

▶ **Classify the item precisely.** The narrower your class, the clearer your meaning. *Stress* is classified as an applied force; to say that stress "is what . . ." or "takes place when . . ." fails to denote a specific classification. Diabetes is precisely classified as a *metabolic disease*, not as a *medical term*.

▶ **Differentiate the item accurately.** If the distinguishing features are too broad, they will apply to more than this one item. A definition of *brief* as a "legal document used in court" fails to differentiate briefs from all other legal documents (wills, affidavits, and the like).

▶ **Avoid circular definitions.** Do not repeat, as part of the distinguishing feature, the word you are defining. "Stress is an applied force that places stress on a body" is a circular definition.

▶ **Expand your definition selectively.** Begin with a sentence definition and select the best expansion strategy or combination of expansion strategies for your audience and purpose.

▶ **Use visuals to clarify your meaning.** No matter how clearly you explain, as the saying goes, a picture can be worth a thousand words—even more so when used with readable, accurate writing.

▶ **Know "how much is enough."** Don't insult people's intelligence by giving needless details or spelling out the obvious.

▶ **Consider the legal implications of your definition.** What does an *unsatisfactory job performance* mean in an evaluation of a company employee: that the employee could be fired, required to attend a training program, or given one or more chances to improve (Performance Appraisal 3-4)? Failure to spell out your meaning invites a lawsuit.

▶ **Consider the ethical implications of your definition.** Be sure your definition of a fuzzy or ambiguous term such as *safe levels of exposure, conservative investment,* or *acceptable risk* is based on fair and accurate interpretation of the facts. Consider, for example, a U.S. cigarette company's claim that cigarette smoking in the Czech Republic promoted *fiscal benefits*, defined, in this case, by the fact that smokers die young, thus eliminating pension and health care costs for the elderly!

▶ **Place your definition in an appropriate location.** Allow users to access the definition and then return to the main text with as little disruption as possible.

▶ **Cite your sources, as needed.** See Appendix A.

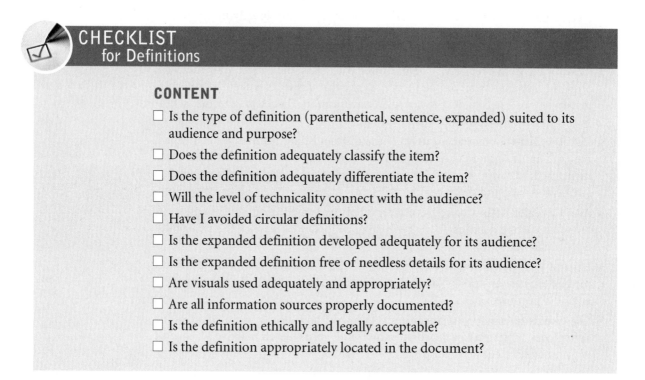

CHECKLIST
for Definitions

CONTENT

☐ Is the type of definition (parenthetical, sentence, expanded) suited to its audience and purpose?

☐ Does the definition adequately classify the item?

☐ Does the definition adequately differentiate the item?

☐ Will the level of technicality connect with the audience?

☐ Have I avoided circular definitions?

☐ Is the expanded definition developed adequately for its audience?

☐ Is the expanded definition free of needless details for its audience?

☐ Are visuals used adequately and appropriately?

☐ Are all information sources properly documented?

☐ Is the definition ethically and legally acceptable?

☐ Is the definition appropriately located in the document?

APPLICATIONS

GENERAL APPLICATION

Choose a situation and an audience, and prepare an expanded definition specifically designed for this audience's level of technical understanding. Use at least four expansion strategies, including at least one visual. In preparing your expanded definition, consult no fewer than four outside references. Cite and document each source as shown in Appendix A.

TEAM APPLICATION

Divide into groups by majors or interests. Appoint one person as group manager. Decide on an item, concept, or process that would require an expanded definition for laypersons; some examples follow:

From computer science: an algorithm, binary coding, or systems analysis

From nursing: a pacemaker, coronary bypass surgery, or natural childbirth

Complete an Audience and Purpose Profile (page 53). Once your group has decided on the appropriate expansion strategies, the group manager will assign each member to work on one or two specific strategies as part of the definition. As a group, edit and incorporate the collected material into an expanded definition, revising as often as needed. The group manager will assign one member to present the definition in class.

GLOBAL APPLICATION

Any definition you write may be read by someone who may not speak English as a first language. Locate an expanded definition on Wikipedia that may be difficult for a non-American or non–native English speaker to understand for one reason or another (use of idioms, use of abbreviations, use of American metaphors such as sports metaphors not used in other countries). Explain how the definition could be reworded so that most readers would be able to understand it.

COMPUTER/WEB-BASED APPLICATION

Convert your expanded definition from the previous General Application into a Web page. Include links to your information sources.

For additional technical writing resources that will help you master the chapter objectives, go to **www.mytechcommlab.com.**

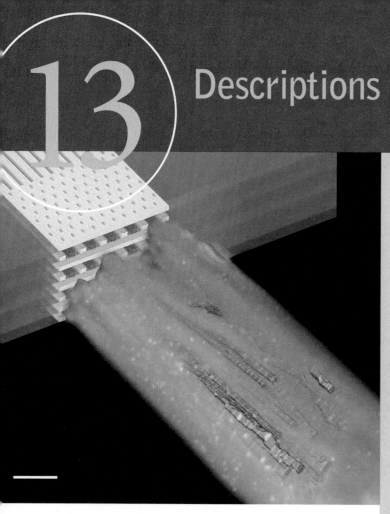

13 Descriptions

LEARNING OBJECTIVES FOR THIS CHAPTER

▸ Understand the importance of descriptions
in workplace communication

▸ Maintain objectivity in descriptions

▸ Differentiate between product descriptions
and process descriptions

▸ Write a long product or process description

▸ Differentiate product or process descriptions
from specifications

▸ Compose a set of specifications

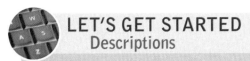

LET'S GET STARTED
Descriptions

Suppose your company has invented a useful gadget—such as a staple remover or paper punch (or some other ordinary but somewhat complex item with multiple parts). Choose such an item—one that you can get your hands on and study, weigh, measure, and possibly take apart. Begin describing this object by assigning descriptive details to it, recording every detail on a piece of paper or in a word-processed document. Weed out the subjective details (such as "pretty" or "ugly") from the objective details (such as—for a staple remover— "prongs," "finger grips," and "spring mechanism"). Then decide on the most logical sequence for describing this item: bottom-to-top, exterior to interior, and so on (such as—for the staple remover—"plastic finger grips" to "hollow metal prongs with pointed tips" to "coil-spring extensor mechanism," and so on). Finally, compose a full description of the product, using visuals as needed.

Questions to ask about the description you wrote as you review the material in this chapter:

▸ Were you able to maintain objectivity when writing your description?

▸ Does your description contain all of the typical elements?

▸ Did you include appropriate visuals?

▸ Did you follow the appropriate descriptive sequence(s) for your purpose and audience?

At the end of this chapter, review your initial Let's Get Started description with your instructor or with a group of students to see how much you might change or modify the description based on what you have learned from the chapter.

Descriptions are essential in workplace writing because, like definitions, they help ensure that readers understand the full meaning of any technical document. Descriptions and definitions often go hand in hand. For example, to return to the *myocardial infarction* example in the previous chapter (page 219), a medical student reading a document about myocardial infarctions would need to know not

Meaning and importance of descriptions

only that a myocardial infarction is a form of heart attack (definition) but also what causes such a heart attack (description).

This chapter will explore how to write technical descriptions from a variety of angles and for a variety of purposes.

AUDIENCE AND PURPOSE OF DESCRIPTIONS

As with any technical document, consider your audience and your document's purpose carefully before writing a description.

Audience considerations

✳ Explore the Concept with the Case Study on Description Writing at mytechcommlab

While definitions answer the questions "What is it?" or "What does it entail?" descriptions often include definitions first, and then must answer the additional questions "What does it look like?" "What are its parts?" "What does it do?" "How does it work?" or "How does it happen?"

Assume that most readers won't be familiar with the product or process you are describing and write your description at the appropriate level of technicality. An audience of medical technicians will easily understand jargon related to their field, but nonexperts will need language with which they are familiar. For example, the sentence "A tumor is a neoplasm" would make sense to most medical professionals; however, for an audience outside that field, you would need to use more accessible language, such as "A tumor is a growth of cells that occurs independently of surrounding tissue and serves no useful function."

Purpose considerations

Consider exactly what you want readers to know and why they need to know it. You may want to write out a purpose statement before you start writing your description, such as: "The purpose of this description is to help plumbing apprentices understand the parts of the Heatwave home water heater and how those parts work together to produce hot water."

OBJECTIVITY IN DESCRIPTIONS

Subjective versus objective descriptions

A description can be mainly *subjective* (based on feeling) or *objective* (based on fact). Subjective descriptions do more than simply convey factual information; subjective descriptions use sensory and judgmental ideas such as "The weather was miserable" or "The room was terribly messy." In contrast, objective descriptions present an impartial view, filtering out personal impressions and focusing on details any viewer could observe ("All day, we had freezing rain and gale-force winds").

Why descriptions should be objective

Except in cases of promotional writing, descriptions should be objective. Pure objectivity is, of course, humanly impossible. Each writer filters the facts and their meaning through his or her own perspective, and therefore chooses what to include and what to omit. Nonetheless, when writing descriptions, you should communicate the facts as we know and understand them. Even positive claims made in promotional writing (for example, "reliable," "rugged") should be based on objective and verifiable evidence.

Being objective does not, however, mean forsaking personal evaluation in cases in which a product or process may be unsafe or unsound. An ethical communicator, in the words of one expert, "is obligated to express her or his opinions of products, as long as these opinions are based on objective and responsible research and observation" (MacKenzie 3).

One way to maintain objectivity when writing descriptions is to always provide details that are visual, not emotional. Ask yourself what any observer would recognize, or what a camera would record. For example, instead of saying, "His office has a depressing atmosphere" (not everyone would agree), say "His office has broken windows looking out on a brick wall, missing floorboards, broken chairs, and a ceiling with chunks of plaster missing."

A second way to maintain objectivity is to use precise and informative language. For instance, specify location and position, exact measurements, weights, and dimensions, instead of using inexact and subjective words like *large*, *long*, and *near*. Be careful, though, not to confuse precise language with overly complicated technical terms or needless jargon. For example, don't say *phlebotomy specimen* instead of *blood*, *thermal attenuation* instead of *insulation*, or *proactive neutralization* instead of *damage control*. General readers prefer nontechnical language—as long as the simpler words do the job.

ELEMENTS OF DESCRIPTIONS

All descriptions should include a forecasting title, an orienting introduction, a logical sequence of topics, clarifying visuals, and a summarizing conclusion.

Title

Promise exactly what the document will deliver—no more nor less. For example, assume you are describing the braking mechanism of a particular brand and type of bicycle: Be clear in your title by referring to the exact brand and type of bicycle, and be limited in your title by indicating that you will only describe the braking mechanism. The title "A Description of a Bicycle" is neither clear nor limited. A better title would be "A Description of the Velo Racing Bicycle's Center-Pull Caliper Braking Mechanism."

Introduction

Descriptions rarely call for a standard topic or thesis statement, because the goal of these documents is to catalog details to help readers visualize the product or process. Any description, however, should begin by telling readers what to look for. If you have written a purpose statement to help you orient yourself prior to writing the description, simply reuse it here. For example, you might say in your introduction,

Descriptions have ethical implications

How to be objective

Analyze the Brief Description at mytechcommlab

Analyze the Long Description at mytechcommlab

Provide a clear and limiting title

Provide an introduction that orients readers

"The goal of this description is to introduce apprentice road construction workers to the parts and function of a standard jackhammer." You may also simply want to start with a brief definition of what you will describe.

Sequence of Topics

Provide a logical and appropriate sequence of topics

For longer descriptions, choose the sequence, or organizational pattern that is most logically consistent with your purpose.

Spatial sequence: How something looks

To describe how something looks, including its parts, use a *spatial* sequence. Follow the same spatial patterns readers would follow when viewing the item. Do you want to move from top to bottom, inside to outside, right to left, or follow some other pattern? For example, when describing a laptop keyboard, you might follow an outside to inside spatial sequence, first describing the "on/off" and mouse keys, and then moving inward to the "page up," "page down," "shift," "tab," "caps lock" and function keys, and finally to the interior number, letter, and punctuation keys.

Functional sequence: How something works

To describe how something works, use a *functional* sequence. Describe the workings (functions) of the device in the order in which the parts function. For example, if you want to describe how a solar home heating system works, proceed from source to outlet: from the heat collectors on the roof through intermediate components to the heating vents.

Chronological sequence: How something is assembled or occurs

To describe how something is assembled, use a *chronological* sequence. Parallel the order in which parts are assembled or stages occur. For example, if you want to describe how to put together a small desk, describe how to put together the main parts first and the smaller, more decorative parts last.

Combine sequencing when appropriate

Spatial, functional, and chronological sequencing are not mutually exclusive; you can combine these sequences as needed. For example, in describing the appearance, use, and assembly of an atomic alarm clock, you would employ a spatial sequence to help users recognize this item, a functional sequence to show how it works, and a chronological sequence to help users assemble it correctly.

Visuals

Provide visuals to enhance and clarify prose descriptions

You can explain a product or process as clearly as you like in words, but a clear diagram or other visual can show your readers the actual look and feel of the product or process. The diagram (top view) in Figure 13.1 adds much-needed visual impact to what would be a complicated prose description. In addition to the picture, labels help users interpret what they are seeing.

Conclusion

Provide a concise conclusion to give readers a sense of finality

A conclusion should be short and to the point and not introduce any new material. It should provide readers with a brief summary of what the description has attempted

FIGURE 13.1
**A descriptive
visual**

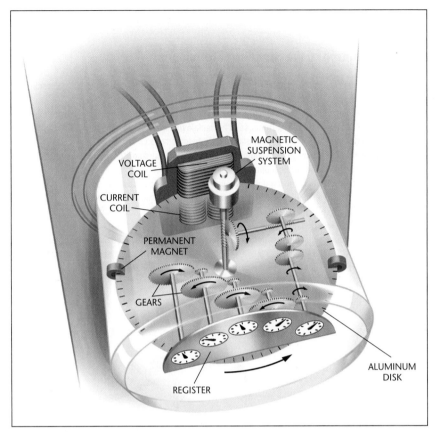

Source: "Description of an Electricity Meter" illustration by George Retseck, from
"Electricity Meters" by Les Rosenau, from *Scientific American*, March 2000,
Volume 108. Reprinted with permission.

to accomplish. It also should give readers a sense that they now understand everything
they need to know about the product or process.

PRODUCT AND PROCESS DESCRIPTIONS

Descriptions generally divide into two broad categories: *product descriptions* and
process descriptions. Anyone learning the parts of a particular device (say, a standard microscope) relies on a product description. Anyone wanting to understand
the steps or stages in a complex event (say, how lightning is produced) relies on a
process description.

    For example, the product description in Figure 13.2 gives beginning paramed-
ical or nursing students a clear image of the overall device (a stethoscope) and its
parts. The process description in Figure 13.3, on the other hand, helps surveyors or
environmentalists understand the steps or stages by which contaminants may be
removed from the soil using the "lasagna process."

Product and process
descriptions

✳ **Explore the Concept**
with the Activity on
Description Writing
at **mytechcommlab**

FIGURE 13.2
**A product
description**

A Description of the Standard Stethoscope

The stethoscope is a listening device that amplifies and transmits body sounds to aid in detecting physical abnormalities.

This instrument has evolved from the original wooden, funnel-shaped instrument invented by a French physician, R. T. Lennaec, in 1819. Because of his female patients' modesty, he found it necessary to develop a device, other than his ear, for auscultation (listening to body sounds).

This description explains to the beginning paramedical or nursing student the structure, assembly, and operating principle of the stethoscope.

The standard stethoscope is roughly 24 inches long and weighs about 5 ounces. The instrument consists of a sensitive sound-detecting and amplifying device whose flat surface is pressed against a bodily area. This amplifying device is attached to rubber and metal tubing that transmits the body sound to a listening device inserted in the ear.

The stethoscope's Y-shaped structure contains seven interlocking pieces: (1) diaphragm contact piece, (2) lower tubing, (3) Y-shaped metal piece, (4) upper tubing, (5) U-shaped metal strip, (6) curved metal tubing, and (7) hollow ear plugs. These parts form a continuous unit (Figure 1).

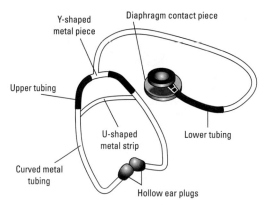

FIGURE 1 Stethoscope with Diaphragm Contact Piece (Front View)

The seven major parts of the stethoscope provide support for the instrument, flexibility of movement for the operator, and ease in use.

In an operating cycle, the diaphragm contact piece, placed against the skin, picks up sound impulses from the body's surface. These impulses cause the plastic diaphragm to vibrate. The amplified vibrations, in turn, are carried through a tube to a dividing point. From here, the amplified sound is carried through two separate but identical series of tubes to hollow ear plugs.

**FIGURE 13.3
A process
description**

The Lasagna Process

Dubbed the "lasagna" process because of its layers, this technology cleans up liquid-borne organic and inorganic contaminants in dense, claylike soils. Initial work is focused on removing chlorinated solvents.

Because clay is not very permeable, it holds ground water and other liquids well. Traditional remediation for this type of site requires that the liquid in the soil (usually ground water) be pumped out. The water brings many of the contaminants with it, then is chemically treated and replaced—a time-consuming and expensive solution.

The lasagna process, on the other hand, allows the soil to be remediated *in situ* (on site) by using low-voltage electric current to move contaminated ground water through treatment zones in the soil. Depending on the characteristics of the individual site, the process can be done in either a vertical or horizontal configuration. (See figure below.)

The first step in the lasagna process is to "fracture" the soil, creating a series of zones. In a vertical configuration, a vertical borehole is drilled and a nozzle inserted; a highly pressurized mixture of water and sand (or another water/ solid mix) is injected into the ground at various depths. The result: a stack of pancake-shaped, permeable zones in the denser, contaminated soil. The top and bottom zones are filled with carbon or graphite so they can conduct electricity. The zones between them are filled with treatment chemicals or microorganisms that will remediate the contaminants.

When electricity is applied to the carbon and graphite zones, they act as electrodes, creating an electric field. Within the field, the materials in the soil migrate toward either the positive or negative electrode. Along with the migrating materials, pollutants are carried into the treatment zones, where they are neutralized or destroyed.

The horizontal configuration works in much the same way, differing only in installation. Because the electrodes and treatment zones extend down from the surface, this configuration does not require the sophisticated hydraulic fracturing techniques that are used in the vertical configuration.

Schematic Diagram of the Lasagna Process

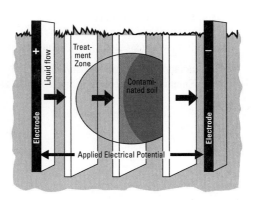

Source: Adapted from Japikse, Catharina. "Lasagna in the making." *EPA Journal*, 20.3 (1990): 27. Print.

A COMPLEX PRODUCT DESCRIPTION

Figure 13.4 is a complex product description. The audience for the standard bumper jack description would be car and truck owners and other general readers. This audience needs to know only the basics—what it is, what it looks like, what its parts are, and how, generally, it works—before actually using the jack safely and effectively.

To plan this description, the writer has created an outline for what details to include and how to organize the material. Also, the writer has determined what *not* to include: for example, basic dimensions and measurements are included, but they are not the precise and detailed dimensions and measurements an engineering audience might require. Finally, the writer has kept the language simple and free of jargon that this audience might not understand.

Writer's outline for planning the complex description →

I. Introduction: General Description
   A. Definition, Function, and Background of the Item
   B. Purpose (and Audience—for classroom only)
   C. Overall Description (with general visuals, if applicable)
   D. Principle of Operation (if applicable)
   E. List of Major Parts

II. Description and Function of Parts
   A. Part One in the Descriptive Sequence
      1. Definition
      2. Shape, dimensions, material (with specific visuals)
      3. Subparts (if applicable)
      4. Function
      5. Relation to adjoining parts
      6. Mode of attachment (if applicable)
   B. Part Two in the Descriptive Sequence (and so on)

III. Summary and Operating Description
   A. Summary (used only in a long, complex description)
   B. Interrelation of Parts
   C. One Complete Operating Cycle

FIGURE 13.4 A complex product description

1

Description of a Standard Bumper Jack

Introduction—General Description

The standard bumper jack is a portable mechanism for raising the front or rear of a car through force applied with a lever. This jack enables even a frail person to lift one corner of a 2-ton automobile.

The jack consists of a molded steel base supporting a free-standing, perpendicular, notched shaft (Figure 1). Attached to the shaft are a leverage mechanism, a bumper catch, and a cylinder for insertion of the jack handle. Except for the main shaft and leverage mechanism, the jack is made to be dismantled. All its parts fit neatly in the car's trunk.

The jack operates on a leverage principle, with the operator's hand traveling 18 inches and the car only $\frac{3}{8}$ of an inch during a normal jacking stroke. Such a device requires many strokes to raise the car off the ground but may prove a lifesaver to a motorist on some deserted road.

Five main parts make up the jack: base, notched shaft, leverage mechanism, bumper catch, and handle.

Description of Parts and Their Function

Base. The rectangular base is a molded steel plate that provides support and a point of insertion for the shaft (Figure 2). The base slopes upward to form a platform containing a 1-inch depression that provides a stabilizing well for the shaft. Stability is increased by a 1-inch cuff around the well. As the base rests on its flat surface, the bottom end of the shaft is inserted into its stabilizing well.

Shaft. The notched shaft is a steel bar (32 inches long) that provides a vertical track for the leverage mechanism. The notches, which hold the mechanism in position on the shaft, face the operator.

The shaft vertically supports the raised automobile, and attached to it is the leverage mechanism, which rests on individual notches.

Leverage Mechanism. The leverage mechanism provides the mechanical advantage needed for the operator to raise the car. It is made to slide up and down the notched shaft. The main body of this pressed-steel mechanism contains two units: one for transferring the leverage and one for holding the bumper catch.

The leverage unit has four major parts: the cylinder, connecting the handle and a pivot point; a lower pawl (a device that fits into the notches to allow forward and prevent backward motion), connected directly to the cylinder; an upper pawl, connected at the pivot point; and an "up-down" lever,

Clear and limiting title tells readers exactly what to expect

Introduction orients readers via a definition

Overall description of the product uses spatial sequencing ("What does it look like?")

Description of parts uses chronological sequencing ("How is it assembled?")

FIGURE 13.4 *(Continued)*

2

Clearly labeled
visual enhances
prose descriptions
of parts

FIGURE 1 A Side View of the Standard Bumper Jack

which applies or releases pressure on the upper pawl by means of a spring
(Figure 1). Moving the cylinder up and down with the handle causes the
alternate release of the pawls, and thus movement up or down the
shaft—depending on the setting of the "up-down" lever. The movement is
transferred by the metal body of the unit to the bumper catch holder.

   The holder consists of a downsloping groove, partially blocked by a wire
spring (Figure 1). The spring is mounted in such a way as to keep the
bumper catch in place during operation.

Bumper Catch. The bumper catch is a 9-inch molded plate that attaches the
leverage mechanism to the bumper and is bent to fit the shape of the
bumper. Its outer $\frac{1}{2}$ inch is bent up to form a lip (Figure 1), which hooks
behind the bumper to hold the catch in place. The two sides of the plate are
bent back 90 degrees to leave a 2-inch bumper contact surface, and a bolt
is riveted between them. This bolt slips into the groove in the leverage
mechanism and provides the attachment between the leverage unit and the
car.

Jack Handle. The jack handle is a steel bar that serves both as lever and
lug bolt (or lugnut) remover. This round bar is 22 inches long, $\frac{5}{8}$ inch in
diameter, and is bent 135 degrees roughly 5 inches from its outer end. Its outer

FIGURE 13.4 *(Continued)*

3

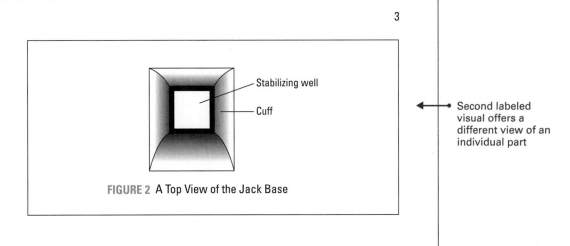

FIGURE 2 A Top View of the Jack Base

Second labeled visual offers a different view of an individual part

end is a socket wrench made to fit the wheel's lug bolts. Its inner end is beveled to form a bladelike point for prying the wheel covers and for insertion into the cylinder on the leverage mechanism.

Conclusion and Operating Description

One quickly assembles the jack by inserting the bottom of the notched shaft into the stabilizing well in the base, the bumper catch into the groove on the leverage mechanism, and the beveled end of the jack handle into the cylinder. The bumper catch is then attached to the bumper, with the lever set in the "up" position.

As the operator exerts an up-down pumping motion on the jack handle, the leverage mechanism gradually climbs the vertical notched shaft until the car's wheel is raised above the ground. When the lever is in the "down" position, the same pumping motion causes the leverage mechanism to descend the shaft.

Conclusion uses functional sequencing ("How does it work?")

FIGURE 13.4 *(Continued)*

A COMPLEX PROCESS DESCRIPTION

Figure 13.5 is an example of a complex process description. The writer has determined that the audience for the description of the acid rain process will be a nontechnical group of readers. The purpose of the document is to explain the threat posed by acid rain. To plan how to describe a scientific process to a nonscientific audience, the writer has created an outline and has used simple, jargon-free language.

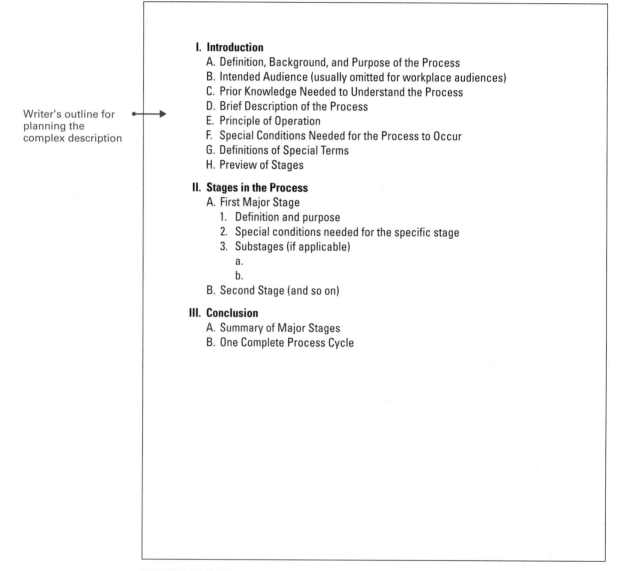

Writer's outline for planning the complex description

I. Introduction
   A. Definition, Background, and Purpose of the Process
   B. Intended Audience (usually omitted for workplace audiences)
   C. Prior Knowledge Needed to Understand the Process
   D. Brief Description of the Process
   E. Principle of Operation
   F. Special Conditions Needed for the Process to Occur
   G. Definitions of Special Terms
   H. Preview of Stages

II. Stages in the Process
   A. First Major Stage
      1. Definition and purpose
      2. Special conditions needed for the specific stage
      3. Substages (if applicable)
         a.
         b.
   B. Second Stage (and so on)

III. Conclusion
   A. Summary of Major Stages
   B. One Complete Process Cycle

FIGURE 13.5 A long process description

1

HOW ACID RAIN DEVELOPS, SPREADS, AND DESTROYS

Introduction
Acid rain is environmentally damaging rainfall that occurs after fossil fuels burn, releasing nitrogen and sulfur oxides into the atmosphere. Acid rain increases the acidity level of waterways because these nitrogen and sulfur oxides combine with the air's normal moisture. The resulting rainfall is far more acidic than normal rainfall. Acid rain is a silent threat because its effects, although slow, are cumulative.

Power plants burning oil or coal are primary causes of acid rain. The burnt fuel is not completely expended, and residue enters the atmosphere. Although this residue contains several potentially toxic elements, sulfur oxide and, to a lesser extent, nitrogen oxide are the major problems: These chemical culprits combine with moisture to form sulfur dioxide and nitric acid, which then rain down to earth.

The Process

HOW ACID RAIN DEVELOPS. Once fossil fuels have been burned, their usefulness ends. It is here that the acid rain problem begins (Figure 1).

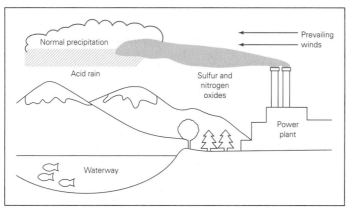

Figure 1 How Acid Rain Develops and Spreads

Acid level is measured by pH readings. The pH scale runs from 0 through 14—a pH of 7 is neutral. (Distilled water has a pH of 7.) Numbers above 7 indicate increasing alkalinity. (Household ammonia has a pH of 11.) Numbers below 7 indicate increasing acidity. Movement in either direction on the scale means multiplying by 10. Lemon juice, with a pH value of 2, is 10 times more acidic than apples, with a pH of 3, and 1,000 times more acidic than carrots, with a pH of 5.

FIGURE 13.5 (Continued)

Annotations (right margin):

- Clear title tells readers what to expect and also promotes awareness of the issue
- Introduction orients readers via a definition
- Initial description of the process uses functional sequencing ("How does it work?"), as does the remainder of the description
- Headers in "The Process" section mirror and follow through on the description's title
- Clearly labeled visual enhances prose description of process
- Additional definition introduces a new concept ("pH")

FIGURE 13.5
(Continued)

2

Because of carbon dioxide (an acid substance) normally present in air, unaffected rainfall has a pH of 5.6. At this time, the pH of precipitation in the northeastern United States and Canada is between 4.5 and 4. In Massachusetts, rain and snowfall have an average pH reading of 4.1. A pH reading below 5 is considered abnormally acidic, and therefore a threat to aquatic populations.

HOW ACID RAIN SPREADS. Although we might expect areas containing power plants to be most severely affected, acid rain can in fact travel thousands of miles from its source. Stack gases escape and drift with the wind currents, traveling great distances before they return to earth as acid rain (Figure 1).

For roughly two to five days after emission, the gases follow the prevailing winds far from the point of origin. About 50 percent of the acid rain that affects Canada originates in the United States; conversely, 15 to 25 percent of U.S. acid rain originates in Canada.

The tendency of stack gases to drift makes acid rain a widespread menace. More than 200 lakes in the Adirondacks, hundreds of miles from any industrial center, cannot support life because their water has become so acidic.

HOW ACID RAIN DESTROYS. Acid rain causes damage wherever it falls. It erodes various types of building rock such as limestone, marble, and mortar. Damage to buildings, houses, monuments, statues, and cars is widespread. Many priceless monuments have already been destroyed, and even trees of some varieties are dying.

More crucial is damage to waterways (Figure 2). Acid rain gradually lowers the pH in lakes and streams, eventually making a waterway so acidic that it dies. In areas with natural acid-buffering elements such as limestone, the dilute acid has less effect. The northeastern United States and Canada, however, lack this natural protection, and so are most vulnerable.

Second labeled
visual provides
graphic illustration
of the process

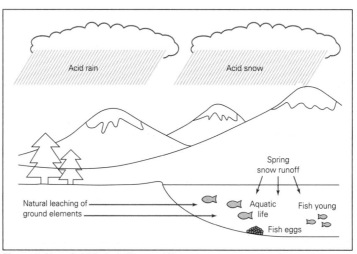

Figure 2 How Acid Rain Infiltrates Waterways

FIGURE 13.5
(Continued)

3

The pH level in an affected waterway drops so low that some species cease to reproduce. A pH of 5.1 to 5.4 means that entire fisheries are threatened: once a waterway reaches a pH of 4.5, fish reproduction ceases.

In the northeastern United States and Canada, the acidity problem is compounded by the runoff from acid snow. During winter, acid snow sits with little melting, so that by spring thaw, the acid released is greatly concentrated. Aluminum and other heavy metals normally present in soil are also released by acid rain and runoff. These concentrated toxins leach into waterways, affecting fish in all stages of development.

Summary

Acid rain develops from nitrogen and sulfur oxides emitted by the burning of fossil fuels. In the atmosphere, these oxides combine with ozone and water to form precipitation with a low pH. This acid precipitation returns to earth miles from its source, damaging waterways that lack natural buffering agents. The northeastern United States and Canada are the most severely affected areas in North America.

Conclusion summarizes the process and implicitly solicits audience support

STRATEGIES
for Descriptions

▶ **Take a look at the product or process.** Study your subject. For a product description, get your hands on the item if you can; weigh it, measure it, take it apart. For a process description, observe the process yourself, if possible.

▶ **Analyze your audience.** Determine your primary and secondary audiences. Then ask yourself exactly what your audience needs to know: "What does it look like?" "What are its parts?" "What does it do?" "How does it work?" or "How does it happen?" Decide upon the appropriate level of technicality for your audience.

▶ **Analyze your purpose.** Ask yourself why your audience needs your description.

▶ **Maintain objectivity.** Think in terms of visual (not emotional) details and specific language when describing location, measurements, weights, and dimensions.

▶ **Be concise.** Provide only what your audience needs.

▶ **Include all necessary parts.** Include a clear and limiting title, an orienting introduction, the appropriate sequence of topics (spatial, functional, chronological—or a combination), and a conclusion that brings readers full circle.

▶ **Incorporate visuals.** Enhance your verbal description using visuals, particularly if the product or process is too complicated to describe only in words.

SPECIFICATIONS

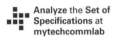

Specifications (or "specs") are a type of description used by professionals. Specifications build on definitions and descriptions by asking the question "How is this process or procedure performed according to regulations?" Airplanes, bridges, computer software, medical procedures, and nearly all modern products and processes are produced according to specifications. The minimum standards are identified; then, the specific methods or materials for meeting those standards are proposed, reviewed, and revised until they are approved. Specifications are vital because they prescribe standards for consistency, quality, and safety.

Specifications are important when everyone in your audience needs to understand and agree on what is to be done and how it is to be done. In other words, specifications ensure consistency, helping prevent misunderstandings that may lead to errors, slowdowns, or even lawsuits. For example, Figure 13.6 shows partial specifications drawn up by an architect designing a medical clinic (these specs are for the exterior of the building only; additional specs would be written for the interior). These specifications help ensure that contractors, architects, landscapers, and others have a consistent master plan regarding parts, materials, and designs that everyone can interpret identically.

Specifications describe features such as methods for manufacturing, building, or installing a product; materials and equipment used; and size, shape, and weight. Professionals must therefore carefully consider the quality of the product they produce. They must ask themselves "Does this product exceed or at the very least meet governmental standards?" "How do the standards compare with those of others in the field?" and "How will our standards be perceived by our customers?" In the medical clinic specifications (Figure 13.6) for example, the quality of materials must not only meet government regulations but also the medical profession's requirements for quality. As a result, those specifications call for a reinforced foundation, exterior, and roof; high-quality insulated windows; and a relaxing landscape that will appeal to both highly stressed medical staff and patients.

Perhaps most important, specifications are always written with public safety in mind. For example, the U.S. Department of Energy (DOE) issues specifications that prescribe minimum design requirements for the shipping containers (or casks) used to transport (via rail or road) spent nuclear fuel to permanent storage facilities. In the private sector, any product that fails to meet federal or industry specifications may provide grounds for a lawsuit.

When injury or death results (as in a bridge collapse or an airline accident), a product will be inspected to be sure it was designed and maintained according to the appropriate specifications. If not, the contractor, manufacturer, or supplier may be liable. The architectural specifications in Figure 13.6, for instance, must meet government standards for building safety as well as the medical profession's standards for a building in which patient safety is paramount.

FIGURE 13.6
**Specifications
to ensure
consistency,
quality, and
safety**

**Ruger, Filstone, and Grant
Architects**

SPECIFICATIONS FOR THE POWNAL CLINIC BUILDING

Foundation

footings: 8" x 16" concrete (load-bearing capacity: 3,000 lbs. per sq. in.)
frost walls: 8" x 4' @ 3,000 psi
slab: 4" @ 3,000 psi, reinforced with wire mesh over vapor barrier

Exterior Walls

frame: eastern pine #2 timber frame with exterior partitions set inside posts
exterior partitions: 2" x 4" kiln-dried spruce set at 16" on center
sheathing: 1/4" exterior-grade plywood
siding: #1 red cedar with a 1/2" x 6' bevel
trim: finished pine boards ranging from 1" x 4" to 1" x 10"
painting: 2 coats of Clear Wood Finish on siding; trim primed and finished
with one coat of bone white, oil base paint

Roof System

framing: 2" x 12" kiln-dried spruce set at 24" on center
sheathing: 5/8" exterior-grade plywood
finish: 240 Celotex 20-year fiberglass shingles over #15 impregnated felt
roofing paper
flashing: copper

Windows

Anderson casement and fixed-over-awning models, with white exterior
cladding, insulating glass and screens, and wood interior frames

Landscape

driveway: gravel base, with 3" traprock surface
walks: timber defined, with traprock surface
cleared areas: to be rough graded and covered with wood chips
plantings: 10 assorted lawn plants along the road side of the building

Audience for specifications

Specifications may be written for a wide range of readers, including customers, designers, contractors, suppliers, engineers, programmers, and inspectors. If your audience consists primarily of technical experts (such as architects) you can use specialized language and brief explanations. But if your audience is mixed, you may need to include more detail, or refer readers to other sources of information, such as a glossary, appendix (see page 328), or Web site.

STRATEGIES
for Specifications

▸ **Analyze your audience.** Determine who will be reading the specs.

▸ **Know the minimum governmental and industry standards.** If your product is for specific customers, also consider the standards they will expect you to meet.

▸ **Keep consistency, quality, and safety at the forefront.** Specifications fulfill all three purposes. Everyone who reads the document needs to be "on the same page" (consistency); the product you describe must meet minimal quality requirements; and it must also meet safety requirements.

▸ **Use a standard format when applicable.** If your organization uses a standard format for specifications, follow that format.

▸ **Include a brief introduction or descriptive title.** Include some kind of overview, be it a one- or two-sentence introduction, a brief summary, or an abstract (see Chapter 15 for more on summaries and abstracts). For an audience completely familiar with the material, a clear and descriptive title will suffice.

▸ **List component parts or materials.** List all the parts or materials your readers will need to know about. Group items into categories if needed.

▸ **Refer to other documents or specs, as needed.** Often one set of specifications will refer to another set, or to government or industry standards. If your specifications are online, link to other specifications you refer to.

▸ **Use a consistent terminology.** Use the same terms for the same parts or materials throughout your specifications. If you refer to an "ergonomic adapter" in one section, do not substitute "iMac mouse adapter" in a later section.

▸ **Include retrieval aids.** Especially in longer specifications, some readers may be interested in only one portion. For example, someone working on a subset of a larger project may want to look up technical details for his or her part of the project only. Use clear headings and a table of contents.

▸ **Keep it simple.** People look at specifications because they want quick access to items, parts, technical protocols, and so on. If you can, limit your specs to short lists, using longer prose passages only as necessary.

▸ **Check your use of technical terms.** Use terms that are standard for the field.

CHECKLIST
for Descriptions and Specifications

PRODUCT OR PROCESS DESCRIPTIONS

- ☐ Have I studied the product or process to get a clear view of how it looks or what it does?
- ☐ Have I recorded the details of the product or process objectively?
- ☐ Have I written a clear purpose statement upon which to base my description?
- ☐ Does the title promise exactly what the description delivers?
- ☐ Have I provided an introduction based on my purpose statement (and a definition, if necessary)?
- ☐ Have I written the description using a spatial, functional, or chronological sequence, or a combination of sequences?
- ☐ Are relationships among parts or stages clearly explained?
- ☐ Do visuals appear whenever they can provide clarification?
- ☐ Have I provided a conclusion to bring readers full circle?
- ☐ Is the use of technical terminology appropriate for this audience?

SPECIFICATIONS

- ☐ Are the specifications appropriately detailed for the audience?
- ☐ Do the specifications meet the requirements for consistency, quality, and safety?
- ☐ Do the specifications adhere to prescribed standards?
- ☐ Do the specifications follow a standard format, if applicable?
- ☐ Have I included a brief introduction or descriptive title?
- ☐ Have I listed the component parts or materials?
- ☐ Are other specifications or documents referred to, if needed?
- ☐ Is my terminology consistent?
- ☐ Are the specifications easy to navigate, with clear headings and other retrieval aids?
- ☐ Do I provide short lists instead of long prose passages wherever possible?
- ☐ Are technical terms standard for the field?

APPLICATIONS

GENERAL APPLICATIONS

1. Choose a product requiring a description. Identify the audience and purpose, and prepare a description for this audience's level of technical understanding. As you prepare your description, refer to the Strategies on page 247. Be sure to include a clear and limiting title; an orienting introduction; a spatial, functional, or chronological sequence of topics; at least one visual; and a conclusion. Also remain as objective as possible.

2. Select a specialized process that you understand well and that has several distinct steps. Begin by analyzing your audience and purpose. Using the process description on page 245 as a model, explain this process to classmates who are unfamiliar with it.

3. The bumper-jack description in this chapter is aimed toward a general audience. Evaluate its effectiveness for this audience. In one or two paragraphs, discuss your evaluation and suggest revisions.

4. How do specifications function in your workplace or home? Find one example of specifications used in your home or workplace and analyze it in terms of its usability. Are the specifications written for consistency, quality, and safety? How? What could the writers have done to improve the usability of this document?

TEAM APPLICATIONS

1. Divide into groups. Assume your group works in the product development division of a diversified manufacturing company. Your division has just thought of an idea for an inexpensive consumer item with a potentially vast market (choose a simple mechanism, such as nail clippers or a stapler). Your group's assignment is to prepare three descriptions of this invention:

   a. one for company executives who will decide whether to produce and market the item

   b. one for the engineers, machinists, and so on, who will design and manufacture the item

   c. one for the customers who might purchase and use the item

   Before writing for each audience, complete an Audience and Purpose Profile sheet (page 53). Appoint a group manager, who will assign tasks to members (visuals, typing, etc.). When the descriptions are prepared, the group manager will appoint one member to present the documents and explain their differences in class.

2. Select a specialized process you understand well or which you can learn about quickly by searching the Web (e.g., how gum disease develops, how an earthquake

occurs, how steel is made, how a computer compiles and executes a program). Write a brief description of the process, incorporating at least one visual. Exchange your description with a classmate. Study your classmate's description for 15 minutes and then write the description in your own words. Now, evaluate your classmate's version of your original description. Does it show that your description was understood? If not, why not? Discuss your conclusions in a memo to your instructor, submitted with all samples. Be sure to document your information sources.

3. Assume your group is an architectural firm designing buildings at your college. Develop a set of specifications for duplicating the interior of the classroom in which this course is held. Focus only on materials, dimensions, and equipment (whiteboard, desk, etc.), and use visuals as appropriate. Your audience includes the firm that will construct the classroom, teachers, and school administrators. Use the same format as in Figure 13.6, or design a better one. Appoint one member to present the completed specifications in class. Compare versions from each group for accuracy and clarity.

GLOBAL APPLICATION

Descriptions, especially those for nonspecialized or nontechnical audiences, are often written by comparing the item being described to an item that is already familiar to readers. For instance, the human heart is often described as a pump and compared to a pump people already know about (the pump on a swimming pool or a car's water pump). While descriptions based on these types of comparisons can be useful, they can also be problematic if your readers are from different countries and cultures. For instance, if you describe the human heart in relation to the pump on a swimming pool, people from countries or parts of the U.S. that don't have pools would not be able to understand the comparison. Working with 2–3 other students, pick an item for which you'd like to write a description that will be distributed both within the U.S. and to at least one other country. Discuss whether or not to use a comparison and how you would decide which comparisons to use.

COMPUTER/WEB-BASED APPLICATION

Use the Internet to search for a description of a product or process that is related to your field of study. Look for places where the description might be confusing for general readers, and rewrite the description for their understanding.

For additional technical writing resources that will help you master the chapter objectives, go to **www.mytechcommlab.com**.

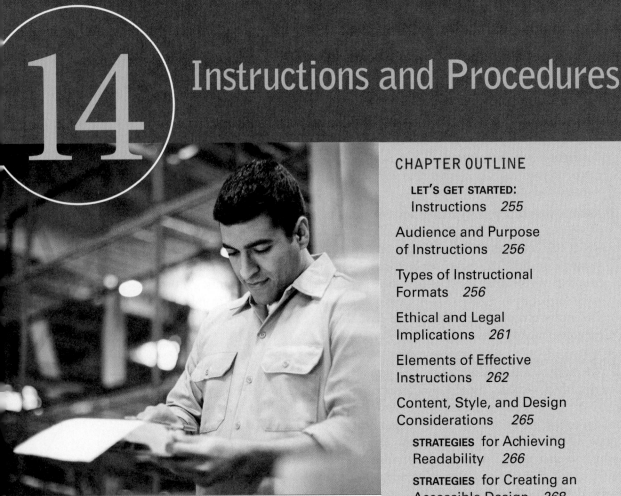

14 Instructions and Procedures

LEARNING OBJECTIVES FOR THIS CHAPTER

- ▶ Identify various types of instructions and their uses

- ▶ Understand the ethical and legal implications of instructions

- ▶ Understand the components of instruction

- ▶ Determine the level of detail and technicality necessary for a given set of instructions

- ▶ Write instructions with a readable style and accessible design

- ▶ Understand the components of procedures

- ▶ Write a set of procedures

- ▶ Test instructions and procedures for usability

LET'S GET STARTED
Instructions

Almost everyone writes instructions. Think about the last time someone asked you how to get to your apartment or house. You may have told them to look it up on Google maps, but you probably also gave them some simple step-by-step instructions ("Get off at Exit 12. Turn left. Go about 1/2 mile. . . ."). Before reading the material in this chapter, write instructions that tell a new student how to get from your classroom to the student union (or to a good pizza place, or similar).

Questions to ask about the instructions you wrote as you review the material in this chapter:

▶ Did I provide enough of an introduction?

▶ Are steps listed in order?

▶ Are the steps visually easy to follow?

▶ Am I using imperative verb forms?

▶ Am I providing enough detail, or too much?

At the end of this chapter, review your initial Let's Get Started instructions with your instructor or with a group of students to see how much you might change or modify the instructions based on what you have learned from the chapter.

Instructions spell out the steps required for completing a task or series of tasks (for example, installing printer software on your hard drive or operating an electron microscope). The audience for a set of instructions might be someone who doesn't know how to perform the task or someone who has performed the task but can't remember how or wants to perform it more effectively. In any case, well-written and carefully designed instructions enable users to get the job done safely and efficiently.

> Definition of instructions
>
> ⊙ **Watch** the Video on Creating a Set of Instructions at **mytechcommlab**

Procedures, a special type of instructions, serve as official guidelines for people who typically are already familiar with a given task (say, firefighters who are evacuating a high-rise building). Procedures ensure that all members of a group coordinate their activities when performing a task. More so than instructions, procedures may need to be reviewed and approved by an official body of

> Definition of procedures

some sort. For example, official surgical procedures may need to be approved by a hospital's safety and ethics board.

Instructions and procedures can be written and designed in a wide variety of formats, from brochures and print materials to PDFs available on the Internet to instructions that come on a CD with a product. The format should be chosen based on the people who will be using the material and the environment where the material will be used. For example, instructions for connecting a battery charger to your car's battery should not be provided on a CD, since most people will not have a laptop computer handy while performing this task. Instead, these instructions should be printed directly on the charger itself, with a longer brochure (containing safety information) included in the box.

This chapter will first explore various aspects of instructions, followed by procedures.

AUDIENCE AND PURPOSE OF INSTRUCTIONS

Before writing instructions, find out how much your readers already know about the task. For instance, if you are writing for technicians who have done a similar task with a different piece of equipment, you may not need as much detail or context. If on the other hand, you are writing for a general audience, such as consumers who are trying to assemble a new stereo cabinet or use a new Bluetooth headset, you will need more details but in a less technical presentation. If you have a mixed audience (some experienced users, some new users), you will need a layered approach, offering a "quick start up" document for those in the know and a more comprehensive user guide for the new users.

Readers across the globe, some who may not speak English as a first language, might use your instructions. Therefore, write in a straightforward style with plenty of visuals, and remain sensitive to cultural differences.

The purpose of instructions is simply to help users perform a task or series of tasks. As you write, keep the following questions in mind: "How is the task done?" "What materials are needed in order to complete the task?" "In which order should the steps in the task be completed?" "What could go wrong?" and "Are any safety issues involved?" Ask yourself if the primary purpose is to allow users to complete the task quickly (as when people are trying to assemble a new stereo cabinet and don't want to take all day), or to complete the task incrementally and over a longer period (as when people are using a kit to test for radon in their homes).

TYPES OF INSTRUCTIONAL FORMATS

As discussed above, instructions and procedures alike come in many formats. The most common formats for instructions are instructional brochures, user manuals, quick reference cards, hyperlinked instructions, and computer instructions.

Instructional Brochures

Instructional brochures can be posted, handed out, mailed, put on a Web site, or otherwise distributed to a broad audience. Typically, brochures contain both text and visuals, which helps increase the audience appeal. Figure 14.1 shows an instructional brochure. Notice its user-friendly design: In addition to the cartoon illustration at the top, which immediately catches a reader's attention, clear visuals reinforce each main section ("Clean," "Separate," "Cook," and "Chill"). Each main section also begins with an action verb, includes a brief introduction, and uses bulleted lists (which also use action verbs) to break up the text into easy-to-digest chunks. Finally, a Web address at the end points readers to further information.

Features of effective instructional brochures

✴ **Explore the Concept** with the Case Study on Pictorial and Textual Instructions at **mytechcommlab**

BAC (foodborne bacteria) could make you and those you care about sick. In fact, even though you can't see BAC—or smell him, or feel him—he and millions more like him may have already invaded the food you eat. But you have the power to *Fight BAC!*®.

Foodborne illness can strike anyone. Some people are at a higher risk for developing foodborne illness, including pregnant women, young children, older adults and people with weakened immune systems. For these people the following four simple steps are critically important:

 CLEAN: *Wash hands and surfaces often*

Bacteria can be spread throughout the kitchen and get onto hands, cutting boards, utensils, counter tops and food. To *Fight BAC!*®, always:

- Wash your hands with warm water and soap for at least 20 seconds before and after handling food and after using the bathroom, changing diapers and handling pets.
- Wash your cutting boards, dishes, utensils and counter tops with hot soapy water after preparing each food item and before you go on to the next food.
- Consider using paper towels to clean up kitchen surfaces. If you use cloth towels wash them often in the hot cycle of your washing machine.
- Rinse fresh fruits and vegetables under running tap water, including those with skins and rinds that are not eaten.
- Rub firm-skin fruits and vegetables under running tap water or scrub with a clean vegetable brush while rinsing with running tap water.

 SEPARATE: *Don't cross-contaminate*

Cross-contamination is how bacteria can be spread. When handling raw meat, poultry, seafood and eggs, keep these foods and their juices away from ready-to-eat foods. Always start with a clean scene—wash hands with warm water and soap, and wash cutting boards, dishes, countertops and utensils with hot water and soap.

- Separate raw meat, poultry, seafood and eggs from other foods in your grocery shopping cart, grocery bags and in your refrigerator.
- Use one cutting board for fresh produce and a separate one for raw meat, poultry and seafood.
- Never place cooked food on a plate that previously held raw meat, poultry, seafood or eggs.

 COOK: *Cook to safe temperatures*

Food is safely cooked when it reaches a high enough internal temperature to kill the harmful bacteria that cause illness. Refer to the chart on the back of this brochure for the proper internal temperatures.

- Use a food thermometer to measure the internal temperature of cooked foods. Make sure that meat, poultry, egg dishes, casseroles and other foods are cooked to the internal temperature shown in the chart on the back of this brochure.
- Cook ground meat or ground poultry until it reaches a safe internal temperature. Color is not a reliable indicator of doneness.
- Cook eggs until the yolk and white are firm. Only use recipes in which eggs are cooked or heated thoroughly.
- When cooking in a microwave oven, cover food, stir and rotate for even cooking. Food is done when it reaches

the safe internal temperature as measured with a food thermometer.

- Bring sauces, soups and gravy to a boil when reheating.

 CHILL: *Refrigerate promptly*

Refrigerate foods quickly because cold temperatures slow the growth of harmful bacteria. Do not over-stuff the refrigerator. Cold air must circulate to help keep food safe. Keeping a constant refrigerator temperature of 40°F or below is one of the most effective ways to reduce the risk of foodborne illness. Use an appliance thermometer to be sure the temperature is consistently 40°F or below. The freezer temperature should be 0°F or below.

- Refrigerate or freeze meat, poultry, eggs and other perishables as soon as you get them home from the store.
- Never let raw meat, poultry, eggs, cooked food or cut fresh fruits or vegetables sit at room temperature more than two hours before putting them in the refrigerator or freezer (one hour when the temperature is above 90°F).
- Never defrost food at room temperature. Food must be kept at a safe temperature during thawing. There are three safe ways to defrost food: in the refrigerator, in cold water, and in the microwave. Food thawed in cold water or in the microwave should be cooked immediately.
- Always marinate food in the refrigerator.
- Divide large amounts of leftovers into shallow containers for quicker cooling in the refrigerator.
- Use or discard refrigerated food on a regular basis. Check USDA cold storage information at **www.fightbac.org** for optimum storage times.

FIGURE 14.1 An instructional brochure

Source: "Four Simple Steps to Food Safety" from *Fight BAC!* Copyright © 2011 by the Partnership for Food Safety Education. Reprinted with permission.

User Manuals

User manuals tend to be the most comprehensive form of instructions: Manuals often contain instructions for using a product, along with descriptions and specifications, warnings, maintenance and troubleshooting advice, and any other information the reader is likely to need. For complex products (for example, a spreadsheet program), the user manual can be a sizable book. Given the cost of printing and distributing such a large book and keeping print material current, companies are increasingly providing smaller ("Getting Started") manuals that contain the basic operating tips and then placing the more lengthy information on a Web site. In some cases (for legal or other reasons), full-scale user manuals are still being produced, but the trend is toward smaller documents.

Figure 14.2 illustrates an overview and table of contents for a photocopier user manual. Although most people will gravitate directly to the section on making copies, the other sections are available for reference in case of special needs (two-sided copies) or problems (misfeed removal). Note how this manual provides basic information first, followed by more technical information, with specifications at the very end.

FIGURE 14.2
An overview and table of contents from a user manual

Source: Introduction and Table of Contents from the *Sharp Compact Copier Operation Manual.* Reprinted with permission.

Quick Reference Materials

Quick reference materials are a form of instructions typically written and designed to fit on a single sheet of paper, a small or wallet-sized card, or a Web page. The instructions focus on the basic steps for users who only want enough information to perform a specific task rapidly and continue on with their work.

Figure 14.3 shows a quick reference Web page for performing basic Internet Explorer tasks using keyboard commands. Notice how it is organized into logical categories so that users can find what they need quickly, how it uses action verbs to describe each task across concisely, and how the layout (two columns, alternating white and color rows, plenty of white space) is easy to navigate.

Features of effective
quick reference
materials

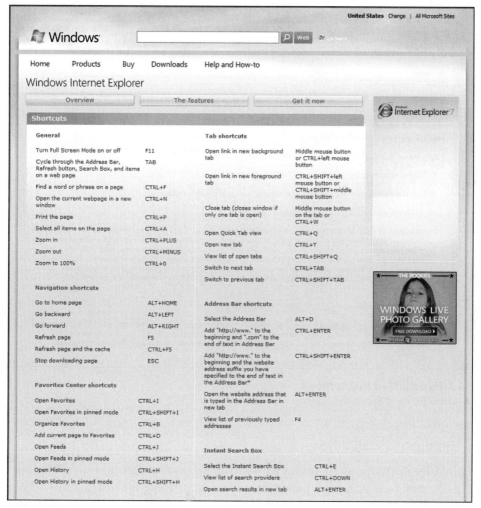

FIGURE 14.3
A quick-reference Web page (partial view)

Source: Microsoft product screen shot reprinted with permission from Microsoft Corporation.

Hyperlinked Instructions

Features of effective hyperlinked instructions

Online instructions that contain hypertext (links within the text) allow readers to explore various layers of information without losing their place on the page. Hyperlinked instructions allow companies to keep the material on their Web sites current by easily updating as needed.

Figure 14.4 shows hyperlinked instructions. This Web page contains the main instructions, but readers can learn more about a particular portion of the main instructions by clicking on the hyperlink (e.g., "eligibility requirements").

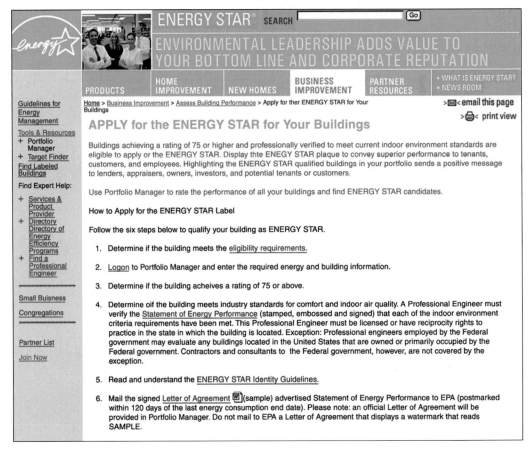

FIGURE 14.4 Hyperlinked instructions
Source: U.S. Environmental Protection Agency.

Computer Instructions

Features of effective computer instructions

Computer instructions are found within your software rather than on a Web site. This format does away with paper entirely by embedding the instructions within the product. For example, if you are using Microsoft Word or WordPerfect and don't remember how to create a table of contents or make a word italic or bold, you simply type your question into the "help" box to access the instructions.

Just like instructions in a printed book, computer instructions (as in Figure 14.5) usually offer an index you can use to look up a topic. Notice how the instructions in Figure 14.5 pop up on the screen without totally obscuring the document, allowing users to read the instructions and view part of the document at the same time.

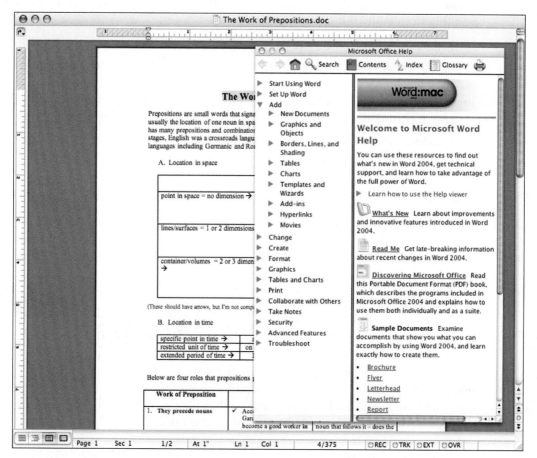

FIGURE 14.5 Computer instructions
Source: Microsoft product screen shot reprinted with permission from Microsoft Corporation.

ETHICAL AND LEGAL IMPLICATIONS

Instructional documents carry profound ethical and legal obligations on the part of those who prepare them. Among all technical documents, therefore, instructions involve the strictest requirements for accurate information in an accessible format.

Ethical implications
of instructions

Countless injuries result from misuse of products such as power tools, car jacks, or household cleaners. This type of misuse is often caused by defective instructions. Clear, easy-to-follow instructions that contain just the right amount of detail can provide the difference between the unsafe and safe use of a product.

Legal implications
of instructions

Any person injured because of unclear, inaccurate, or incomplete instructions can sue the writer as well as the manufacturer. Courts have ruled that a writing defect in product support literature carries the same type of liability as a design or manufacturing defect in the product itself (Girill 37). Some of the legal liabilities resulting from faulty instructions include

- Failure to instruct and caution users about the proper use of a product: for example, a household cleaning product that should not be mixed with other products

- Failure to warn against hazards from proper use of a product: for example, the risk of cutting one's fingers on a vegetable slicer

- Failure to warn against the possible misuses of a product: for example, the danger of improperly installing a child safety seat

ELEMENTS OF EFFECTIVE INSTRUCTIONS

✳ Explore the Concept
with the Case Study
on Writing Instructions
at mytechcommlab

All instructions must include a title, a brief overview or introduction, a body section (including the required steps involved in following the instructions), and a conclusion. In addition, most instructions should also include visuals as well as notes, cautions, warnings, and/or danger notices.

Title

Include a clear
and exact title

✳ Explore the Concept
with the Activity on
Writing Instructions
at mytechcommlab

Be sure your title provides a clear and exact preview of the required task. For example, the title "Instructions for Cleaning the Drive Head of a Laptop Computer" tells people what to expect: instructions for a specific procedure involving one selected part. But the title "The Laptop Computer" gives no such forecast; a document with a general title like this might contain a history of the laptop, a description of each part, or a wide range of related information.

Overview or Introduction

Provide a brief
overview or
introduction to orient
readers before they
begin the task

Explain the purpose of the instructions and describe what they cover. You don't want to bury users in an overly long overview/introduction, nor do you want to set them loose without adequate preparation. Know your audience—what they need and don't need. For example, you might begin with a short paragraph:

> These instructions provide complete information for the use of the lab's electron microscope. The first section explains the set-up steps, and the second section describes how to create a slide and view it with the microscope.

Body

Explain each step and substep in the correct order. Insert notes, cautions, warnings, dangers, and visuals as needed (see below for more on these elements). Begin each step with a definition or a purpose statement, as appropriate. Users who understand the reasons for a step will do a better job. Segment the steps with a numbered list. Begin each substep of a complex process on a new line.

Include a body section with task steps in correct order

Conclusion

The conclusion of a set of instructions might summarize the main steps of the task, describe the results users should experience, offer follow-up advice, or provide troubleshooting tips. You might do all of these things in the conclusion —or none of them. If the body section has given users all they need, omit the conclusion altogether.

Wrap up with a conclusion, if appropriate

Visuals

Visuals in instructions play a vital role: They show what to do, attract the reader's attention, and help keep words to a minimum. (For more, see Chapter 9.) Visuals can illustrate any step that might be hard for people to picture. For instance, describing in words how to locate something is a lot less effective than simply showing the location with a drawing or photograph. Visuals can also help tell the whole story—offer users the "big picture"—in one glance, something that would be far less effective using words only. Figure 14.6 enables users to visualize a task. Figure 14.7 shows users the complete process at a glance.

Provide visuals to enhance usability

FIGURE 14.6
A visual that illustrates a task (how to apply weatherstrip caulking)

Source: From U.S. Department of Energy
<www.nrel.gov/docs/fy01osti/28039.pdf>.

FIGURE 14.7
A visual that shows the full picture (how to build a boulder wall) in one glance

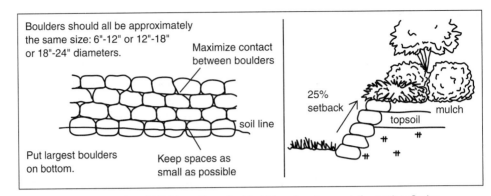

Source: From University of Michigan Sustainable Urban Landscape Information Series website, <www.sustland.umn.edu>. Copyright © 2006 by University of Minnesota Extension. Reprinted with permission.

Notes, Cautions, Warnings, and Danger Notices

Always include notes, cautions and warnings for user safety

Notes provide additional information, while cautions, warnings, and danger notices prevent damage, injury, or even death. Use these items only when needed. Overuse will dull their effect, and readers may overlook their importance.

When to use notes

A note clarifies a point, emphasizes vital information, or describes options or alternatives. For example:

> NOTE: If you don't name a newly initialized disk, the computer automatically names it "Untitled."

When to use cautions

Notes are designed to enhance performance and prevent errors; cautions, warnings, and danger notices are used for safety reasons.

Cautions prevent possible mistakes that could result in injury or equipment damage. For example:

> CAUTION: A momentary electrical surge or power failure will erase the contents of internal memory. To avoid losing your work, every few minutes save on a backup file what you have just typed into the computer.

When to use warnings

Warnings alert users to potential hazards to life or limb. For instance:

> WARNING: To prevent electrical shock, always disconnect your printer from its power source before cleaning internal parts.

When to use a danger notice

Danger notices identify an immediate hazard to life or limb. For example:

> DANGER: The red canister contains DEADLY radioactive material. Do not break the safety seal under any circumstances.

When you include cautions, warnings, or danger notices, be sure to provide the appropriate visual symbol or icon to indicate these conditions, as in Figure 14.8.

FIGURE 14.8
Caution, warning, and danger symbols

CONTENT, STYLE, AND DESIGN CONSIDERATIONS

In addition to including all the necessary elements in a set of instructions, you also need to decide about matters of content, style, and design.

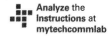

Analyze the Instructions at mytechcommlab

Detail and Technicality

Readers who know a great deal about the product or task(s) to be covered don't need a lot of detail and can typically handle a high level of technical information. But readers who are new to the situation need more detail and fewer technical terms. Use the techniques described in Chapter 4 to determine how much your readers already know.

Provide an adequate level of detail and technicality

Unless you learn that your audience has the relevant background and skills, write for more general readers. For example, if you are writing instructions for providing first aid to a victim of electrical shock, you might write the following for an audience with extensive medical background:

Instructions for a technical audience

> FIRST AID FOR ELECTRICAL SHOCK
> 1. Check vital signs.
> 2. Establish an airway.
> 3. Administer CPR as needed.
> 4. Treat for medical shock.

But for an inexperienced audience, not only will the above details be inadequate, but also terms such as "vital signs" and "CPR" will be too technical. Such instructions posted for workers in a high-voltage area who are not medically trained would be useless. Illustrations and explanations would be needed, as demonstrated in Figure 14.9.

Style

Instructions must always be clear and easy to follow upon first reading because people usually take immediate action. Follow the Strategies on p. 266.

Write with a readable style

FIGURE 14.9
Adequate detail and technicality for a general audience

Methods of Cardiopulmonary Resuscitation (CPR)

Mouth-to-Mouth Breathing

Step 1: If there are no signs of breathing or there is no significant pulse, place one hand under the victim's neck and gently lift. At the same time, push with the other hand on the victim's forehead. This will move the tongue away from the back of the throat to open the airway. If available, a plastic "stoma," or oropharyngeal airway device, should be inserted now.

Step 2: While maintaining the backward head tilt position, place your cheek and ear close to the victim's mouth and nose. Look for the chest to rise and fall while you listen and feel for breathing. Check for about 5 seconds.

Step 3: Next, while maintaining the backward head tilt, pinch the victim's nose with the hand that is on the victim's forehead to prevent leakage of air, open your mouth wide, take a deep breath, seal your mouth around the victim's mouth, and blow into the victim's mouth with four quick but full breaths. For an infant, give gentle puffs and blow through the mouth and nose *and* do not tilt the head back as far as for an adult.

If you do not get an air exchange when you blow, it may help to reposition the head and try again.

If there is still no breathing, give one breath every 5 seconds for an adult and one gentle puff every 3 seconds for an infant until breathing resumes.

If the victim's chest fails to expand, the problem may be an airway obstruction. Mouth-to-mouth respiration should be interrupted briefly to apply first aid for choking.

Step 1

Step 2

Step 3

STRATEGIES
for Achieving Readability

▶ **Use direct address, active voice, and imperative mood.** To emphasize the reader's role, write in the second person, as direct address. Begin all steps and substeps with action verbs, using the active voice and imperative mood. In certain cases, you may want to provide a clarifying word or phrase that precedes the verb:

Say this	Not this
Insert the disk. *or* [To run the program,] insert the disk.	You should insert the disk.
Key in your access code. *or* [To log on,] key in your access code.	The user keys in her access code.
Plug in the power cord. *or* [When you are ready to power up,] plug in the power cord.	The power cord is plugged in.

▶ **Use short and logically shaped sentences.** Use short sentences—one sentence for each step—so that readers can perform one step at a time. If a single step covers two related actions, describe these actions in their required sequence:

> Before switching on the computer, insert the CD in the drive.
>
> *OR*
>
> Insert the CD in the drive. Then switch on the computer.

▶ **Use parallel phrasing.** Parallelism is especially important in instructions because the repeating grammatical forms emphasize the step-by-step organization. Notice how all the sentences below are structured identically:

> To log on to the VAX 380, follow these steps:
>
> 1. Switch the terminal to "on."
> 2. Press the CONTROL key and the C key simultaneously.
> 3. Type "logon" and then press the ESCAPE key.
> 4. Type your user name, and then press the ESCAPE key.

▶ **Use affirmative phrasing.** Negative phrasing is harder to understand.

Say this	Not this
Examine your disk for dust contamination.	Verify that your disk is not contaminated with dust.

▶ **Use transitions to mark time and sequence.** Transitional expressions provide a bridge between related ideas. Some transitions ("first," "next," "meanwhile," "finally," "after," "then") mark time and sequence and are therefore especially useful in instructions, emphasizing their step-by-step nature:

> First, plug in the power cord, and then turn on the printer.
>
> After the printer warms up, insert the paper in the paper slot.
>
> Finally, hit the "print" button.

Design

Create an accessible
design

Instructions rarely receive undivided attention. The reader, in fact, is doing two activities more or less at once: interpreting the instructions and performing the required task.

An effective instructional design conveys the sense that the task is within a qualified user's range of abilities. Therefore, design your instructions so that users can leave and return to the document as needed and easily find their place.

STRATEGIES
for Creating an Accessible Design

▸ **Use informative headings.** Clear headings tell readers what to expect, emphasize what is most important and provide cues for navigation. A heading such as "How to Initialize Your Compact Disk" is more informative than "Compact Disk Initializing."

▸ **Arrange all steps in a numbered list.** Unless the procedure consists of simple steps, list and number each step. Numbered steps not only announce the sequence of required actions, but also help users remember where they left off.

▸ **Separate each step visually.** Single-space within steps and double-space between.

▸ **Make cautions, warnings, and danger notices highly visible.** Use ruled boxes or highlighting and plenty of white space to make these items stand out. Also, include symbols if possible; if not, use bold text and capital letters for emphasis.

▸ **Make visual and verbal information redundant.** Let the visual repeat, restate, or reinforce the prose, rather than provide entirely new information.

▸ **Place visuals and prose steps that are connected close together.** If room allows, place a visual that goes with a step right beside the step; if not, right after the step. Set off the visual with plenty of white space.

▸ **Keep the design simple and easy to navigate.** Readers may be overwhelmed by an excessively complex or inconsistent design.

▸ **For lengthy instructions, consider a layered approach.** In a complex manual, for instance, you might add a "Quick-Use Guide" for getting started or a table of contents with page references to more detailed and technical information.

Figure 14.10 shows instructions that have been prepared for general readers who need to make a common home repair.

1

FIGURE 14.10
**A complete set
of instructions**

HOW TO REPLACE A WORN FAUCET WASHER

◄———●

Introduction

A leaking faucet, caused by a worn washer, can lose up to fifteen gallons of water per day. This loss can result in a higher water bill, overuse of the septic system and well pump, an increase in your hot-water bill, and rust or chlorine deposits in your sink basin. These instructions detail how to replace the washer. No special knowledge or skills are necessary.

◄———●

Overview

The typical faucet consists of a round knob or a handle (Figure 1) which, when turned, causes the stem to screw down until the washer sits snugly over the seat. With the washer in place, the flow of water is stopped. A worn washer loses the ability to form a tight seal, causing a leak or drip to develop. Replacing the worn washer eliminates the leak.

◄———●

Figure 1. Typical faucet in exploded view

◄———●

Equipment and Material Needed

- pliers
- regular or Phillips (crossed head) screwdriver
- new washer of same size and shape as worn washer
- valve for shutting off water supply

◄———●

> ***Note and Caution*** *These instructions only apply to faucets that have washers. Avoid using any excessive force on the threaded parts, because they are made of soft metal and could easily strip.*

◄———● Note and caution
alert users before
they take action

INSTRUCTIONS

◄———● The body section
provides step-by-
step guidance

1. **Shut off the water supply.** Look under the sink or fixture for the shutoff valve. If you are unable to find a valve in this location, use the main shutoff valve located in the basement or beneath the house. The water pipe (one-half to one inch in diameter) usually originates from an inside cellar wall. Locate the shutoff valve by following the pipe from the wall to an attached valve, usually within a few feet of the wall (Figure 2). Turn this valve fully clockwise. With your water supply shut off, you can take the faucet apart.

FIGURE 14.10
(Continued)

2

Figure 2. Location of main shut-off valve

2. Disassemble the faucet. Before removing the handle, open the faucet to allow remaining water in the pipe to escape. Using your screwdriver, remove the screw on top of the handle. If a cap covers the screw, pry it off (Figure 1). Remove the handle.

Next, remove the packing nut, using pliers to turn the nut counter-clockwise. The flat circular nut washer can now be lifted from the faucet base. With packing nut and washer removed, screw the stem out of the base by turning the faucet in the "open" direction. Lift the stem out of the base and proceed to step 3.

3. Replace the worn washer. Using your screwdriver, remove the screw holding the washer at the base of the stem (Figure 1). Remove the worn washer and replace it with a new one of the same size, using the washer screw to hold it in place. (Washers of various sizes can be purchased at any hardware store.) If the washer screw is worn, replace it. When the new washer is fixed in place, proceed to step 4.

4. Reassemble the faucet. To reassemble your faucet, reverse the sequence described in step 2. *Caution: Do not overtighten the packing nut!*

Caution precedes step

Using pliers, screw the stem into the base until it ceases to turn. Next, place the packing washer and nut over the threads in the collar. Tighten the packing nut using the strength of one hand. Finally, secure the handle with your screwdriver. When the faucet is fully assembled, turn the handle to the "off" position and proceed to step 5.

5. Turn on the water supply. First, check to see that your faucet is fully closed. Next, turn the water on slowly (about one-half turn each time) until the shutoff valve is fully open. These slow turns prevent a sudden buildup of pressure, which could damage the pipes. Your faucet should now be as good as new.

Because the body section has given readers all they need, no conclusion is required

PROCEDURES

Procedures provide rules and guidance for people who are required to follow accepted practice. For example, different people in your organization might perform the same task (say, monitoring groundwater pollution) at different times, with different equipment, or under different circumstances. This task may need to be standardized to ensure that all work is done with the same accuracy and precision.

Function of procedures

✳ Explore the Concept with the Case Study on Writing Procedures at mytechcommlab

Audience and Purpose Considerations

Unlike instructions, which will be read mostly by users unfamiliar with the given task, procedures may be used by people already familiar with the task but who need to follow a standard. For example, if apprentice chefs in a famous restaurant who normally prepare salads and appetizers are asked to take over on the preparation of special sauces, those workers probably already know the basics but would need more information on the specific sauces required, amounts of ingredients, reduction techniques, and so on.

Consider your audience

 Analyze the Procedures at mytechcommlab

Determine how your readers will use these procedures. Will they be following the procedures in a hurry while evacuating a building? Would the procedures be better distributed on paper or via computer? Once you know exactly how the procedures will be used, you can make decisions about the document's length, format, level of detail, and medium.

Consider your purpose

✳ Explore the Concept with the Activity on Writing Procedures at mytechcommlab

Types of Procedures

The most common types of procedures are standard operating procedures (SOPs), general safety procedures, and medical or health procedures.

Standard operating procedures are formal procedures designed to give an organization an official record of the procedure and how it should be performed. SOPs, kept up to date and in a location or format available to employees, are required by law in many workplace environments, including those that deal with chemicals or industrial waste. SOPs are also written to inform the public about how a particular procedure is performed.

Standard operating procedures

Safety procedures, as in Figure 14.11, are required in many settings. Hotel rooms typically list fire exit procedures on the back of the entry door. Most organizations have official procedures for dealing with emergencies.

Safety procedures

Medical procedures can be written for medical professionals or for consumers. Procedures for medical professionals might include SOPs on hand washing, surgical techniques, and other steps involved in patient care in the hospital. Today, with the vast amount of medical information available on the Internet, many medical procedures are written for nonexperts.

Medical procedures

FIGURE 14.11
A set of procedures (safety procedures)

Title ("Evacuating High-Rise Buildings") is clear and easy to spot

Overview/introduction section defines the issue and provides background

Headings in the form of reader questions help people find the information they need

Bullets, instead of numbered lists of steps, are appropriate for this document

OSHA **FACT**sheet

Evacuating High-Rise Buildings

The National Fire Protection Association defines "high-rise building" as a building greater than 75 feet (25 m) in height where the building height is measured from the lowest level of fire department vehicle access to the floor of the highest occupiable story. Appropriate exits, alarms, emergency lighting, communication systems, and sprinkler systems are critical for employee safety. When designing and maintaining exits, it is essential to ensure that routes leading to the exits, as well as the areas beyond the exits, are accessible and free from materials or items that would impede individuals from easily and effectively evacuating. State and local building code officials can help employers ensure that the design and safety systems are adequate.

When there is an emergency, getting workers out of high-rise buildings poses special challenges. Preparing in advance to safely evacuate the building is critical to the safety of employees who work there.

What actions should employers take to help ensure safe evacuations of high-rise buildings?

■ Don't lock fire exits or block doorways, halls, or stairways.
■ Test regularly all back-up systems and safety systems, such as emergency lighting and communication systems, and repair them as needed.
■ Develop a workplace evacuation plan, post it prominently on each floor, and review it periodically to ensure its effectiveness.
■ Identify and train floor wardens, including back-up personnel, who will be responsible for sounding alarms and helping to evacuate employees.
■ Conduct emergency evacuation drills periodically.
■ Establish designated meeting locations outside the building for workers to gather following an evacuation. The locations should be a safe distance from the building and in an area where people can assemble safely without interfering with emergency response teams.
■ Identify personnel with special needs or disabilities who may need help evacuating

and assign one or more people, including back-up personnel, to help them.
■ Ensure that during off-hour periods, systems are in place to notify, evacuate, and account for off-hour building occupants.
■ Post emergency numbers near telephones.

What should workers know before an emergency occurs?

■ Be familiar with the worksite's emergency evacuation plan;
■ Know the pathway to at least two alternative exits from every room/area at the workplace;
■ Recognize the sound/signaling method of the fire/evacuation alarms;
■ Know who to contact in an emergency and how to contact them;
■ Know how many desks or cubicles are between your workstation and two of the nearest exits so you can escape in the dark if necessary;
■ Know where the fire/evacuation alarms are located and how to use them; and
■ Report damaged or malfunctioning safety systems and back-up systems

What should employers do when an emergency occurs?

■ Sound appropriate alarms and instruct employees to leave building.
■ Notify police, firefighters, or other appropriate emergency personnel.
■ Take a head count of employees at designated meeting locations, and notify emergency personnel of any missing workers.

What should employees do when an emergency occurs?

■ Leave the area quickly but in an orderly manner, following the worksite's emergency evacuation plan. Go directly to the nearest fire-free and smoke-free stairwell recognizing that in some circumstances the only available exit route may contain limited amounts of smoke or fire.

Source: U.S. Occupational Safety and Health Administration.

USABILITY TESTING

Any technical document must be written and designed for the right audience. With instructions and procedures, however, accuracy and ease of use are especially important. Otherwise, readers could make costly and dangerous errors.

To identify which parts of the document work or don't work, conduct a usability analysis, using the Basic Usability Survey in Figure 14.12. The survey is designed for both the writers and the readers. Essentially it asks one main question (broken into more specific questions): "Do these instructions or procedures enable you to carry out the task safely, efficiently, and accurately?" Notice how the phrasing encourages responses containing examples instead of merely yes or no answers.

The importance of usability testing of instructions and procedures

What a basic usability survey asks

 View the Basic Usability Survey at mytechcommlab

STRATEGIES
for Instructions and Procedures

▸ **Analyze your audience.** For instructions, assume a general audience that does not know how to perform a task. For procedures, assume that your audience does know something about the procedure but needs a set of standard guidelines.

▸ **Analyze your purpose.** Consider where the document will be used and how to present the information for maximum usability.

▸ **Always remember the ethical and legal implications.** Instructions and procedures must always be written with the reader safety at the forefront.

▸ **Use standard organization and include all needed elements.** Always include a clear and exact title; include an overview or introduction for instructions (but only if appropriate for procedures); include a body section (in numbered list format for instructions, but not necessarily for procedures); and include visuals, notes, cautions, warnings, danger notices, and a conclusion as appropriate.

▸ **Provide an appropriate level of detail and technicality.** Do not give readers too much or too little detail, and use only as much technical language as your audience will understand.

▸ **Write with a readable style.** Refer to the Strategies for Achieving Readability (pages 266–267).

▸ **Design for maximum accessibility.** Refer to the Strategies for Creating an Accessible Design (page 268).

▸ **Always test for usability.** Instructions and procedures must be easy to grasp in one reading, lead to successful completion of a task or procedure, and ensure reader safety. Make sure every word and image are just right.

Basic Usability Survey

1. Briefly describe why this document is used. _____
    _____

2. Evaluate the *content:*
    *   Identify any irrelevant information. _____
        _____

    *   Indicate any gaps in the information. _____
        _____

    *   Identify any information that seems inaccurate. _____
        _____

    *   List other problems with the content. _____
        _____

3. Evaluate the *organization:*
    *   Identify anything that is out of order or hard to locate or follow. _____
        _____

    *   List other problems with the organization. _____
        _____

4. Evaluate the *style:*
    *   Identify anything you misunderstood on first reading. _____
        _____

    *   Identify anything you couldn't understand at all. _____
        _____

    *   Identify expressions that seem wordy, inexact, or too complex. _____
        _____

    *   List other problems with the style. _____
        _____

5. Evaluate the *design:*
    *   Indicate any headings that are missing, confusing, or excessive. _____
        _____

    *   Indicate any material that should be designed as a list. _____
        _____

    *   Give examples of material that might be clarified by a visual. _____
        _____

    *   Give examples of misleading or overly complex visuals. _____
        _____

    *   List other problems with design. _____
        _____

6. Identify anything that seems misleading or that could create legal problems or
    cross-cultural misunderstanding. _____

7. Please suggest other ways of making this document easier to use. _____
    _____

FIGURE 14.12 A basic usability survey

Source: Adapted from Carliner 258; Daugherty 17–18; Hart 53–57.

CHECKLIST
for Instructions and Procedures

INSTRUCTIONS

☐ Have I determined what type of instructional format I should use?

☐ Have I assessed the ethical and legal implications of my instructions?

☐ Have I provided a clear and exact title?

☐ Have I included an orienting overview or introduction?

☐ Have I provided step-by-step instructions in the body?

☐ Have I used visuals to enhance usability?

☐ Have I included notes, cautions, warnings, and dangers whenever necessary?

☐ Have I provided the appropriate level of detail and technicality for my audience?

☐ Have I followed the strategies for writing with a readable style?

☐ Have I followed the strategies for creating an accessible design?

☐ Have I performed a Basic Usability Survey?

PROCEDURES

☐ Have I considered my audience and purpose?

☐ Have I provided a clear and exact title?

☐ Have I provided a clear introduction and numbered steps or visuals if appropriate?

☐ Have I included notes, cautions, warnings, and dangers whenever necessary?

☐ Have I provided a conclusion?

☐ Have I provided an appropriate level of detail, a readable style, and an accessible design?

☐ Have I performed a Basic Usability Survey?

APPLICATIONS

GENERAL APPLICATION

Select part of a technical manual in your field—or instructions or procedures for a general audience—and make a copy of the material. Using the Checklist on page 275, evaluate the sample. In a memo to your instructor, discuss the document's strong and weak points or be prepared to explain them in class.

TEAM APPLICATION

Divide into small groups and visit your computer center, library, or any place on campus or at work where you can find operating manuals for computers, lab or office equipment, or the like. (Or look through the documentation for your own computer hardware or software.) Locate fairly brief instructions that could use revision for improved content, organization, style, or format. Make sure the instructions cover a task that you will be able to carry out. Make a copy of the instructions. Test these instructions for usability and revise as needed. Submit all materials to your instructor, along with a memo explaining the improvements, or be prepared to discuss your revision in class.

GLOBAL APPLICATION

In many cultures, the use of imperative mood is considered impolite or too direct. For instance, instructions that state "Place the disk into the disk drive" may sound bossy and inconsiderate. Find a set of instructions that use imperative mood (for example, Figure 14.10 in this chapter) and rewrite these for a cross-cultural audience where the imperative mood would be offensive. For instance, you might use an indirect imperative ("Be sure to insert the disk into the drive").

COMPUTER/WEB-BASED APPLICATION

Think of a product that you have at home, one for which you no longer have the user manual. For instance, you have may have a coffee maker, a snowblower, or a laser printer. Use the Internet to locate the product's user manual. In what format is the manual: a Web page? a PDF document? Would the document be easier to use if it were in print? If so, why? Write and design a much shorter quick reference manual that can be printed and used with the device.

For additional technical writing resources that will help you master the chapter objectives, go to **www.mytechcommlab.com**.

15

Summaries

LEARNING OBJECTIVES FOR THIS CHAPTER

▸ Summarize a long document using step-by-step strategies

▸ Identify the purpose and placement of the four types of summaries: closing summaries, informative abstracts, descriptive abstracts, and executive summaries

▸ Recognize ethical issues when writing summaries

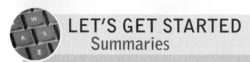

LET'S GET STARTED
Summaries

Locate a technical article related to your undergraduate major that begins with a summary (the summary may use the name "summary," "abstract," or "executive summary"). For instance, if you are majoring in electrical engineering, use the library to find an article from a journal in that field. Most peer-reviewed articles begin with a brief summary of the article. Read this summary and make notes about the use of language, the order in which information is presented, and the level of technicality. See if you can understand the entire article simply by reading the summary. Then read the entire article.

Questions to ask about the summary you've located as you review the material in this chapter may include the following:

▶ What role does the summary play for the readers of this journal?

▶ How well does the summary characterize the full report or article?

▶ What decisions did the writer make about word choice, and why?

As you read this chapter, come back to your notes and the answers to the above questions and modify them based on what you learn from the chapter and in-class discussion.

Definition of summary

A *summary* is a restatement of the main ideas in a longer document. Summaries are used to convey the general meaning of the ideas in the original source without all the specific details or examples that may appear in the original. When you write a summary, take care to provide the essential information clearly and concisely in your own words, leaving out anything that isn't absolutely central to an understanding of the original.

AUDIENCE AND PURPOSE OF SUMMARIES

Audience considerations

Formal reports and proposals (discussed in Chapters 17 and 18) and other long documents are typically submitted to busy people: researchers, developers, managers, vice presidents, customers, and so on. For readers who must act quickly or only need to know the "big picture," reading an entire long report may not only be too time-consuming but also irrelevant. As a result, most long reports, proposals, and other long documents are commonly preceded by a summary.

The purpose of summaries, then, is to provide only an overview and the essential facts. Whether you summarize your own writing or someone else's, your summary should do three things for readers: (1) describe, in short form, what the original document is all about; (2) help readers decide whether to read all of the long document, parts of it, or none of it; and (3) give readers a framework for understanding the full document that will follow if they do plan to read it.

To get a basic idea of how summaries fulfill audience needs, consider the examples in Figures 15.1 and 15.2.

Purpose of summaries

> Scientists know with virtual certainty that human activities are changing the composition of Earth's atmosphere. Increasing levels of greenhouse gases like carbon dioxide (CO_2) since pre-industrial times are well-documented and understood. The atmospheric buildup of CO_2 and other greenhouse gases is largely the result of human activities such as the burning of fossil fuels. Increasing greenhouse gas concentrations tend to warm the planet. A warming trend of about 0.7 to 1.5°F occurred during the 20th century in both the Northern and Southern Hemispheres and over the oceans. The major greenhouse gases remain in the atmosphere for periods ranging from decades to centuries. It is therefore virtually certain that atmospheric concentrations of greenhouse gases will continue to rise over the next few decades.

Source: Adapted from *State of Knowledge*, by the U.S. Environmental Protection Agency.

FIGURE 15.1
A passage to be summarized

Figure 15.2 shows a summary of the complex passage in Figure 15.1. Note how it captures the original's main ideas but in a compressed and less technical form that busy readers and general audiences would appreciate. The summary does not, however, change the essential meaning of the original—it merely boils the original down to its basic message.

> Scientists are virtually certain that greenhouse gases largely produced by human activities are warming the planet. Temperatures have risen worldwide during the 20th century and undoubtedly will continue.
>
> *Source:* From *State of Knowledge*, by the U.S. Environmental Protection Agency.

FIGURE 15.2
A summarized version of Figure 15.1

ELEMENTS OF EFFECTIVE SUMMARIES

Whether you summarize your own document or someone else's, always keep in mind that all summaries have four key characteristics: accuracy, completeness, conciseness, and nontechnical style.

Four characteristics of summaries

Accuracy

Readers expect a precise sketch of the content, emphasis, and line of reasoning used in the original document. Be careful not to alter the essential meaning of the original. For example, in Figure 15.2, on page 279, the summary uses different wording but remains true to the original document's central point (scientists feel that global warming is "virtually certain," not "somewhat certain"), retains the emphasis made in the original (the fact that human activity is responsible), and follows the same logical sequence (global warming has and will continue to occur).

Completeness

Readers will also expect your summary to include everything essential in the original document—everything they need at a glance to grasp its full meaning. For example, in Figure 15.2, nothing has been left out to prevent readers from getting a complete overview of the original. Readers will know exactly what to expect from the longer document, only in fuller detail.

Conciseness

Readers expect a summary to exclude superfluous details—as well as any new details, examples, or opinions—not found in the original. Although the summary in Figure 15.2 doesn't omit anything essential, it does omit lesser details such as statistics ("0.7 to 1.5°F"), examples (set off by "like," "such as," "and other"), and overly long passages ("in both the Northern and Southern Hemispheres and over the oceans" is replaced with "the planet"). Also the summary in no way embellishes upon the original content.

Nontechnical Style

Unless your readers are all experts (and most of the time they will not be), always summarize a document using plain English rather than carrying the original's technical jargon or scientific and mathematical data into the summary. The summary in Figure 15.2, for example, omits expressions such as "atmospheric buildup" and "greenhouse gas concentrations," while also leaving out the specific temperatures mentioned.

WRITING SUMMARIES STEP-BY-STEP

Step-by-step nature of summaries

Watch the Video on Summarizing an Article at mytechcommlab

More so than for other types of documents, writing summaries involves a straightforward process: reading and rereading the original document, marking the key information, and writing and revising your summary while checking it against the original. The Strategies for Summaries on page 290 provide an overview of these steps, along with audience and purpose considerations.

Step 1: Read the Original Document

Before you can effectively summarize a document, you need a solid understanding of what it says. Read the original from start to finish, without highlighting or taking notes. An initial read will give you a general understanding of the document's main point and key subpoints.

Do an initial read to get the big picture

Step 2: Reread and Mark Essential Material

Read the document again, this time using a highlighter or pen (if working on hard copy) or your computer's highlighting feature (after copying and pasting the document into a word processing file). Pay close attention to cues to help you identify the essential points. In Figure 15.3, key sentences are underlined, while the less important information is not.

Reread and highlight for a sharper understanding

Step 3: Cut and Paste the Key Information

If you are working from a hard copy of the original, rekey the material you highlighted into a new document. If you are working from an electronic version of the original, copy and paste only the highlighted portions into a new file. Don't worry about the overall organization or sentence construction at this point; just gather everything you need.

Create a new document from the highlighted information

Step 4: Redraft the Information into Your Own Organizational Pattern and Words

At this point, reorganize the material from the original source into patterns that work well in a smaller space. Use your own wording to express the original concepts. Don't worry about length just yet. You just want to get your own wording down on paper.

Turn the cut-and-paste version into your own version

Step 5: Edit Your Draft

In the previous step, the goal was to get your own wording down on paper. Now, edit your version. Keeping sentences clear and grammatical, cross out needless words; get rid of any asides; combine related concepts; and look for any repetitions. Note how Figure 15.4 is as pared down as it can be.

Focus on shortening your version

Step 6: Compare Your Version with the Original Document

As a final step, double-check that you have not altered the meaning, intent, or emphasis of the original document. Reread the original and then immediately reread your own version. As you can see, Figure 15.4 remains true to the original source but is only about 25% of the original's length.

Make sure you preserve the intent of the original

FIGURE 15.3
An article to be summarized

Open with basic claim

Omit background details

Include key comparison

Omit inessential detail

Include essential definition

Compress list of examples

Omit repetition and inessential statistic

Include key fact

Compress list of benefits

Include key comparison

Include key point

Dietary Fats and Your Health

Scientific evidence shows that consumption of <u>saturated fat, trans fat, and dietary cholesterol raises low-density lipoprotein (LDL), or "bad" cholesterol levels, which increases the risk of coronary heart disease (CHD).</u> According to the National Heart, Lung, and Blood Institute of the National Institutes of Health, more than 12.5 million Americans have CHD, and more than 500,000 die each year. That makes CHD one of the leading causes of death in the United States.

The <u>Food and Drug Administration has required that saturated fat and dietary cholesterol be listed on food labels since 1993. With trans fat added to the Nutrition Facts panel, you will know for the first time how much of all three—saturated fat, trans fat, and dietary cholesterol—are in the foods you choose.</u> Identifying saturated fat, trans fat, and dietary cholesterol on the food label gives you information you need to make food choices that help reduce the risk of CHD. This revised label will be of particular interest to people concerned about high blood cholesterol and heart disease. However, everyone should be aware of the risk posed by consuming too much saturated fat, trans fat, and dietary cholesterol.

But what is trans fat, and how can you limit the amount of this fat in your diet?

What Is Trans Fat?
Basically, <u>trans fat is made when manufacturers add hydrogen to vegetable oil—a process called hydrogenation.</u> Hydrogenation increases the shelf life and flavor stability of foods containing these fats. <u>Trans fat can be found in vegetable shortenings, some margarines, crackers, cookies, snack foods, and other foods made with or fried in partially hydrogenated oils.</u> Unlike other fats, the majority of trans fat is formed when food manufacturers turn liquid oils into solid fats like shortening and hard margarine. <u>A small amount of trans fat is found naturally, primarily in dairy products, some meat, and other animal-based foods.</u>

Trans fat, like saturated fat and dietary cholesterol, raises the LDL cholesterol that increases your risk for CHD. Americans consume on average 4 to 5 times as much saturated fat as trans fat in their diets. Although saturated fat is the main dietary culprit that raises LDL, trans fat and dietary cholesterol also contribute significantly.

Are All Fats Bad?
Simply put: <u>No. Unsaturated fat is a major source of energy for the body and aids in the absorption of vitamins A, D, E, and K, and carotenoids.</u> Both animal- and plant-derived food products contain fat, and when eaten in moderation, <u>unsaturated fat is important for proper growth, development, and maintenance of good health.</u> As a food ingredient, unsaturated fat provides taste, consistency, and stability and helps you feel full. In addition, parents should be aware that unsaturated <u>fats are an especially important source of calories and nutrients for infants and toddlers</u> (up to 2 years of age), who have the highest energy needs per unit of body weight of any age group.

<u>While unsaturated fats (monounsaturated and polyunsaturated) are beneficial when consumed in moderation, saturated and trans fats are not.</u> Saturated fat and trans fat raise LDL cholesterol levels in the blood. Dietary cholesterol also raises LDL cholesterol and may contribute to heart disease even without raising LDL. Therefore, it is advisable to <u>choose foods low in saturated fat, trans fat, and dietary cholesterol as part of a healthful diet.</u>

< continued >

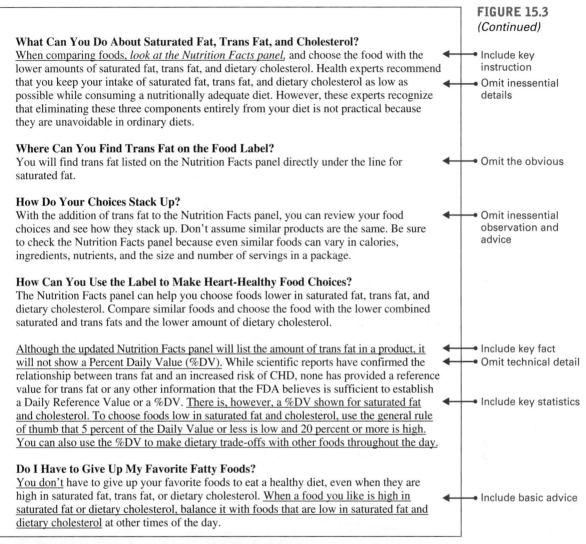

FIGURE 15.3
(Continued)

What Can You Do About Saturated Fat, Trans Fat, and Cholesterol?
When comparing foods, *look at the Nutrition Facts panel,* and choose the food with the
lower amounts of saturated fat, trans fat, and dietary cholesterol. Health experts recommend
that you keep your intake of saturated fat, trans fat, and dietary cholesterol as low as
possible while consuming a nutritionally adequate diet. However, these experts recognize
that eliminating these three components entirely from your diet is not practical because
they are unavoidable in ordinary diets.

— Include key instruction
— Omit inessential details

Where Can You Find Trans Fat on the Food Label?
You will find trans fat listed on the Nutrition Facts panel directly under the line for
saturated fat.

— Omit the obvious

How Do Your Choices Stack Up?
With the addition of trans fat to the Nutrition Facts panel, you can review your food
choices and see how they stack up. Don't assume similar products are the same. Be sure
to check the Nutrition Facts panel because even similar foods can vary in calories,
ingredients, nutrients, and the size and number of servings in a package.

— Omit inessential observation and advice

How Can You Use the Label to Make Heart-Healthy Food Choices?
The Nutrition Facts panel can help you choose foods lower in saturated fat, trans fat, and
dietary cholesterol. Compare similar foods and choose the food with the lower combined
saturated and trans fats and the lower amount of dietary cholesterol.

Although the updated Nutrition Facts panel will list the amount of trans fat in a product, it
will not show a Percent Daily Value (%DV). While scientific reports have confirmed the
relationship between trans fat and an increased risk of CHD, none has provided a reference
value for trans fat or any other information that the FDA believes is sufficient to establish
a Daily Reference Value or a %DV. There is, however, a %DV shown for saturated fat
and cholesterol. To choose foods low in saturated fat and cholesterol, use the general rule
of thumb that 5 percent of the Daily Value or less is low and 20 percent or more is high.
You can also use the %DV to make dietary trade-offs with other foods throughout the day.

— Include key fact
— Omit technical detail
— Include key statistics

Do I Have to Give Up My Favorite Fatty Foods?
You don't have to give up your favorite foods to eat a healthy diet, even when they are
high in saturated fat, trans fat, or dietary cholesterol. When a food you like is high in
saturated fat or dietary cholesterol, balance it with foods that are low in saturated fat and
dietary cholesterol at other times of the day.

— Include basic advice

Source: Excerpt from *FDA Consumer* Sept.–Oct. 2003: 12–18.

SPECIAL TYPES OF SUMMARIES

In preparing a report, proposal, or other document, you might summarize the
work of other people as part of your presentation. The previous sections have
described how to summarize documents written by others. But in other situations,
you will often need to summarize your own material. Various types of reports,
proposals, and other long documents require internal summaries. Depending
on the length, purpose, and audience, your document might include one or
more of four special types of summaries, in different locations, with different
levels of detail. These four types of summaries are (1) closing summaries,

FIGURE 15.4
A summary
of Figure 15.3

Dietary Fats and Your Health (A Summary)

Saturated fat is a principal cause of bad cholesterol (LDL, or low density lipoprotein), but dietary cholesterol and trans fat also play a role. High LDL is a major risk factor for coronary heart disease, a leading killer in the United States. In addition to the listing of saturated fat and dietary cholesterol on food labels, the Food and Drug Administration (FDA) now requires that trans fat be listed.

Although small amounts of trans fat exist naturally in dairy products and other animal-based foods, most trans fat is a byproduct of hydrogenation, the addition of hydrogen to vegetable oil. This process increases shelf life and stabilizes the flavor of foods such as hard margarine, crackers, snack foods, and foods fried in hydrogenated oil.

Not all fats are bad. In fact, unsaturated fat serves as a major energy source, promotes vitamin absorption, enhances food taste, and helps us feel full. Consumed in moderation, unsaturated fat is essential to health and provides a vital calorie source for infants. However, saturated fats and trans fats, along with dietary cholesterol, should be avoided as much as possible.

To make wise choices about fats and cholesterol, read the Nutrition Facts label on packaged foods. Note the serving size, number of servings in the package, and the Percent Daily Value (%DV) of each ingredient. Although no Daily Value is yet established for trans fat, avoid foods with a high saturated fat or cholesterol DV (greater than 20 percent per serving), unless you can balance these with low DV foods during the day.

Source: Excerpt from *FDA Consumer* Sept.–Oct. 2003: 12–18.

(2) informative abstracts, (3) descriptive abstracts, and (4) executive summaries. Figure 15.5 illustrates each of these types of summaries, their placement, and their purpose. The following sections discuss and illustrate each type in more detail.

FIGURE 15.5
Special types
of summaries

Source: Adapted from Vaughan, David.

Closing Summaries

A *closing summary* appears in the concluding section of a formal report or proposal. The closing summary helps readers review and remember the major findings that have preceded it. This look back at "the big picture" also helps readers appreciate the conclusions and recommendations that typically follow the closing summary. Figure 15.6 shows a closing summary at the end of a report that analyzes the feasibility of a career in technical marketing. This summary appears just before the "Recommendations" portion that ends the report.

Purpose and placement of closing summaries

Summary of Findings
Technical marketing and sales requires solid technical background, motivation, communication skills, and interpersonal skills. This career offers job diversity and excellent income potential, balanced against hard work and relentless pressure to perform.

College graduates interested in this field confront four entry options: (1) direct entry with on-the-job training, (2) a formal training program, (3) prior experience in a technical specialty, and (4) graduate programs. Each option has benefits and drawbacks based on immediacy of income, rate of advancement, and long-term potential.

FIGURE 15.6
A closing summary

Informative Abstracts

An *informative abstract* is a capsule version of a formal report or proposal that appears on a separate page, just after the document's title page. Informative abstracts provide readers with a snapshot of a long document—a clear picture of what is to come. Some readers, such as busy executives, may want just the "bottom line" without having to read the entire report or proposal. The informative abstract summarizes what the full document says: it identifies the need or issue that prompted the document; it describes the research methods used; it reviews the main facts and findings; and it condenses the conclusions and recommendations. (See page 329 of the formal report in Chapter 17 or page 354 of the formal proposal in Chapter 18 for an example.) An informative abstract may simply be labeled as an "abstract."

Purpose and placement of informative abstracts

Descriptive Abstracts

More compressed than an informative abstract, a *descriptive abstract* is usually only one to three sentences long and appears on the title page of a report or proposal. A descriptive abstract merely states what a document *covers*; it doesn't get

Purpose and placement of descriptive abstracts

FIGURE 15.7
A descriptive
abstract

> The origin of trans fat, its relation to saturated fat and dietary cholesterol, and its causative role in heart disease is explained, and advice for consumers is provided.

into detail about what the document contains. Such an abstract helps people decide whether to read the report. Compare, for example, the descriptive abstract in Figure 15.7 with the article summary in Figure 15.4. The descriptive abstract conveys only the basic nature and extent of the longer document.

Executive Summaries

Purpose and placement of executive summaries

An *executive summary* is similar to an informative abstract; however, it not only summarizes the long document but also tells readers what they should think about it. Placed on a separate page just after a long document's title page (just like an informative abstract), an executive summary is aimed at decision-makers rather than technical audiences. Unlike informative abstracts, executive summaries are written to persuade readers to act on the information. Executive summaries are crucial in cases when readers have no time to read the entire original document and when they expect the writer to help guide their thinking ("Tell me how to think about this," instead of, "Help me understand this"). Unless the readers (the organization or company) stipulate a specific format, organize your executive abstract to answer the following questions:

Questions to answer in an executive summary

- What is the issue?
- What was found?
- How was it found?
- What does it mean?
- What should be done?

The executive summary in Figure 15.8 falls at the beginning of a 55-page report. These three pages summarize the much longer, more detailed report. Notice how the executive summary answers all the above questions.

ETHICAL CONSIDERATIONS IN SUMMARIZING INFORMATION

Summaries in the information age

Information in summary format is increasingly attractive to today's readers, who often feel bombarded by more information than they can handle. Consider, for example, the popularity of the *USA Today* newspaper, with its countless news items offered in brief snippets for overtaxed readers. In contrast, the *New York Times* offers lengthy

(*Text continues on p. 289.*)

ECSTASY: WHAT WE KNOW AND DON'T KNOW ABOUT MDMA A SCIENTIFIC REVIEW

EXECUTIVE SUMMARY

A number of our nation's best monitoring mechanisms have detected an alarming increase in the popularity of MDMA (3,4-methylenedioxymethamphetamine), particularly among young Americans. This report, _Ecstasy: What We Know and Don't Know About MDMA_, represents a scientific review of what research has discovered about how this drug works in the brain and what requires further study to fully understand the consequences of using this illicit substance.

Much of this report is based on a scientific conference – _MDMA/Ecstasy Research: Advances, Challenges, Future Directions_ – that was sponsored by the National Institute on Drug Abuse (NIDA) and the National Institutes of Health and held July 19-20, 2001. Information in this report was supplemented by an exhaustive review of the extensive published scientific literature on MDMA, particularly that which has appeared in scientific and medical journals during the past five years.

MDMA, a relatively simple chemical belonging to the amphetamine family of compounds, has properties of both stimulants and hallucinogens. While MDMA does not cause true hallucinations, many people have reported distorted time and perception while under the influence of this drug. The vast majority of people take MDMA orally, and its effects last approximately four to six hours. Many users will "bump" the drug, taking a second dose when the effects of the initial dose begin to fade. The typical dose is between one and two tablets, with each containing approximately 60-120 milligrams of MDMA. However, tablets of what users call Ecstasy often contain not only MDMA but a number of other drugs, including methamphetamine, caffeine, dextromethorphan, ephedrine, and cocaine.

One of the more alarming facts about MDMA is that despite its known detrimental effects, there are increasing numbers of students and young adults who continue to use the drug. Results from the 2000 Monitoring the Future survey indicate that MDMA use increased among students in the 12th, 10th, and 8th grades.

Effects of Acute Doses of MDMA
Controlled studies in humans have shown that MDMA has potent effects on the cardiovascular system and on the body's ability to regulate its internal temperature. Of great concern is MDMA's adverse effect on the pumping efficiency of the heart – in the presence of MDMA, increased physical activity increases heart rate significantly, but the heart does not respond in its normal manner, which is to increase the efficiency with which it pumps blood. Since MDMA use is often associated with sustained, strenuous activity, such as dancing, MDMA's effects on the heart could increase the risk of heart damage or other cardiovascular complications in susceptible individuals.

Long-Term Consequences of MDMA: Neurochemical and Developmental
Acute doses of MDMA produce marked changes in both dopamine and serotonin systems within the brain. Though the changes in dopaminergic neurons appear transient, the data suggest that the changes in the serotonergic system are longer lasting. In addition, examinations of more global brain function have shown that the effects of acute doses of MDMA extend to regions of the brain that are thought to be involved in higher thought processes. These findings have raised concern about possible long-term effects on both infrequent and regular users of MDMA.

< continued >

FIGURE 15.8
A three-page executive summary from a much longer (55 page) report

Answers the question "What is the issue?"

Answers the questions "What was found?" and "How was it found?"

Answers the question "What does it mean?"

FIGURE 15.8
(Continued)

Since younger brains may have an increased susceptibility to the neurotoxic effects of MDMA, it may be that the youngest, fastest developing brains – those of a developing fetus – could be particularly vulnerable to the effects of this apparent serotonin neurotoxin. Since most MDMA users are young and in their reproductive years, it is possible that some female users may take MDMA when they are pregnant, either inadvertently or intentionally, because of the misperception that it is a safe drug. Studies in animals have shown that MDMA has little effect on the physical development of the young brain.

Behavioral and cognitive studies in laboratory animals, however, have identified significant adverse cognitive effects from pre and neonatal exposure to MDMA. This effect was not due to serotonergic neurotoxicity; the mechanisms underlying the development of these cognitive deficits are not known yet. Though the rodent experiments have predictive value, it is not known whether human fetuses exposed to MDMA when their mothers abuse the drug will develop persistent and learning memory deficits.

Long-Term Functional Consequences of MDMA:
Behavioral, Mood, Psychiatric, and Cognitive
Because MDMA produces long-term deficits in serotonin function, and because serotonin function has been implicated in the etiology of many psychiatric disorders including depression and anxiety, investigators have suspected that MDMA users may experience more psychopathology than nonusers. Indeed, a number of investigators have found that heavy MDMA users experience a constellation of psychiatric changes, scoring significantly higher on measures of obsessive traits, anxiety, paranoid thoughts, and disturbed sleep, among others.

There is a large and growing body of evidence from a variety of studies with humans that MDMA use can have long-lasting effects on memory. Moreover, the relationship between memory problems and MDMA use appears to have a dose-dependent relationship, that is, the more MDMA used, the greater the deficit.

In attempting to answer the question of whether MDMA causes permanent damage to human memory abilities, there is no one study that provides a resounding, definitive yes. To be sure, no study provides any evidence that MDMA is a beneficial drug or even that it is safe when taken in moderation. In fact taking MDMA at any dose carries with it the risk of inducing physiological, psychological, and cognitive damage in vulnerable users.

Methodological Issues
As much as the data collected so far largely supports the proposition that MDMA damages the serotonin system in the brain and produces long-lasting behavioral deficits, researchers agree that methodological issues, such as limited sample size and difficulties controlling for the possible influence of other illicit substances, have made it difficult to move beyond generalities and unequivocally prove a cause and effect relationship between MDMA use and specific cognitive or psychological damage in humans.

Since there seem to be few, if any, young people who use MDMA without also abusing other drugs, this will continue to be a confounding factor in future studies. Self-reporting also means that it is not possible to determine with complete confidence or accuracy how much a person has consumed, either on a particular occasion or over a lifetime of use. This uncertainty arises for two reasons: MDMA content is not constant across all tablets, and user memory of how much and how often a person took MDMA over many years is far from reliable.

< continued >

FIGURE 15.8
(Continued)
Answers the
question "What
should be done?"

Challenges and Future Directions

Though the data presented at this conference and in the literature support the hypothesis that MDMA produces acute behavioral and physiological effects, there is still more to be determined about factors that precipitate severe acute toxicity. For example, are there predisposing genetic factors that increase the risk for acute toxicity? Is overall health status important? Which organs and systems are the primary targets of MDMA toxicity? Are interactions with other drugs important? Does MDMA use lead to tolerance, withdrawal, and craving?

Source: Excerpt from National Institute on Drug Abuse <archives.drugabuse.gov/ PDF/MDMAconf.pdf>.

text that is information rich but more time-consuming to digest. Summaries are especially adaptable to the hypertext-linked design of Web-based documents. Instead of long blocks of text, Web pages are often designed with concise modules, or "chunks," of information that stand alone, are easy to scan, and require little or no scrolling (see Chapter 21 for more on Web page design). Moreover, magazine Web sites such as *Forbes* or *The Economist* offer email summaries of their hard copy articles.

While such capsules or "digests" of information are an efficient way to stay informed, summaries carry with them potential pitfalls, as media critic Ilan Greenberg points out (65):

Ethical pitfalls of summaries

- A condensed version of a complicated document may provide a useful overview, but this superficial treatment often fails to communicate the document's full complexity—that is, the complete story. Whoever summarizes a lengthy document makes decisions about what to leave out and what to leave in, what to emphasize, and what to ignore. During the selection process, the original message could very well be distorted. Therefore, be careful that any summary (except a descriptive abstract) conveys the full picture of what the original document says.

- In a summary of someone else's writing, the tone or "voice" of the original author often disappears—along with that writer's way of seeing. Be careful that you not only carry the essential facts of an original document into your summary, but that in the process of condensing you don't distort the original writer's intent. If a writer says, as in Figure 15.1, "Scientists know with virtual certainty" that human activities are leading to global warming, make sure that this critical point carries into your summary. Downplaying ("some scientists suspect") or overplaying ("scientists are 100% certain") the original writer's intent is a distortion.

Although summaries do have their place in our busy world, the more complex the topic, the more that readers need the whole story.

STRATEGIES
for Summaries

▸ **Start the summary process by reading the original document.** Read the document all the way through without highlighting or taking notes, to get a clear sense of its main point and most important subpoints.

▸ **Reread the original while highlighting essential information.** A second read, combined with highlighting or underlining, will give you a sharper picture of important points.

▸ **Save only the key information.** Delete the inessential information from the original document to create a rough draft of the original document's wording.

▸ **Rewrite the key information in your own words.** Initially don't worry about length. Avoid using any of the original document's words unless a key term or phrase is indispensable. If you must quote a passage directly, use quotation marks around the quoted words.

▸ **Edit your version.** When you have included everything readers need, edit your work for conciseness, getting rid of wordiness, combining related ideas, and eliminating repetition.

▸ **Finally, check your version against the original.** Verify that you have added no personal observations (unless you are writing an executive abstract) and have not altered the meaning, intent, or emphasis of the original.

▸ **Indicate the exact source of the summarized material.** When you are summarizing someone else's work, immediately follow your summary with a reference to the original source.

▸ **Use the appropriate types of summaries in your own formal documents.** Formal reports and proposals always include informative abstracts (when the intent is simply to provide a snapshot) or executive summaries (when the intent is to persuade readers how to think about the longer document). Closing summaries are always helpful in such reports. Descriptive abstracts can be helpful when included on the title page of a formal report or proposal.

▸ **Remain aware of ethical considerations.** A summary that adds material not found in the original document or omits critical information from the original is misleading and unethical. Likewise, misrepresenting the original document's point of view is unethical.

CHECKLIST
for Summaries

☐ Can the summary stand alone?

☐ Is the summary accurate when checked against the original?

☐ Is the summary free of needless details?

☐ Is the summary concise yet clear and comprehensive?

☐ Is the source of this summary documented?

☐ Does the descriptive abstract merely tell what the original is about?

☐ Is the level of technicality appropriate for its audience?

☐ Does the executive summary tell readers how to think about the information?

APPLICATIONS

GENERAL APPLICATIONS

1. Find an article about your major field or area of interest and write both an informative abstract and a descriptive abstract for the article.

2. Find a long article (at least five pages) and summarize it, following the step-by-step process described in this chapter, and keeping accuracy, completeness, conciseness, and nontechnical language always in mind. Capture the essence and main points of the original article in no more than one-fourth the length. Use your own words, and do not distort the original. Submit a copy of the original along with your summary.

TEAM APPLICATION

Organize into small groups and choose a topic for discussion: an employment problem, a campus problem, plans for an event, suggestions for energy conservation, or the like. (A possible topic: Should employers have the right to require lie detector tests, drug tests, or AIDS tests for their employees?) Discuss the topic for one class period, taking notes on significant points and conclusions. Afterward, organize and edit your notes in line with the directions for writing summaries. Write a summary of the group discussion in no more than 200 words. As a group, compare your individual summaries for accuracy, emphasis, conciseness, and clarity.

GLOBAL APPLICATION

Find a long article (longer than five pages) from a technical, scientific, financial, or similar publication. Pick an article that deals with an issue that is global in scope (for instance, an article about the use of pesticides in different countries or an article about the ways in which financial decisions have worldwide impacts). Summarize this article for an audience of nonspecialists, but for two different groups: one group of United States citizens and another group of citizens in a different country. Learn what you can about the other country by looking on the Internet and determining key scientific, political, or financial issues. Or bring knowledge you have from your own travel (such as a study abroad experience) or background, or from a class that you took. What will you highlight in the summary for the U.S. readers, and what will you highlight in the article for the non-U.S. readers, and why? Bring both copies to class to discuss with others.

COMPUTER/WEB-BASED APPLICATION

In class, form teams who have similar majors or interests. Decide on a related topic currently in the news. Using a combination of Web-based and hard-copy versions of news coverage, compare summarized versions with more detailed coverage. For example:

- a headline summary from the *New York Times* "Quick News" and "Page Plus" links versus the original article
- a summarized cover story from "The Daily News Info" link on *Newsweek*'s Web site versus the original article

Each team member should compare the benefits and drawbacks of the story's shorter and longer versions, making a copy of each. Are there instances in which the shorter version simply is ethically inadequate as a sole source of information? Using your sample documents, explain and illustrate. As a full team, assemble and discuss the collected findings, and select one member to present the findings to the class.

For additional technical writing resources that will help you master the chapter objectives, go to **www.mytechcommlab.com**.

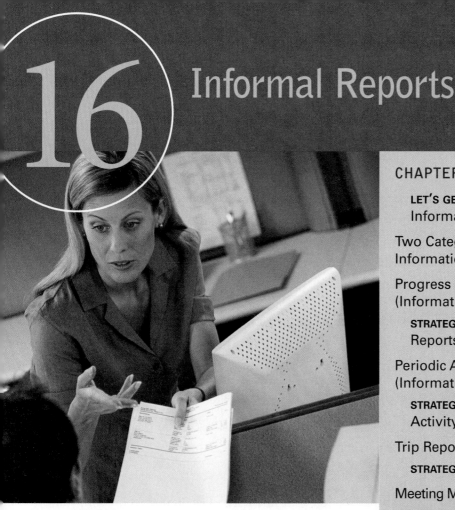

16

Informal Reports

LEARNING OBJECTIVES FOR THIS CHAPTER

▸ Define and understand the role
  of informal reports

▸ Identify the difference between informational
  and analytical reports

▸ Plan and write effective informational reports

▸ Plan and write effective analytical reports

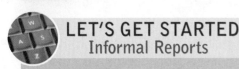

LET'S GET STARTED
Informal Reports

You have probably written a short informal report at one time or another (at school, for an internship, or on the job). Make some notes about that situation and then think about a different real-life situation for which you might need to write a short informal report. For instance, you may need to write a short progress report for your employer about what you accomplished this week. Or you may want to write a feasibility report addressed to your instructor, explaining and justifying the final project you propose to do for class. Use a memo format to write your short report.

Questions to ask about the short report you wrote as you review the material in this chapter:

▸ Is the purpose of the report clear (status update, recommendation, other)?

▸ Have I used headings and bullets, and if so, are these used appropriately?

▸ Is the tone of my short report personal enough, yet professional?

▸ Is the report's length appropriate?

▸ Is the subject line clear?

At the end of this chapter, review your initial Let's Get Started report with your instructor or with a group of students, to see how much you might change or modify the report based on what you have learned from the chapter.

Definition
of informal reports

When you think of reports, you probably picture long, formal documents that contain many pages of research, information, charts and graphs, footnotes, and other details. Yet in the workplace, for every long, formal report dozens of shorter reports are written, reports focused on only one or two very specific issues. These *informal reports* help people make informed decisions on matters such as the most comfortable office chairs to buy or the best recruit to hire for management training. Unlike long formal reports (discussed in Chapter 17), most informal reports require no extended planning, are prepared quickly, contain little or no background information, and have no *front* or *end matter* (title page, table of contents, glossary, works cited, index).

Despite being so focused and concise, informal reports do provide the information and analysis that readers need every day on the job. Although various formats can be used, informal reports most often take the form of a memorandum. Informal memo reports are usually written using word-processing software and distributed as email attachments. Recipients can read the documents on their computer screens or print hard copies. Often, to ensure that the formatting of the document will remain consistent, the memo will be converted into a PDF file. In some organizations, it might be customary to distribute informal reports by hard copy (print), too.

Format of informal reports

TWO CATEGORIES OF REPORTS: INFORMATIONAL AND ANALYTICAL

In the professional world, decision makers rely on two types of informal reports: some reports focus primarily on information ("what we're doing now," "what we did last month," "what our customer survey found," "what went on at the department meeting"), while others may also include analysis ("what this information means for us," "what courses of action should be considered," "what we recommend, and why").

Informational versus analytical reports

The purpose of an *informational report* is to inform; that is, to provide data and other information to answer basic questions, such as how much progress has been made on a project (progress reports), what activity has taken place over the course of a certain period of time (activity reports), what activity occurred during a business trip (trip reports), or what discussions took place in a meeting (meeting minutes). These reports help keep an organization running from day to day by providing short, timely updates on important activities.

Purpose of informational reports

✳ Explore the Concept with the Case Study on Informational Reports at **mytechcommlab**

Unlike informational reports, *analytical reports* offer both information and conclusions based on the information. Analysis is the heart of technical communication. Analysis involves evaluating information, interpreting it accurately, drawing valid conclusions, and making persuasive recommendations. Although gathering and reporting information are essential workplace skills, analysis is ultimately what professionals do to earn their pay. Analytical reports analyze and evaluate whether a project or situation is feasible (feasibility reports), make recommendations on how to proceed (recommendation reports), or constructively critique the work of others (peer review reports).

Purpose of analytical reports

PROGRESS REPORTS (INFORMATIONAL)

Organizations depend on *progress reports* (also called status reports) to monitor progress and problems on various projects. Progress reports may be written either for internal personnel or outside clients. In the case of internal audiences, managers use progress reports to evaluate projects, monitor employees, decide how to

Purpose, audience, and frequency of progress reports

allocate funds, and keep track of delays or expense overages that could dramatically affect outcomes and project costs. In the case of external audiences, progress reports explain to clients how time and money are being spent and how difficulties have been overcome. The reports can therefore be used to assure the client that the project will be completed on schedule and on budget.

Many contracts stipulate the dates and stages when progress will be reported. Failing to report on time may invoke contractual penalties. Some organizations require regular progress reports (daily, weekly, monthly), while others only use such reports as needed, such as when a project milestone has been reached.

Elements of progress reports

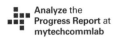

Analyze the
Progress Report at
mytechcommlab

Figure 16.1 shows a progress report from a training manager to a company vice president. Because the audience is internal, the writer has chosen memo format. A report like this to an external client might be written in letter format and on company letterhead as a legal record. Notice also how the report provides only those details essential to the reader. In addition, it follows a timeline structure, beginning with a summary of progress on the project (or since the last progress report) and concluding with the next steps to be completed. The text of this report (without the heading guide, company logo, and copy notation) also appears on pages 96–97.

STRATEGIES
for Progress Reports

▸ **Choose an appropriate format.** Routine, regular reports may be delivered in email format, whereas more infrequent reports might be better delivered via a signed memo (or a letter, when the report is for an external client).

▸ **Provide a clear subject line.** All progress reports should clearly identify their purpose in the subject line of a memo or email, or in the introduction to a letter.

▸ **Present information efficiently.** Because readers of progress reports are managers or clients who want the bottom line information as quickly as possible, chunk the information into logically headed sections and use bulleted or numbered lists. Leave out information readers will already know, but do not omit information they need to know.

▸ **Make sure your report answers the anticipated questions.** First identify what has been accomplished since the last report; then discuss any important details such as outcomes of meetings, problems encountered and solutions implemented or proposed, deadlines met or missed, resources/materials needed, and so on. Conclude with steps to be completed in time for the next report, with specific dates, if available.

FIGURE 16.1
A progress report

BETA National

MEMORANDUM
To: P. J. Stone, Senior Vice President
From: B. Poret, Group Training Manager *B.P.*
Date: June 6, 20xx
Subject: *Progress Report: Equipment for New Operations Building* ← • Subject line identifies exact purpose of the report

Work Completed
Our training group has met twice since our May 12 report. In our first meeting, ← • Summarizes first achievement
we identified the types of training we anticipate.

Types of Training Anticipated
- Divisional Systems Training
- Divisional Clerical Training (Continuing)
- Divisional Clerical Training (New Employees)
- Divisional Management Training (Seminars)
- Special/New Equipment Training

In our second meeting, we considered various areas for the training room.

Training Room Assignment and Equipment   ← • Summarizes second achievement
The frequency of training necessitates having a training room available daily. The
large training room in the Corporate Education area (10th floor) would be ideal.
Please confirm that this room can be assigned to us on a full-time basis.
To support the training programs, we purchased this equipment:
- Audioviewer
- LCD monitor
- CD recorder and monitor
- Software for computer-assisted instruction
- Tape recorder

This equipment will allow us to administer training in varied modes, ranging from
programmed and learner-controlled instruction to seminars and workshops.

Work Remaining   ← • Describes work remaining
To support the training, we need to furnish the room appropriately. Because the types
of training will vary, the furniture should provide a flexible environment. Outlined here
are our anticipated furnishing needs.
- Tables and chairs that can be set up in many configurations. These would allow ← • Bulleted list breaks up dense information
  for individual or group training and large seminars.
- Portable room dividers. These would provide study space for training with
  programmed instruction, and allow for simultaneous training.
- Built-in storage space for audiovisual equipment as well as training supplies.
  This storage space should be multipurpose, providing work or
  display surfaces.
- A flexible lighting system, for audiovisual presentations and individualized study.

The project is on schedule. As soon as we receive your approval of these specifications, ← • Concludes with request for approval of next phase
we will send out bids for room dividers and have plans drawn for built-in storage.

The next example (Figure 16.2) is a progress report written by a student. As you work on a longer report or term project, your instructor might require a progress report. In this example, the student writer documents the progress she has made on her term project: a causal analysis examining the impact of a recently formed town committee.

PROGRESS REPORT

TO: Dr. J. Lannon

FROM: T. Fitzgerald, Student *T.F.*

DATE: April 27, 20XX

SUBJECT: Analytical Report

             A STUDY OF THE IMPACT OF THE SANDWICH HISTORIC DISTRICT COMMITTEE ON THE TOWN'S ARCHITECTURAL CHARACTER

WORK COMPLETED TO DATE

    March 22:   Completed report on Sandwich Historic District Committee.

    April 11:   Obtained maps of Sandwich, legislation, certificates of appropriateness, exemption, and appeals from Town Hall.

    April 12, 14, 15:   Investigated district area by car, noted differences in historic and nonhistoric areas.

    April 18:   Photographed sampling of areas in district. Twenty photos taken, fifteen returned by developer.

    April 19:   Divided master map into sections, redefining district.

    April 20:   Completed tentative outline.

    April 22:   Interviewed chairman of Committee, Donald Bourne. Received new set of rules and regulations for district.

WORK IN PROGRESS: Drawing maps of present district and redefined area.

WORK TO BE COMPLETED

    April 28:   Interview Edward Cain, committee member.

    May 2:   Interview Gary Sosa committee member.

DATE FOR COMPLETION: May 11, 20XX

FIGURE 16.2 Progress report on a term project

PERIODIC ACTIVITY REPORTS (INFORMATIONAL)

Periodic activity reports resemble progress reports in that they summarize activities over a specified period. But unlike progress reports, which summarize specific accomplishments on a particular project, periodic activity reports summarize general activities during a particular period. Periodic activity reports are almost always internal, written by employees to keep their supervisors up to date on their activities as a whole, in order to help managers monitor workload. In many companies, these reports, usually written weekly or monthly, are called "status reports."

Figure 16.3 shows a periodic activity report, in the form of a weekly status report. Notice how Laura Hardin presents the most vital information first (the ongoing user manuals project) and ends with necessary but less pressing details (vacation time and "other"). The report contains only the information and level of detail her supervisor needs.

Purpose, audience, and frequency of periodic activity reports

Elements of periodic activity reports

STRATEGIES
for Periodic Activity Reports

▶ **Choose an appropriate format.** Periodic activity reports are usually written in email or memo format to a supervisor. However, some organizations may require a predesigned form.

▶ **Provide a clear subject line.** As with any report, identify the exact purpose of a periodic activity report by providing a subject line, such as "Monthly activity report for August."

▶ **Present information efficiently.** All report readers want the bottom line. Omit minor details but include all the essentials. Use headers to chunk information, and bulleted and numbered lists to break up dense prose for easier reading.

▶ **Make sure your report answers the expected questions.** Begin by describing your most important accomplishments during the period (such as progress on an ongoing project). Then describe any other relevant activity since the last report, (such as completion of one-time projects, attendance at meetings, supplies needed, conflicts or problems encountered, schedule changes, vacation time taken or upcoming, and so forth).

TRIP REPORTS (INFORMATIONAL)

Trip reports resemble periodic activity reports in that they detail activities during a given period, but they focus specifically on business-related travel rather than a variety of workplace activities. These reports, like periodic

Purpose and audience of trip reports

Email format
indicates routine
nature of report

Subject line clearly
indicates purpose
of report

Progress on most
important ongoing
projects presented
first

Bold introductions
and double spaces
between items
highlight and
separate categories
of information

Less vital
information
presented at
the end

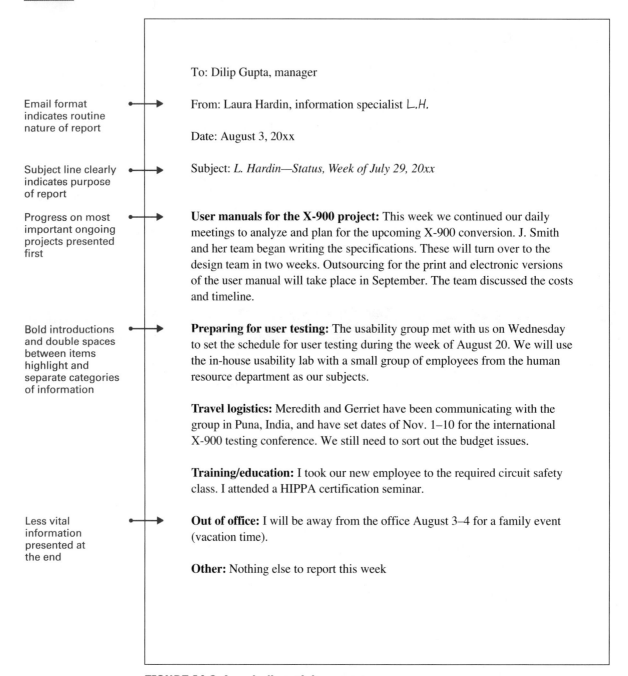

To: Dilip Gupta, manager

From: Laura Hardin, information specialist L.H.

Date: August 3, 20xx

Subject: *L. Hardin—Status, Week of July 29, 20xx*

User manuals for the X-900 project: This week we continued our daily meetings to analyze and plan for the upcoming X-900 conversion. J. Smith and her team began writing the specifications. These will turn over to the design team in two weeks. Outsourcing for the print and electronic versions of the user manual will take place in September. The team discussed the costs and timeline.

Preparing for user testing: The usability group met with us on Wednesday to set the schedule for user testing during the week of August 20. We will use the in-house usability lab with a small group of employees from the human resource department as our subjects.

Travel logistics: Meredith and Gerriet have been communicating with the group in Puna, India, and have set dates of Nov. 1–10 for the international X-900 testing conference. We still need to sort out the budget issues.

Training/education: I took our new employee to the required circuit safety class. I attended a HIPPA certification seminar.

Out of office: I will be away from the office August 3–4 for a family event (vacation time).

Other: Nothing else to report this week

FIGURE 16.3 **A periodic activity report**

activity reports, are written to help a supervisor monitor employee activities. In the case of trip reports, when employers pay for employee travel, managers need to know that the company is getting its money's worth. Managers also need to know what employees learn through their travels.

Explore the Tutorial on Trip Reports at mytechcommlab

Figure 16.4 shows a trip report written by an employee who has traveled to a branch office to inspect the site and interview those employees about absenteeism and hiring problems at that branch. Because the report is informational, not analytical, it sticks only to the facts. Note also that Bill Moskowicz begins the report with a purpose statement, accounts for how he spent his time, identifies the people with whom he met, offers a summary of what he learned, and provides a conclusion.

Elements of trip reports

For more on Trip Reports, see the Strategies below.

STRATEGIES
for Trip Reports

▶ **Take good notes and make accurate transcriptions of interviews.** If you must interview people, either ask their permission to record the conversation or take careful notes. Transcribe interviews immediately, while the discussion is still fresh in your mind. If you investigate a location or site, take careful notes of what you observe.

▶ **Write down the names of people and places.** Make sure you are able to indicate who you spoke with (spelling their names correctly and getting their job titles right) and the names of places visited.

▶ **Account for times and locations.** Demonstrate a good use of your time by accounting for it (but not exhaustively). If you visit more than one location, be clear about what occurred at each.

▶ **Provide a clear title and purpose statement.** A clear title indicates exactly which trip you are referring to, including date(s), while a purpose statement at the beginning of the report prevents any possible confusion as to your reasons for taking the trip.

▶ **Use a format that is easy to navigate.** As you would in any report, provide clear headings to break up chunks of information and use bulleted/numbered lists, double spacing, and so on, for ease of readability.

▶ **Describe findings completely and objectively.** Don't omit vital information or include irrelevant information, and don't insert personal impressions—stick to the facts.

▶ **Offer to follow up.** Because trip reports may lead to further questions from a supervisor, indicate that you are available to help answer those questions. Unless you have been asked to do so, do not make recommendations.

FIGURE 16.4
A trip report

Subject line
identifies trip
and date

Starts with a
purpose statement

Provides an
accounting of how
time was spent

Includes discussion
of what was learned

Uses bulleted list
(and headings) to
break up text and
identify key points

To: Monica Herrera, Director of Human Resources, Boston office
From: Bill Moskowicz, Human Resources Specialist *B. M.*
Date: March 30, 20xx
Subject: *Visit to the Eastfield Office*

PURPOSE

On March 20th, I visited the Eastfield office to explore these two issues:

• Higher than average rate of employee absenteeism at that office
• Difficulties hiring qualified employees to work and live in or near the
  Eastfield Fort Channel area

To pinpoint the causes of these problems, I decided to interview three individuals
face-to-face, in hopes of getting more candid and detailed responses than I would
via phone or email, particularly regarding the sensitive absenteeism problem.

SCHEDULE

I spoke with the following people individually: Susan Sheehan, Director of
HR (9:00 a.m.–10:00 a.m.); Sammy Lee, Marketing Manager for the gourmet
desserts division (10:00 a.m.–11 :00 a.m.); and Megan Fields, an Administrative
Assistant in the distribution division (11:00 a.m.–12:00 p.m.). Then we all had
lunch and continued the discussion between noon and 2:00 p.m., at which time
I transcribed my recordings and headed back to Boston.

INTERVIEWS

The interviews were illuminating. Essentially all three pointed out how the
absenteeism and hiring problems are not entirely separate issues; in fact, they
are closely linked. While once a thriving, safe, and low-crime city (including
the branch's Fort Channel area), Eastfield has now fallen upon difficult
economic times, particularly in the last year. All three employees identified
the following problems:

• Increased gang activity and vagrancy in the Fort Channel area
• Lack of safe public transportation to and from the office or a secure, on-site
  parking facility

FIGURE 16.4
(Continued)

- An increasing decline in amenities, especially lunch venues or safe public areas nearby
- Decreased security resulting from a busy police force and high security guard turnover

While Susan and Sammy can both afford to occasionally take cabs and leave the Fort Channel area for lunch, Megan pointed out her limitations due to salary and an insufficient reimbursement program.

The Fort Channel area's problems have all had a direct impact on employee hiring in recent months. Both Susan and Sammy reported losing promising potential employees following interviews. According to Susan, while United Foods manufactures and distributes gourmet products, attracting those who wish to work in an upscale environment, potential employees are often frightened away, preferring employment at either the Boston office or with competitors located elsewhere in the state. At the same time, very few have opted to relocate from the Boston to Eastfield offices to help account for imbalances.

CONCLUSION

While the goal of this trip was not for me to make recommendations, I have some specific ideas. I would be glad to speak with you further to answer any questions and to share those ideas with you.

Provides an offer to follow up

MEETING MINUTES (INFORMATIONAL)

Purpose, audience, and distribution of meeting minutes

Many team or project meetings require someone to record the proceedings. *Meeting minutes* are the records of such meetings. Copies of minutes usually are distributed (often via email) to all members and interested parties, to track the proceedings and to remind members about their responsibilities. Usually one person is appointed to record the minutes. Often, the person assigned will type minutes on a laptop computer and email them out as soon as the meeting is completed. Be sure to proofread the minutes, check the spelling of the attendees' names, and consider how you have described any politically sensitive or confidential issues before sending. Remember, email can travel widely.

Figure 16.5 shows minutes from a personnel manager's meeting.

STRATEGIES
for Meeting Minutes

- **Take good notes during the meeting.** Don't rely on your memory, even if you write up the minutes immediately after the meeting. Write down who said what, especially if a particularly important point was raised.

- **Complete the minutes immediately after the meeting.** Even if you take good notes, you may forget the context of a particular point if you wait too long. Write up the minutes immediately.

- **Include a clear title, with the meeting date.** A clear title should indicate the meeting's exact purpose ("sales conference planning meeting"), and always include the meeting date to prevent confusion with similar meetings.

- **List attendees.** List everyone who attended. If the meeting was chaired or moderated, indicate by whom.

- **Describe all agenda items.** Make sure all topics discussed are recorded. Your own memory of meeting topics and that of other meeting attendees is usually fleeting.

- **Record all decisions or conclusions.** If everyone agreed on a point, or if a vote was taken, be sure to include those results in your minutes.

- **Make sure the minutes are easy to navigate.** Use headings, lists, and other helpful design features.

- **Make sure the minutes are precise and clear.** Describe each topic fully yet concisely. Don't leave out important nuances, but stick to the facts.

- **Keep personal commentary, humor, and "sidebar" comments out of meeting minutes.** Comments ("As usual, Ms. Jones disagreed with the committee") or judgmental words ("good," "poor," "irrelevant") are not appropriate.

Minutes of Personnel Managers' Meeting
October 5, 20xx

Members Present

Harold Tweeksbury, Jeannine Boisvert, Sheila DaCruz, Ted Washington, Denise Walsh, Cora Parks, Cliff Walsh, Joyce Capizolo

Agenda

1. The meeting was called to order Friday, October 5 at 10 A.M. by Cora Parks.

2. The minutes of the September meeting were approved unanimously.

3. The first new business was to approve the following Christmas season policies:

   a. Temporary employees should list their ID numbers in the upper-left corner of their receipt envelopes to help verification. Discount Clerical assistant managers will be responsible for seeing that this procedure is followed.

   b. When temporary employees turn in their envelopes, personnel from Discount Clerical should spot-check them for completeness and legibility. Incomplete or illegible envelopes should be corrected, completed, or rewritten.

4. Jeannine Boisvert moved that we also hold one-day training workshops for temporary employees in order to teach them our policies and procedures. The motion was seconded. Joyce Capizolo disagreed, saying that on-the-job training (OJT) was enough. The motion for the training session carried 6–3. The first workshop, which Jeannine agreed to arrange, will be held October 25.

5. Joyce Capizolo requested that temporary employees be sent a memo explaining the temporary employee discount procedure. The request was converted to a motion and seconded by Cliff Walsh. The motion passed by a 7–2 vote.

6. Cora Parks adjourned the meeting at 11:55 A.M.

Annotations (right margin):
- Clear title indicates the purpose of the meeting, along with its date
- Tells who attended
- Summarizes discussion of each item
- Tells who said what
- Explains decisions made or conclusions reached

FIGURE 16.5 Meeting minutes

FEASIBILITY REPORTS (ANALYTICAL)

Feasibility reports are used when decision makers need to assess whether an idea, plan, or course of action is realistic and practical. Sometimes an idea may make perfect sense from one perspective, but may not be feasible at the moment for one reason or another, usually because of timing. For example, a manufacturing company may want to switch to a more automated process, which would greatly reduce costs over the long term. But in the short term, the resulting layoffs would have a negative impact on morale.

Purpose of feasibility reports

Analyze the Feasibility Report at mytechcommlab

Typical questions about feasibility

A feasibility report provides answers to questions such as these:

- What is the problem or situation, and what is the best approach to solving or dealing with it?
- Is this course of action likely to succeed?
- Do the benefits outweigh the drawbacks or risks?
- What are the pros and cons, and what are the alternatives?
- Should anything be done at all? Should it wait? Is the timing right?

The answers are based on the writer's careful research.

Audience for feasibility reports

Managers and other decision makers are the primary audience for feasibility reports. These busy people want to see the recommendation or answer at or near the beginning of the document, followed by supporting evidence and reasoning. In other words, a feasibility report should use the "bottom line first" organizational pattern: here is the situation; here is our recommendation; and here is why this approach is feasible at this time.

Elements of feasibility reports

Figure 16.6 shows a feasibility report in which a securities analyst for a state pension fund reports to the fund's manager on the feasibility of investing in a rapidly growing computer maker. Notice how it starts with background, provides a direct recommendation, provides information that supports the recommendation, and ends with a call to action.

STRATEGIES
for Feasibility Reports

- ▶ **Make sure the subject line is clear.** Always use the word "feasibility" (or a synonym) in the title ("Subject: Feasibility of . . .").
- ▶ **Provide background information.** Your readers may not always need background information, but if they do, make it short.
- ▶ **Offer the recommendation near the beginning of the report.** Because readers of feasibility reports are interested primarily in the "bottom line," state it explicitly at the very beginning of the report, or just after the background information.
- ▶ **Provide the details, data, and criteria after the recommendation section.** Include supporting data, such as costs, equipment needed, results expected, and so on. Don't overdo the supporting data, but include everything directly relevant that will persuade readers to support your recommendation.
- ▶ **Explain why your recommendation is the most feasible of all the possible choices.** Your readers may prefer other choices. Persuade them that yours is the best choice.
- ▶ **End with a call to action.**

State Pension Fund

MEMORANDUM

To: Mary K. White, Fund Manager

From: Martha Mooney MM

Date: April 1, 20xx

Subject: *The Feasibility of Investing in WBM Computers, Inc.*   ← Clear subject line leaves no doubt as to purpose of report

Our Treasury bonds, composing 3.5 percent of the Fund's investment portfolio, mature on April 15. Current inflationary pressures make fixed-income investments less attractive than equities. As you requested, I have researched and compared investment alternatives based on these criteria: market share, earnings, and dividends. ← Gives brief background

Recommendation

Given its established market share, solid earnings, and generous dividends, WBM Computers, Inc. is a sound and promising company. I recommend that we invest our maturing bond proceeds in WBM's Class A stock. ← Makes a direct recommendation

Market Share

Though only ten years old, WBM competes strongly with established computer makers. Its market share has grown steadily for the past five years. This past year, services and sales ranked 367th in the industrial U.S., with orders increasing from $750 million to $1.25 billion. Net income places WBM 237th nationally, and 13th on return to investors. ← Explains the criteria supporting the recommendation

Earnings

WBM's net profit on sales is 9 percent, a roughly steady figure for the past three years. Whereas 1998 earnings were only $.09 per share, this year's are $1.36 per share. Included in these ten-year earnings is a two-for-one stock split issued November 2, 2004. Barring a global sales downturn WBM's outlook for continued strong earnings is promising.

Dividends

Investors are offered two types of common stock. The assigned par value of both classes is $.50 per share. Class A stock pays an additional $.25 per share dividend but restricts voting privileges to one vote for every ten shares held by the investor. Class B stock does not pay the extra dividend but carries full voting rights. The additional dividend from Class A shares would enhance income flow into our portfolio.

WBM shares now trade at 14 times earnings and current share price of $56.00, a bargain in my estimation. An immediate investment would add strength and diversity to our portfolio. ← Encourages reader action

FIGURE 16.6 A feasibility report

RECOMMENDATION REPORTS (ANALYTICAL)

Purpose and audience of recommendation reports

While a feasibility report sets out to prove that a particular course of action is the right one to take, a *recommendation report* shortens or even skips the feasibility analysis (since it has already taken place or been discussed) and gets right to the point of making a recommendation. Recommendation reports, like feasibility reports, may include supporting data, but they also state an affirmative position ("Here's what we should do and why") rather than examining whether the approach will work ("Should we do it?"). Like feasibility reports, recommendation reports are for the eyes of decision makers, and these documents take a direct stance.

Elements of recommendation reports

Figure 16.7 shows a recommendation report from a health and safety officer at an airline company to a vice president, regarding the workstation comfort of the company's reservation and booking agents. Notice that it is organized similarly to a feasibility report, but takes a more authoritative stance based on previous analysis, emphasizing expected rather than possible benefits. Also, a description of the problem and its causes precedes the recommendations.

Analyze the **Recommendation Report** at **mytechcommlab**

This is just one example of countless short reports used to examine a workplace problem and recommend a solution.

STRATEGIES
for Recommendation Reports

▸ **Provide a clear subject line.** As always, make sure the subject of the report is brief and directly to the point.

▸ **Keep background information short.** Keep the background history brief, but do discuss how feasibility has already been determined.

▸ **Discuss the problem or situation prior to making recommendations.** In addition to the brief background information, outline the problem or situation that the recommended actions will resolve. Then discuss the recommendations in as much detail as necessary.

▸ **Use an authoritative tone.** Take a strong stance and write with confidence, knowing that the recommendation has already been determined to be feasible.

▸ **Use headings and make them as informative as possible.** Instead of using the vague heading "Problem," be specific ("Causes of Agents' Discomfort"). Don't forget that you are writing to a "bottom line" audience.

▸ **End with a list of benefits for taking action.** Rather than appealing for action, assume that it will be taken by reemphasizing the benefits.

MEMORANDUM

To: R. Ames, Vice President, Personnel

From: B. Doakes, Health and Safety *B.D.*

Date: August 15, 20xx

Subject: **Recommendations for Reducing Agents' Discomfort**

In our July 20 staff meeting, we discussed physical discomfort among reservation and booking agents, who spend eight hours daily at workstations. They complain of headaches, eyestrain, blurred or double vision, backaches, and stiff joints. This report outlines the apparent causes and recommends ways of reducing discomfort.

Causes of Agents' Discomfort

For the time being, computer display screens can be ruled out as a cause of headaches and eye problems for the following reasons:

1. Our new display screens have excellent contrast and no flicker.

2. Research about effects of low-level radiation from computer screens is inconclusive.

The headaches and eye problems seem to be caused by excessive glare on display screens from background lighting.

Other discomforts, such as backaches and stiffness, apparently result from the agents' sitting in one position for up to two hours between breaks.

Recommended Changes

We can eliminate much discomfort by improving background lighting, workstation conditions, and work routines and habits.

Background Lighting. To reduce the glare on display screens, I recommend these changes in background lighting:

1. Decrease all overhead lighting by installing lower-wattage bulbs.

2. Keep all curtains and adjustable blinds on the south and west windows at least half-drawn, to block direct sunlight.

3. Install shades to direct the overhead lighting straight downward, so that it is not reflected on the screens.

Workstation Conditions. I recommend the following changes in the workstations:

1. Reposition all screens so light sources are neither at front nor back.

2. Wash the surface of each screen weekly.

3. Adjust each screen so the top is slightly below the operator's eye level.

4. Adjust all keyboards so they are 27 inches from the floor.

5. Replace all fixed chairs with pneumatic, multi-task chairs.

<continued>

**FIGURE 16.7
A recommendation report**

• Subject line directly states exact purpose of report

• Provides immediate orientation by giving brief background and main point

• Statement of problem or situation precedes recommendations

• Makes general recommendations

• Expands on each recommendation

FIGURE 16.7
(Continued)

Work Routines and Habits. These are recommended changes in agents' work routines and habits:

1. Allow frequent rest periods (10 minutes hourly instead of 30 minutes twice daily).
2. Provide yearly eye exams for agents, as part of our routine healthcare program.
3. Train agents to adjust screen contrast and brightness whenever the background lighting changes.
4. Offer workshops on improving posture.

Discusses benefits of following the recommendations →

These changes will give us time to consider more complex options such as installing hoods and antiglare filters on display screens, replacing fluorescent lighting with incandescent, covering surfaces with nonglare paint, or other disruptive procedures.

cc: J. Bush, Medical Director
     M. White, Manager of Physical Plant

PEER REVIEW REPORTS (ANALYTICAL)

Purpose and audience of peer review reports

Peer review reports are written between employees, providing a way for people (peers) to give each other constructive criticism and feedback. Because peer review reports are shared by colleagues wishing to preserve good workplace relationships, they must be written with tact.

Figure 16.8 illustrates the use of constructive criticism in peer review and can serve as a model for reviewing the work of other students in the classroom.

STRATEGIES
for Peer Review Reports

▸ **Start with the positives.** Briefly state the good points of the reviewed document as a way of leading into and balancing against the criticisms.

▸ **Organize by topic area.** Provide separate sections for suggestions about the reviewed document's writing style, design, use of visuals, and other areas.

▸ **Always provide constructive criticism.** Remember that you are reviewing the work of a colleague or colleagues. Review their work tactfully, as you would want them to review your work. However, don't ignore problem areas.

▸ **Support your criticisms with examples and advice.** Point to particular examples in the reviewed document as you discuss them. Suggest alternatives, if possible. Point to helpful resources, if applicable.

▸ **Close positively.** End with a friendly, encouraging tone. If the reviewed document is particularly problematic, state as much—but diplomatically.

FIGURE 16.8
**A peer review
report**

TO: Catie Noll, Advertising Associate
FROM: David Summer, Advertising Supervisor D.S.
DATE: May 1, 20xx
SUBJECT: Review of Your Feasibility Report for the Garvey Account

I have reviewed the first draft of your report for the Garvey account. Thank you for your good work! You have done a great job organizing the material and getting started. I would like to offer the following suggestions:

Voice: You use passive voice in a number of places where active voice would be more appropriate. For instance, at the bottom of page 7, you might want to change "A mistake was made" to "We made a mistake." I would recommend that you review the entire draft for this usage.

Organization: As a reader, I did not know what you were recommending in this report until I reached the very end. I would suggest that you move your recommendation up to the beginning of the report, then follow it with the supporting data. Our supervisors will want to know the bottom line right away.

Research: I noticed that most of your research was based on commercial Web sites. You should probably look at more reliable peer-reviewed sources, such as well-respected business newspapers, journal articles, and online publications of professional organizations.

Visuals/font: Great use of images, especially the maps on page 9. You might want to increase the font size of the base text.

I hope my recommendations are helpful as you complete this project. Your report is well on the way, offering solid reasons that should persuade the managers to try winning the Garvey account from our competitors. Please let me know if you have any questions.

Report starts with a friendly tone and says something positive before offering suggested changes.

Suggested changes are clear and organized by area

Writer provides rationale behind suggestions

Writer provides specific advice to help the writer improve the reviewed document

Report uses a polite closing

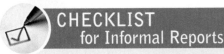

CHECKLIST
for Informal Reports

☐ Have I determined the right report type (status report, recommendation report, etc.) for this situation?

☐ When preparing a progress or status report, have I determined how much detail is necessary to include?

☐ When taking minutes for a meeting, have I included all the key decisions and discussion items and left out unnecessary detail?

☐ If I have decided to write a recommendation report, has the feasibility of the project or idea already been determined, or is a feasibility study and report more appropriate at this time?

☐ For all forms of informal reports, have I used a memo format?

☐ Is the subject line clear?

☐ Is the tone professional and polite but direct?

☐ For any report, have I done enough research so that my position is credible?

☐ Have I reviewed the Strategies boxes for my specific report type?

APPLICATIONS

GENERAL APPLICATIONS

1. For this or another class, write a progress report to your instructor, describing the progress you've made on a project you are working on (your final project, for instance). Use the strategies suggested in this chapter. Or, write a peer review report of a classmate's draft of an upcoming assignment.

2. For a current or past job or internship, write a periodic activity report in which you report on the past week's activities (actual or typical). Be sure to follow the strategies for periodic activity reports in this chapter.

3. Take notes at the next group event or meeting that you attend. Write up minutes for the meeting, thinking about how much detail to include and what kinds of information will be useful to the other members of the team.

TEAM APPLICATIONS

1. With two or three other classmates, identify a dangerous or inconvenient area or situation on campus or in your community (endless cafeteria lines, an unsafe

walkway, slippery stairs, a bad campus intersection). Observe the problem for several hours during a peak use period. Write a recommendation report to a specifically identified decision maker (the head of campus security, for example) describing the problem, listing your observations, and making a recommendation.

2. Convert the same report into a feasibility report by discussing several different approaches that might be taken and then recommending the feasibility of the approach you prefer.

GLOBAL APPLICATION

Assume that you are a team leader of a company that is based in the United States but has offices worldwide. You have been assigned a new manager who is a citizen of another country. This week you need to write a report recommending that all the staff on your team receive bonuses. You know the tone you would take if your manager were from the United States, but you are uncertain about what tone or level of politeness is appropriate for this new manager. Pick a country and do some research on the Internet about tone, style, and politeness in different cultures, remembering that not everyone in a country or culture is exactly alike. Write a short memo to your instructor explaining what you have learned and how you would shape your recommendation report in this situation.

COMPUTER/WEB-BASED APPLICATION

Many Web-based recommendation reports are not in the brief memo or email format described in this chapter. Take a look at some Web-based recommendation reports and write a description of the differences in length, format, look, and feel for these Web-based reports. For instance, the page at <www.cdc.gov/mmwr/preview/mmwrhtml/rr5704a1.htm> is a report about the prevention of certain diseases in pregnant women and infants. Why did the Center for Disease Control choose to use a Web-based format and not a shorter memo report? Write a short memo to your instructor answering this question.

For additional technical writing resources that will help you master the chapter objectives, go to **www.mytechcommlab.com**.

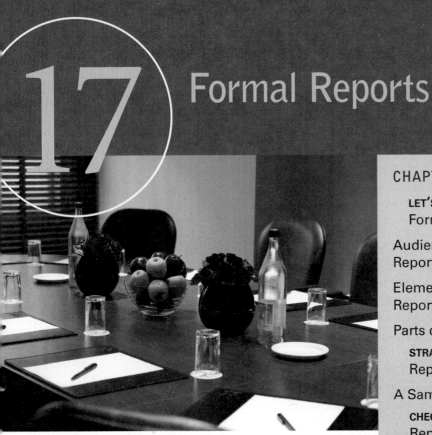

17 Formal Reports

LEARNING OBJECTIVES FOR THIS CHAPTER

▸ Differentiate between informal and formal reports

▸ Determine the audience and purpose
of a formal report

▸ Identify the characteristics of the three analytical
approaches: comparative, causal, and feasibility

▸ Write a formal report that incorporates
all the vital elements

▸ Include all the essential parts in a formal
report (front matter, text elements, end matter)

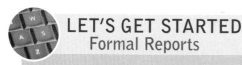

LET'S GET STARTED
Formal Reports

Formal reports are more complex and longer than informal reports (discussed in Chapter 16). Whether written for the workplace or for a class, formal reports are usually the culmination of many weeks or months of research, planning, drafting, and revising.

Think about a situation where you will need to write a formal report (for work, for this class, or for another class). Draft an initial plan by writing a 1–2 page memo to your instructor. In your plan consider the intended audience, purpose of the report, intended use of the report, main question(s) the report is intended to answer, the research and sources of information you will need to look at, and so on. Also create a rough outline for your report.

Questions to ask about the formal report as you review the material in this chapter may include the following:

- ▶ Who is my audience?

- ▶ Are there any secondary audiences (other readers)?

- ▶ What is the purpose of the report? To inform? To persuade?

- ▶ What would be the right length for this report?

- ▶ Should I use visuals? What kind?

- ▶ What types of research will I need to undertake?

At the end of this chapter, review your Let's Get Started report planning memo with your instructor or with a group of students and determine how much you might change or modify your plan based on what you have learned in this chapter.

M uch like the shorter analytical reports (feasibility and recommendation reports) discussed in Chapter 16, long, formal reports are analytical reports that often lead to recommendations. The formal report format replaces the informal memo format when the topic requires lengthy discussion. Formal reports generally include a title page, a table of contents, a system of headings, a list of references or works cited, and other front-matter and end-matter supplements.

Formal versus informal reports

An essential component of workplace problem solving, formal reports are designed to answer these questions:

- Based on the information gathered about this issue, what do we know?
- What conclusions can we draw?
- What should we do or not do?

Scenario for a formal report

For instance, imagine you work on a team of alternative energy experts (engineers, policy analysts, technical writers, lawyers), and the state department of energy has asked your organization for a report on the feasibility of producing biodiesel fuel in your state. First you will have to learn everything you can about the nature of the energy situation in your state at this time. Then you will need to compare the advantages and disadvantages of various options based on the *criteria* you are using to assess feasibility, such as cost-effectiveness, time required versus time available to begin biodiesel production, potential risk to the public and the environment, and so on. As you consider all the factors, you might find that the cheapest biodiesel option might also pose the greatest environmental risk; on the other hand, the most environmentally friendly option might be too expensive.

The importance of research in formal reports

This type of situation requires critical thinking and research. Aside from the technical knowledge about biodiesel production that your team already has, you may need additional research about the state or about the relationship of biodiesel to other sectors of the agricultural economy. Sources for this research may be available using secondary research (online or through the library), or you may need to answer these questions through primary research (surveys and interviews). For more information on how to conduct research, review Chapter 3.

AUDIENCE AND PURPOSE OF FORMAL REPORTS

Audience considerations

Because of their major impact on the decision-making process, formal reports are almost always written for an audience of decision makers: for example, government officials, corporate managers. You need to know who you are writing for and whether the report will be read primarily by an individual, a team, or a series of individuals with differing roles in the company.

Purpose considerations

To determine the purpose of the report, consider what question or questions it will ultimately answer. Also, consider why this particular topic is timely and useful to the intended audience. Use the Audience and Purpose Profile Sheet on page 53 to begin mapping out your audience and purpose for the report.

Next, determine which of the following three analytical categories best fits your purpose: the comparative analysis ("Which is better, X or Y?"), the causal analysis ("Why does X occur?"), or the feasibility analysis ("Is X a good idea?"). Note that not all formal reports fall neatly into one of these categories. Some reports blend two or all three. For instance, some reports will present a feasibility analysis but will also offer a great deal of comparative information.

Comparative Analysis

Comparative analysis rates similar items on the basis of specific criteria. For example, you may need to answer a question such as "Which type of security procedure—firewall or encryption—should we install in our company's computer system?"

Features of a comparative analysis

For a comparative analysis, base the comparison on clear and definite criteria: costs, uses, benefits/drawbacks, appearance, results. Identify your specific criteria and then rank these in order of importance. Give each item balanced treatment. Support and clarify the comparison or contrast through credible examples. Use research, if necessary, for examples that readers can visualize.

In a report titled "A Comparison of Different Methods for Uploading Digital Photographs," the abstract of which is shown in Figure 17.1, Christina Romano compares three different upload methods. Romano, a freelance photographer, was asked to write this report for a local photography club. Notice how the abstract makes clear the comparative approach of the report.

Abstract

This report compares three different methods for uploading digital photographs from camera to computer. Each method has strengths and weaknesses, depending on the needs and skill level of the photographer.

The first method involves connecting the camera to the computer with a USB cable, then uploading the photographs through whatever software is used (Picasa, iPhoto, other). This method is the easiest but does not give users very much control on where the photo files are stored.

The second method requires users to remove the storage card from the camera, insert it into a device called a card reader, and then connect the card reader to the computer's USB or firewire port. This method is quicker than the first one described, but it is also more complicated for users not experienced with the directories on their computer.

The final method uses the camera and computer's Bluetooth wireless communication feature. This method does not require any cables or card readers, but it can be slow.

For beginning photographers, this report recommends the first method. For more advanced photographers, the second method is often preferred.

FIGURE 17.1 Abstract for a formal report that takes a primarily comparative approach

Causal Analysis

Causal analysis explains the causes or the effects of an event, a problem, or a decision. For example, medical researchers may need to explain why so many apparently healthy people have sudden heart attacks. Or you might need to anticipate the possible effects of a proposed corporate merger on employee morale.

Features of a causal analysis

For a causal analysis, be sure the cause fits the effect. Faulty causal reasoning is extremely common, especially when people ignore other possible causes or when they confuse mere coincidence with causation. Make the links between effect and cause clear. Identify the immediate cause (the one most closely related to the effect) as well as the distant cause(s) (the ones that precede the immediate cause). For example, the immediate cause of an airplane crash might be a fuel-tank explosion, caused by a short circuit in frayed wiring. This wiring defect, it turns out, was caused by faulty design or poor quality control by the manufacturer. Discussing only the immediate cause merely scratches the surface of the problem.

The sample formal report by Crystal Cunningham, "Recommendation for a New Study of the Effects of Periodontal Disease on Preterm Low Birth Weight Babies," provided later in this chapter (see pages 326–337), takes a primarily causal approach. The writer examines the research literature on the question of whether periodontal disease in mothers might cause low birth weight in babies.

Feasibility Analysis

Feasibility analysis assesses the practicality of an idea or plan. For example, if your company needs to know whether increased business will justify the cost of maintaining a corporate blog for customers, you would do some research and describe your findings in a formal feasibility report. In some cases, you (the writer) can't actually determine the feasibility; all you can do is provide enough information so that the readers of your report can make the final decision.

For a feasibility analysis, consider the strength of supporting reasons. Choose the best reasons for supporting the action or decision being considered—based on your collected evidence. Also consider the strength of opposing reasons. Remember that people usually see only what they want to see. Avoid the temptation to overlook or downplay opposing reasons, especially for an action or decision you have been advocating. Consider alternate points of view and examine and evaluate all the evidence. After weighing the pros and cons, recommend a realistic and well-reasoned course of action.

In their report "A Study on the Feasibility of Biodiesel Production in Georgia" (the conclusion section is shown in Figure 17.2), Professor George A. Shumaker and his coauthors provide decision makers with the information needed to decide on a vital component of one state's energy policy. Their conclusion is a good example of how a feasibility study can take into account criteria that would have to be met (in this case cost effectiveness) for a proposed plan to be feasible.

ELEMENTS OF EFFECTIVE FORMAL REPORTS

Readers expect a report that is based on thorough research, critical analysis of the evidence, and clear presentation of the material.

FIGURE 17.2
Conclusion of
a formal report
that takes a
feasibility
approach

Conclusion

There exist a variety of potential feedstocks both in Georgia and nearby states that could be utilized to produce biodiesel. These feedstocks vary significantly in price depending on supply and demand conditions, as well as market structural conditions. Feedstock costs represent between 50 and 75 percent of the cost of producing biodiesel, and thus a reliable source of low priced feedstocks is critical to success. A 15 million gallon biodiesel plant would require about 27% of the vegetable and animal fats currently available within the State of Georgia. This facility would produce 750 million gallons of 2% blend for approximately twice the state demand. A 20% blend will create 75 million gallons of B20 or roughly 20% of the Georgia diesel market.

The processing technology for producing biodiesel is well established and presents little technological risk. The production of biodiesel is a very efficient process, returning about 3.2 units of energy for each unit used in production. Biodiesel is thus an excellent renewable fuel source. Biodiesel can be very easily integrated into the existing petroleum distribution system from the handling, chemical, physical, and performance perspectives.

Lacking government mandates or subsidies, a feedstock cost of about 10 cents per pound or less, given current diesel fuel prices, is needed for biodiesel to be cost effective.

Source: From "A Study on the Feasibility of Biodiesel Production in Georgia" by Professor George A. Shumaker, et al. Copyright © 2003 by The University of Georgia's Center on Agribusiness & Economic Development. Reprinted with permission.

Accurate, Appropriate, and Clearly Interpreted Data

Make sure your information is accurate and, to the best of your ability, unbiased. Use reputable information sources (particularly for statistical data), such as government documents, peer-reviewed sources, and sound reporting from nationally respected newspapers and similar sources. Make sure you interpret information fairly and provide valid conclusions based on your best research. Assume, for example, that you are writing a report to recommend the best brand of chain saw for a logging company. If, in reviewing test reports on various chain saw brands, you learn that one brand, Bomarc, is the easiest to operate but also has the fewest safety features, include both pieces of information in your report—even if you personally prefer this brand.

Choose and interpret the source material critically

Clearly Identified Purpose Statement

Begin by defining the primary question the report will need to answer, and then identify any secondary questions. The biodiesel report discussed earlier may have begun with a question from a state legislator: "Will producing biodiesel benefit the state of Georgia?" Answering this question is the report's primary purpose (feasibility analysis); however, this question leads to others, such as "What are the advantages and drawbacks of biodiesel use versus other types of fuels?" (comparative analysis), or "How does biodiesel fuel affect the environment?" (causal analysis). Create a purpose statement that addresses both primary and secondary purpose, such as

Address both primary and secondary purposes in the purpose statement

"The purpose of this report is to examine the feasibility of biodiesel production in the state of Georgia by comparing biodiesel fuels to other alternatives and assessing their environmental effects."

Understandable Structure

Use outlining, chunking, sequencing, paragraphing, and heading strategies

Structure your report for ease of navigation. Begin by outlining your report and adjusting that outline as you go. Then, chunk the text so that large passages of dense information don't overwhelm your readers. Next, sequence all your data in a logical order (spatial, chronological, problem-solution, cause and effect). After that, order information within your paragraphs for maximum readability. Finally, use clarifying headings and subheadings to announce what each section contains. For example, the heading "Data Analysis" does not really say much, whereas the heading "Physiological Effects and Health Risks" offers a clear, informative preview.

Readable Style

Write clearly, concisely, fluently, and personably

Readers don't want to be bogged down with cumbersome prose. Make your writing clear by avoiding ambiguous pronoun references and modifiers, using active voice, avoiding nominalizations, unstacking modifying nouns, and avoiding unnecessary jargon. Make your writing concise by avoiding wordiness and eliminating repetition and redundancy. Make your writing fluent by combining related ideas, varying sentence construction and length, and using parallel structure. Write personably by choosing the appropriate tone, and avoiding sexist and biased language. Ask a colleague or editor to copyedit your report before it is printed. Proofread the final version carefully.

Audience-centered Visuals

Use graphs, tables, charts, illustrations, diagrams, and photographs as appropriate

Provide as much visual information as appropriate to make complex statistics and numeric data easy to understand. Graphs are especially useful for analyzing rising or falling trends, levels, and long-term forecasts. Tables and charts are helpful for comparing data. Illustrations, diagrams, and photographs are an excellent way to show a component or special feature. Place each visual near the accompanying text and be careful not to overuse visuals. The biodiesel feasibility study mentioned earlier uses visuals effectively. For instance, on page 18 of the report (see Figure 17.3), the writers quantify the reduction in emissions when biodiesel fuel is used. In that example, a table provides an excellent way to compare information without the requirement of reading a lot of dense prose.

User-friendly Design

Design for consistency, cohesiveness, navigation, and emphasis

Remember that a well-designed document demonstrates consistency and cohesiveness via grid patterns, margins, paragraphs, justification, line spacing, font style, and font size. A good design also aids navigation and adds emphasis via headings, color, shading, bold, italic, underlining, color, bulleted and numbered lists, and running heads and feet (see Chapter 9).

FIGURE 17.3
**Effective use
of a visual in a
formal report**

18

Gelling of biodiesel varies depending upon the chemical composition of the feedstock used in its production. The higher the saturated fat of the feedstock, such as in animal fats, the higher the temperature at which gelling occurs. The converse is also true. Canola oil, with low levels of saturated fats, derived biodiesel provides the lowest gelling temperature biodiesel. Pure biodiesel should be stored and transported at temperatures above 50 F and blending temperatures should be above 40 F.

Environmental Impacts of Biodiesel Use

Studies completed by the Environmental Protection Agency (NREL/TP 2001) state that a 20% blend is "basically a trade off between cost, emissions, cold weather, material compatibility and solvency issues". Researchers believe the 20% blend to be the best blend for general use without encountering major issues. Higher blends often cause problems in winter and with nitrogen oxide emissions.

Table 10. Emission Changes with Biodiesel Fuels.

Emission	100% Biodiesel*	20% Biodiesel Blend*
Carbon Monoxide	-43.2%	-12.6%
Hydrocarbons	-56.3%	-11%
Particulates	-55.4%	-18%
Nitrogen Oxides	+5.8%	+1.2%
Air Toxics	-60% to -90%	-20%
Mutagenicity	-80% to -90%	-20%
Carbon Dioxide**	-78.3%	-15.7%

* Average of data from 14 EPA FTP Heavy duty test cycle tests, variety of stock engines
** Life Cycle Emission

It would appear that the use of biodiesel can be an effective means for reducing exhaust emissions. The relevant question becomes, how does the cost of reducing emission using biodiesel compare to other means of obtaining the same level of emission reduction? The answer to that question is beyond the scope of this inquiry.

Impact Analysis

Impact analysis is a key component of any feasibility study. An impact analysis indicates the effect of a new venture on the economy. Building a new biodiesel facility in Georgia will impact the economy on two levels. The new plant will generate output as it begins selling biodiesel and its by-products. These sales will, in turn, generate additional sales as the plant purchases inputs. The suppliers to the plant will increase the purchase of their inputs, thus

← • The table enables
readers to compare
data easily

Source: From "A Study on the Feasibility of Biodiesel Production in Georgia" by Professor George A. Shumaker, et al. Copyright © 2003 by The University of Georgia's Center on Agribusiness & Economic Development. Reprinted with permission.

PARTS OF FORMAL REPORTS

Most formal reports consist of the front matter, the text of the report, and the end matter. (Some parts of the front and end matter may be optional.) The following sections describe these various parts.

Letter of Transmittal

Many formal reports include a letter of transmittal, addressed to a specific reader or readers, which precedes the report. This letter might acknowledge individuals or organizations that helped with the report, refer readers to sections of special interest, discuss any limitations of the study or any problems in gathering data, offer personal (or off-the-record) observations, or urge readers to take immediate action. See page 326 (Figure 17.4) for a sample letter of transmittal.

Front Matter

Preceding the text of the report is the front matter: the title page, table of contents, list of tables and figures if appropriate, and abstract or executive summary.

Title Page. The title page provides the report title, the names of all authors and their affiliations (and/or the name of the organization that commissioned the report), and the date the report was distributed to readers. The title announces the report's purpose and subject by using descriptive words such as *analysis, proposal, feasibility,* or *recommendation.* Be sure the title fully describes your report, but avoid an overly long and involved title. Design the page so that the title is the most prominent item, highest on the page, followed by the name of the recipient(s), the author(s), and the date of submission. See page 327 (Figure 17.4) for a sample title page.

Table of Contents. A table of contents is essential for any long report, helping readers find what they seek by providing the page number for each major section, including any front matter that falls after the table of contents. (Do not include the letter of transmittal, title page, or the table of contents itself, but do include the list of tables and figures, along with the abstract or executive summary.)

Indicate page numbers for front matter in lowercase Roman numerals (i, ii, iii). Note that the title page, though not numbered itself or listed on the table of contents, is counted as page i. Number the report text pages using Arabic numerals (1, 2, 3), starting with the first page of the report. Number end matter using Arabic numerals continuing from the end of the report's text.

Make sure headings and subheadings in the table of contents match exactly the headings and subheadings in the report. Indicate headings of different levels (a-level, b-level, c-level) using different type styles or indentations. Use *leader lines* (........) to connect headings with their page numbers. For a sample table of contents, see page 328 (Figure 17.4).

List of Tables and Figures. On a separate page following the table of contents (or at the end of the table of contents, if it fits), list the tables and figures in the report. If the report contains only one or two tables and figures, you may skip this list. Because Figure 17.4 contains no illustrations, it includes no such list in the front matter.

Abstract or Executive Summary. Instead of reading an entire formal report, readers interested only in the big picture may consult the abstract or executive summary that commonly precedes the report proper (see Chapter 15). The purpose of this summary is to explain the issue, describe how you researched it, and state your conclusions (and, in the case of an executive summary, indicate what action the conclusions suggest). Busy readers can then flip through the document to locate sections important to them.

Make the abstract or executive summary as brief as you can. Summarize the report without adding new information or leaving out critical information. Write for a general audience and follow a sequence that moves from the reason the report was written, to the report's major findings, to conclusions and recommendations. For an example of an abstract, see page 329 (Figure 17.4).

Text of the Report

The text of the report consists of the introduction, the body, and the conclusion.

Introduction. The introduction engages and orients the audience and provides background as briefly as possible. Readers don't generally need a long history lesson. In your introduction, identify the topic's origin and significance, define or describe the problem or issue, and explain the report's purpose. Briefly identify your research methods (interviews, literature searches, and so on). List working definitions, but if you have more than five, place definitions in a glossary. Finally, if you have not done so in the abstract or executive summary, state your conclusion. Don't make readers wade through the entire report to find out what you are recommending or advising. For a sample introduction to a formal report, see page 330 (Figure 17.4).

Body. The body describes and explains your findings. Present a clear and detailed picture of the evidence, interpretations, and reasoning on which you will base your conclusion. Divide topics into subtopics, and use informative headings as aids to navigation, as described earlier in this chapter. The body of your report will vary greatly, depending on the audience, topic, purpose, and situation. The body of Figure 17.4 begins after the introduction on page 1 of the report and ends with the recommendation on page 4 of the report (pages 330–334 in this book).

Conclusion. The conclusion is vital, because it answers the questions that originally sparked the analysis. In the conclusion, you summarize, interpret, and recommend. Although you have interpreted evidence at each stage of your analysis, your conclusion presents a broad interpretation and suggests a course of action (where appropriate). Your conclusion should provide a clear and consistent perspective on the whole document. Don't introduce new ideas, facts, or statistics. See page 333 (Figure 17.4) for a sample conclusion.

End Matter

Following the text of the report (as needed) is the end matter, which may include a list of references cited in your report, a glossary, and/or appendixes. Users can refer to any of these supplements or skip them altogether, according to their needs.

References or Works Cited List. If you have used outside sources in your report (and typically you should), you must provide a list of References (per APA style) or of Works Cited (per MLA style) just after the text of the report or on a separate page. For detailed advice on documenting sources using APA or MLA style, see Appendix A of this book. The long report in Figure 17.4 uses APA style and includes a References list (page 334).

Glossary. Use a glossary if your report contains more than five technical terms that may not be understood by all intended readers. If five or fewer terms need defining, place them in the report's introduction as working definitions, or use footnote definitions. If you do include a separate glossary, announce its location when you introduce technical terms defined there ("see the glossary at the end of this report"). Figure 17.4 includes working definitions in the appendix (page 335).

Appendices. If you have large blocks of material or other documents that are relevant but will bog readers down, place these in an appendix. For example, if your report on the cost of electricity at your company refers to another report issued by the local utility company, you may wish to include this second report as an appendix. Other items that belong in an appendix might include complex formulas, interview questions and responses, maps, photographs, questionnaires and tabulated responses, texts of laws and regulations, and the like.

Do not stuff appendices with needless information or use them to bury bad or embarrassing news that belongs in the report itself. Title each appendix clearly: "Appendix A: Projected Costs." Mention the appendices early in the introduction, and refer readers to them at appropriate points in the report: ("see Appendix A"). The sample report in Figure 17.4 includes an appendix on pages 335–337.

STRATEGIES
for Formal Reports

▸ **Determine your audience.** Be sure that you understand what your audience needs to know or do as a result of reading your report.

▸ **Determine your analytical approach.** Decide whether the primary purpose of the report is to compare items, look for a cause, or determine feasibility. Because formal reports are complex, also consider if the report will have a secondary purpose or purposes.

▸ **Do your research and document your sources.** For a long, formal report, research is paramount. Strive for accurate, appropriate, and clearly interpreted data. Always think critically about the sources you consult during the research process. Document all your sources within the report (using parenthetical citation—see pages 434, 446) and at the end of the report (in a References or Works Cited list—see pages 435, 447).

▸ **Work from a clear purpose statement.** You may need to revise your purpose statement during the research process as you uncover new information, but make sure the statement is finalized before you start writing your final draft of the report.

▸ **Use an understandable structure.** Follow the strategies in Chapter 6 for outlining, chunking, sequencing, paragraphing, and using headings.

➡

▸ **Write with a readable style.** Follow the strategies in Chapter 7 to write with a clear, concise, fluent, and personable style.

▸ **Include audience-centered visuals.** Follow the strategies in Chapter 8 for using graphs, tables, charts, illustrations, diagrams, and photographs as appropriate to enhance, not decorate, the report.

▸ **Create a user-friendly design.** Follow the strategies in Chapter 9 for consistency, cohesiveness, navigation, and emphasis.

▸ **Include all appropriate front matter.** If appropriate, include a letter of transmittal. Always include a title page as well as a table of contents and an abstract or executive summary. If your report contains plentiful visuals, include a list of tables and figures.

▸ **Provide an introduction, body, and conclusion.** In the text of the report, include an introduction to orient readers and provide background; a body with a clear and detailed presentation of findings; and a conclusion that answers the question or questions posed by the report, possibly with recommendations.

▸ **Include the appropriate end matter.** Always include a list of References (APA style) or of Works Cited (MLA style) on a separate page at the report's end. If your report includes more than five technical terms to be defined, place them in a glossary after the Works Cited or References page; otherwise, define the terms in your introduction or via footnotes in the report. Relevant secondary information that will not fit within the report (surveys, complex formulas, interviews, maps, and so on) belongs in an appendix at the very end.

▸ **Proofread.** If possible, get someone else to read and edit your report.

A SAMPLE FORMAL REPORT

Figure 17.4 is a formal report. Its author, Crystal Cunningham, was a student in the B.S. program in dental hygiene at the University of Minnesota. For a final project in her technical writing class, she chose a real life research situation that fit nicely with her major. Crystal chose to examine the relationship between periodontal disease in mothers and low birth weights in their babies. Her research is aimed at other dental hygiene experts; in particular, she wants to send her report to a professor in her department who might wish to continue this research.

With this audience in mind, Crystal makes appropriate choices about technical language, statistical analysis, and reference to scientific articles. While these approaches would not be suitable for a nonexpert audience, they are just right for an audience of other scientists. She understands that her primary purpose is to see if the literature can show a causal relationship. Another purpose is to convince her readers to take her work seriously so that her work might be continued and possibly published in a scientific journal.

FIGURE 17.4
A sample formal report

Letter of transmittal targets and thanks specific reader and provides additional context

28 August, 20xx
15 Timber Drive
St. Paul, MN 55666

Professor Janet Belding
University of Minnesota
School of Dentistry
Minneapolis, MN 55444

Dear Dr. Belding:

Thank you for providing me with this opportunity to research the potential impacts of periodontal disease on birth weights. Enclosed in this envelope is my final report, "Recommendation for a New Study on the Effects of Periodontal Disease on Preterm Low Birth Weight Babies." In this report, I recommend that further studies be undertaken to explore this potential causal connection.

If I can provide any other information as you review this report, please don't hesitate to contact me. I look forward to meeting with you at a later date to hear your thoughts. I hope this report is useful in your research program.

Yours truly,

Crystal Cunningham

Crystal Cunningham, B.S., Dental Hygiene

FIGURE 17.4
(Continued)

Recommendation for a New Study of the Effects of Periodontal Disease on Preterm Low Birth Weight Babies

← Title is clear and encompasses entire focus of the report

for
Professor Janet Belding
University of Minnesota
School of Dentistry

← Name and affiliation of intended recipient is given

by
Crystal Cunningham
University of Minnesota
Division of Dental Hygiene

← Author provides name and affiliation

March 15, 20xx

← Date of distribution of the report appears on the title page

FIGURE 17.4
(Continued)

Table of contents
helps readers find
information and
visualize the
structure of the
report

Recommendation Report   ii

Table of Contents

FIGURE 17.4
(Continued)

Abstract

The purpose of this report is to assess ten recent studies concerning periodontal disease and its association with preterm and low birth weight infants and to recommend, based on the inconclusiveness of these studies, that a new study be undertaken at the University. A number of these studies have found a correlation between periodontal disease and premature birth/low birth weight. However, a number of them have been limited in their scope and the results have been contradictory, indicating the need for the new comprehensive study I propose at the end of this report.

Abstract fully summarizes the content of the report

FIGURE 17.4
(Continued)

Introduction sets
up the problem
and clearly
indicates the
report's causal
analytical approach

Background
section provides
helpful but not
overly detailed
context

Clear purpose
statement leads
into the body
of the report

Subheads within
the Methodologies
section make the
section easy to
follow

Introduction

In the last ten to fifteen years, interesting findings in dental and obstetric research have linked periodontal disease in mothers to preterm low birth weight conditions in their babies. Many studies have found a correlation, while adequately controlling for confounding variables; the variables include age, smoking, diabetes and other factors already contributing to preterm low birth weight babies. However a definitive link has yet to be found. This report examines the existing studies, charting their methodologies and results, and concludes with a recommendation for a new, comprehensive study of the possible correlation.

Background

The world has seen a rise in preterm low birth weight births in the last few decades. This fact has alarmed many physicians and obstetricians, because there have been so many advancements in the medical field aiming to promote the health and longevity of life. Many reasons have been proposed to explain the reasons for preterm low birth weight births, but no conclusive answers have yet emerged. In the last ten years, some researchers have suggested that gingivitis and periodontal disease may be to blame for this occurrence. One possible cause could be the increase in harmful bacteria entering the bloodstream.

Preterm birth is considered to be any birth that occurs before 37 weeks of gestation; low birth weight is recognized as a weight of fewer than 2,500 grams. Many studies since the middle 1990s have attempted to find a correlation between periodontal disease and preterm low birth weight babies. However, research related to the possibility that periodontal disease increases the risk for preterm low birth weight babies has varied immensely over the years.

This report is an assessment of ten peer-reviewed journal articles that seek to examine whether periodontal disease has any correlation with preterm low birth weight babies. The goal of this report is to find a correlation between gingivitis/periodontal disease and preterm low birth weight infants in previous studies and offer a recommendation to conduct a new study.

Methodologies of the Studies

Following is a summary of the methodologies used in the various studies:

Time

Studies by Farrell, Ide, and Wilson (2006) and Dortbudak, Eberhardt, Ulm, and Persson (2005) examined women during pregnancy. In the Farrell et al. study, pregnant women were recruited at 12 weeks of gestation (p. 116). Subjects were excluded if gestational age was below 10 weeks or above 15 weeks. The Dortbudak et al. study maintained that it was crucial to examine patients during weeks 15–20 of gestational age, because a sample of amniotic fluid is needed to assess for particular bacteria (p. 46). However, most studies waited to collect fluid samples until immediately after the birth.

FIGURE 17.4
(Continued)

Recommendation Report   2

Setting

Most of these studies were conducted in hospital settings. The remaining studies were conducted after the subjects returned home from the hospital and were either instructed to return to their dental office or wait for an examiner to visit their home within 48 hours after birth. Some studies had a lengthier time frame to collect data following the birth, such as 72 hours, or five days as in a UK study (Buduneli et al., 2005, p. 176; Moore, Randhawa, & Ide, 2005, p. 3).

Sentence variety and clear prose give the report a readable style

Examiners

Examiners in these studies were calibrated, blind, and often a single examiner was used (Alves & Ribeiro, 2006, p. 322; Bassani, Olinto, & Kreiger, 2007, p. 37; Gazolla et al., 2007, p. 844; Jarjoura et al., 2005, p. 516; Moliterno, Monteiro, Figueredo, & Fischer, 2005, p. 887; Moore et al., 2005, p. 2). The study by Farrell et al. (2006) involved three examiners, which allowed more subjects to be evaluated (p. 117).

Exclusion Criteria

A questionnaire/interview was given to patients (Bassani et al., 2007, p. 32; Bosnjak, Relja, Vucicevic-Boras, Plasaj, & Plancak, 2006, p. 712; Farrell et al., 2006, p. 117; Jarjoura et al., 2005, p. 516; Moliterno et al., 2005, p. 888; Moore et al., 2005, p. 3). These questions pertained to socioeconomic status, race, education, occupation, marital status, smoking, drinking, medications, pregnancies, preterm deliveries, and prenatal care (Gazolla et al., 2007, p. 843).

Writer uses accurate and clearly interpreted data

    The information gathered from questions and patients' medical records excluded many subjects from the study. Exclusion criteria included diabetes, anemia, cardiovascular disorders, hepatic deficiency, high blood pressure, TB, cancer, seizure disorders, psychopathology, asthma, STD, HIV, fetal or uterine anomalies, cervical incompetence, labor induction, and multiple birth pregnancies (Buduneli et al., 2005, p. 177; Gazolla et al., 2007, p. 844; Jarjoura et al., p. 516; Moliterno et al., p. 887; Moore et al., p. 4). Another common exclusion involved subjects who required prophylactic antibiotics prior to dental treatment (Farrell et al., p. 117; Jarjoura et al., p. 513; Moore et al., p. 3).

No year needed for work that follows closely after the initial reference

Data Collection

The most common measurements in each trial were pocket depths, clinical attachment levels, and bleeding on probing. A periodontal probe of varying markings was used to assess the extent of periodontal involvement. A few studies included a plaque index along with the previously mentioned tests (Farrell et al., 2006, p. 117; Jarjoura et al., 2005, p. 515; Moore et al., 2005, p. 3). One study, by Alves and Ribeiro, also included calculus detection (2006, p. 319). DMFT scores were taken into account in two other studies (Bosnjak et al., 2006, p. 712; Buduneli et al., 2005, p. 176).

All information from outside sources is documented in text

    Most of the studies gathered periodontal measurements from six different sites on one tooth throughout the entire dentition (Alves & Ribeiro, 2006, p. 319; Bassani et al., 2007, p. 36; Buduneli et al., 2005, p. 176; Gazolla et al., 2007, p. 845;

Writer not only describes but critiques the previous studies examined

FIGURE 17.4
(Continued)

Moliterno et al., 2005, p. 887). However other studies assessed fewer sites, for example mesial, distal, buccal and lingual surfaces (Bosnjak et al., 2006, p. 711; Dortbudak et al., 2005, p. 47). Columbia University collected data from three sites; mesiobuccal, midbuccal, and distobuccal in two randomly selected quadrants (Jarjoura et al., 2005, p. 514). The fewest measurements were taken from one tooth at only two sites, in a UK study. These sites were midbuccal and mesiobuccal in the maxillary, and midlingual and mesiolingual in the mandibular (Moore et al., 2005, p. 3).

Three studies included a subgingival plaque sample from the mesial and distal aspect of certain teeth. The sample was obtained by placing a paperpoint into the sulcus and analyzing the type of bacteria collected (Buduneli et al., 2005, p. 177; Dortbudak et al., 46; Jarjoura et al., 518).

An interesting study was conducted by Dortbudak et al. A periodontal exam was completed as in other studies; however, this study included collection of amniotic fluid at 15–20 weeks. These women were already scheduled to have amniocentesis tests for medical purposes. Two milliliters of additional fluid were collected and analyzed for particular bacteria. The results concluded that an increased number of certain bacteria from the fluid placed these women at a higher risk for premature birth. An obvious limitation to this study, however, was that women undergoing an amniocentesis are already at an increased risk for problems during their pregnancy, or they would not be having the test in the first place (p. 51).

Results of the Studies

The research analyzed for this report demonstrates varying degrees of correlation between periodontal disease and birth weight of preterm low weight babies (PTLWB). See Table 1 for summary.

Writer provides bottom line results of previous studies

Table 1. Results of major studies

Correlation	Correlation percentages	Comments
High correlation :		
Alves and Ribeiro 2005,p.323.	84.21%	High correlation found.
Bosnjak et al. 2006, p.716.	73.26%	Similar correlation found between PTLWB and tobacco use (p.716).
Dortbudak et al. 2005, p. 52.	83%	No bacteria found in amniotic fluid: authors still believe maternal periodontitis could be causal.
Jarjoura et al. 2005, p. 522; Moliterno et al. 2005, p.890.	No percentages given.	Both found statistically significant casual connections.
Low correlations:		
Bassani et al. 2007, p. 39.	No significant correlation.	While 59% of subjects had periodontal disease, causality was not established.
Buduneli et al. 2005, p.181; Farrell et al. 2006, pg.120.	No significant correlation.	No differences established.
Gazolla et al. 2007, pg 879.	No significant correlation.	Note that the group not treated with scaling/ root planning had 79% PTLWB.

FIGURE 17.4
(Continued)

Recommendation Report 4

As summarized in Table 1 (previous page), recent studies offer conflicting results about the relationship between periodontal disease and the birth of preterm low weight babies. The two studies to establish high, statistically significant correlations are Aalves and Ribeiro 2005 and Dortbudak et al.2005, but as noted, Dortbudak et al. did not actually find bacteria in the amniotic fluid, thus requiring the authors to make something of casual leap. As noted in the next section, there were also other limitations to all these studies.

Limitations of the Studies

All these studies involved limitations, the most obvious being the sample size. Two studies had a sample of less than 100 subjects (Alves & Ribeiro, 2006, p. 318; Dortbudak et al., 2005, p. 45). Another limitation was the location of the studies. Many well-known studies were conducted outside the United States, in countries such as Croatia, United Kingdom, Turkey, and two in Brazil.

Almost all of these studies were conducted in lower socioeconomic areas, in developing countries, with more uniform ethnic and racial groups. Pregnant Croatian women were studied because they tend to develop more pronounced periodontal disease (Bosnjak et al., 2006, p. 710).

Limitations in only a couple cases were the ages of the subjects. It is well known that having a child above or beneath a certain age poses potential problems for the mother and child, not to mention the strong correlation between age and increased periodontal disease. Only two studies imposed a restriction on age. One study only allowed an age range of 18 to 35 years (Buduneli et al., 2005, p. 174); another only allowed an age range of 18 to 30 years (Gazolla et al., 2007, p. 842).

The writer is careful to list the limitations of previous studies

Conclusion

In conclusion, several studies found a correlation between periodontal disease and preterm low birth weight babies, even when accounting for possible confounding variables. On the other hand, many found no correlation between periodontal disease and preterm low birth weight babies. These researchers make the argument that their counterparts who did find a correlation did not account for all confounding variables.

The research conducted pertaining to the correlation between preterm low birth weight babies and periodontal disease, then, continues to result in conflicting conclusions. More research is needed in order to arrive at definitive conclusions.

Conclusion provides a summary of the report

Because the report takes the causal approach, writer is careful to show that correlation does not always equal causation

Recommendation

The research question is whether periodontal disease has an effect on preterm low birth weight babies. I propose a new study using different methods of data collection to explore a possible correlation between periodontal disease and

This report includes a recommendation section

FIGURE 17.4
(Continued)

Writer
cross-references
to emphasize
importance
of Appendix

preterm low birth weight babies. (See the Appendix for the specifics of this proposed new study.) This study will measure six surfaces on every tooth, and most importantly, it will gather a baseline periodontal reading within eight weeks after conception. Using this approach, the examiners can measure to see if there has been a significant difference in periodontal disease during pregnancy, or if the subject has always had the same level of disease. This more exacting approach should increase the accuracy and reliability of test findings.

Reference page
immediately
follows the report
and lists all sources
consulted in APA
style

References

Alves, R. T., & Ribeiro, R. A. (2006). Relationship between maternal periodontal disease and birth of preterm low weight babies. *Pesquisa Odontologica Brasileira, 20*(4), 319–323.

Bassani, D. G., Olinto, M. T., & Kreiger, N. (2007). Periodontal disease and perinatal outcomes: a case-control study. *Journal of Clinical Periodontology, 34*(1), 32–39.

Bosnjak, A., Relja, T., Vucicevic-Boras, V., Plasaj, H., & Plancak, D. (2006). Pre-term delivery and periodontal disease: a case-control study from Croatia. *Journal of Clinical Periodontology, 33*(10), 710–716.

Buduneli, N., Baylas, H., Buduneli, E., Turkoglu, O., Kose, T., & Dahlen, G. (2005). Periodontal infections and pre-term low birth weight: a case-control study. *Journal of Clinical Periodontology, 32*(2), 174–181.

Dortbudak, O., Eberhardt, R., Ulm, M., & Persson, G. R. (2005). Periodontitis, a marker of risk in pregnancy for preterm birth. *Journal of Clinical Periodontology, 32*(1), 46–52.

Farrell, S., Ide, M., & Wilson, R. F. (2006). The relationship between maternal periodontitis, adverse pregnancy outcome and miscarriage in never smokers. *Journal of Clinical Periodontology, 33*(2), 116–120.

Gazolla, C. M., Ribeiro, A., Moyses, M. R., Oliveira, L. A., Pereira, L. J., & Sallum, A. W. (2007). Evaluation of the incidence of preterm low birth weight in patients undergoing periodontal therapy. *Journal of Periodontology, 78*(5), 842–849.

Jarjoura, K., Devine, P. C., Perez-Delboy, A., Herrera-Abreu, M., D'Alton, M., & Papapanou, P. N. (2005). Markers of periodontal infection and preterm birth. *American Journal of Obstetrics and Gynecology, 192*(2), 513–522.

Moliterno, L. F., Monteiro, B., Figueredo, C. M., & Fischer, R. G. (2005). Association between periodontitis and low birth weight: a case-control study. *Journal of Clinical Periodontology, 32*(8), 887–890.

Moore, S., Randhawa, M., & Ide, M. (2005). A case-control study to investigate an association between adverse pregnancy outcome and periodontal disease. *Journal of Clinical Periodontology, 32*(1), 2–4.

FIGURE 17.4
(Continued)

Appendix

Terms of Proposed New Study

Detailed data that
might bog down the
body of the report
goes into an
appendix

Method/Procedures/Materials

The purpose of this study is to determine whether a correlation exists between mothers with periodontal disease and preterm low birth weight babies.

Research Design

The research design of this study involves no manipulation of subjects; patients are only observed for changes in their periodontal status. Therefore, the design of this study is quantitative, non-experimental, and correlational.

Research Question

The following is the research question for the proposed research study: When accounting for confounding variables, is there a relation between mothers with periodontal disease and delivering a preterm low birth weight child?

Variables

Attribute Variables: The attribute variables are women who are 18–35 years of age. This study accepts women from all different educational levels, socioeconomic levels and race. One does not need to have prior periodontal disease to be included in the study.

Working Definitions

Preterm: Birth before 37 weeks of gestation.
Low birth weight: A weight below 2500 g.
Gingivitis: Inflammation of the gums, characterized by redness, swelling, and tendency of bleeding.
Periodontal disease: Disease of the supporting structures of the teeth. Common symptoms are bleeding gums and loosening of the teeth.
Mild periodontal disease: A periodontal reading of 3–4 mm.
Moderate periodontal disease: A periodontal reading of 5–6 mm.
Severe periodontal disease: A periodontal reading of 7 mm and above.

Threats to Internal Validity

There are many threats to internal validity, such as selection, pregnancy complications, losing the baby, instrumentation, testing, women dropping out of the study, newly identified systemic diseases, among others. These threats will be reduced by having professionally trained and calibrated examiners conduct the examinations, testing, and instrumentation.

FIGURE 17.4
(Continued)

Sample

The sample will include 500 women from the Twin Cities Area. Women cannot be more than eight weeks pregnant to be included in the study. Exclusion criteria include women with diabetes and other systemic illnesses, previous birth complications, and previous abuse of alcohol or other illegal substances.

Data Collection Instrument

The data collection instruments will be a probe and scale to measure the infant's weight. The probe will be made of different colored incremental markings, increasing by two millimeters. The scale used must have the ability to weigh in ounces. A form will need to be used to chart periodontal recordings. Six measurements will be taken on each tooth. Reliability will be ensured by having examiners cross-examine each other every fifth subject. Validity will be ensured by only using periodontal probes and scales specifically designed to measure pocket depths for this study.

Scales of Measurement

The patient will be placed in one of three categories depending on the severity of their periodontal condition. The first assessment will take place before the eighth week of pregnancy, and the second assessment will be taken following the delivery of the baby. The classifications are as follows: mild periodontal disease is 3–4 mm, moderate is 5–6 mm, and severe is considered 7 mm and above.

Procedure

Pregnant women will be identified as they come to the University of Minnesota Medical Clinic for their first visit. Women who are not above the eighth week of pregnancy will be approached to participate in the study. A consent form will be given to the potential subject. If the pregnant woman agrees to participate, then she will need to sign at the bottom of the consent form.

The baseline periodontal reading will be taken the same day the subject first visits the hospital. Periodontal measurements will be recorded and the readings will place each mother into the category of mild, moderate, or severe. Periodontal measurements will be taken again following the birth of the child, as well as the weight of the baby. The level of periodontal disease will be reassessed to reassign each subject to a new category if necessary. This reassessment needs to be done within 72 hours after birth.

Statistical Analysis

Variables	Level of Measurement	Measure of Central Tendency	Measure of Dispersion
Pregnant mothers	Nominal	Mode	Range
Number of surfaces with periodontal disease	Interval/ratio	Mean	Standard Deviation

FIGURE 17.4
(Continued)

Number of teeth	Interval/ratio	Mean	Standard Deviation
Preterm birth	Interval/ratio	Mean	Standard Deviation
Low birth weight	Interval/ratio	Mean	Standard Deviation
Periodontal category ranking	Ordinal	Median	Percentile

Significance

Most earlier research has only taken periodontal measurements after the child has been born. The goal is to take measurements earlier than previous studies have done, to more accurately seek a correlation between gingivitis/periodontal disease and preterm low birth weight infants.

Dissemination

The results of this proposed study will be sent to the *Journal of Dental Hygiene*, *Dimensions of Dental Hygiene*, and the *American Dental Hygienist Association* for further review.

Budget and Justification

Type of Cost	Amount of Money	Justification
3 Computers/printers/ paper office supplies	$12,000	Computers are needed to insert data. Professionally made forms are needed to record the information prior to entering the data into the computer. They also function as a back-up.
Personnel/travel expenses	$20,000	This is needed for non-volunteering, paid staff.
Dental instruments/scales	$1,000	To measure variables.
Payment to subjects	$75,000	This is to offset their travel expenses and time to participate.

Credentials of Project Personnel

Crystal Cunningham is a recent graduate from the school of dentistry at the University of Minnesota, Division of Dental Hygiene. She is well prepared to perform a study in this particular area due to the extensive background research she has completed in this area. As the project director, who will also be working in collaboration with highly educated professionals from the University of Minnesota, the author anticipates that this research will be successfully carried out.

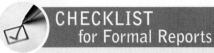

CHECKLIST
for Formal Reports

☐ Have I determined the audience for this report?

☐ Have I decided on the purpose, and have I chosen the right analytical approach (comparative, causal, feasibility) to fit this purpose?

☐ Did I evaluate all sources consulted while researching?

☐ Is my data accurate, appropriate, and clearly interpreted?

☐ Does my report have a clearly defined purpose statement, early in the report?

☐ Is the structure of the report logical and appropriate for this setting?

☐ Is the writing style clear and professional?

☐ If there are visuals in my report, are the visuals supportive of what is in the text?

☐ Are the pages well designed and easy to follow?

☐ Is there a distinct introduction, body, and conclusion?

☐ Does the introduction provide enough of an orientation to the issue or problem, without being too long?

☐ Does the body of the report offer a clear picture of the issue or problem?

☐ Does the conclusion answer the question that originally sparked the analysis?

☐ Have I included all the required and appropriate front and end matter?

☐ Have I documented all my sources both in text and in a References or Works Cited list?

APPLICATIONS

GENERAL APPLICATIONS

1. Choose a specific audience and purpose, based on a real-life situation at school or at work, and write out some ideas for how you would determine whether this situation is an appropriate one for a formal report. List all possible readers (audience members) and all possible purposes. List the kinds of questions your report will need to answer, and then list the kinds of research you will need to do in order to write the report. Bring this document to class for a discussion.

2. Prepare a formal report using causal, comparative, or feasibility analysis (or some combination). As you prepare your report, refer to the Strategies for Formal Reports on pages 324–325, the Checklist, and other materials in this chapter.

TEAM APPLICATION

In the workplace, it is common for reports to be written not by one individual but in teams. Thinking of an idea you might have for a report for this class, ask yourself whether this report might be a team project. How would you divide the tasks and ensure that the work was being done fairly? What are the advantages and disadvantages of a team approach to a report? In groups of 2–3, discuss these issues. If your instructor indicates that your report is to be team-based, write a memo (as a team) to your instructor indicating the role of each team member and the timeline.

GLOBAL APPLICATION

Use the Internet to look for reports written in English by government agencies of different countries. See if you can use the material from this chapter to determine if the reports fall into causal, comparative, or feasibility categories. Look for similarities to the reports you are familiar with within the United States (or the one you are preparing for class), as well as differences in features such as structure and organization, word choice, formatting, use of visuals, levels of politeness, and so on.

COMPUTER/WEB-BASED APPLICATION

Many reports, particularly government reports, are turned into PDF documents and are available on the Web. When you have a draft of your report, experiment with turning it into a PDF document or uploading it to a file sharing site (such as *Google Docs* or *iWork.com*) and sending it to others on your team (or to your instructor if this is not a team assignment). What changes happened to your document as a result of the uploading, and how could you avoid these changes in the future?

For additional technical writing resources that will help you master the chapter objectives, go to **www.mytechcommlab.com**.

18 Proposals

LEARNING OBJECTIVES FOR THIS CHAPTER

▶ Differentiate between solicited and
unsolicited proposals

▶ Differentiate between informal and
formal proposals

▶ Understand the different functions of
planning, research, and sales proposals

▶ Write an informal proposal

▶ Write a formal proposal

LET'S GET STARTED
Proposals

Most people have had experience making verbal proposals. For instance, a student may want a new computer but will need to propose that his or her parents share the cost. ("If I contribute XX$ from my summer job, will you help me with the rest of the payment?") Workplace proposals require a more detailed, research-oriented approach, but the concept is the same: you are proposing a particular plan of action and you need to make your best case. Before reading this chapter, think of a proposal you may wish to make to your manager, the supervisor of your internship, or your instructor. What exactly, would you like to see happen and why and how? After specifying your goal, make a list of the supporting reasons that you think will be most persuasive in this case.

Questions to ask about your proposal ideas as you review the material in this chapter may include the following:

▶ Do I have a strong enough case?

▶ How will my audience react?

▶ What other ideas might they counterpropose, and am I ready for these arguments?

▶ Did someone ask for my proposal or does it originate from me?

▶ What sort of format (number of pages, uses of visuals, organizational structure) is best suited to my plan?

At the end of this chapter, review your initial Let's Get Started list with your instructor or with a group of students, to see how much you might change or modify it based on what you have learned from the chapter.

*P*roposals encourage an audience to take some form of direct action: to authorize a project, purchase a service or product, or support a specific plan for solving a problem. Although proposals often contain the same basic elements as reports (see Chapters 16 and 17), they have *one* specific purpose: to persuade the audience to say "Yes, let's move ahead with this plan." This purpose may sound similar to the purpose of a recommendation report. However, while a recommendation report answers the question "What should we do, and why?" a proposal maps out

How proposals and reports differ

✳ Explore the Concept with the Case Study on Brief Proposals at mytechcommlab

the steps for getting it done: "Here's what we should do and here's how we can do it." (Note the difference, for example, between the recommendations made in the long report on birth weight in Chapter 17 and the proposed study outlined in that report's appendix.)

Proposals are called for in a variety of situations: a request to fund a training program for new employees, a suggestion to change the curriculum of your English or biology department, a bid to the U.S. Defense Department on a missile contract, and so on. Depending on the situation, proposals may be short (informal) or long (formal), and may be written in the form of a report, a letter, or a memo. As a student or as an intern at a nonprofit agency, you might submit a formal grant proposal, requesting financial support for a research or community project. If your job depends on funding from outside sources, proposals might be the most important documents you produce.

✳ Explore the Concept with the Case Study on Formal Proposals at mytechcommlab

AUDIENCE AND PURPOSE OF PROPOSALS

Audience considerations

In science, business, industry, government, and education, proposals are written for any number of audiences: managers, executives, directors, clients, board members, or community leaders. Inside or outside the organization, these people review various proposals and then decide whether the plans are worthwhile, the projects will materialize, and the services or products are useful.

Purpose considerations

The singular purpose of proposals is to persuade your audience to say yes to your plan.

TYPES OF PROPOSALS

Solicited and unsolicited proposals

Proposals may be either *solicited* or *unsolicited*. Solicited proposals are those that have been requested by a manager, client, or customer. For example, if you represent an engineering firm specializing in highway construction, you may receive a request for proposal (RFP) from a local township asking you to bid on a road project. Typically, an RFP is issued to numerous companies, and your proposal will need to stack up against all the others. Unsolicited proposals are those that have not been requested. If you are a new advertising agency in town, you may send out short unsolicited proposals to local radio stations suggesting that they use your agency for their advertising needs.

Because the audience for a solicited proposal has made a specific request, you will not need to spend time introducing yourself or providing background on the product or service. For an unsolicited proposal (sometimes termed a "cold call" in sales), you will need to catch readers' attention quickly and provide incentives for them to continue reading: perhaps by printing a price comparison of your fees on the first page, for example.

Informal and formal proposals

Proposals may also be *informal* or *formal*. Informal proposals, like informal reports, can take the form of an email or memo (if distributed within an organization), or a letter (when sent outside of an organization). Formal proposals, meanwhile, take on the same format as formal reports (see Chapter 17), including front matter, the text of the report, and end matter, if applicable. Formal proposals will be discussed later in this chapter.

Both solicited and unsolicited proposals, whether informal or formal, fall into three categories: planning proposals, research proposals, and sales proposals.

Planning Proposals

Planning proposals offer solutions to a problem or suggestions for improvement. A planning proposal might be a request for funding to expand the campus newspaper (as in the formal proposal at the end of this chapter), an architectural plan for new facilities at a ski area, or a plan to develop energy alternatives to fossil fuels.

Figure 18.1 is a solicited, informal planning proposal that will be used by bank loan officers when deciding whether or not to grant a construction loan. Because this document is addressed to external readers, it is cast as a letter. For specific advice on how to approach planning proposals, read the annotations accompanying Figure 18.1 and see the Strategies for Proposals on pages 349–350.

Characteristics of planning proposals

 View the Planning Proposal at mytechcommlab

Research Proposals

Research (or grant) proposals request approval and funding for research projects. For example, a chemist at a university might address a research proposal to the Environmental Protection Agency for funds to identify toxic contaminants in local groundwater. Research proposals are solicited by many agencies, including the National Science Foundation and the National Institutes of Health. Each agency has its own requirements and guidelines for proposal format and content. Successful research proposals follow these guidelines and carefully articulate the goals of the project. In these cases, proposal readers will generally be other scientists, so writers can use language that is appropriate for other experts (as in the Appendix to Figure 17.4, page 335).

Figure 18.2 is a solicited, informal research proposal from an employee in the marketing and research department to her supervisor, proposing to conduct research into management–employee relations at a single location of the company that has experienced problems in this area. Because this document is addressed to an internal reader (the instructor), it has been cast as a memo. It could also have taken the form of an email. For specific advice on how to approach research proposals, read the annotations accompanying Figure 18.2 and see the Strategies for Proposals on pages 349–350.

Characteristics of research proposals

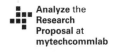 **Analyze** the **Research Proposal** at mytechcommlab

Sales Proposals

Sales proposals offer services or products and may be solicited or unsolicited. If solicited, several firms may be competing for the same contract, so submitted

Characteristics of sales proposals

(*Text continues on p. 346.*)

FIGURE 18.1
A planning proposal

P.O. Box 185
Amherst, MA 01002

March 15, 20xx

Ambrose Savings Bank
South Haley Street
Weaton, MA 09758

Provides a clear subject line →

SUBJECT: PROPOSAL TO ERECT A NEW DWELLING

Dear Mr. Smith:

Introduction states purpose, identifies plan, gives background, and provides a timetable →

As we discussed in our meeting on March 6, this letter is in application for a construction loan in the amount of $300,000, on an interest-only basis, for the construction of the described residence (plans and specifications are enclosed) on Lot #6 of my Leverett property. Anticipated sales price of the completed home is $398,000, including the standard realtor's commission. I have already completed clearing work and some excavation, and I expect weather conditions to permit the commencement of foundation work within the next three weeks. Construction time is projected at approximately five months, with completion targeted for September 1, 20xx.

Body paragraph spells out details (what will be done, qualifications, obtaining permits) →

The quality of construction materials and workmanship will be comparable to the adjacent three homes, which you have inspected. Exterior woodwork will be executed in Western Red Cedar, while interior finishes will comprise masonry, dry-wall, and Philippine mahogany. All sashes, doors, flooring, cabinets, and special millwork will be designed and custom fabricated. Water supply and waste disposal will be handled on-site; the appropriate permits have already been obtained. The heating system will be oil-fired hot air, ducted for the later addition of air conditioning. All windows and skylights will be double-glazed and insulation will be maximized.

Concluding paragraph thanks the reader and encourages acceptance of the proposal →

Thank you for giving this proposal your immediate attention. I will be pleased to provide any additional information you may require.

Very truly yours,

Gerald A. Jackson

Gerald A. Jackson

GAJ/ch

Enclosures: architect's drawings
                    specifications

FIGURE 18.2
**A research
proposal (memo
format)**

MEMORANDUM

To: James Granger, Vice President, Marketing and Research Division
From: Anne Hickett, Analyst, Marketing and Research Division *A.H.*
Date: March 4, 20xx
Subject: Report Proposal Regarding the South Dennis Location

Proposed Study

In answer to your March 2 request for a research report due May 10, I propose to study the ongoing problem of low employee morale at our Foodstuff Supermarket in South Dennis. Following are the specifications:

• Opens with general description of the problem and a proposed study

Statement of Problem

During my two years as a part-time employee at Foodstuff, I worked at a location with similar problems. I have witnessed firsthand the high turnover and general employee dissatisfaction over the work situation and store management policies. Because we have heard continuing complaints about management–employee relations at the South Dennis location, including from top management, I propose to research the situation and offer potential solutions.

• Describes the problem in detail, as well as the writer's qualifications

Scope of Proposed Study

My study will explore the following issues:

1. An assessment of the efficiency of Foodstuff's South Dennis management by drawing parallels and contrasts between the actual management operation and principles of effective management that I will identify and collect from my secondary sources.
2. A consideration of the direct or indirect effects that any management problem might have on employee morale.
3. An assessment of the management's effectiveness in employee motivation.
4. An assessment of the role of effective communication in all management–employee relations.

• Details overall scope of study

Methods and Data Sources

My secondary research will include library resources on the topic of management, as well as reliable Web resources. Primary research will include personal observation at the South Dennis site, which I will visit next Thursday; a survey (see attached) to be distributed to all of the South Dennis management and employees; and interviews with both employee and management representatives at the South Dennis location. All conclusions and any recommendations for positive change will be based on the collected evidence in my report.

• Details specific approaches to the research

If you have any further questions, I will be happy to discuss this proposal with you at your convenience.

• Encourages reader acceptance

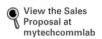
View the Sales
Proposal at
mytechcommlab

proposals may be ranked by a committee. Sales proposals can be cast as letters if the situation calls for them to be brief. If the situation requires a longer proposal, include the various parts and elements of formal proposals. A successful sales proposal persuades customers that your product or service surpasses those of any competitors. What you include in a sales proposal is determined by the guidelines from the client or by a thorough analysis of the kinds of information your audience needs.

Figure 18.3 is an example of a solicited, informal sales proposal, in which the writer explains why her machinery is best for the job, what qualifications her company can offer, and what costs are involved. As with Figure 18.1, because this document is addressed to external readers, it is cast as a letter. For specific advice on how to approach sales proposals, read the annotations accompanying Figure 18.3 and see the Strategies for Proposals on pages 349–350.

ORGANIZATION OF INFORMAL AND FORMAL PROPOSALS

Follow a problem-solution or situation-resolution pattern

No matter the type, all proposals must move in a logical direction from problem/situation to solution/resolution. All effective proposals typically include a clear title or subject line; background information; a statement of the problem or situation; a description of how to solve the problem or resolve the situation; a breakdown of costs, timing, or qualifications (if applicable); and a conclusion that induces readers to act.

Include front matter and end matter as needed

Formal proposals typically require *front matter* including a title page, table of contents, abstract or executive summary, and possibly a letter of transmittal. *End matter* would include appendixes and a list of sources cited (if the formal proposal has entailed research, which it usually will). For more information on these components, see Chapter 17 (pages 321–324); front matter and end matter are presented in the same way in a formal proposal as in a formal report.

Clear Title or Subject Line

Clearly announce your proposal

State the proposal's purpose with a clear and complete title, such as "Recommended Wastewater Treatment System for the MudPie Resort and Spa" (for a formal proposal) or a subject line (in an informal proposal). Avoid being vague or overly general. An overworked decision-maker facing a stack of proposals might very well decide that one that lacks a clear, focused title or subject line probably will be unclear and unfocused in its content.

FIGURE 18.3
A sales proposal

Modern Landscaping
23–44 18th Street
Sunnyside, NY 11104

October 4, 20xx

Martin Haver
35–66 114th Avenue
Jamaica, NY 11107

Subject: *Proposal to Dig a Trench and Move Boulders at Bliss Site*

Dear Mr. Haver:

I've inspected your property and would be happy to undertake the landscaping
project necessary for the development of your farm. ← • Describes the subject and purpose

The backhoe I use cuts a span 3 feet wide and can dig as deep as 18 feet—more
than an adequate depth for the mainline pipe you wish to lay. Because this backhoe is on
tracks rather than tires and is hydraulically operated, it is particularly efficient in moving
rocks. I have more than twelve years of experience with backhoe work and have
completed many jobs similar to this one. ← • Gives the writer's qualifications

After examining the huge boulders that block access to your property, I am
convinced they can be moved only if I dig out underneath and exert upward
pressure with the hydraulic ram while you push forward on the boulders with your
D-9 Caterpillar. With this method, we can move enough rock to enable you to farm
that now inaccessible tract. Because of its power, my larger backhoe will save you
both time and money in the long run. ← • Explains how the job will be done / • Maintains a confident tone throughout

This job should take 12 to 15 hours, unless we encounter subsurface ledge
formations. My fee is $200 per hour. The fact that I provide my own dynamiting crew
at no extra charge should be an advantage to you because you have so much rock
to be moved. ← • Gives a qualified cost estimate

Please phone me any time for more information. I'm sure we can do the job
economically and efficiently. ← • Encourages reader acceptance by emphasizing economy and efficiency

Sincerely yours,
Sharon Ingram
Sharon Ingram

Background Information

A background section can be brief or long. In Figure 18.1, the writer's opening sentence ("As we discussed in our meeting on March 6 . . .") provides a quick reminder of the context for the project. This sentence is brief because the reader is already familiar with the project. For a new audience or in an unsolicited proposal, you may need to provide a longer paragraph (or in the case of a formal proposal, a full introduction) with background information on the project. If the topic warrants, the background section may take up several pages.

Statement of Problem or Situation

The problem or situation and its resolution form the backbone of any proposal. Describe the problem or situation statement in either the background portion of your proposal or in its own headed section. For example, a good statement of the problem or situation might be: "Complaints about noise in our college library call for a plan that will make areas of the library quiet enough for serious study."

Description of Solution or Resolution

The bulk of the proposal should map out your plan to solve the problem or resolve the situation. Include in this section as much detail as needed for your audience to evaluate the soundness of your plan. If the plan is vague or unrealistic, the proposal will be rejected.

Costs, Timing, and Qualifications

If your proposal involves financial outlay, timing sensitivity, or proof of your qualifications, provide separate sections dealing with these factors. Make sure that your breakdown of costs and timing is accurate, easy to understand, and realistic. If you work with an accountant or other financial specialist, ask that person to check your cost figures. If the proposal is solicited, make sure you follow the client's guidelines for establishing a budget and/or schedule.

Conclusion

The conclusion reaffirms the need for your plan and induces the audience to act. A conclusion does not need to be more than a sentence or two in an informal proposal (longer, of course, in a formal proposal), but no matter the length, always end on a strong note, with a conclusion that is assertive, confident, and encouraging.

STRATEGIES
for Proposals

▸ **Consider your audience and purpose.** Remember that your audience consists of decision-makers; therefore, the purpose of any proposal must be to convince the decision makers to say yes to what you propose.

▸ **Understand the audience's needs.** The proposal audience wants specific suggestions to meet their specific needs. Their biggest question will be "What will this plan do for me?" Make your proposal demonstrate a clear understanding of the audience's problem or situation, and then offer an appropriate solution or resolution.

▸ **Perform research as needed.** To make your plan convincing, do your research. For example, you might research the very latest technology for solving a problem or resolving a situation; compare the costs, benefits, and drawbacks of various approaches; contact others in your field for their suggestions; find out what competitors are up to; and so on.

▸ **Be sure to credit information sources and contributors.** Complex proposals rarely emerge from thin air, and proposals are often a result of a team effort. If anything in your proposal represents the work or input of others, document the sources or acknowledge fellow contributors.

▸ **Use an appropriate format.** For an informal proposal distributed internally, use email or memo format. For an informal proposal distributed externally, use letter format. For a formal proposal, include all the required components, including a title page, table of contents, abstract or executive summary, introduction, body, and conclusion. If applicable, include a letter of transmittal and appendixes.

▸ **Provide a clear title or subject line and background information.** Draw readers into your proposal with a title or subject line that describes the content of the proposal exactly, and orient your readers with the appropriate background information.

▸ **Follow a problem-to-solution or situation-to-resolution organizational pattern.** All proposals should move in this sequence from beginning to end.

▸ **Spell out the problem (and its causes) or situation clearly and convincingly.** Provide enough detail for your audience to appreciate the importance of the problem or situation. Answer the implied question, "Why is this such a big deal?"

▸ **Point out the benefits of solving the problem.** Answer the implied question, "Why should we spend time, money, and effort to do this?"

▸ **Offer a realistic solution or resolution.** Stick to claims or assertions you can support. Answer the implied question, "How do we know this will work?" If the solution or resolution involves accounting for costs, budgeting time, or proving your qualifications, include this information.

➡

▶ **Address anticipated objections to your solution.** Decision makers typically approach a proposal with skepticism, especially if the project will cost them money and time. Answer the implied question, "Why should we accept the things that seem wrong with your plan?"

▶ **Include all necessary details, but don't overload.** Include as much supporting detail as you need to induce readers to say yes to your proposal. Leave nothing to guesswork. At the same time, don't overload your readers with information that is not directly relevant.

▶ **Write clearly and concisely.** Make sure your document is easy to read, uses action verbs, and avoids puffed-up language or terms that are too technical for your audience. If necessary for a mixed audience with differing technical levels, include a glossary.

▶ **Express confidence.** You are trying to sell yourself, your ideas, or your services to a skeptical audience. Be up front about the supporting facts ("For the third year in a row, our firm has been ranked as the number 1 architecture firm in the Midwest") and state your case directly ("We know you will be satisfied with the results").

▶ **Make honest and supportable claims.** Because they often involve large sums of money, investments of time, and contractual obligations, proposals require a solid ethical and legal foundation. False promises not only damage the writer's or company's reputation but also invite lawsuits. If the solutions you offer have limitations, make sure you say so.

▶ **Induce readers to act.** Decide exactly what you want readers to do, and give reasons why they should be the ones to act. In your conclusion, answer the implied question, "What action am I supposed to take?"

A SAMPLE FORMAL PROPOSAL

Figure 18.4 has been written because a state university's newspaper is struggling to meet rising costs. The paper's yearly budget is funded by the Student Fee Allocation Committee, which disburses money to various campus organizations. Because of drastic budget cuts for all state schools, the newspaper has received no funding increase for three years. Bill Trippe, the *Torch*'s business manager, must justify a requested increase of 20.6 percent for the coming year's budget.

Before drafting his proposal, Bill constructed a detailed profile of his audience and purpose: he determined that the primary audience (the Allocation Committee) would use the document as perhaps the sole basis for deciding whether to grant the additional funds, and that his primary purpose must be to provide a convincing rationale. To achieve his goal, he has included a detailed plan for reducing existing operating costs, a section outlining next year's projected costs, and an appendix comparing the *Torch*'s performance with that of other nearby college newspapers. All these materials demonstrate how Bill has anticipated his audience's possible objections.

FIGURE 18.4
**A formal
proposal**

The SMU *Torch*

Old Westport Road
North Dartmouth, Massachusetts 02747

May 1, 20XX

Charles Marcus, Chair
Student Fee Allocation Committee
Southeastern Massachusetts University
North Dartmouth, MA 02747

Dear Dean Marcus:

No one needs to be reminded about the effects of increased costs on our
campus community. We are all faced with having to make do with less.

Accordingly, we at the *Torch* have spent long hours devising a plan to cope with
increased production costs—without compromising the newspaper's tradition
of quality service. I think you and your colleagues will agree that our plan is
realistic and feasible. Even the "bare-bones" operation that will result from our
proposed spending cuts, however, will call for a $7,710.27 increase in next
year's budget.

We have received no funding increase in three years. Our present need is
absolute. Without additional funds, the *Torch* simply cannot continue to function
as a professional newspaper. I therefore submit the following budget proposal
for your consideration.

Respectfully,

William Trippe

William Trippe
Business Manager, SMU *Torch*

Letter of transmittal
provides additional
context and
persuasion

FIGURE 18.4
(Continued)

Provides
a clear title

Writer, affiliation,
and date always
appear on the title
page

A Funding Proposal
for
The SMU *Torch*
(20XX–XX)

Prepared for
The Student Fee Allocation Committee
Southeastern Massachusetts University
North Dartmouth, Massachusetts

by
William Trippe
Torch Business Manager

May 1, 20XX

FIGURE 18.4
(Continued)

iii

TABLE OF CONTENTS

PAGE

Table of contents
orients readers and
demonstrates
proposal's structure

FIGURE 18.4
(Continued)

INFORMATIVE ABSTRACT

Abstract accurately
encapsulates entire
document

The SMU *Torch*, the student newspaper at Southeastern Massachusetts University, is crippled by inadequate funding, having received no budget increase in three years. Increased costs and inadequate funding are the major problems facing the *Torch*. Increases in costs of technology upgrades and in printing have called for cutbacks in production. Moreover, our low staff salaries are inadequate to attract and retain qualified personnel. A nominal pay increase would make salaries more competitive.

Our staff plans to cut costs by reducing page count and by hiring a new press for the *Torch*'s printing work. The only proposed cost increase (for staff salaries) is essential.

A detailed breakdown of projected costs establishes the need for a $7,710.27 budget increase to keep the paper a weekly publication with adequate page count to serve our campus.

Compared with similar newspapers at other colleges, the *Torch* makes much better use of its money. The comparison figures in the Appendix illustrate the cost-effectiveness of our proposal.

FIGURE 18.4
(Continued)

Funding Proposal 1

INTRODUCTION

Overview

Our campus newspaper faces the contradictory challenge of surviving ever-growing production costs while maintaining its reputation for quality. The following proposal addresses that crisis. This plan's ultimate success, however, depends on the Allocation Committee's willingness to approve a long-overdue increase in the *Torch*'s upcoming yearly budget.

→ Opens with an overview of the situation

Background

In ten years, the *Torch* has grown in size, scope, and quality. Roughly 6,000 copies (24 pages/issue) are printed weekly for each fourteen-week semester. Each week, the *Torch* prints national and local press releases, features, editorials, sports articles, announcements, notices, classified ads, a calendar column, and letters to the editor. A vital part of university life, our newspaper provides a forum for information, ideas, and opinions—all with the highest professionalism. This year we published a Web-based version as well.

→ Provides relevant background

Statement of Problem

With much of its staff about to graduate, the *Torch* faces next year with rising costs in every phase of production, and the need to replace outdated and worn equipment.

→ Describes the problem concisely

Our newspaper also suffers from a lack of student involvement: Despite gaining valuable experience and potential career credentials, few students can be expected to work without some kind of remuneration. Most staff members do receive minimal weekly salaries: from $20 for the distributor to $90 for the Editor-in-Chief. But salaries averaging barely $3 per hour cannot possibly compete with the minimum wage. Since more and more SMU students must work part-time, the *Torch* will have to make its salaries more competitive.

The newspaper's operating expenses can be divided into four categories: hardware and software upgrades, salaries, printing costs, and miscellaneous (office supplies, mail, and so on). The first three categories account for nearly 90 percent of the budget. Over the past year, costs in all categories have increased: from as little as 2 percent for miscellaneous expenses to as much as 19 percent for technology upgrades. Printing costs (roughly one-third of our total budget) rose 9 percent in the past year, and another price hike of 10 percent has just been announced.

FIGURE 18.4
(Continued)

Funding Proposal   2

Proposes a logical
solution to the
problem based on
evidence

Need

Despite growing production costs, the *Torch* has received no increase in its yearly budget allocation ($37,400) in three years. Inadequate funding is virtually crippling our newspaper.

Previews the plan
before getting into
the details

Scope

The following plan includes

1. Methods for reducing production costs while maintaining the quality of our staff
2. Projected costs for technology upgrades, salaries, and services during the upcoming year
3. A demonstration of feasibility, showing our cost-effectiveness
4. A summary of attitudes shared by our personnel

PROPOSED PLAN

This plan is designed to trim operating costs without compromising quality.

Itemizes realistic
ways to save money
and retain staff

Methods

We can overcome our budget and staffing crisis by taking these steps:

Reducing Page Count. By condensing free notices for campus organizations, abolishing "personal" notices, and limiting press releases to one page, we can reduce page count per issue from 24 to 20, saving nearly 17 percent in production costs. (Items deleted from hard copy could be linked as add-ons in the *Torch*'s Web-based version.)

Reducing Hard-Copy Circulation. Reducing circulation from 6,000 to 5,000 copies barely will cover the number of full-time SMU students, but will save nearly 17 percent in printing costs. The steadily increasing hits on our Web site suggests that more and more readers are using the electronic medium. (We are designing a fall survey that will help determine how many readers rely on the Web-based version.)

Hiring a New Press. We can save money by hiring Arrow Press for printing. Other presses (including our present printer) bid at least 25 percent higher than Arrow. With its state-of-the art production equipment, Arrow will import our "camera-ready" digital files to produce the hard-copy version. Moreover, no other company offers the rapid turnover time (from submission to finished product) that Arrow promises.

FIGURE 18.4
(Continued)

Upgrading Our Desktop Publishing Technology. To meet Arrow's specifications for submitting digital files, we must upgrade our equipment. Upgrade costs will be largely offset the first year by reduced printing costs. Also, this technology will increase efficiency and reduce labor costs, resulting in substantial payback on investment.

Increasing Staff Salaries. Although we seek talented students who expect little money and much experience, salaries for all positions must increase by an average of 25 percent. Otherwise, any of our staff could earn as much money elsewhere by working only a little more than half the time. In fact, many students could exceed the minimum wage by working for local newspapers. To illustrate: The *Standard Beacon* pays $60 to $90 per news article and $30 per photo; the *Torch* pays nothing for articles and $6 per photo.

A striking example of low salaries is the $4.75 per hour we pay our desktop publishing staff. Our present desktop publishing cost of $3,038 could be as much as $7,000 or even higher if we had this service done by an outside firm, as many colleges do. Without this nominal salary increase, we cannot possibly attract qualified personnel.

Costs

Our proposed budget is itemized in Table 1, but the main point is clear: If the *Torch* is to remain viable, increased funding is essential.

Provides detailed breakdown of costs—the central issue in the situation

Table 1 Projected Costs and Requested Funding for Next Year's *Torch* Budget

PROJECTED COSTS

Hardware/Software Upgrades

Macintosh G5 (1.8 GHz) Processor	$2,494.98
23-inch Apple™ HD Display (w/rebates)	1,499.98
LaCie™ 160 GB 7200 RPM USB Hard Drive	219.99
Olympus™ Stylus 410 4MP Digital Camera	349.99
Mikrotek™ ScanMaker 6100 Pro	299.99
Extensis™ Photo Imaging Suite	499.98
Microsoft™ Office 2007 Professional-Upgrade	289.97
QuarkEXPress™ 6 software (discounted)	729.97
Adobe™ Photoshop™ CS-Upgrade	169.97
Adobe™ Illustrator™ CS-Upgrade	169.99
Macromedia™ Dreamweaver™ MX2004-Upgrade	199.98
Subtotal	**$6,924.79**

FIGURE 18.4
(Continued)

Funding Proposal   4

Wages and Salaries

Desktop-publishing staff (35 hr/wk at $6.00/hr x 28 wk)	$5,880.00
Editor-in-Chief	3,150.00
News Editor	1,890.00
Features Editor	1,890.00
Advertising Manager	2,350.00
Advertising Designer	1,575.00
Webmaster	2,520.00
Layout Editor	1,890.00
Art Director	1,260.00
Photo Editor	1,890.00
Business Manager	1,890.00
Distributor	560.00
Subtotal	**$26,745.00**

Miscellaneous Costs

Graphics by SMU art students (3/wk @ $10 each)	$ 840.00
Mailing	1,100.00
Telephone	1,000.00
Campus print shop services	400.00
Copier fees	100.00
Subtotal	**$3,440.00**

Fixed Printing Costs (5,000 copies/wk x 28/wk)	**$24,799.60**

TOTAL YEARLY COSTS	**$61,909.39**
Expected Advertising Revenue ($600/wk x 28 wks)	**($16,800.00)**
Total Costs Minus Advertising Revenue	**$45,109.39**

TOTAL FUNDING REQUEST	**$45,109.39**

FIGURE 18.4
(Continued)

Feasibility

Beyond exhibiting our need, we feel that the feasibility of this proposal can be measured through an objective evaluation of our cost-effectiveness: Compared with newspapers at similar schools, how well does the *Torch* use its funding?

→ Assesses probability of success

In a survey of the four area college newspapers, we found that the *Torch*—by a sometimes huge margin—makes the best use of its money per page. Table 1A in the Appendix shows that, of the five newspapers, the *Torch* costs students the least, runs the most pages weekly, and spends the least money per page, *despite a circulation two to three times the size of the other papers.*

The *Torch* has the lowest yearly cost of all five newspapers, despite having the largest circulation. With the requested budget increase, the cost would rise by only $0.88, for a yearly cost of $9.00 to each student. Although Alden College's newspaper costs each student $8.58, it is published only every third week, averages 12 pages per issue, and costs more than $71.00 yearly per page to print—in contrast to our yearly printing cost of $55.65 per page. As the figures in the Appendix demonstrate, our cost management is responsible and effective.

Personnel

The *Torch* staff is determined to maintain the highest professionalism. Many are planning careers in journalism, writing, editing, advertising, photography, Web design, or public relations. In any *Torch* issue, the balanced, enlightened coverage is evidence of our judicious selection and treatment of articles and our shared concern for quality.

→ Addresses important issue of personnel

CONCLUSION

As a broad forum for ideas and opinions, the *Torch* continues to reflect a seriousness of purpose and a commitment to free and responsible expression. Its role in campus life is more vital than ever during these troubled times.

→ Reemphasizes need and encourages action

Every year, allocations to student organizations increase or decrease based on need. Last year, for example, eight allocations increased by an average of $4,332. The *Torch* has received no increase in three years.

Presumably, increases are prompted by special circumstances. For the *Torch*, these circumstances derive from increasing production costs and the need to update vital equipment. We respectfully urge the Committee to respond to the *Torch*'s legitimate needs by increasing next year's allocation to $45,109.39.

FIGURE 18.4
(Continued)

Funding Proposal   6

APPENDIX (Comparative Performance)

Table 1A Allocations and Performance of Five Local College Newspapers

Appendix provides
detailed breakdown
of cost comparisons

	Stonehorse College	Alden College	Simms University	Fallow State	SMU
Enrollment	1,600	1,400	3,000	3,000	5,000
Fee paid (per year)	$65.00	$85.00	$35.00	$50.00	$65.00
Total fee budget	$104,000	$119,000	$105,000	$150,000	$325,000
Newspaper budget	$18,300	$8,580	$36,179	$52,910	$37,392
					$45,109[a]
Yearly cost per student	$12.50	$8.58	$16.86	$24.66	$8.12
					$9.00[a]
Publication rate	Weekly	Every third week	Weekly	Weekly	Weekly
Average no. of pages	8	12	18	12	24
Average total pages	224	120	504	336	672
					560[a]
Yearly cost per page	$81.60	$71.50	$71.78	$157.47	$55.65
					$67.12[a]

[a]These figures are next year's costs for the SMU *Torch.*

Source: Figures were quoted by newspaper business managers in April 20XX.

CHECKLIST
for Proposals

☐ Have I identified whether my proposal is solicited or unsolicited, and have I planned accordingly?

☐ Have I determined whether my proposal should be informal or formal?

☐ Have I identified whether my proposal is a planning, research, or sales proposal?

☐ Does my proposal follow a problem-solution or situation-resolution pattern?

☐ Have I done adequate research?

☐ Have I provided a clear title or subject line?

☐ Is the problem or situation clearly identified in the introduction?

☐ Is the background section appropriate for this audience's needs?

☐ Does the proposal maintain a clear focus on benefits?

☐ Is the proposed solution or resolution appropriate and realistic?

☐ Is the cost, budget, and/or qualifications section accurate and easy to understand?

☐ Are my claims honest and supportable?

☐ Are all foreseeable limitations identified?

☐ Are visuals, if needed, used effectively?

☐ Is my writing style clear, concise, and confident?

☐ Does the proposal end with a call to action?

APPLICATIONS

GENERAL APPLICATIONS

1. After identifying your primary and secondary audience, write a short planning proposal for improving an unsatisfactory situation in the classroom, on the job, or in your dorm or apartment (e.g., poor lighting, drab atmosphere, health hazards, poor seating arrangements). Choose a problem or situation whose solution or resolution is more a matter of common sense and lucid observation than of intensive research. Be sure to (a) identify the problem clearly, give a brief background, and stimulate interest; (b) clearly state the methods proposed to solve the problem; and (c) conclude with a statement designed to gain audience support.

2. Write a research proposal to your instructor (or an interested third party) requesting approval for your final term project (a formal analytical report or formal

proposal). Verify that adequate primary and secondary sources are available. Convince your audience of the soundness and usefulness of the project.

3. As an alternate term project to the formal analytical report (Chapter 17), develop a long proposal for solving a problem, improving a situation, or satisfying a need in your school, community, or job. Choose a subject sufficiently complex to justify a formal proposal, a topic requiring research (mostly primary). Identify an audience (other than your instructor) who will use your proposal for a specific purpose. Complete an Audience and Purpose Profile.

TEAM APPLICATION

Working in groups of four, develop an unsolicited planning proposal for solving a problem, improving a situation, or satisfying a need in your school, community, or workplace. Begin by brainstorming as a group to come up with a list of possible issues or problems to address in your proposal. Narrow your list, and work as a group to focus on a specific issue or idea. Your proposal should address a clearly identified audience of decision makers and stakeholders in the given issue. Complete an Audience and Purpose Profile.

GLOBAL APPLICATION

Compare the sorts of proposals regularly done in the United States with those created in other countries. For example, is the format the same? Are there more proposals for certain purposes in the United States than in another country? You can learn about this topic by interviewing an expert in international business (someone you meet on the job, during an internship, or through your adviser). You can also search the Web for information on international technical communication. Describe your findings in a short memo that you will share with your classmates.

COMPUTER/WEB-BASED APPLICATION

Solicited proposals are usually written in response to a formal "request for proposal" (RFP). Most RFPs are available on the Web. For instance, the National Science Foundation's site <www.nsf.gov/funding> has links for all sorts of research funding opportunities. There is a link for undergraduate students, for graduate students, for K–12 educators, and for many program areas such as engineering, geosciences, and so on. Go to this site, click on a link that interests you, and locate the RFP. Write a memo to your instructor explaining why you are interested in this research and what focus your proposal would take. For instance, you might have a good idea for a proposal in response to the Research Experiences for Undergraduates (REU) RFP. What topic would you choose and how would you make your best case?

For additional technical writing resources that will help you master the chapter objectives, go to **www.mytechcommlab.com**.

19 Email and Text Messages

LEARNING OBJECTIVES FOR THIS CHAPTER

- ▶ Identify advantages of using email in the workplace

- ▶ Determine if email is the correct form of communication in a given situation

- ▶ Write a well-organized, stylistically appropriate email

- ▶ Identify advantages and disadvantages of using text messages in the workplace

- ▶ Conduct a successful workplace communication using text messages

- ▶ Recognize basic issues about copyright and privacy in digital communication

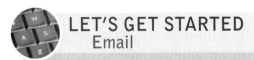

LET'S GET STARTED
Email

Think about how quickly most email messages are written and sent. Before reading this chapter, compose an email message to a professor whom you have never met, asking for more information about a course that she or he is teaching next semester. Consider that the professor probably receives a lot of email, doesn't know you, and is busy with current students.

Questions to ask about the email you wrote as you review the material in this chapter:

▸ What did I write in the subject line?

▸ Is my tone informal, formal, or in between?

▸ Is my request clear?

▸ Did I use any emoticons (such as smiley faces)?

▸ What differences should be considered between an email sent to a friend and an email sent to a professor, potential employer, or current employer?

At the end of this chapter, review your initial Let's Get Started email with your instructor or with a group of students, to see how much you might change or modify the document based on what you have learned from the chapter.

In the past, the bulk of everyday workplace correspondence occurred over the telephone, face to face, or via printed documents such as memos and letters; today's workplace communication, however, occurs mostly in electronically mediated form—usually via email. More recently, text messages, typically via cell phone, are also used for shorter forms of communication. This chapter explores email and text messages in detail.

EMAIL

Email has become the most common form of workplace communication, often replacing paper memos and letters. Unlike paper documents, email can quickly address an individual, a group within an organization, interested people from outside the organization, or a mix of people. One email message can reach thousands of readers in seconds, and these readers can forward the email to others.

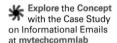
Explore the Concept with the Case Study on Informational Emails at **mytechcommlab**

■ ■ ■ Analyze the
■ ■ ■ Workplace
■ Email at
mytechcommlab

Email is also useful when people are in different time zones or have different working schedules: You can send an email at 2:00 A.M. if you are a night owl, and your early-bird colleague can read it in the morning. Email also provides an electronic paper trail for legal reasons or a record of ongoing conversation. Finally, email allows people to include attachments—even scanned attachments of print documents— thus replacing fax machines.

Email messages tend to be conversational and typically are used for routine, simple messages, such as quickly letting a coworker know the status of a project or asking your boss a simple question. Even writers who are extremely careful with traditional paper correspondence sometimes ignore spelling and grammar as they dash off various emails. However, as the uses for email broaden and as the software evolves, workplace emails are starting to look more polished. Writers are paying greater attention to style and correctness, and making their email look more professional.

The changing
character of email

Audience and Purpose of Email

Unlike paper documents, with email you have little control over the final audience. You might send your message to only a small group, but because of easy forwarding, your audience could turn out much larger. People also tend to be more casual and off-the-cuff on email, sometimes more than in person; therefore, audience considerations become crucial.

Audience
considerations

■ ■ ■ Analyze the
■ ■ ■ Informal Email at
■ mytechcommlab

Suppose, for example, that after a long week of work on a particularly tough engineering design project, you send a quick email to another manager. In your message, you complain about one of the engineers not holding up his end. You quickly press "Send" and head out for the weekend. At a Monday status meeting, you are surprised to find that your message was forwarded to several other engineers. Clearly, your original message was not intended for them, but—inadvertently or deliberately—someone forwarded it along.

Be sure you understand a cardinal rule about email correspondence: Always assume that your message will travel far beyond its intended recipient, and never send anything private or confidential via email.

Email accomplishes various purposes: to schedule meetings, update team members on a project, send simple memos in electronic form, and send attached documents to colleagues both within and outside of an organization.

Purpose
considerations

■ ■ ■ Analyze the
■ ■ ■ Formal Email at
■ mytechcommlab

Always think carefully about whether email is the best medium for the given message. If you want the message to be private or confidential choose another medium. Also, consider sending a complex or important memo as a print document because an electronic memo may be ignored when sent to full in-boxes. Finally, do not attach highly formal documents (such as long reports, proposals, or legal correspondence) to your email—unless your recipient has specifically requested such an attachment.

Components and Organization of Email

A standard email resembles a combination of a paper memo and a letter (Chapter 11). Like a memo, an email begins with a heading guide with "To," "From," "Date," and "Subject" lines. Like a letter, an email can include optional features, such as copy notation, enclosure notation, sender's contact information, and complimentary closing. Unlike a letter, the copy notation appears as a "CC" (courtesy copy) or "BCC" (blind courtesy copy) in the heading guide; an email attachment (signaled by an icon or the word "attachment" below the heading guide) takes the place of an enclosure notice; and the sender's contact information—the signature block—appears at the bottom of the page. A complimentary closing (e.g., "Sincerely, Lynn") at email's end provides a personal touch.

Email components

Like any other workplace document, a typical email message has a brief introduction that gets right to the point, a clear body section with transitions between each, and a brief conclusion that usually asks the reader to take action (such as, "please send me back your thoughts"). Also, to break the information into chunks, emails often include headings, bullets, and other graphic highlights.

Email organization

Figure 19.1 illustrates the components and organization of a standard workplace email.

Style and Netiquette of Workplace Email

Personal email often contains deliberately misspelled or abbreviated words, a disregard for grammatical rules, a lax attitude toward proper punctuation, a highly informal tone, and an emphasis on brevity over completeness. Workplace email, however, should use proper spelling, grammar, and punctuation and should avoid words or phrases in all capital letters, as well as text-message style abbreviations ("LOL," "imho," and the like) and emoticons (facial expressions, such as smiley faces, created using type). In addition, adopt a professional, respectful tone and express complete thoughts. An email that is too casual (e.g., using such words as "uh huh," "whatever," and "cool") or is incomplete will undermine the writer's professionalism.

Workplace email style

Explore the Concept with the Case Study on Diplomatic Emails at **mytechcommlab**

Netiquette, jargon for "Internet etiquette," encompasses not only email tone, but also the physical ways in which people respond to and forward email messages. To practice netiquette, avoid *flaming* (angry, sarcastic, insulting messages that will only lead to repercussions), using sexist or otherwise biased language that demeans or excludes some potential readers, and blaming others. Also, do not forward a particularly sensitive email without permission, edit a forwarded email, or send enormous attachments. Respond to an email as soon as possible.

Workplace email etiquette

Figure 19.2 shows an email that violates style and netiquette rules. Although the writer and recipient are close personal friends in addition to their employee–supervisor relationship, an email like this should never be written in the workplace.

(*Text continues on p. 370.*)

**FIGURE 19.1
A workplace
email**

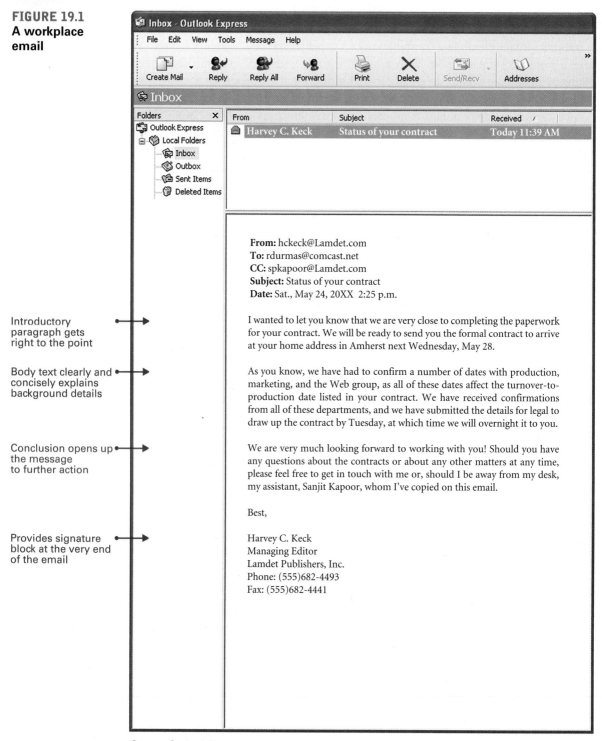

Introductory
paragraph gets
right to the point

Body text clearly and
concisely explains
background details

Conclusion opens up
the message
to further action

Provides signature
block at the very end
of the email

From: hckeck@Lamdet.com
To: rdurmas@comcast.net
CC: spkapoor@Lamdet.com
Subject: Status of your contract
Date: Sat., May 24, 20XX 2:25 p.m.

I wanted to let you know that we are very close to completing the paperwork for your contract. We will be ready to send you the formal contract to arrive at your home address in Amherst next Wednesday, May 28.

As you know, we have had to confirm a number of dates with production, marketing, and the Web group, as all of these dates affect the turnover-to-production date listed in your contract. We have received confirmations from all of these departments, and we have submitted the details for legal to draw up the contract by Tuesday, at which time we will overnight it to you.

We are very much looking forward to working with you! Should you have any questions about the contracts or about any other matters at any time, please feel free to get in touch with me or, should I be away from my desk, my assistant, Sanjit Kapoor, whom I've copied on this email.

Best,

Harvey C. Keck
Managing Editor
Lamdet Publishers, Inc.
Phone: (555)682-4493
Fax: (555)682-4441

Source: Outlook Express frame used with permission from Microsoft.

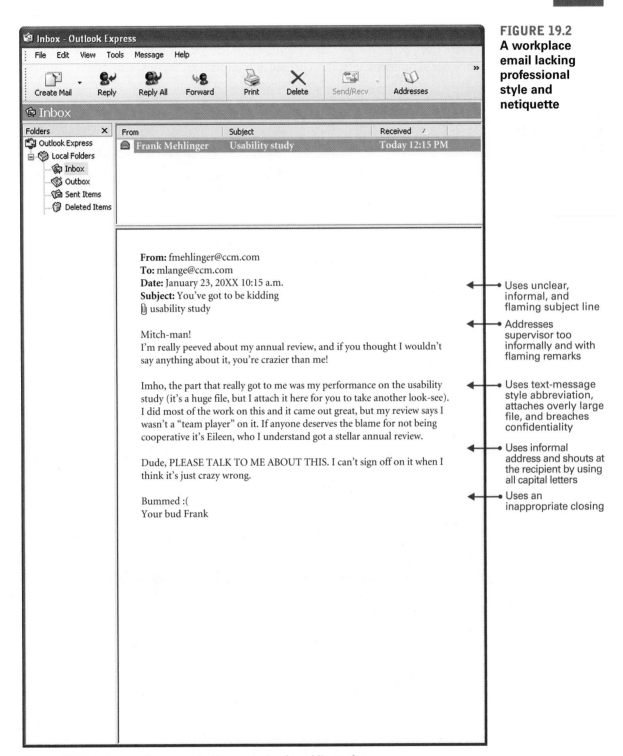

FIGURE 19.2
A workplace email lacking professional style and netiquette

Email content shown in figure:

From: fmehlinger@ccm.com
To: mlange@ccm.com
Date: January 23, 20XX 10:15 a.m.
Subject: You've got to be kidding
📎 usability study

Mitch-man!
I'm really peeved about my annual review, and if you thought I wouldn't say anything about it, you're crazier than me!

Imho, the part that really got to me was my performance on the usability study (it's a huge file, but I attach it here for you to take another look-see). I did most of the work on this and it came out great, but my review says I wasn't a "team player" on it. If anyone deserves the blame for not being cooperative it's Eileen, who I understand got a stellar annual review.

Dude, PLEASE TALK TO ME ABOUT THIS. I can't sign off on it when I think it's just crazy wrong.

Bummed :(
Your bud Frank

Callout annotations:
- Uses unclear, informal, and flaming subject line
- Addresses supervisor too informally and with flaming remarks
- Uses text-message style abbreviation, attaches overly large file, and breaches confidentiality
- Uses informal address and shouts at the recipient by using all capital letters
- Uses an inappropriate closing

Source: Outlook Express frame used with permission from Microsoft.

Not only does the message in Figure 19.2 have legal implications in terms of the writer's job performance and future employment, but it also violates another employee's confidentiality. It is also much too informal for any workplace document.

STRATEGIES
for Email

▶ **Consider your audience.** If you are writing to a customer, client, or superior in your organization, use a more formal tone with a coworker or immediate supervisor. If you know your recipient well, use an informal salutation ("Hello") and an informal closing ("Regards," "Best"). However, for someone you don't know or someone in authority, use a formal salutation ("Dear Dr. Gomez") and a formal closing ("Sincerely").

▶ **Consider your purpose.** Don't use email when a more personal medium is preferable. Sometimes an issue is best resolved by talking face-to-face, making a phone call, or even just leaving a voice mail. Don't use email to apply for or resign from a job, send a thank-you letter following a job interview, request a raise, respond to a formal letter, or respond to something that may have legal implications.

▶ **Consider confidentiality.** Email is not the medium for sending legal documents, confidential company files, or anything else that should remain private. Also, before forwarding a message, obtain permission from the sender, who may have intended the message for you only.

▶ **Assume that your email is permanent and readable by anyone at any time.** "Forensic software" can find virtually any file that has been deleted, so don't make promises you cannot keep or expect anything else you say to disappear forever.

▶ **Write a clear subject line.** Instead of "Test Data" or "Data Request," be specific: "Request for Beta Test Data for Project 18." This line helps recipients decide whether or not to read the message immediately, and it helps for filing and future reference.

▶ **Use appropriate formatting.** Provide a brief introduction, details in the body, and a conclusion. Use bullets, headings, numbered lists, italics, and other formatting features to make your message easy to read.

▶ **Keep it short.** Readers are impatient and don't want to scroll through long screens of information. If you must send a complex message, keep longer details in an email attachment.

▶ **Use informal language, emoticons, and abbreviations sparingly.** Even in an informal message, use proper spelling, grammar, and mechanics (avoid using only lower case letters or all capital letters). Emoticons should be used only in informal

➡

messages to coworkers or people you know very well. The same goes for common abbreviations (FYI, ASAP, OMG).

▶ **End with a signature block.** In most cases, include the name and address of your organization or department, your telephone and fax number, and other contact information by using an automatic signature block.

▶ **Proofread thoroughly before hitting "send."** Every message reflects your image, so double-check any email with your name on it. Also be careful that the email goes only to your intended recipients.

▶ **Observe netiquette.** Check your emails daily and reply in timely fashion; give email recipients reasonable time to reply to your emails; avoid flaming (angry or personal attacks) and sexist or biased language; do not edit forwarded emails without the sender's permission; and do not send large attachments.

TEXT MESSAGES

A faster medium than email, text messages (often called "texts" for short) allow you to communicate quickly using a cell phone or smart phone (such as Black-berry, Droid or iPhone). When you send a text, it is received almost immediately. Texts can be sent to one person or to several. Long popular for personal communication, texting has recently become common in the workplace for short, quick exchanges (e.g., to let someone know you'll be late for a meeting or tell a colleague your plane has landed). Although few rules govern the use of texting on the job, many companies recognize the value of short, instantaneous messages and are increasingly accepting the text message as legitimate communication.

Advantages of workplace text messages

Similar to text messages, instant messages (IMs, also called "chats" or "chatting") allow for text-based conversations in real time, using a computer or tablet (iPad, for example) instead of a cell phone. The user types a message into a pop-up box or other interface, and the recipient can respond instantly. Instant messaging can be used one-to-one or with groups, allowing people to converse and collaborate from various locations. One advantage of IMs over text messaging is that typically, IM conversations can be captured on the screen, whereas text messages on cell phones disappear after a short time.

Audience and Purpose of Workplace Text Messages

Consider your audience carefully before deciding to use text messaging for workplace communication. Texting can be useful in place of a phone call for short questions or notifications. But keep in mind that most people receive text

Audience considerations

messages on their personal cell phone number and may be charged a fee per message, so only send text messages if the recipient has agreed to communicate this way.

Purpose considerations

In most cases, defer to using email, which requires timely, but not instant and rapid-fire responses. Texting is not a good medium for the kind of written communication that requires careful planning, composing, and editing. For such messages, consider using email or print instead of texting. Also, most texting programs do not allow you to send attachments. And, importantly, text messages are typically not archived, so if you should need to review a message weeks or months later, you may not be able to find the information.

STRATEGIES
for Text Messages

▶ **Consider your audience and purpose.** Use texts to communicate with people who are comfortable with this medium or who don't mind texts interrupting their work. Use texts for quick conversations on single topics that don't require a paper trail.

▶ **Keep each text conversation separate.** Stick to the topic at hand.

▶ **Keep text messages short.** Texting is more informal than email, so feel free to use abbreviations, as long as everyone understands them.

▶ **Stay connected if you are in the middle of a communication.** Texting requires you to stay connected until you complete your text conversation. If you need to end a conversation, alert the other people involved.

▶ **Know when to end the conversation.** Don't digress. When you've exhausted the topic, say goodbye.

▶ **Observe applicable rules of netiquette.** Avoid flaming and sexist or biased language, maintain confidentiality, and respond to messages quickly.

COMPARING EMAIL AND TEXT MESSAGING

Email and text messaging are common forms of communication, both personally and on the job. Yet when deciding which one to use for a workplace situation, you may want to take a moment and consider a more detailed comparison about audience, purpose, and style. Table 19.1 will help you compare email and text messaging so you can choose the most appropriate tool for the situation.

TABLE 19.1 When to choose a text message or an email

Audience	Purpose	Writing style and content	Email or text?
Student	Let someone know you'll be late for a meeting	Brief, timely, to the point	Text message (short, no need for permanent record)
Instructor/professor	Ask about your grade on a quiz	Brief, but polite	Email (provides a record, is more accessible because most instructors don't give out cell numbers)
Your manager	Indicate that you'd like to take a vacation day	Business-like, to the point	Email unless your manager has specifically requested the use of texting
Coworkers	Start a discussion about a new project	Professional style and content	Email, in most instances
Customers or clients	Send a thank you note	Polite, with some detail	Email (or even paper letter)

COPYRIGHT AND PRIVACY IN DIGITAL COMMUNICATION

Because the various forms of digital communication discussed in this and the next two chapters are often written quickly and distributed widely, you need to keep in mind the importance of copyright and privacy issues.

Copyright is a system of legal protection for original works of authorship (books, photographs, user manuals, music) that are "fixed in a tangible medium." In other words, copyright applies when an idea becomes recorded or written down or otherwise fixed, as in a printed book, an email message, a Web site, or a recorded piece of music.

Copyright protects many forms of work including digital communication

In technical writing and communication, especially with digital communication, there are a few key aspects of copyright to be aware of. In the workplace, if you are a full-time employee, most of what you write and create is typically owned by the company. So be careful about posting material to a blog or Web site without first obtaining permission from the company. Also, you may find a photograph or piece of music or image on a Web site and think it's the perfect visual for the report you are writing. But unless your use is for educational purposes or the piece is clearly marked as "copyright free" or "in the public domain," you probably need to seek permission to use the item. (See pages 399 and 459 for more on Fair Use.)

If you are unsure about the copyright status of a work, it's best to consult with a librarian or with the author of the material, keeping in mind that sometimes the author is a corporate, not individual author.

All digital communications are, to a degree, private

Digital communications also raise privacy issues. For example, avoid forwarding an email without checking with the sender first. Likewise, don't forward proprietary information (information that originates in your company) to unauthorized recipients outside the company. Texts are not always archived, but they can still be used to violate a sender's privacy or a company's confidential information.

BE PREPARED FOR TECHNOLOGY TO FAIL

Have a backup plan when communicating digitally

Digital communication is "virtual" and can therefore disappear temporarily or permanently when technology fails. Before the advent of the Internet, paper copies and written notes allowed for a permanent record. Barring some disaster, once something was recorded, a physical document would be retrievable from the file cabinet.

Today we often rely—perhaps too much—on technology to preserve everything for us. However, computer crashes, server failures, faulty flash drives, and viruses compromise the permanence of virtual communications. So, have a backup plan. Use email rather than texts to record important ongoing conversations, and print out or back-up all digital work to an external hard drive or server routinely. Don't rely on continuous access to the Internet. Along with regular electronic backups, make regular print copies, too.

CHECKLIST
for Email and Text Messages

EMAIL

☐ Have I determined if email is the best medium in this situation?

☐ Did I write a clear subject line?

☐ Have I kept my message short and to the point?

☐ Have I included a brief introduction, details in the body, a conclusion, and a complimentary closing and signature block?

☐ Is my email appropriately informal or formal, depending on my audience?

☐ Have I used emoticons, abbreviations, and text-speak sparingly (or not at all in a formal email)?

☐ Does my email follow all the rules of netiquette?

➜

CHECKLIST *continued*

☐ Have I maintained confidentiality?

☐ Did I proofread my email and check the distribution list before sending?

TEXT MESSAGES

☐ Have I determined if text messaging is the best medium in this situation?

☐ Have I kept my message very short and on topic?

☐ Have I remained connected throughout the conversation?

☐ Did I conclude the topic when appropriate?

☐ Have I observed the rules of netiquette that apply to text messaging?

 APPLICATIONS

GENERAL APPLICATIONS

1. Choose a topic and an audience, and write an email complaining about something that bothers you, written in a way that follows proper email format, includes all the required components, and avoids flaming.

2. Do some online research to learn how corporations are using text messaging for workplace communication. Write a brief recommendation report, arguing that your company or organization or department (you can invent a company or organization if you are not currently on the job) should or should not allow text messaging.

TEAM APPLICATION

Work with a team to write a collaborative version of the complaint email (Application 1, in General Applications).

GLOBAL APPLICATION

Copyright and privacy are subject to the laws of a country or region. The Internet and other technologies complicate matters because data can easily travel around the world without regard for borders. The World Intellectual Property Organization (WIPO) is an international group that oversees the global implications of intellectual property issues. (You can learn more about WIPO by visiting its Web site at <www.wipo .org>.) If you can, talk to a communication professional who deals with international audiences. Ask about any difficulties the person has encountered with copyright or privacy. Review the WIPO Web site with this professional, and ask how the information on this site might affect the way she or he would write, design, and distribute various digital communications.

COMPUTER/WEB-BASED APPLICATION

Work collaboratively in teams of two and discuss a workplace situation in which text messaging would be appropriate. If you have cell phones with you (and won't incur any charges), exchange a series of messages about this situation, following the strategies in this chapter.

For additional technical writing resources that will help you master the chapter objectives, go to **www.mytechcommlab.com.**

20 Blogs, Wikis, and Social Networks

LEARNING OBJECTIVES FOR THIS CHAPTER

▸ Differentiate between internal and external blogs

▸ Understand how to write for blogs and wikis

▸ Recognize the difference between social networking for personal use and for workplace use

▸ Understand how to use social networking for workplace communication

▸ Identify social networking sites specific to job search and career advancement

▸ Understand appropriate ways of presenting yourself on social networks

LET'S GET STARTED
Blogs, Wikis, and Social Networks

Blogs, wikis, and social networks can be useful tools to help companies and other organizations stay in touch with customers and reach potential new employees. Think of a group you are involved with—a club, a volunteer organization, a study group, a part-time or full-time job—and, in teams of three people, compile a list of ideas about how you might use a blog, wiki, or social network to increase visibility for your organization.

Questions to ask may include the following:

▶ Why would we use a blog? A wiki? A social network?

▶ Which social network (Facebook? LinkedIn?) would make sense?

▶ What tone and style should we use when writing for these sites?

▶ Should we include visuals?

At the end of this chapter, review your initial Let's Get Started list with your instructor to see how much you might change or adapt your initial strategy based on what you have learned here.

Advantages of blogs, wikis, and social networking

◉ Watch the Video on External Blogs at mytechcommlab

Blogs (short for Web logs) began as forums for people to read about and discuss political topics, hobbies, and other mutual interests. Soon, commercial entities began to see the benefits of launching their own blogs to share information and bring people together. Corporate blogs play an increasing role in mainstream workplace communication. Major companies use blogs to help employees network with each other (internal blogs) and to communicate with customers and clients (external blogs). Wikis (to be discussed) are special types of blogs. Social networks are Web sites that connect people to each other and to topics they may be interested in (hobbies, products, volunteer organizations). Social networking, which began as a way for students and friends to stay in contact, has turned into a popular and powerful way for companies to stay in touch with customers and for people to connect about jobs and careers.

INTERNAL CORPORATE BLOGS

How a blog can enhance a company's internal conversation

Internal corporate blogs enhance workflow and morale. In large organizations, blogs can provide an alternative to email for routine in-house communication. Anyone in the network can post a message or comment on other messages. In the blogging environment, meetings can be conducted without the time and location constraints of face-to-face meetings. Employee training can be delivered, and updates about company developments can be circulated. Blogs are especially useful for collaborating. For example, someone in a company's engineering department can create a forum to discuss various solutions to a technical problem.

EXTERNAL CORPORATE BLOGS

In the public arena, external blogs facilitate customer feedback on products and services, enhance marketing and public relations, and help personalize a large corporation in the eyes of customers and consumers. Blogs give businesses a chance to show a personal, informal side, to respond amiably and quickly to customer concerns, and to allow customers to provide ideas and feedback. Tone, of course, is critical in a corporate blog; it needs to sound friendly, welcoming, and sincere.

How a blog can enhance a company's public conversation

Figure 20.1 is a corporate blog from Marriott hotels. The most prominent feature on the page, as on any blog, is the daily post, featuring a dated news item directly

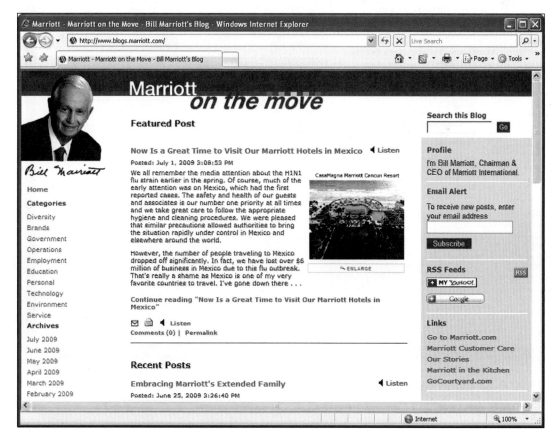

FIGURE 20.1 An external corporate blog

Source: Reproduced with permission of Marriott International, Inc.

FIGURE 20.2 An access page for RSS feeds

Source: USA.gov

linked to the company's business, with an option for anyone to comment. In addition, this blog (like most) includes a brief orienting introduction, a search engine, and links to other parts of the site. This particular blog also offers the options to subscribe to an RSS feed and to listen to an audio version of the blog post. An RSS feed (short for Really Simple Syndication and also known as a Web feed or a news feed) is a retrieval program that delivers summaries of blog or news items to subscribers.

The Marriott blog offers readers the option to subscribe to Marriott's RSS feed. People who are interested in keeping up with information from a variety of sources may also want to subscribe to an RSS aggregator, such as the U.S. Government RSS Library (see Figure 20.2) or Google Reader, which gathers RSS feeds and sends them to subscribers based on their preselected interests.

CORPORATE WIKIS

A wiki (from the Hawaiian phrase *wiki wiki*, meaning "quick") is a type of blog used primarily to collect information and keep it updated. Most people are familiar with Wikipedia, an online encyclopedia for which anyone can write or revise the content. Corporate wikis, also known as enterprise wikis, are similar, in that they allow for the sharing and updating of content, but they serve a different function—to allow employees within a company (or outside the company, if given password access) to update information. Each person with access may log on to the wiki and make changes to content, overwriting previous versions. Despite the potential for abuse created by such alterations, a well-managed wiki can be a valuable resource among trustworthy contributors. To ensure that serial edits do not end up distorting the original posting, copies of the original along with each subsequent edit are saved for later reference.

How wikis enhance team communication

SOCIAL NETWORKS

Social networks have become popular ways of connecting people with each other and with activities, interests, companies, non-profits, and other organizations. Some of the more popular social networking sites and tools include the following:

Types of social networks

- Facebook, originally developed for college students but now used by friends, family, professional associates, businesses, and other organizations.
- MySpace, originally used by young people and still a popular site for artists and independent musicians.
- LinkedIn, used specially for professional networking and job hunting.
- Twitter, used to send short messages (called "tweets") to people who subscribe to a particular Twitter feed.

Two important business uses of social networks are for workplace communication and for job searches and career advancement.

Social Networking and Workplace Communication

Although social networking began as a way for friends to stay in contact, the workplace is rapidly embracing such media for business purposes. Many companies and organizations maintain a Facebook page, and employers routinely check out the Facebook entries of potential employees. Social networking has also become a popular way to reach people in specific interest groups.

Social network use in organizational communication

Organizations such as Dell Computer, the New York Times, and NASA use social networks for outreach and marketing by creating a page and inviting people to join. This use of social networking promotes the organization's name and ideas.

Corporate uses of social media marketing

Companies such as Ford Motor Company are hiring people who specialize in social media marketing. The head of their social media group keeps a blog and discusses strategies for measuring online customer behavior, including how often people click on a given link, view a Web page, or search parts of a site (Monty).

Social Networking and Your Career

Explore social networking career sites

Social networking sites can help you stay connected, discover job openings, and advertise yourself. One popular professional networking site is LinkedIn (see Figure 20.3). On this and similar sites, you can keep your profile (work experience,

FIGURE 20.3 LinkedIn, a Professional Networking Site LinkedIn and similar sites let you connect with potential employers as well as with other people in your field.

references, and so forth) updated and make this profile available to professional contacts, potential employers, and job recruiters. Importantly, you can connect with former colleagues and classmates. These people are often your best bet for learning about job openings. Don't be shy about contacting people you don't know firsthand but with whom you have some mutual connection through a third party (a former coworker, for example).

Twitter is also becoming a popular tool for employment-related communication. Many companies use Twitter to announce job openings. By using Twitter, companies can reach hundreds of potential employees quickly and inexpensively.

STRATEGIES
for Blogs, Wikis, and Social Networking

BLOGS AND WIKIS

▸ **When writing for blogs and wikis, keep content brief, to-the-point, and concise.** Avoid wordiness and repetition.

▸ **Write differently for internal versus external audiences.** Internal audiences do not require as much background. External audiences may need more explanation.

▸ **For an external blog, focus on the customer's priorities and needs.** A friendly, encouraging tone goes a long way in good customer relations.

▸ **Check blog and wiki entries for credibility.** Check the content to see when it was last updated (usually under the "history" tab on a wiki)

SOCIAL NETWORKING

▸ **Write with a friendly yet professional tone.** It's always nice to be friendly, but a professional tone will make your message more credible.

▸ **Keep ideas focused and specific.** Social networks let you narrow your message down to a targeted audience (say, customers who use a specific model of laptop).

▸ **Be discreet about what you post.** When posting to your personal Facebook or other page, remember to omit private or potentially damaging information. It may be fun to tell your friends how many parties you've attended, but when you apply for a job, this information may come back to haunt you.

▸ **Keep global readers in mind.** Social networking pages can typically be viewed by readers from across many countries and cultures. Keep the content accessible to a wide audience (see Chapter 2 for more on global audiences).

CHECKLIST
for Blogs Wikis, and Social Networking

☐ Have I determined if a blog or wiki should be internal (for employees only) or external (for outside audiences)?

☐ Are blog or wiki entries written clearly, avoiding wordiness and repetition?

☐ Have I checked blog or wiki entries for credibility and truthfulness?

☐ For external blogs or wikis, have I provided enough background and context for this audience?

☐ For external blogs or wikis, is the tone friendly, welcoming, and sincere?

☐ Have I determined if the blog or wiki should include an RSS feed?

☐ When creating a social networking site for a company or organization, have I written content and used images that are professional and appropriate?

☐ When creating a social networking site for myself, have I used the right site for the right purpose (e.g., LinkedIn for professional networking and job hunting)?

☐ For personal sites, such as Facebook, does the information I've posted portray me in a way that I would want a potential employer to see?

APPLICATIONS

GENERAL APPLICATIONS

1. Locate one or more blogs related to technical communication or to your major. Follow the discusson for a few days, and write a brief analysis of the chosen blog, its intended audience, content areas, and its value to members in the field.

2. Explore several professional networking sites (e.g., LinkedIn, Ryze, Spoke). What are the differences among these three sites. For instance, all three offer to help you see your network of professional contacts—does one of these sites offer a better visual display of connections? Do all of these sites let you upload your resume and provide a list of references? If you have an account with any of these, look at your profile to see how well it reflects your current experience and career goals. Make a list of five to six qualities that students should consider when writing and posting to professional networking sites.

TEAM APPLICATION

In teams of two, look at your Facebook page and the Facebook page of your class-mate. Imagine that you are managers interested in hiring new college students for a trainee position in your department. What do these Facebook pages tell you about these potential employees? What aspects of Facebook pages—pictures, text, connections—should college students consider during their transition from being a student to being a potential employee? Write a short summary of your thoughts and share with class.

GLOBAL APPLICATION

Blogs, wikis, and social networks have global reach—you can use these tools to col-laborate with team members from other countries. Locate a wiki related to your major. See if the wiki is available in languages other than English. Write a memo to your instructor explaining what you found.

COMPUTER/WEB-BASED APPLICATIONS

1. Set up an account on Blogger or some other site that hosts blogs and create a mock corporate blog. What kinds of subjects would you include on the site? What links would you provide to other corporate sites?

2. Review the material in Chapter 10 (Resumes and Other Employment Material), especially the discussion about electronic resumes (pages 170–171). Take a look at LinkedIn and other professional networking sites to see what options they provide for uploading resumes. Do resumes need to be in any special format or layout? Present your findings to class.

PEARSON

For additional technical writing resources that will help you master the chapter objectives, go to **www.mytechcommlab.com**.

21

Web Pages and Online Videos

LEARNING OBJECTIVES FOR THIS CHAPTER

▸ Recognize the advantages of offering information on Web pages rather than in printed form

▸ Consider audience and purpose before designing and writing a Web page

▸ Identify the various Web page elements

▸ Design and write an effective Web page

▸ Script and record an online video for a Web page

▸ Weigh the ethical and legal issues involved in creating Web pages

▸ Understand in which situations PDF files may be appropriate on a Web page

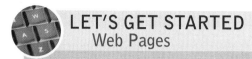

LET'S GET STARTED
Web Pages

Think of a situation for which you and some classmates or colleagues might need a Web site. Perhaps the student organization to which you belong needs a site. Or maybe your team at work could use a Web site to publicize the project you are working on. Before reading this chapter, make a list of the audience characteristics of people you think will be the primary audience for this site. Then look online for examples that seem like good models for the site you are considering.

Questions to ask about your Web site ideas may include the following:

▸ What audience features are important considerations when writing for a Web environment?

▸ How much time will people spend on the site?

▸ Do I want people to simply read the site, or should the site be interactive?

▸ What features do I think are most important about this Web site?

At the end of this chapter, review your initial Let's Get Started list with your instructor or with a group of students to see how much you might change or modify the list based on what you have learned from the chapter.

Although workplace communication continues to use both print and digital formats, Web pages can offer several advantages over hard copy. When documents are printed on paper, their contents remain fixed. If information needs to be updated, a new (and costly) print run is required. But web-based content can be updated at minimal cost and can even be updated automatically. Another advantage of Web pages is that hard-copy documents take up physical space and can be expensive to print (especially in color), whereas web-based information requires only server space and can be far less expensive to create. Web pages also allow for interactivity: people can provide feedback, interact with others, download files, and place orders. Figure 21.1 shows an interactive Web page from the U.S. Food and Drug Administration on the topic of bug bites and bee stings. Interactive features include a list of consumer updates (links) in the left margin, a list of frequently asked questions (such as "When is medical attention needed?"), and a resources section that provides email and RSS updates.

FIGURE 21.1
An interactive Web page

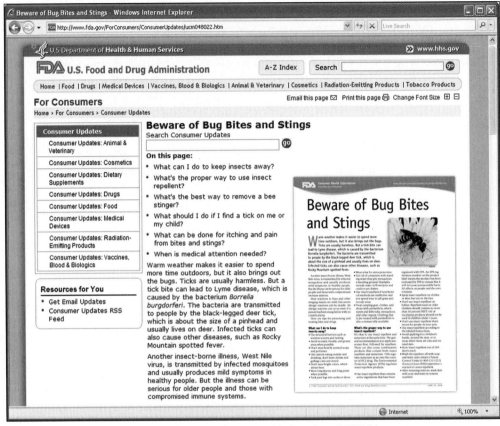

Source: From <www.fda.gov/ForConsumers/ConsumerUpdates/ucm048022.htm>

Web site development in the workplace

✳ **Explore the Concept** with the Case Study on Planning Web Pages at **mytechcommlab**

Web site development is a complex process that changes as related technologies change. Professional Web site development requires training in visual communication, information design, and programming. Moreover, Web development is primarily a collaborative process, often involving content providers, information architects, graphic designers, computer programmers, and marketers. Nevertheless, especially in small businesses and nonprofit organizations, writing and designing for the Web often becomes the responsibility of everyday employees. This chapter introduces the basics of writing and designing Web pages. The Strategies on pages 401–402 provide a basic overview of the process.

AUDIENCE AND PURPOSE OF WEB PAGES

As with any technical documents you must first think carefully about your intended audience and purpose before designing and writing a Web page.

Consider the audience for a Web page by filling out an Audience and Purpose Profile Sheet (see Chapter 4). Does the primary audience consist of potential customers or others who are seeking information, or people buying a product or service, or customers needing product support, or some combination? Who is the secondary audience?

Will your audience be proficient at navigating a complex Web page, or will they need a help menu and a feedback mechanism (email address, phone number) if they have questions? Will the page be read by audiences fluent in English or non-native speakers of English or nonspeakers of English? Unless your page is aimed at a highly technical audience, use plain, noncolloquial English that is easily understood by anyone with basic English proficiency and easily translatable into other languages.

Is the Web page's purpose to publish information, explain a task, sell a product or promote an idea, solicit customer feedback, or some combination? If you want to sell something to technologically savvy young audiences, the page will need to convey a cutting-edge image, employing the latest Web technologies (animation, interaction, complex design). Begin by writing a purpose statement, such as "The purpose of this Web page is to both sell our new mp3 and video players to a young, hip audience and to provide instructions, contact information, downloads, and feedback options for those who already own one."

> **Audience considerations**

> **Purpose considerations**

ELEMENTS OF EFFECTIVE WEB PAGES

Both print documents and Web pages must follow the same basic principles of understandable structure (Chapter 6), readable style (Chapter 7), audience-centered visuals (Chapter 8), and a user-friendly design (Chapter 9). However, because Web pages and print pages are read differently, some of these elements play out differently in the online environment. As you read though this section, refer to Figure 21.3, a user-friendly Web home page, and note how structure, style, visual, and design elements both resemble and differ from print pages.

> **Print documents versus Web pages**

> **Analyze the Web page at mytechcommlab**

Structure

As discussed in Chapter 6, the three approaches in planning a print document's structure are outlining, chunking, and sequencing. This section discusses how these approaches apply to Web pages.

Outlining (Storyboarding).

For a simple print document you would create a basic introduction-body-conclusion outline. A longer print document would require a

> **Create a storyboard rather than an outline**

FIGURE 21.2
A storyboard sketch for a home page

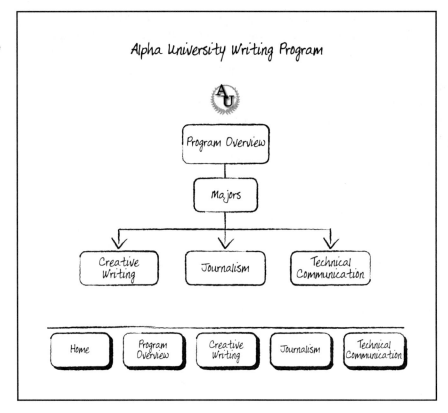

more detailed formal outline using alphanumeric notation, as in Figure 6.3 in Chapter 6. But instead of outlining a Web page, create a storyboard (a handwritten sketch of the page, as in Figure 21.2). This type of storyboard for a Web site is often called a site map.

Most of us have visited Web pages that have no apparent logical organization. A well-designed Web page is storyboarded in advance so that readers can follow the information flow and locate what they seek. The page should be organized so that its main purpose stands out.

In Figure 21.3 the "News for July 1, 2009" header stands prominently toward the top of the page, in orange text and in a large font. It grabs reader attention and signals them to move to the text below. Other information on the page has been storyboarded into categories of special interest to various readers.

Chunking. Readers expect information to be in small and easy-to-digest chunks. Computers are associated with speed, and users are impatient with long blocks of online information. Also, the flickering light patterns of computer screens tire the eyes.

Why storyboards are important

Explore the Concept with the Activity on Storyboarding at **mytechcommlab**

Always chunk information into small segments

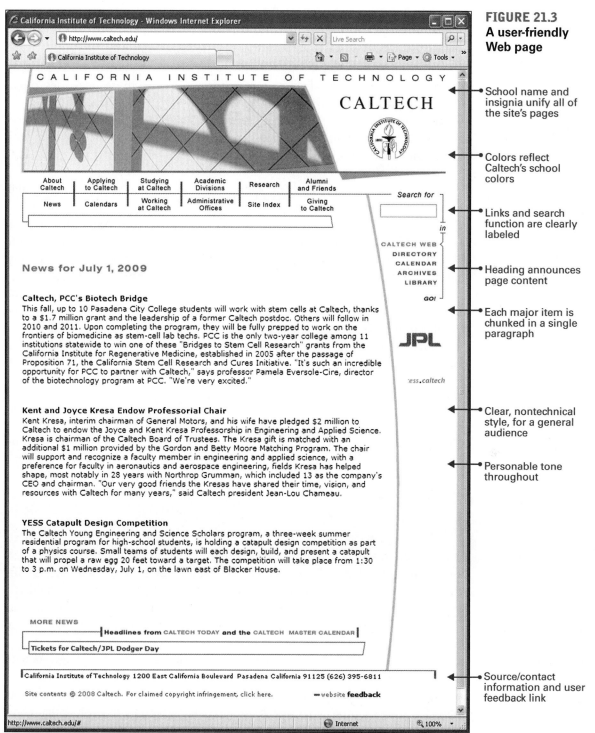

FIGURE 21.3
A user-friendly Web page

School name and insignia unify all of the site's pages

Colors reflect Caltech's school colors

Links and search function are clearly labeled

Heading announces page content

Each major item is chunked in a single paragraph

Clear, nontechnical style, for a general audience

Personable tone throughout

Source/contact information and user feedback link

Source: From <www.caltech.edu>. Reproduced with permission by California Institute of Technology or Caltech.

Analyze the Web page at mytechcommlab

How you chunk the information depends on how your audience will interact with the site. Imagine that you are writing text for a Web site intended to explain a medical procedure to patients. You decide to organize this information by questions users might ask: "How long will the surgery last?" or "When will I be able to return to work?" You would chunk your information into those categories, possibly making each an individual link.

In Figure 21.3, each new item is presented in a single-paragraph chunk. Were the news items longer, the page would likely provide a summary of each item with links to the full articles.

Use logical sequencing, but don't expect users to follow it

Sequencing. A print document follows a logical, linear sequence: spatial, chrono-logical, problem-solution, or cause-and-effect. A Web page should also follow a logical sequence even though people tend not to read Web pages in linear fashion. A typical site displays information in a hypertext format, allowing users to move from link to link, often randomly. Each chunk of text on a Web page must therefore make sense by itself, regardless of its order in the original sequence.

Explore the Concept with Activity on Web Site Analysis at mytechcommlab

Because Figure 21.3 presents three distinct items, sequencing patterns don't apply. However, if the purpose of the page were to provide instructions for applying to Caltech, the instructions would follow a chronological sequence, and readers could link, as needed, to various subsections ("personal statement," "recommendations," or the like).

Style

Follow the style guidelines for print documents

As explained previously, information on the Web must be presented in small, easy-to-digest chunks. Be especially attentive to conciseness by avoiding wordiness and eliminating repetition and redundancy. As in any effective document, the news items in Figure 21.3 are all written in a clear, concise, fluent, and personable style (see Chapter 7).

Visuals

Use, but don't overuse, visuals

As discussed in Chapter 8, use visuals to perform a function rather than merely dress up the page. Figure 21.3 has only two visuals, but each serves a purpose: the school insignia serves as a brand that ties all the site's pages together, whereas a revolving series of images at the top of the page (the screen capture here can only show one) conveys a flavor of the school—from its landscape to its architecture to its students, faculty, and staff.

Select simple, complementary colors

Color is an important visual component, particularly on a Web page. As with the "News for July 1, 2009" header in Figure 21.3, color can direct reader attention to where it is intended. Color also can be used to create a mood. The colors in Figure 21.3, for example, are Caltech's school colors. Select a few colors that complement each other well, and keep your choices simple.

Design

Like printed documents, Web pages must be designed for consistency, cohesiveness, navigation, and emphasis (see Chapter 9); however, some individual design elements serve a different function online than in print documents.

Explore the Concept with the Case Study on Designing Web Pages at **mytechcommlab**

Grid Patterns. Web pages typically use a combination of horizontal and vertical grid patterns, as in Figure 21.3. The key information on the page is presented horizontally and takes visual precedence, whereas links to other pages appear in a vertical column to the right or left.

Combine grid patterns as needed

Margins. In print documents and on Web pages, margins serve the same purpose: they prevent the page from looking crowded and when used consistently they lend cohesiveness to the entire document or site. In Figure 21.3, the margins to the left and right of the news items prevent information from blurring at the screen edges. Other pages on the Caltech Web site use margins of approximately the same width to unify the entire site visually.

Provide ample and consistent margins

Justification. Text set unjustified right is easier to read on a screen than text set justified right. Most Web pages, such as Figure 21.3, use unjustified text on the right.

Use consistent justification, usually unjustified right

White Space. Readers get frustrated with Web pages that have a cluttered look, where too many elements are crammed together without space between. Figure 21.3, on the other hand, has an open feel. Each element—not just the individual news items, but also elements at the top, right, and bottom of the page—is surrounded by plenty of white space.

Provide ample white space between all page elements

Line Spacing and Indentation. Though not required, you may want to use double spacing to make the online reading experience easier. Because material on the Web is chunked into small portions, you need not indent lines. Instead, double space between multiple paragraphs that fall within the same chunk of text.

Use consistent and readable line spacing, and double space between paragraphs

Font Style and Size. Use a consistent base font style and size throughout the site. In addition, choose a font style and size that will be easy on readers' eyes. Prefer a sans serif font in a 10- to 12-point or larger size.

Use a readable font style and size, and use it consistently

In Figure 21.3, the font size appears smaller in the capture than it actually is on the computer screen, where it is about 11 points in size. Meanwhile, the font itself is a simple sans serif that looks professional. Note also how the font styles of various site elements complement each other.

Headings. In Figure 21.3, headings set off each news item and links enable readers to connect to separate pages they want to view.

Use headings to chunk text on a single page, and links to connect to other pages

Use color, shading, and italic for emphasis, but use bold or underlining for hyperlinks only

Color, Shading, Italic, Bold, and Underlining. On a Web page, use color, shading, or italic (but sparingly) to emphasize particular words or phrases, but do not use bold or underlining, which signifies a hyperlink.

Use bulleted and numbered lists to further chunk text

Bulleted and Numbered Lists. Bulleted and numbered lists enhance readability by extracting from a dense paragraph interrelated items or items that fall into a sequence or process. Because the Web environment calls for small chunks of texts and ease of reading on a screen, use lists generously.

Don't use running heads and feet, but clearly identify each page's purpose

Running Heads and Feet. Web pages use links to move from page to page, so running heads and feet are not necessary. However, Web sites with multiple pages should still provide cues to help readers identify their location on the site. Make sure the purpose of each page is clearly labeled in some way, usually at the top or otherwise prominent on the page. Because Figure 21.3 is the home page for Caltech, it isn't labeled, but all pages linking from the home page ("About Caltech," "Applying to Caltech") are clearly labeled.

Use link lists and search options instead of tables of contents and indexes

Tables of Contents and Indexes. A Web site's home page might include a link to a site index (as in Figure 21.3), which may resemble a table of contents without page numbers; however, most Web pages rely on Web-specific forms of navigation, such as a search engine and a list of links. The Caltech home page in Figure 21.3 keeps navigation simple—it provides a list of links (this list must be the same on every page in the site to maintain consistency and prevent confusion) and one search option by category (which likewise must follow the same format across the entire site).

✳ **Explore the Concept** with Activity on Web Site Design at **mytechcommlab**

ONLINE VIDEOS

Uses of online videos

For years, companies used films, audio tape, video cassettes, CDs, or DVDs to train employees. Today, the technology for making and publishing videos is inexpensive and easy to use, and many companies are placing videos, especially instructional videos, directly on their Web sites.

Multimodality

Online videos are what communication experts call "multimodal," meaning that video can take advantage of a full range of communication modes including sound, movement, color, speech, narration, and text. You can actually show how something is done or assembled or produced. Research suggests that *showing* is a powerful teaching technique. We've all had this experience: for example, imagine the last time you tried to assemble a new desk or some other item using the printed instructions, but you just couldn't seem to figure out how to attach certain parts as described in the instructions. In this case, a video, packed on a CD or available on the company's Web site, would be a useful supplement to the written instructions.

Scripting Online Videos

Begin your video project by writing a script that outlines the narration, images, motion, and other features that will constitute the complete video. For an instructional video, you might begin by writing a printed set of instructions (see Chapter 14). Then you can adapt the print instructions to a video format: deciding on background and foreground details, determining camera placement, deciding where and when to include music or text, and writing out the full narrative to be delivered on camera.

The video should be scripted (and then edited) to provide separate segments that orient the reader, list the parts, give detailed step-by-step instructions, and offer a conclusion (such as a shot of the assembled product in action and a closing remark). Any unnecessary background or foreground clutter should be removed. Camera placement should always keep the object or procedure at the center of the frame, at a distance that allows viewers to see exactly what is being shown. Music should be kept to a minimum, usually only at the beginning and end. When text is used, it should be easy to read on the screen—concise, clear, and to the point. Finally, each step should be narrated clearly and slowly, with adequate transitions between steps.

Figure 21.4 features nine stills from a student-made online video for a fictional product (a "Blend-O-Matic 2000" blender made out of Tinkertoys), posted online. Script would look something like the following. (For brevity, the script shown here only goes through shots 1–5. Also, this script omits full dialogue, which would be written out separately.)

The scripting function

Elements of an instructional video script

- Shot 1 (approx. 7 seconds): Opening piano music over side shot of assembled product. Camera moves around the product from side to front view, as title fades in ("Blend-o-Matic 2000 Video Instruction Manual").

- Shots 2 and 3 (approx. 40 seconds): Cut to full view straight-on shot of Blend-o-Matic 2000 parts arranged on table. Fade music. Begin narration ("Welcome to the video instruction manual for the Blend-o-Matic 2000—for all your blending needs"). Hold shot. Presenter points to each part as she discusses them ("These are the parts that should have been included with your product package ...").

- Shot 4 (approx. 4 minutes): Cut to high-angle shot of presenter sitting at the table, with working space in front of her and parts lined up in view. Start narration ("First, be sure to find a level surface on which to assemble the Blend-o-Matic 2000").

- Shot 5 (approx. 5 seconds): Begin assembling the device, starting with the base and first cross piece.

1

Orienting shot for student
instructional video

2

As with written instructions, the
video begins with a complete
parts list

3

Presenter points to each part,
guiding the user along

4

Video directions are provided
step by step

5

Presenter takes ample time and
speaks slowly during each step

6

Presenter moves product in
multiple angles, providing viewers
with context and motion

FIGURE 21.4 Stills from an online instructional video created by students

Source: Gruel, Daniel; Harrison, Holly; Wickler, Allison. *Blend-O-Matic 2000 Video Instruction Manual.* Minneapolis, MN. 2009.

FIGURE 21.4
(Continued)

7

As each part is inserted, the video illustrates the exact direction and shape

8

As the final parts are inserted, users can see how the completed product looks

9

Presenter demonstrates the use of the product, as a way to conclude the video

STRATEGIES
for Online Videos

▶ **Determine your audience.** Consider whether your audience will prefer an online video over another medium or as a supplement to print. Make sure your audience has the appropriate technical background.

▶ **Determine your purpose.** Online videos are most often instructional, but they can also be informational or persuasive. If your purpose is to instruct, consider using written instructions if the product or process is simple. Video is ideal for longer or more complex instructions. If your purpose is to inform or persuade, again think about whether another form of communication might be more appropriate; if you do use video, keep it short to maintain viewer attention.

▸ **Consider teamwork issues.** Because most videos are made by teams (scriptwriter, presenter, cameraperson, editor), determine early on what role each team member will play.

▸ **Do your research.** If there are safety or other issues that need to be mentioned in the video, do careful research to provide accurate information.

▸ **Write a detailed script.** Think through and plan out everything in advance, including the overall structure (introduction-body-conclusion), background and foreground details, camera placement and movement, music, text, and narrative.

▸ **Use a good video camera.** The camera that comes with your cell phone is fine for capturing vacation shots but typically not powerful enough to create a professional-looking online video. If you need a truly high-end video, hire a professional.

▸ **Test your video.** Play back your video and fix any technical problems. Then show the video to a group—coworkers, customers, managers, or some combination—and solicit their feedback.

▸ **Provide backup documents, if necessary.** Determine whether it would be useful to provide viewers with a printed or downloadable written document or a set of PowerPoint slides, so that users have something to follow for later reference.

ETHICAL AND LEGAL CONSIDERATIONS

The power of a Web page to convey information instantaneously and worldwide increases the writer or designer's need for sound ethical and legal judgment.

Ethical Considerations

How a Web page can be unethical

Consider the speed of the Internet, its global reach, and a Web page's ability to combine sound, color, images, text, and interactivity. These features create the potential for manipulation and distortion. Imagine a Web site for an herbal remedy that some people feel is helpful for anxiety. This herbal remedy may not have Food and Drug Administration approval, and may have harmful side effects. But a Web site promoting this product could easily, and at very little cost, be set up to look extremely scientific and factual. Fancy logos from quasi-scientific organizations might give the page a sense of professional credibility. Statistics, charts, and links to other Web sites might create the appearance of a valid medical site. As a communicator setting up such a site, you need to question the possible risks for users.

Legal Considerations

Legal considerations in preparing Web pages include copyright infringement and invasion of privacy. (See page 373 for more about copyright and privacy.)

Verify the ownership of everything you include on a Web page. If you have located a bar chart elsewhere on the Web that you'd like to insert, it is technically very easy to cut and paste or download the bar chart to your page. But is this use legal? Even if the chart has no copyright symbol (©), in the United States all expressions fixed in a tangible medium are copyrighted. The © symbol is not absolutely necessary. Therefore, downloading and including the chart in your document could be a copyright infringement. You should first consider whether your inclusion of this material falls within the boundaries of *fair use* (Figure 21.5). When in doubt, obtain written permission, even if you are only linking from your Web page to another Web page.

Copyright infringement

These four factors are what courts consider when determining if a particular use of copyrighted material falls under fair use. Fair use is part of U.S. copyright law and may not be the same internationally.

(1) the *purpose* and *character* of the use, including whether such use is of a commercial nature or is for nonprofit educational purposes

(2) the *nature* of the copyrighted work (for instance, if the work is published or unpublished)

(3) the *amount* and *substantiality* of the portion used in relation to the copyrighted work as a whole

(4) the *effect* of the use upon the potential *market* for or *value* of the copyrighted work

FIGURE 21.5
Guidelines for determining fair use of copyrighted materials

Source: "Copyright Law of the United States of American and Related Laws Contained in Title 17 of the United States Code." Circular 92. <www.copyright.gov/title17>.

Web pages raise important privacy concerns as well, especially in regard to gathering the personal information of visitors to the site. Many organizations create privacy statements that can be accessed on their Web sites (Figure 21.6). Such statements let readers know how information will be used and what rights readers have. Privacy statements should be readily available on a site, and they should be

Invasion of privacy

written in language that anyone can understand. As a technical communicator, you may be asked to help write such a privacy statement.

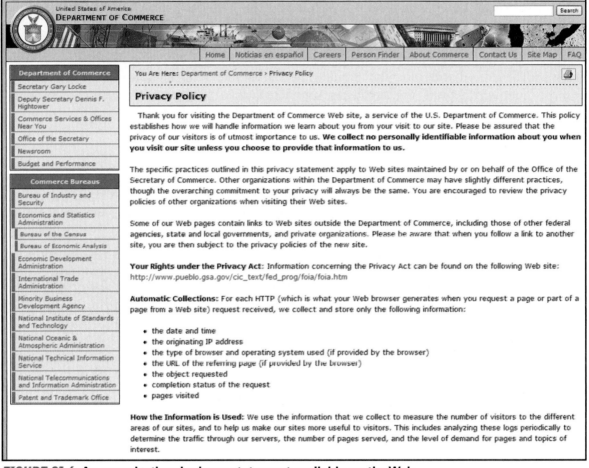

FIGURE 21.6 An organizational privacy statement available on the Web
Source: U.S. Department of Commerce.

PDF FILES

Function of PDFs

PDF stands for "portable document format." PDF files are electronic documents that can be placed on the Web or sent as email attachments. They can be read by anyone who downloads Adobe Reader (which is available for free). PDF documents retain their formatting and appear exactly as they were designed, both on the screen and when printed out. This feature has turned out to be a useful and efficient way for companies to make user documentation, product manuals, reports, and other documents available on the Web. If you purchase a product from a friend or find a used item at a garage sale and the manual is missing, you can usually visit the company Web site, search for the exact product and model number, and find the original documentation.

In addition, PDFs can be format-protected so the content cannot be altered or manipulated in any way (unprotected PDFs can be altered using special software). As such, PDFs serve a legal function. They also provide a way for Web sites to post longer documents that were originally in print form without chunking the information for the Web environment; and they can be archived for later retrieval if needed.

STRATEGIES
for Web Pages

▶ **Identify the intended audience.** Who is the primary audience? Who is the secondary audience? Will your audience be Web savvy? Will the audience include worldwide readers?

▶ **Decide on the page's purpose.** Is the purpose to inform, instruct, persuade, or some combination?

▶ **Decide what the page will contain.** Will it display print only or a combination of print and graphics? Will it include audio and video? Will links be provided and, if so, how many and to where? Will user feedback be solicited and, if so, in what form: surveys, email comments, or other?

▶ **Visit other Web sites for design ideas.** When you find an attractive, navigable site (or the opposite), analyze what works or doesn't work in terms of structure, style, visuals, and design. For a look at award-winning Web sites, go to *Webby Awards* at <www.webbyawards.com> or The University of Wisconsin–Madison's Internet Scout Project at <www.scout.wisc.edu>.

▶ **Create an understandable structure.** Map out your Web page with a storyboard that illustrates which parts of the page will go where, and that provides ways to navigate. Chunk information into short passages that are easy to access and quick to read. Provide a logical sequence (even if readers won't necessarily follow the given sequence).

▶ **Write with a readable style.** Write clearly, concisely, fluently, and personably, with special emphasis on conciseness.

➡

► **Use visuals.** Include visuals that serve a useful purpose, not merely a decorative one. Select simple and complementary colors.

► **Design a Web-friendly page.** Combine grid patterns as needed; provide ample margins, consistent justification, plenty of white space, consistent line spacing, and a simple and readable font. Use headings to chunk text on a single page, color/shading/italic for emphasis, and lists whenever appropriate. Label the purpose of every Web page and provide search windows and lists of links.

► **Proofread your page.** Verify the accuracy of numbers, dates, and data; check for spelling or grammar errors.

► **Attend to ethical and legal considerations.** Consider whether your page in any way exploits users. If you use copyrighted information, be aware of fair use guidelines (page 000). When in doubt, request permission. If your page asks individuals for private information, display a privacy statement.

► **Test your page for usability.** Test with unfamiliar users and record their problems and questions. What do users like and dislike? Can they navigate effectively to get to what they need? Are the icons recognizable? Is the site free of needless complexity or interactivity?

► **Maintain your page.** Review and update the page often and redesign as needed.

DIFFERENCES IN MEDIA TYPES

Literacy affordances

To choose whether to use a Web page on its own or with a combination of PDF files and video, you need to consider the literacy affordances of different types of media. *Literacy affordances* refers to the features and characteristics that are built into the user experience of different communication technologies. For instance, the literacy affordances of print documents include easy access without needing batteries, limited distribution compared to the Internet, and slow/careful/linear readability. Other features of print documents include limited interactivity, navigation via table of contents/index/headings, and access to additional information via outside sources only. Compare these affordances with those of reading a Web page or watching a video, as illustrated in Table 21.1. You might ask, for example, whether a goal of your Web page is to enable readers to interact with the content. If so, video is probably not the right choice. But if you want your readers to have a full picture of how to assemble a product, an online video is easy to distribute and provides for rich detail.

	Print documents/PDFs	Web pages	Online videos
Accessibility	No technical or electrical requirements to view, unless in PDF format.	Computer, electricity or battery, and Internet connection required to view.	Computer, electricity or battery, and high-speed Internet connection required to view.
Distribution	Distribution limited unless published.	Worldwide distribution, unless password-protected.	Worldwide distribution, unless password-protected.
Readability	Designed to be read slowly, carefully, and in a linear fashion. Text and fixed visuals only.	Designed to be read quickly and in a nonlinear fashion. Combines text, fixed visuals (sometimes animations), and limited audio.	Designed to be viewed in real time and in a linear fashion, but nonlinear access possible using rewind and fast forward. Combines audio, moving visuals, and limited text.
Interactivity	Limited interactivity (marginal notes only). No interactivity for PDFs.	Depending on features provided, can be highly interactive.	No interactivity.
Ability to correct and update	Changes can be made only by redistributing the document, distributing a separate set of corrections, or making corrections in a reprint.	Changes can be made and uploaded easily and inexpensively at any time.	Changes can only be made through reediting or adding new material at the beginning or end of the video.
Navigability	Table of contents, index, headings, and running heads/feet aid navigation.	Hyperlinks allow for easy navigation throughout the document.	Fast forward and rewind only.
Ability to access additional information	Must consult outside sources for additional information. Works Cited or References page can provide direction.	Easy access to additional information via hyperlinks, links posted on the Web page, or Web searches.	No hyperlinks within video, but Web page on which the video is posted may provide links, or a Web address shown during the video can lead to further information.

TABLE 21.1 Literacy affordances of different communication technologies

CHECKLIST
for Web Pages

☐ Have I assessed my audience and purpose before planning the Web page?

☐ Did I create a storyboard to plan the overall structure?

☐ Have I chunked information into small pieces for ease of reading on the Web?

☐ Did I sequence the information logically (even if it may not be read in its original order on the Web)?

☐ Have I followed the same style guidelines that apply to print documents, with special attention to conciseness?

☐ Did I use (but not overuse) visuals, including color?

☐ Have I used consistent grid patterns when creating multiple Web pages for the same site?

☐ Does the Web page provide ample margins?

☐ Did I use consistent justification, with text on the right unjustified?

☐ Have I provided ample white space?

☐ Have I used a consistent and readable font style and size?

☐ Did I use headings to chunk text on a single Web page and links to navigate to other pages?

☐ Does the page include any color, shading, and italics to highlight key information?

☐ Have I avoided the use of bold and underlining, except to indicate hyperlinks?

☐ Did I use bullets and numbered lists as often as possible, to break up text?

☐ Have I provided a search option and links to other pages within or outside of my site?

☐ Have I attended to ethical and legal considerations?

☐ Have I considered whether to add an online video to this Web site?

☐ If necessary, have I provided links to PDF documents?

☐ Have I proofread the page before going "live"?

APPLICATIONS

GENERAL APPLICATIONS

1. With a classmate, locate one or two Web sites you might use as research sources for a project. Using the guidelines in this chapter, assess these Web sites for the quality of their structure, style, use of visuals, and design. Write up your findings in an email message to your instructor. Include the Web address for each of the sites you used.

2. Workplace communicators are frequently asked to prepare multiple versions of a document, adapting similar content for presentation on a Web site, in a printed manual, or for a corporate digital archive, for example. Each version may have different purposes and audiences. The word-processing software installed on your computer, for instance, probably offers both online help and a paper user's manual. (Most companies post PDF versions of their printed user documentation on their Web sites if you do not have the hard copy available.)

   Compare your software's online or on-screen help information to the information in the paper (or PDF) manual. Notice in particular the use of chunking. Is the online information organized differently from the paper version? Which is easier to use? Which allows you to find a topic more quickly and accurately? Write a short report comparing the two types of information. Include both online and hard-copy examples.

3. Design a new Web page for your major. *Note*: Do not use any such existing page on your school or department Web site as a model.

TEAM APPLICATION

Divide into groups by major. As a team, look for a Web site that uses online video for instructional purposes. Watch the video and determine if you would be able to assemble the product or perform the task by video alone, or whether you might also need a print copy of the instructions as well. If the video does not come with print instructions, create some and turn the file into a PDF.

GLOBAL APPLICATION

Find Web sites that are in different languages or based in different countries. Besides differences in language, note any other differences between non-U.S. Web sites and those that originate in the United States. Here are some features you might look for:

- Use of color. Different cultures often associate unique meanings with certain colors. For example, the color red may be used in India to mean procreation or life, while red in the United States is often associated with danger or warnings (Hoft 267).

- Issues of privacy. U.S. sites often send out *cookies* (files sent to your computer that give Web site providers information about you), but other countries, such as Germany, take a different approach, allowing no personal information to be used without an individual's permission. Note if any of the sites mention their privacy policy in this regard.

Keep track of what you find, and present your findings in class.

COMPUTER/WEB-BASED APPLICATION

Do some research to develop your own "top 10" list of effective Web design principles. Begin by reviewing this chapter and exploring the two Web sites listed here. Then find other resources on Web style and Web design. Based on what you find, assemble your list. Using your list as a guide, find three Web sites that exemplify the principles of effective Web design and style. Prepare a short presentation on your exemplary sites, and explain why you selected them as examples of good design.

- <www.webstyleguide.com>: *Web Style Guide*, by Lynch and Horton, widely regarded as a "bible" of Web design.

- <www.useit.com/papers/webwriting>: *Writing for the Web*, by Jakob Nielsen, a leading Web usability expert.

For additional technical writing resources that will help you master the chapter objectives, go to **www.mytechcommlab.com**.

22 Oral Presentations

LEARNING OBJECTIVES FOR THIS CHAPTER

▶ Analyze the audience and purpose of an oral presentation

▶ Organize an oral presentation logically

▶ Prepare for an oral presentation

▶ Use presentation software effectively

▶ Deliver a confident, professional oral presentation

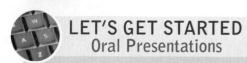

LET'S GET STARTED
Oral Presentations

Most workplace professionals are required at some point to give an oral presentation. Before reading this chapter, take an informal report, formal report, or proposal that you have written, and use it as a basis for a presentation that you would give in class or at work. Create an outline for the oral presentation.

Questions to ask as you write the outline may include the following:

- ▶ Who is the audience, and how will my presentation make the content interesting and understandable for this audience?

- ▶ Do I need any additional research?

- ▶ What is the primary purpose of this presentation: informative, instructive, or persuasive? If persuasive, am I trying to persuade the audience to accept a point, take action, or buy something?

- ▶ Is the purpose of my presentation clear right from the start?

- ▶ Does my introduction create interest and provide an overview of the presentation?

- ▶ Are the transitions between sections clear?

- ▶ Have I created a clear, brief conclusion?

At the end of this chapter, review your initial Let's Get Started outline with your instructor or with a group of students, to see how much you might change or modify the outline based on what you have learned from the chapter.

The importance of oral presentations in the workplace

In addition to being good writers and designers, technical communicators need to present their ideas effectively in person. The skills required to give an effective oral presentation include thorough research, strong organization, and stage presence. You may be asked to make oral presentations at meetings in your department or company (status reports, team meetings, and so on), at professional conferences or meetings, to your community, or in the classroom.

The interactive nature of oral presentations

Unlike written documents, oral presentations are interactive. Face-to-face communication is arguably the richest form of interaction because you can give and receive information via body language, vocal inflection, eye contact, and other physical means. Moreover, there is room for give and take, which does not happen with written documents. Oral presentations allow you to see how your audience reacts. You can get immediate feedback, and you can change or amend your ideas on the spot.

Most professionals use presentation software such as Microsoft PowerPoint or Apple Keynote when giving a presentation. But despite the visual appeal and easy-to-use templates such products offer, you still need to create a presentation that is well researched, clearly organized, and professionally delivered.

Presentations involve careful preparation

AUDIENCE AND PURPOSE OF ORAL PRESENTATIONS

Analyzing audience and purpose is a slightly different proposition when speaking rather than writing. Therefore, use the amended version of the Audience and Purpose Profile Sheet provided in Figure 22.1

Do all you can to find out exactly who will be attending your presentation. Determine their roles within the organization. Learn about their attitudes and personal experiences regarding your subject. For example, managers may focus on the bottom line, while engineers may care more about the difficulties involved in the project you are proposing. Oral presentations are often delivered to a mixed group, so consider the attitudes of the group as a whole and speak to the needs of various factions. The group is also likely to consist of people from various cultural and linguistic backgrounds, so be sure to account for these differences.

Audience considerations

✴ Explore the Concept with the Case Study on Oral Presentations at mytechcommlab

Determine whether your purpose is to inform, instruct, or persuade. Does your audience simply need some vital information? If so, provide enough detail and explanation for people to understand the information clearly. Will they use your information to perform a task? If so, focus on the task itself and send background and other information via email after the presentation. Is your goal to influence your audience's thinking or sell them something? If so, be sure to have all the specifications, costs, and other data that will help them make their decision. In short, knowing clearly what you wish to accomplish will help you formulate a definite plan for your presentation.

Purpose considerations

✴ Explore the Tutorial on Presentations at mytechcommlab

TYPES OF ORAL PRESENTATIONS

Your primary purpose will determine the type of presentation required: an informative presentation, a training presentation, a persuasive presentation, an action plan presentation, or a sales presentation.

The five types of oral presentations

Informative Presentations

Informative presentations are often given at conferences, product update meetings, briefings, or class lectures. Your goal is to be as impartial as possible and to

Informative presentations provide facts and explanations

FIGURE 22.1
Audience and purpose profile sheet for an oral presentation

View the Audience and Purpose Profile Sheet for an Oral Presentation at mytechcommlab

AUDIENCE

Primary audience members:_____
(names, titles)

Secondary audience members:_____
_____

Are most attendees of this presentation members of the same team or group?
Y   N

Relationship with audience members:_____
(client, employer, other)

Technical background of audience:_____
(layperson, expert, other)

Cultural background of audience:_____

How many people will attend: 2–6   7–12   12–20   more than 20

PURPOSE

Primary purpose:_____(informative, training,

persuasive, action plan, sales)

Secondary purpose(s):_____

Intended use of presentation:_____ (to inform or

educate; to persuade; to propose an action; to sell something)

ROOM or LOCATION for presentation

Conference table_____

Theater style_____

TECHNOLOGY REQUIRED

PowerPoint or other presentation software

Overhead projector

Flip chart

Whiteboard or chalkboard

provide the best information you can locate. If your primary purpose is informative, observe these criteria:

- Keep the title of the presentation clear and factual.
- Stipulate at the outset that your purpose is simply to provide information.
- Be clear about your sources of information.

Training Presentations

Training (or instructional) presentations can cover such topics as how to ensure on-the-job safety, how to use a specific software application, or how to exit a capsized kayak. Some technical communicators specialize in giving training presentations. If your primary purpose is instructional, follow these guidelines:

Training presentations show how to perform a task

- Use a title that indicates the training purpose of the presentation.
- Provide an overview of the learning outcomes—what participants can expect to learn from the presentation.
- Create slides or a handout that participants can reference later, when they are trying to perform the task(s) on their own.

Persuasive Presentations

To influence people's thinking, give a persuasive presentation. For example, an engineer at a nuclear power plant may wish to persuade her peers that a standard procedure is unsafe and should be changed. In a persuasive situation, be sure to perform adequate research so that you are well informed on all sides of the issue. If your primary purpose is persuasive, follow these guidelines:

Persuasive presentations attempt to gain support or change an opinion

- Be clear from the start that you are promoting a point of view.
- Use research and visual data (charts, graphs, etc.) to support your stance.
- Consider and address counterarguments in advance ("Some might say that this approach won't work, but here is why it will"), and be prepared to take questions that challenge your point of view.

Action Plan Presentations

To get something done, give an action plan presentation. For example, if you wanted your company to address a design flaw in one of its products, you would give a presentation that outlined the problem, presented a specific solution, and

Action plan presentations motivate people to take action

encouraged listeners to implement the solution. If your primary purpose is to evoke action, follow these guidelines:

- Be clear up front about your purpose ("My primary purpose today is to ask you to act on this matter").
- Present the research to back up the need for your plan.
- Show that you have considered other plans but that yours is most effective.
- In closing, restate what you want your audience to do.

Sales Presentations

Sales presentations inform and persuade

Technical sales presentations need to be well researched. (At many high-tech companies, technical sales representatives are often scientists or engineers who understand the product's complexities and also are good communicators). If your primary purpose is to sell something, observe these criteria:

- Let the facts tell the story. Use examples to illustrate why your product or service is the right one.
- Know your product or service—and those of your competitors—inside and out. Thorough knowledge and a well-researched competitive analysis will make your presentation that much more persuasive.
- Display sincere interest in the needs and concerns of your customers.
- Provide plenty of time for questions. You may think you have made an airtight case, but you will need extra face-to-face time to field questions and convince skeptical audience members.

PARTS OF ORAL PRESENTATIONS

Like most technical documents, oral presentations should follow an introduction–body–conclusion structure.

Introduction

Set the stage

For introducing most presentations, pay attention to three main tasks:

1. Capture your audience's attention by telling a quick story, asking a question, or relating your topic to a current event or to something else the audience cares about.
2. Establish your credibility by stating your credentials or explaining where you obtained your information.
3. Preview your presentation by listing the main points and the overall conclusion.

An effective introduction might sound like this:

> How many times have you searched for medical information on the Web, only to find that after hours online, you can't locate anything useful? If you're like most Americans polled in a recent survey, you may feel that you are wasting time when it comes to Web-based medical information. My name is Travis Armstrong, and I've been researching this topic for some time. Today, I'd like to share my findings with you by covering three main points: how to search for medical information, how to separate good information from bad, and how to contribute to medical discussions online.

Body

Readers who get confused or want to know the scope of a print document can look back at the headings, table of contents, or previous pages. But oral presentations have no such features. To make your presentation easy to follow, structure the material into small chunks. To signal that you are moving from one main point to another, use transition statements such as, "Now that I've explained how to separate good information from bad, let me suggest how you can contribute to medical discussions on the Internet."

Use small chunks and transitions in the body

Conclusion

Your conclusion should return full circle to your introduction. Remind your audience of the big picture, restate the main points you've just covered, and leave listeners with some final advice or tips for locating more information. You can also distribute handouts at this time.

Tie everything together

PREPARING ORAL PRESENTATIONS

Preparing an oral presentation is a step-by-step process that requires research, planning, and rehearsal.

Research and Connect the Topic to Your Audience

Be prepared to support each assertion, opinion, conclusion, and recommendation with solid evidence. Begin gathering material well ahead of time. Use recognized sources, such as newspaper articles, peer-reviewed journals, industry fact sheets, government documents, and interviews. Check your facts for accuracy. If you will be using presentation software or handouts, you will need to indicate your information sources on the slides or handouts (typically as footnotes at the bottom of the slide or page). Keep track of your sources.

Know your topic

Relate the topic
to your audience

Even the most well-researched presentation won't be effective unless the speaker connects the topic to the interests, backgrounds, and technical levels of the audience. Look back at your Audience and Purpose Profile Sheet and think about ways you can connect to ideas already familiar to your audience.

Create an Outline or Storyboard

Use an outline
to organize your
thoughts

If your presentation is a spoken version of a written report, you can use the outline from the written report. Otherwise, organize your ideas in terms of A- and B-level headings. Indicate on the outline any places where you want to use a visual. If you plan to use presentation software, go to "outline mode" or "outline view" to start laying out your presentation.

Use a storyboard
to accommodate
multiple visuals

If your presentation includes multiple visuals, you might create a storyboard rather than an outline. Storyboards help you see how the visuals will complement the spoken content. A simple storyboard (Figure 22.3) for an oral presentation consists of a double-column format in which your discussion is outlined in the left column, and the specific supporting visuals are described in the right column.

✳ Explore the Concept
with the Activity on
Outlining a Presentation
at **mytechcommlab**

Figure 22.2 is an outline for a typical oral presentation (slides for this presentation appear later in this chapter), whereas Figure 22.3 is a partial storyboard for a longer oral presentation involving many visuals.

FIGURE 22.2
**An outline for
a typical oral
presentation**

I. Introduction

   A. Introduce myself
   B. Open with a question ("What's different about the Web 2.0 generation compared with previous generations of technology users?")
   C. Give audience overview of my presentation's organization

II. Body

   A. Discuss various characteristics of the Web 2.0 generation
   B. Talk about Web 2.0 generation at the University (technologies students use here)
   C. Discuss 2009 survey (what University students expect from technology)
   D. Discuss other advantages current technologies offer to students
   E. Add special emphasis to the importance of social network sites

III. Conclusion

   A. Restate my main points
   B. Tell audience we'll open for questions/discussion for the last 15 minutes

Pollution Threats to Local Groundwater

1.0 Introduce the Problem

    1.1 Do you know what you are drinking when you turn on the tap and fill the glass?

    1.2 The quality of our water is good but not guaranteed to last forever.

    1.3 Cape Cod's rapid population growth poses a serious threat to our freshwater supply.   *(slide: a line graph showing twenty-year population growth)*

    1.4 Measurable pollution in some town water supplies has already occurred.   *(slide: two side-by-side tables showing twenty-year increases in nitrate and chloride concentrations in three town wells)*

    1.5 What are the major causes and consequences of this problem and what can we do about it?   *(poster: a multicolored list that previews my five subtopics)*

2.0 Describe the Aquifer

    2.1 The groundwater is collected and held in an aquifer.

        2.1.1. This porous rock formation creates a broad, continuous arch beneath the entire Cape.   *(slide: a cutaway view of the aquifer's geology)*

FIGURE 22.3 A partial storyboard for a long oral presentation

Determine a Delivery Style

Your presentation's effectiveness will depend largely on how well it connects with listeners. Different styles of delivery (memorized, impromptu, scripted, and extemporaneous) create different connections. *Use an appropriate delivery style*

A memorized delivery takes a long time to prepare, offers no chance for revision during the presentation, and spells disaster if you lose your place. Avoid a memorized delivery style in workplace settings. *Memorized delivery style*

An impromptu (off-the-cuff) delivery style can be a natural way of connecting with listeners—but only when you really know your material, feel comfortable with your audience, and are in an informal speaking situation. Avoid an impromptu delivery style when making complex and formal presentations, no matter how well you know the material. *Impromptu delivery style*

In some formal settings (a speech, a keynote address, a conference paper), it may be appropriate for you to read your material verbatim from a prepared script. A scripted delivery can help you keep strict control over your material and meet time limits, but it offers little chance for audience interaction and it can be boring. If you do plan to read aloud, rehearse until you are able to glance up from the script periodically without losing your place. *Scripted delivery style*

An extemporaneous delivery style is carefully planned, practiced, and based on notes that keep you on track. In this natural way of addressing an audience, you glance at your material and speak in a conversational manner. Extemporaneous delivery is based on key ideas in sentence or topic outline form, often projected as overhead transparencies or as slides generated from presentation software.

An extemporaneous delivery is typically the preferred method for oral presentations in the workplace: it provides somewhat of a script for the speaker and allows the speaker to interact with the audience while following along. However, there are dangers, such as losing track, skipping over a key point, or going over a time limit.

Table 22.1 summarizes the various uses and drawbacks of the latter three delivery styles (memorized style should always be avoided and is therefore not included). In many instances, some combination of methods can be effective. For example, in an orientation for new employees, you might prefer the flexibility of an extemporaneous format but also read a scripted passage aloud from time to time.

Choose Your Technology

Although presentation software is a helpful and popular tool (see the section on presentation software in this chapter), there are other options. For example, you

TABLE 22.1 Advantages and drawbacks of delivery styles

Delivery Method	* Main Uses *	• Main Drawbacks •
IMPROMPTU (inventing as you speak)	* in-house meetings * small, intimate groups * simple topics	• offers no chance to prepare • speaker might ramble • speaker might lose track
SCRIPTED (reading verbatim from a written work)	* formal speeches * large, unfamiliar groups * strict time limit * cross-cultural audiences * highly nervous speaker	• takes a long time to prepare • speaker can't move around • limits human contact • can appear stiff and unnatural • might bore listeners • makes working with visuals difficult
EXTEMPORANEOUS (speaking from an outline of key points)	* face-to-face presentations * medium-sized, familiar groups * moderately complex topics * somewhat flexible time limit * visually based presentations	• speaker might lose track • speaker might leave something out • speaker might exceed time limit • speaker might fumble with notes, visuals, or equipment

might opt for a more natural, extemporaneous presentation in which you use handouts or flip charts. Or you might decide to sketch on a whiteboard or use an overhead projector. Think about your audience: What would work best? What would keep people active, engaged, and listening?

Plan the Use of Visuals

Visuals not only add vigor and impact to a presentation, but they also summarize complex information and set a tone. If you might embed visuals within your slides, include them in handouts, use overhead transparencies, or simply post them somewhere in the room.

Use visuals to enhance the presentation

Although visuals are an important component, they can also be overused or misused. A presentation that simply uses one visual after the other will bore an audience. Likewise, visuals that carry no real meaning or that are hard to see or decipher will frustrate the audience.

Seek a balance of text/speech and visuals that enhance the presentation rather than distracting from it. Notice how the slides in Figure 22.4 (page 419) use visuals sparingly but effectively. The smart phone illustration in slide 3 illustrates the cutting-edge technology at the center of the discussion; the bar graph in slide 4 effectively summarizes the results of a complex survey; and the closing photograph sets a relaxed tone for the questions/discussion portion of the presentation.

Practice the Presentation

On your own or with a volunteer viewer, practice your presentation. This process will give you an idea of how you sound and look while speaking; it will also reveal gaps or wordiness in your presentation and help you get the timing right. If possible, make an audio or video recording of yourself to see if you speak too fast or too slow, or if you gesture too much or look stiff. Try to rehearse with the actual equipment you plan to use, and in the actual setting.

Rehearse to fine-tune

Explore the Concept with the Activity on Presentations at mytechcommlab

STRATEGIES
for Preparing Oral Presentations

▶ **Determine your audience.** Fill out the audience portion of an Audience and Purpose Profile Sheet. Know exactly who your listeners are (primary and secondary), what their attitude is toward the topic, what they already know, and what they need to learn. If you anticipate that different audience members will have different needs, make sure you speak to the entire audience.

▶ **Determine your purpose.** Is the purpose of the presentation to inform, instruct, or persuade? Adjust your presentation to suit its particular purpose.

▸ **Do your research.** Make sure you understand your topic. Anticipate audience questions or objections and prepare answers or responses.

▸ **Decide on your delivery style.** Avoid the memorized style, as you may lose your place. Choose an impromptu, scripted, or extemporaneous style, but recognize the pros and cons of each.

▸ **Organize your presentation.** Include an introduction, body, and conclusion. Prepare an outline (typical presentation) or storyboard (visually complex presentation) to work out what information to discuss and when.

▸ **Choose your technology.** You need not always use presentation software. Consider alternatives such as handouts, flip charts, whiteboards, or overhead projectors.

▸ **Use visuals.** Whenever possible, enhance your presentation by using visuals, but only when they genuinely add to the discussion. Be sure that all your visuals are easy for the audience to see and understand.

▸ **Rehearse your presentation.** Practice, and correct any content or style problems based on your rehearsal.

USING PRESENTATION SOFTWARE

Overview of
presentation
software

Explore the Concept
with the Case Study
on Presentation Software
at mytechcommlab

PowerPoint, a Microsoft product, is still the most widely used presentation software. Yet other software, such as Apple's Keynote or Open Office's Impress, is also used by students and professionals. These products run on a desktop or laptop computer; you can share files via email or a file-sharing site. Another approach is a program called Prezi that requires an Internet connection and offers creative tools for animation and transitions. Google also has a presentation program, available through an Internet connection via Google Docs. Prezi, Google, and other such programs allow you to collaborate on a presentation because everyone on the team can access the same file without searching through old emails to find an attachment.

Analyze the Slide
Presentation at
mytechcommlab

Whatever software you choose, remember that good presentations are based on the qualities discussed previously in this chapter. They must be well researched, carefully planned, well organized, and correctly timed. Excessive material crammed on one slide might help you as you speak but will frustrate your audience. Also, while presentation software helps structure the speaker's story or argument, an overreliance on bulleted items can oversimplify complex issues and distract from the deeper message. In short, use the software as a tool, not as the brains of the operation. Don't let presentation software do the thinking for you.

For specific advice, see the Strategies for Using Presentation Software on page 422. Also, have a close look at Figure 22.4.

FIGURE 22.4
A presentation using software tools

Communicating with the Web

2.0 Generation

Lynn N. Rice
Undergraduate research assistant
Department of Media and Communication

◄ Title page introduces the speaker and topic simply and straightforwardly

1.

Overview

- ☐ The Web 2.0 generation
- ☐ Web 2.0 students at the University
- ☐ Student expectations of digital technology
- ☐ Focus on social network sites
- ☐ Questions and discussion

◄ Overview slide provides a roadmap to key points that will be covered

2.

First body slide corresponds to first bullet in the overview slide

The Web 2.0 Generation

☐ Today's 18-year-olds were born in 1990

- Cell phones are a given
- Texting and IM is the norm
- Email is outdated
- Instant, anytime/anywhere communication is expected

Clip art adds visual interest but does not overwhelm

3.

The Web 2.0 Generation at the University

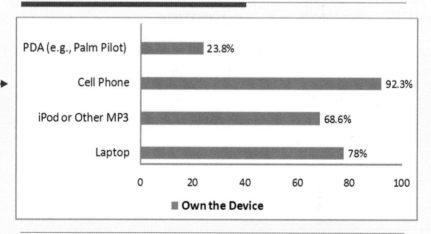

Bar graph summarizes data for audience

PDA (e.g., Palm Pilot) ▬ 23.8%
Cell Phone ▬ 92.3%
iPod or Other MP3 ▬ 68.6%
Laptop ▬ 78%

0   20   40   60   80   100

■ Own the Device

Source: Walker, J.D. & Jorn, L. 2007. *Student Technology Education Survey 2007*. University of Minnesota Digital Media Center, Office of Information Technology.

4.

2007 Survey: What Students Expect from Technology

☐ **Mobility**: majority own mobile devices; the rest want them

☐ **Immediacy**: use IM and text messaging vs. email

☐ **Media-multiplicity**:
use simulations, animations, audio & video technologies

Source: Walker, J.D. & Jorn, L. 2007. *Student Technology Education Survey 2007.* University of Minnesota Digital Media Center, Office of Information Technology.

Key points highlighted with checklist boxes and bold text

Source information set in smaller type at the bottom of the slide

5.

Facebook, MySpace, and Other Social Network (SN) Sites

☐ Students use these more than other Web sites

☐ Schools should not create their own versions

☐ SN sites allow students to form new communities

Reasonable number of lines on the page and words per bulleted item

6.

Photograph makes the slide more inviting and personal

7.

STRATEGIES
for Using Presentation Software

▶ **Don't let the software do the thinking.** Use your own research, sense of audience and purpose, and other original ideas to shape the presentation. Then use the software to help make the material accessible and interesting. The shape and content should come from you, not from the software.

▶ **Have a backup plan in case the technology fails.** Bring handouts to the presentation and be prepared to give the presentation without the software. Don't distribute handouts until you are ready to discuss them; otherwise, people will start reading the handouts instead of paying attention to you.

▶ **Start with an overview slide.** Orient your audience by showing an opening slide that indicates what you plan to cover and in what order.

▶ **Find a balance between text and visuals.** Excessive text is boring; excessive visuals can be confusing. Each visual should serve a purpose: to summarize information, to add emphasis, to set a tone, and so on. Avoid overcrowding the slides: Include no more than 7–9 lines per slide (including the heading) with no more than 6–9 words per bulleted item.

▶ **Avoid using too many slides.** In general, aim for one slide per key point. If you are the kind of person who likes to embellish and enjoys speaking to a crowd, use fewer slides.

➤

▸ **Don't simply read the slides.** The slides are there to keep you and your audience oriented and to highlight key points. But you should elaborate upon each slide, adding and analyzing details.

▸ **Avoid too much flash.** Don't allow the medium (animations, color, sound) to obscure your message.

▸ **Keep viewers oriented.** Don't show a slide until you are ready to discuss it. Present one topic per slide, bringing bullets (subtopics) on one at a time as you discuss them. Let your audience digest the slide data *while* you speak, and not before or after.

▸ **End with a "conclusions" or "questions" slide.** Give your audience a sense of having come full circle. On a "conclusions" slide, summarize the key points. A "questions" slide can simply provide a heading and a visual. Allow time at the end of your presentation for questions and/or comments.

DELIVERING ORAL PRESENTATIONS

Many find that the actual delivery of an oral presentation is the most difficult hurdle. Most people experience anxiety when they must speak in public. If you are particularly nervous, seek additional advice about ways to calm your nerves, such as stretching beforehand and performing deep breathing exercises. You are likely to find that once you have actually spoken your first line, you will settle down quickly. The following Strategies offer further advice.

STRATEGIES
for Delivering Oral Presentations

▸ **Be rehearsed and prepared.** The best way to calm your nerves is to remind yourself of the preparation and research you have done. Practice your delivery so that it is professional and appropriate but natural for you. Also, know your material inside and out.

▸ **Memorize a brief introduction.** If you begin your presentation smoothly and confidently, you won't be as nervous going forward. Do not open by saying "I'm a little bit nervous today" or "I have a slight cold. Can everyone hear me in the back?" Just begin. A memorized introduction will help you avoid having to ad-lib (potentially badly) when you are most anxious.

▸ **Dress for success.** Wear clothes that suggest professionalism and confidence.

▸ **Stand tall and use eye contact.** Good posture and frequent eye contact convey a sense of poise, balance, and confidence. Practice in front of a mirror. If looking people directly in the eye makes you nervous, aim just above people's heads.

Or find a friendly face or two and look at those people first. As you gain confidence, be sure to cast your gaze around the entire room or conference table.

▶ **Take charge.** If you get interrupted but don't want to take questions until the end, remember that you are in control. Be polite but firm: "Thank you for that good question. I'll save it and other questions until the end of my presentation."

▶ **Gesture naturally.** Don't force yourself to move around or be theatrical if this is not your style. But do not stand like a robot, either. Unless you are speaking from a podium or lectern, move around just a bit. And when it's time to take questions, consider moving closer to the audience. In a conference room setting, if everyone else is seated, you should stand.

▶ **Allow time for questions, comments, and discussion.** Announce a time limit; listen carefully; ask for clarification if necessary; provide brief but well-considered replies (if time allows—otherwise continue later and in private). When the time is up, announce that you have time for one more question or comment, and conclude politely.

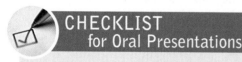

CHECKLIST
for Oral Presentations

☐ Have I analyzed my audience and purpose thoroughly?

☐ Have I done adequate research about the topic, looking into all sides of the problem or issue?

☐ Have I organized my material, using an outline or storyboard?

☐ Have I chosen a delivery style that best suits my skills and the needs of my audience?

☐ Have I decided to use presentation software (e.g., PowerPoint) or to use more basic technology or no technology at all?

☐ Am I using an appropriate number of visuals, as well as visuals that serve a specific purpose?

☐ Have I rehearsed my presentation and ironed out problems with content and delivery?

☐ If using presentation software, have I followed the strategies given in this chapter?

☐ Have I calmed my nerves and gained confidence by following the strategies for delivering presentations in this chapter?

☐ Am I prepared to allow time for questions and comments, and to interact with my audience effectively when doing so?

APPLICATIONS

GENERAL APPLICATIONS

1. Prepare an oral presentation for your class, based on your written formal report or proposal. Develop an outline and a storyboard that includes at least three visuals. Ask your instructor for the time limit of the presentation (15 minutes? 20 minutes?), and practice so that you do not exceed the allotted time. Make note of places where you tend to struggle or places where you speak for too long.

2. At work, on an internship, or at a campus event, observe a lecture or speech, and evaluate it according to the Strategies boxes in this chapter. In a memo to your instructor (without naming the speaker), identify strong and weak areas and suggest improvements.

TEAM APPLICATION

In today's work world, presentations are often prepared by, and sometimes delivered by, more than one person. In groups of three to four people, come up with a simple presentation topic that everyone can work on. (You might want to base this topic on a group writing activity from the semester.) Discuss how, as a team, you will approach the research, planning, and creation of the presentation. For example, will one person be responsible for the research? Will another person put the slides together? Create a brief presentation for your instructor and classmates (using presentation software), describing the process you will take and the decisions that your team made.

GLOBAL APPLICATION

You've been assigned to represent your company at an international conference or before international clients. As you plan and prepare your presentation, what can you do to remain sensitive to various cultural expectations? For example, some cultures might be offended by a presentation that gets right to the point without first observing formalities of politeness. Use the Internet to research issues about intercultural communication, then create a short presentation on this topic for the class.

COMPUTER/WEB-BASED APPLICATION

As noted in the Team Application above, presentations are often created collaboratively. Refer back to the discussion on page 418 ("Using Presentation Software"), and experiment with various options for collaboration. Do the desktop/laptop based programs, such as PowerPoint and Keynote, allow teams to work on a common document? (*Hint:* look for "share" in the menu bar to see what options you have.) What about Web-based programs such as Prezi and Google Doc's presentations program? (You will need a Google account to try the latter.) Decide which approach would work best for a class team project and share your results with the class in a short presentation.

For additional technical writing resources that will help you master the chapter objectives, go to **www.mytechcommlab.com**.

A Documenting Sources

WHAT IS PLAGIARISM?

When creating technical documents, especially more formal, longer documents such as reports, you will need to rely on outside research. To make your case credible, use outside sources wisely and avoid plagiarizing the work of others.

Plagiarism is using someone else's work—words, ideas, or illustrations, published or unpublished—without giving the creator of that work sufficient credit. A serious breach of scholarly ethics, plagiarism can have severe consequences. Students risk a failing grade or disciplinary action ranging from suspension to expulsion; a record of such action can adversely affect future professional opportunities. Scholars and teachers can face public disgrace and even be forced out of a position. Elsewhere in the workplace, plagiarism can lead to a lawsuit as well as permanent career damage.

Plagiarism violates three significant values: preserving intellectual honesty, giving credit to the work of others, and promoting intellectual growth. First, the academic community relies on the reciprocal exchange of ideas and information to advance knowledge and research. Using material without acknowledging its source violates this expectation and consequently makes it harder for researchers to verify and build on others' results. In addition, plagiarism cheats writers and researchers of the credit they deserve for their work and creativity. Even with the writer's permission, presenting another's work as one's own is equivalent to lying: it's a form of dishonesty. Finally, and perhaps most important for students, plagiarizing negates the very reason for attending college. A student who hands in a plagiarized paper has missed an opportunity for growth and learning.

---

*Portions of this appendix were written by Linda Stern, Publishing School of Continuing and Professional Studies, New York University, and adapted by the authors.

Ethical considerations aside, it's hard to get away with plagiarism. Experienced professors can easily tell when a paper is not written in a student's own style or is more professionally prepared than they would expect. In addition, online services can now identify plagiarized papers, and academic institutions are subscribing to such services.

Most plagiarism is unintentional. To avoid plagiarism, you need to do all of the following:

- Identify sources and information to be documented in your paper.
- Take effective and accurate notes.
- Understand how to quote, paraphrase, and summarize properly.
- Know how to document sources both in the text itself and at the end of your report.

Plagiarism is easy to spot

✳ Explore the Podcast on Avoiding Plagiarism at mytechcommlab

Ways to avoid unintentional plagiarism

IDENTIFYING SOURCES AND INFORMATION TO BE DOCUMENTED

Documentation is the key to avoiding plagiarism. The legal doctrine of *fair use* (see page 460) allows writers to quote or paraphrase a limited amount of another's work in their own papers and books. To make sure that they are not plagiarizing someone else's work, writers must therefore take care to document every source they consult accurately and clearly. Documentation involves providing readers with sufficient information about the sources you have consulted; consequently, readers may consult those sources themselves if they so desire. This sort of documentation ordinarily requires two elements: (1) an end-of-report list of sources used in the report (known as a Works Cited or References list), and (2) citations in the text of the report that link to the items in that end-of-report list.

Whenever you use information from an *outside source* (any source that isn't your own brain), you need to document that source. Some major outside sources that researchers often consult are discussed in Chapter 3 and include books, newspapers, magazines, government sources, radio or television programs, material from electronic databases, correspondence, films, plays, interviews, speeches, surveys, and Web sites. The one major exception to this rule is that you do not have to document *common knowledge:* widely known information about current events, famous people, geographical facts, or familiar history. When in doubt, the safest strategy is to provide documentation. (For more on what you should document, see page 433.)

The importance of documentation

What needs to be documented and what does not

TAKING EFFECTIVE AND ACCURATE NOTES

Another key way to avoid unintentional plagiarism is to take notes systematically. Do not rely on your memory to keep track of the sources you consult and the information you want to use from those sources. Take detailed notes that identify the specific material and its sources; otherwise you may forget about a source you learned something from, thereby unintentionally plagiarizing.

Why note-taking is important

Because most research today is done electronically, you need to be especially careful about taking notes if you cut and paste quotations or other material from an electronic source. Whether this source is a Web page, a blog or wiki, or a journal article available in electronic format, be sure to keep track of the author (individual or organizational), Web address, and date when you accessed the information. If the publication is a traditional one in e-format (such as the electronic version of the *New York Times*), record the title, page number, and other publication information needed for the citation.

How to take notes

Using old-fashioned notecards is one way to record your sources and the material you want to use. Figure A.1 shows a notecard entry for a bibliographic citation.

Record each bibliographic citation exactly as it will appear in your final report. ⟶

> Pinsky, Mark A. *The EMF Book: What You Should Know about Electromagnetic Fields, Electromagnetic Radiation, and Your Health.* New York: Warner, 1995.

FIGURE A.1 A bibliographic citation

Researchers also take notes on a laptop computer, using electronic file programs or database management software that allows citations and notes to be filed, shuffled, and retrieved by author, title, topic, date, or keywords. You can also take notes in a single word-processing file and then use the "Find" command to locate notes quickly. Be sure to take your time when cutting and pasting direct quotes and include all citation information.

STRATEGIES for Taking Notes

▶ **Keep copies of your documentation information.** For all sources that you use, keep photocopies or accurate notes of the title and copyright pages and the pages with quotations you need. Highlight the relevant citation information in color. Keep these materials until you've completed your report.

▶ **Create the Works Cited or References list first.** Before you start writing your report, create a working bibliography, a list of possible sources to which you add entries as they emerge. When you finalize your list, you can delete entries for sources that you've decided not to use.

▶ **Record bibliographical information for each source you consult.** Use the citation format that will appear in your document. Record the information accurately so you won't have to track down a source at the last minute. When searching online, print out or save the full bibliographic record for each source or copy and paste the Web address into your document, thereby ensuring an accurate citation.

➡

STRATEGIES *continued*

▶ **Determine whether to quote, paraphrase, or summarize.** When quoting others directly, be sure to record words and punctuation accurately. When restating material in your own words (paraphrasing and summarizing), preserve the original meaning and emphasis. Double-check if any portions of paraphrases or summaries are actually quotations, and insert the necessary quotation marks.

QUOTING, PARAPHRASING, AND SUMMARIZING PROPERLY

To avoid plagiarism, you must use material from outside sources properly. You can integrate outside material into your paper in three ways: by quoting, paraphrasing, or summarizing. Each method must accurately convey the meaning expressed in the original source.

Three ways to use outside sources

Quoting the Work of Others

A *quotation* reproduces a portion of a source, using the exact words, for a purpose of your own: to support a statement or idea, to provide an example, to advance an argument, or to add interest or color to a discussion. A quotation can range in length from a word or phrase to several paragraphs. In general, quote the least amount that gets your point across.

Definition of a quotation

In your notes, place quotation marks around all exact wording you borrow, whether the words were written or spoken (as in an interview or presentation) or appeared in electronic form. Even a single borrowed sentence or phrase or a single word used in a special way requires quotation marks, with the exact source properly cited. These sources include people with whom you collaborate. Figure A.2 shows notes for a quotation. Notes can be taken by typing your information in a word-processing document.

Pinsky, Mark A. pp. 29–30

"Neither electromagnetic fields nor electromagnetic radiation causes cancer per se, most researchers agree. What they may do is promote cancer. Cancer is a multistage process that requires an 'initiator' that makes a cell or group of cells abnormal. Everyone has cancerous cells in his or her body. Cancer—the disease as we think of it—occurs when these cancerous cells grow uncontrollably."

FIGURE A.2
Notes for a quotation

In your notes, place quotation marks around all directly quoted material.

▸ **Use a direct quotation only when absolutely necessary.** Sometimes a direct quotation is the only way to do justice to the author's words or thoughts. Use direct quotations to preserve the original line of reasoning, special phrasing or emphasis, precise meaning, or an especially striking or colorful example. Direct quotes convey the authority and complexity of expert opinion and can capture the original's voice, sincerity, or emotional intensity.

▸ **Copy the material from your source to your document exactly as it appears in the original.** Do not alter the original spelling, capitalization, or punctuation. If a quotation contains an obvious error, you may insert [*sic*], which is Latin for "so" or "thus," to show that the error appeared in the original. Record the exact page numbers, and double-check that you haven't altered the original expression in any way.

▸ **Use ellipses to keep quotations as brief as possible.** Ellipses are three spaced periods (. . .) indicating that words have been omitted within a single sentence. Add a fourth period to indicate the end of a sentence or the omission of more than a sentence. The resulting passage must be grammatical and must not distort the original meaning. (For more on ellipses, see pages 473–474.)

▸ **Use square brackets to insert your own clarifying comments or transitions.** To distinguish your words from those of your source, place them within brackets—for example, "This occupation [campus police officer] requires excellent judgment."

▸ **Integrate quoted material into your writing smoothly and grammatically.** Quotations must blend seamlessly into your text so that the resulting sentence is neither ungrammatical nor awkward, and punctuation must be handled properly (see pages 472–473).

▸ **In your paper, set off long quotations as block quotations.** Avoid relying on long quotations except when you want to provide an extended example or definition, or to analyze or discuss a particular idea or concept. Start on a separate line. Double-space and indent the entire block ten spaces. Do not indent the first line of the passage and do not use quotation marks.

▸ **Cite the source of each quoted passage.** Immediately follow each quotation with a parenthetical reference (see pages 434 and 446) indicating the source.

Paraphrasing the Work of Others

Definition of a paraphrase

Research is a process of independent thinking in which you work with the ideas of others to reach your own conclusions. Therefore, unless the author's exact wording is essential, try to paraphrase instead of quoting borrowed material. A *paraphrase* is a restatement, in your own words and your own sentence structure, of specific ideas or information from a source. The chief purpose of a paraphrase is to *maintain your own writing style* throughout your paper. A paraphrase can be about as long as the original passage.

Paraphrasing means more than changing or shuffling a few words; it means restating the original idea in your own words—sometimes in a clearer, more direct and emphatic way—and giving full credit to the source. To offer as a paraphrase an original passage only slightly altered is plagiarism. Equally unethical is offering a paraphrase, although documented, that distorts the original meaning.

Figure A.3 shows notes in which the quotation in Figure A.2 has been paraphrased. Paraphrased material is not enclosed within quotation marks, but it is documented to acknowledge your debt to the source.

> According to Pinsky, most researchers doubt that cancer is caused by either electromagnetic fields or electromagnetic radiation. These electrical currents, however, may "promote" cancer by initiating the "multistage process" that leads to the proliferation of cancer cells that are otherwise present in small amounts in the healthy human body (29–30).

Signal the beginning of the paraphrase by identifying the source and the end by citing the location.

FIGURE A.3 Notes for a paraphrase

STRATEGIES
for Paraphrasing the Work of Others

▸ **Retain key words from the original to preserve its meaning.** Use quotation marks within your paraphrase to indicate quoted material.

▸ **Use your own words and sentence structure.** Do not duplicate the source's words (unless quoting briefly), and write the sentences in your own style.

▸ **Make sure your readers know when the paraphrase begins and ends.** Identify the source at the start of the paraphrase or as early into it as possible.

▸ **Be sure to preserve the author's original intent.** Check that your paraphrase is an accurate and objective restatement of the source's specific ideas.

▸ **Indicate the exact source of each paraphrased passage.** Immediately follow each paraphrase with a parenthetical reference (see pages 434 and 446) indicating the exact location of the material in the source.

Summarizing the Work of Others

Like a paraphrase, a *summary* is a restatement of the original in your own words. A summary, however, restates a large portion of the original text briefly, rather than restating a small portion of the original in about the same number of words. Figure A.4 shows notes in which the quotation in Figure A.2 has been summarized.

Definition of a summary

For more information on summarizing see Chapter 15.

Signal the beginning of the summary by identifying the source, and the end by citing the location.

> Pinsky explains that electromagnetic waves probably do not directly cause cancer. However, they might contribute to the uncontrollable growth of cancer cells that are normally present—but controlled—in the human body (29–30).

FIGURE A.4 Notes for a summary

STRATEGIES
for Summarizing the Work of Others

▸ **Use your own words and sentence structure.** If you must quote a crucial word or phrase directly, use quotation marks around the quoted words.

▸ **Make sure your readers know when the summary begins and ends.** As with a paraphrase, identify the source early in the summary.

▸ **Make sure your summary is an accurate restatement of the source's main ideas.** Do not add new details or remove essential details from the original.

▸ **Indicate the exact source of the summarized material.** Immediately follow each summary with a parenthetical reference (see pages 434 and 446) indicating the exact location of the material in the source.

DOCUMENTATION: THE KEY TO AVOIDING PLAGIARISM

Proper documentation satisfies professional requirements for ethics, efficiency, and authority.

Why You Should Document

Ethical reasons

Documentation is a matter of *ethics*, in that the originator of borrowed material deserves full credit and recognition. Moreover, all published material is protected by copyright law. Failure to credit a source could make you liable to legal action, even if your omission was unintentional. (For more on copyright, see page 459.)

Efficiency reasons

Documentation is also a matter of *efficiency*. Accurate documentation provides a network for organizing and locating the world's recorded knowledge. If you cite a particular source correctly, your reference will enable interested readers to locate that source themselves.

Authority reasons

Finally, documentation is a matter of *authority*. In making any claim (say, "A Mercedes is more reliable than a Ford") you invite challenge: "Says who?" Data on road tests, frequency of repairs, resale value, workmanship, and owner comments can help validate your claim by showing its basis in *fact*. A claim's credibility increases in relation to the expert references supporting it. For a controversial topic, you may need to cite several authorities who hold various views. Readers of your research report expect the *complete picture*.

What You Should Document

Document any insight, assertion, fact, finding, interpretation, judgment, or other "appropriated material that readers might otherwise mistake for your own" (Gibaldi & Achtert, 3rd ed., 155)—whether the material appears in published form or not. Specifically, you must document these sources:

Document any ideas or works that are not your own

- any source from which you use exact wording
- any source from which you adapt material in your own words
- any visual illustration: charts, graphs, drawings, or the like

Sources that require documentation

In some instances, you might have reason to preserve the anonymity of unpublished sources—say, to allow people to respond candidly without fear of reprisal (as with employee criticism of a company), or to protect their privacy (as with certain material from email inquiries or electronic newsgroups). You must still document the fact that you are not the originator of this material. Using MLA style (see page 434), you would provide a general acknowledgment in the text ("A number of employees expressed frustration with . . ."), along with a general citation in your list of Works Cited ("Interviews with department employees, May 2009"). Using APA style (see page 446), you would cite the confidential source in your text itself ("During interviews with department employees in May 2009 . . .").

How to document a confidential source

As stated previously in this appendix, you don't need to document anything considered *common knowledge* (material that appears repeatedly in general sources). In medicine, for instance, it has become common knowledge that foods containing animal fat (meat, butter, cheese, whole milk) raise blood cholesterol levels. So in a research report on fatty diets and heart disease, you probably would not need to document that well-known fact. But you would document information about how the fat-cholesterol connection was discovered, what subsequent studies have found (say, on the role of saturated versus unsaturated fats), and any information for which some other person could claim specific credit. If the borrowed material can be found in only one specific source and not in multiple sources, document it. When in doubt, document the source.

Common knowledge need not be documented

How You Should Document

Cite borrowed material twice: at the exact place you use that material, and at the end of your report. Documentation practices vary widely, but all systems work

Document in text and at the end of the text

almost identically in the following respect: A brief in-text reference names the source and refers readers to the complete citation at the end of the report, which allows readers to consult the source if they so desire.

This chapter illustrates citations and entries for three styles that are widely used for documenting sources in professional writing:

- Modern Language Association (MLA) style for the humanities
- American Psychological Association (APA) style for social sciences
- Council of Science Editors (CSE) style for natural and applied sciences

Unless your audience or your company has a preference, any style can be adapted to most research writing. Use one style consistently throughout your document.

MLA DOCUMENTATION STYLE

The *MLA Handbook for Writers of Research Papers*, 6th ed. (2003), updated in the third edition of the *MLA Style Manual and Guide to Scholarly Publishing* (2008), requires that you cite a source briefly in your text (parenthetical reference) and fully at the end of the report (in a "Works Cited" list).

MLA Parenthetical References

For clear and informative parenthetical references, observe these guidelines:

- If you name the author in your discussion, do not repeat the name in your parenthetical reference; simply give the page or page range:

Citing page numbers only

> Lederman points out that data provided by 796 colleges indicate that violent crime on campus began increasing rapidly around 1985 (31).

- If you cite two or more works in a single parenthetical reference, separate the citations with semicolons:

Three works in a single reference

> (Jones 32; Leduc 41; Gomez 293–94)

- If you cite two or more authors with the same surname, include the first initial in your parenthetical reference to each author:

Two authors with identical surnames

> (R. Jones 32) (S. Jones 14–15)

- If you cite two or more works by the same author, include the first significant word from each work's title or a shortened version of the title:

Two works by one author

> (Lamont, *Biophysics* 100–01) (Lamont, *Diagnostic Tests* 81)

- If the work is by an institutional or corporate author or if it is unsigned (that is, if the author is unknown), use only the first few words of the institutional name or the work's title in your parenthetical reference:

  | (American Medical Association 2) ("Distribution Systems" 18)

Institutional, corporate, or anonymous author

To avoid distracting the reader, keep each parenthetical reference as brief as possible. One method is to name the source in your discussion and to place only the page number in parentheses.

Keep parenthetical references short

For a paraphrase, place the parenthetical reference *before* the closing punctuation mark. For a quotation in the text, place the reference *between* the final quotation mark and the closing punctuation mark. For a quotation set off (indented) from the text, place the reference *after* the closing punctuation mark.

Where to place a parenthetical reference

MLA Works Cited Entries*

The Works Cited list includes each source that you have paraphrased or quoted. Place your Works Cited list on a separate page at the end of the document. Arrange entries alphabetically by author's surname. When the author is unknown, list the title alphabetically according to its first word (excluding introductory articles). For a title that begins with a numeral, alphabetize the entry as if the number were spelled out. In preparing the list, type the first line of each entry flush with the left margin. Indent the second and subsequent lines 1/2 inch (five spaces). Double-space within and between entries.

How to format the Works Cited list

Following are examples of complete citations as they would appear in the Works Cited list. Shown below each citation is its corresponding parenthetical reference as it would appear in the text. Note the capitalization, abbreviations, spacing, and punctuation in the sample entries. Also note that each citation names the *medium* of publication (print, Web, CD, film, television, and so on) in which you located the material you are citing.

How to cite individual items

Table A.1 provides an overview of the types of citations discussed in this section.

MLA Works Cited Entries for Books.
Any citation for a book should contain the following information (found on the book's title and copyright pages): author, title (in italics), editor or translator, edition, volume number, facts about publication (city, publisher, date), and medium ("Print," "Web," "Lecture," and so on).

What to include in an MLA citation for a book

---

*Our thanks to Cynthia K. Marshall, Wright State University, for the most recent MLA style updates.

TABLE A.1 INDEX TO MLA WORKS CITED ENTRIES

BOOKS

1. Book, single author
2. Book, two or three authors
3. Book, four or more authors
4. Book, anonymous author
5. Multiple books, same author
6. Book, one or more editors
7. Book, indirect source
8. Anthology selection or book chapter

PERIODICALS

9. Article, magazine
10. Article, journal with new pagination each issue
11. Article, journal with continuous pagination
12. Article, newspaper

OTHER SOURCES

13. Encyclopedia, dictionary, other alphabetical reference
14. Report
15. Conference presentation
16. Interview, personally conducted
17. Interview, published

18. Letter, unpublished
19. Questionnaire
20. Brochure or pamphlet
21. Lecture
22. Government document
23. Document with corporate or foundation authorship
24. Map or other visual aid
25. Miscellaneous items (unpublished report, dissertation, and so on)

ELECTRONIC SOURCES

26. Online abstract
27. Print article posted online
28. Reference database
29. Computer software
30. CD-ROM
31. Email discussion group
32. Newsgroup
33. Personal email
34. Home page for a course
35. Blogs, wikis, podcasts, and real-time communications
36. General reference to a Web site

1. Book, Single Author—MLA

Reardon, Kathleen Kelley. *They Don't Get It, Do They? Communication in the Workplace—Closing the Gap between Women and Men.* Boston: Little, 1995. Print.

Parenthetical reference: (Reardon 3-4)

Identify the city of publication; if in the United States, omit the state. If several cities are listed on the title page, give only the first. For Canada, include the province abbreviation after the city. For all other foreign countries, include an abbreviation of the country name.

2. Book, Two or Three Authors—MLA

Aronson, Linda, Roger Katz, and Candide Moustafa. *Toxic Waste Disposal Methods.* New Haven: Yale UP, 2010. Print.

Parenthetical reference: (Aronson, Katz, and Moustafa 121-23)

Shorten publishers' names, as in *Simon* for Simon & Schuster, *GPO* for Government Printing Office, and *Yale UP* for Yale University Press. For page numbers with more than two digits, give only the final two digits for the second number when the first digit is identical.

3. Book, Four or More Authors—MLA

Santos, Ruth J., et al. *Environmental Crises in Developing Countries.*
New York: Harper, 2009. Print.

Parenthetical reference: (Santos et al. 9)

Et al. is the abbreviated form of the Latin *et alia*, meaning "and others."

4. Book, Anonymous Author—MLA

Structured Programming. Boston: Meredith, 2010. Print.

Parenthetical reference: (*Structured* 67)

5. Multiple Books, Same Author—MLA

Chang, John W. *Biophysics.* Boston: Little, 2009. Print.

---. *Diagnostic Techniques.* New York: Radon, 1999. Print.

Parenthetical reference: (Chang, *Biophysics* 123-26) (Chang, *Diagnostic* 87)

When citing more than one work by the same author, do not repeat the author's name; simply type three hyphens followed by a period. List the works alphabetically by title.

6. Book, One or More Editors—MLA

Morris, A. J., and Louise B. Pardin-Walker, eds. *Handbook of New
Information Technology.* New York: Harper, 2009. Print.

Parenthetical reference: (Morris and Pardin-Walker 34)

For more than three editors, name only the first, followed by *et al.*

7. Book, Indirect Source—MLA

Kline, Thomas. *Automated Systems.* Boston: Rhodes, 1999. Print.

Stubbs, John. *White-Collar Productivity.* Miami: Harris, 2002. Print.

Parenthetical reference: (qtd. in Stubbs 116)

When your source (as in Stubbs, above) has quoted or cited another source, list each source in its appropriate alphabetical place in the Works Cited list. Use the name of the original source (here, Kline) in your text, and begin the parenthetical reference with *qtd. in,* or *cited in* for a paraphrase.

8. Anthology Selection or Book Chapter—MLA

```
Bowman, Joel P. "Electronic Conferencing." Communication and
        Technology: Today and Tomorrow. Ed. Al Williams. Denton: Assn.
        for Business Communication, 1994. 123-42. Print.
```

Parenthetical reference: (Bowman 129)

The page numbers in the complete citation are for the selection cited from the anthology.

What to include in an MLA citation for a periodical

MLA Works Cited Entries for Periodicals.
Give all available information in this order: author, article title (in quotation marks), periodical title (in italics), volume and issue, date (day, month, year), and page numbers for the entire article—not just pages cited.

9. Article, Magazine—MLA

```
DesMarteau, Kathleen. "Study Links Sewing Machine Use to Alzheimer's
        Disease." Bobbin Oct. 1994: 36-38. Print.
```

Parenthetical reference: (DesMarteau 36)

No punctuation separates the magazine title and date. Nor is the abbreviation *p.* or *pp.* used to designate page numbers. If no author is given, list all other information:

```
"Video Games for the Next Decade." Power Technology Magazine 18 Oct.
        2009: 18+. Print.
```

Parenthetical reference: ("Video Games" 18)

This article began on page 18 and continued on page 21. When an article does not appear on consecutive pages, give only the number of the first page, followed immediately by a plus sign. A three-letter abbreviation denotes any month spelled with five or more letters.

10. Article, Journal with New Pagination Each Issue—MLA

```
Thackman-White, Joan R. "Computer-Assisted Research." American Library
        Journal 51.1 (2010): 3-9. Print.
```

Parenthetical reference: (Thackman-White 4-5)

Because each issue for that year will have page numbers beginning with 1, readers need the number of this issue: Here 51 is the volume number and 1 is the issue number. Omit *The, A,* or *An* from a journal or magazine title.

11. Article, Journal with Continuous Pagination—MLA

> Barnstead, Marion H. "The Writing Crisis." *Journal of Writing Theory* 12
>
>   (2009): 415-33. Print.

Parenthetical reference: (Barnstead 418)

When page numbers continue from issue to issue, readers won't need the issue number because no other issue in that year repeats the same page numbers. (Include the issue number, however, if you think it will help readers retrieve the article more easily.) Here 12 is the volume number.

    If you are citing an abstract found in a bound collection of abstracts, and not the full article, include the information on the abstracting service right after the information on the original article.   *How to cite abstracts*

> Barnstead, Marion H. "The Writing Crisis." *Journal of Writing Theory* 12
>
>   (2009): 415-33. *Rhetoric Abstracts* 67 (2010): item 1354. Print.

If you are citing an abstract that appears before the printed article, add *Abstract*, followed by a period, immediately after the original work's page number or range.

12. Article, Newspaper—MLA

> Baranski, Vida H. "Errors in Medical Diagnosis." *Boston Times* 15 Jan.
>
>   2010, evening ed., sec. B: 3+. Print.

Parenthetical reference: (Baranski 3)

When a daily newspaper has more than one edition, cite the edition after the date. Omit any introductory article in the newspaper's name (not *The Boston Times*). If no author is given, list all other information. If the newspaper's name does not contain the city of publication, insert it, using brackets: *Sippican Sentinel* [Marion].

MLA Works Cited Entries for Other Sources.

MLA Works Cited Entries for Other Sources. Miscellaneous sources range from unsigned encyclopedia entries to conference presentations to government publications. A full citation should give this information (as available): author, title, city, publisher, date, and page numbers.   *What to include in an MLA citation for a miscellaneous source*

13. Encyclopedia, Dictionary, Other Alphabetical Reference—MLA

> "Communication." *The Business Reference Book.* 2008 ed. Print.

Parenthetical reference: ("Communication")

Begin a signed entry with the author's name. For any work arranged alphabetically, omit page numbers in the complete citation and the parenthetical reference.

For a well-known reference book, include only an edition (if stated) and a date. For other reference books, give the full publication information.

14. Report—MLA

Electrical Power Research Institute (EPRI). *Epidemiologic Studies of*
    Electric Utility Employees. (Report No. RP2964.5). Palo Alto:
    EPRI, Nov. 1994. Print.

Parenthetical reference: (Electrical Power Research Institute [EPRI] 27)

If no author is given, begin with the organization that sponsored the report.

For any report or other document with group authorship, include the group's abbreviated name in your first parenthetical reference and then use only that abbreviation in any subsequent reference.

15. Conference Presentation—MLA

Smith, Abelard A. "Multicultural Stereotypes in Elizabethan Prose
    Fiction." Conference Presentation. *First British Symposium in*
    Multicultural Studies. London, 11-13 Oct. 2007. Ed. Anne Hodkins.
    London: Harrison, 2008. 106-21. Print.

Parenthetical reference: (Smith 109)

The previous example shows a presentation that has been included in the published proceedings of a conference.

For an unpublished presentation, include the presenter's name, the title of the presentation, and the conference title, location, date, and the medium (*Conference presentation*) from which you accessed this material. Do not italicize the conference information.

16. Interview, Personally Conducted—MLA

Nasson, Gamela. Personal interview. 2 Apr. 2010.

Parenthetical reference: (Nasson)

17. Interview, Published—MLA

Lescault, James. "The Future of Graphics." Interview by Carol Jable.
    Executive Views of Automation. Ed. Karen Prell. Miami: Haber,
    2007. 216-31. Print.

Parenthetical reference: (Lescault 218)

The interviewee's name is placed in the entry's author slot.

18. Letter, Unpublished—MLA

```
Rogers, Leonard. Letter to the author. 15 May 2010. Print.
```

Parenthetical reference: (Rogers)

19. Questionnaire—MLA

```
Taynes, Lorraine. Questionnaire sent to 61 college administrators.

    14 Feb. 2009. Print.
```

Parenthetical reference: (Taynes)

20. Brochure or Pamphlet—MLA

```
Career Strategies for the 21st Century. San Francisco: Blount Economics

    Assn., 2010. Print.
```

Parenthetical reference: (Career)

If the work is signed, begin with its author.

21. Lecture—MLA

```
Dumont, R. A. "Androgyny and the Rhetorical Tradition." University of

    Massachusetts at Dartmouth, 15 Jan. 2010. Lecture.
```

Parenthetical reference: (Dumont)

If the lecture title is not known, write *Address, Lecture,* or *Reading* and do not use quotation marks. Include the sponsor and the location if they are available.

22. Government Document—MLA

If the author is unknown, begin with the information in this order: name of the government, name of the issuing agency, document title, place, publisher, and date:

```
Virginia. Highway Dept. Standards for Bridge Maintenance. Richmond:

    Virginia Highway Dept., 2009. Print.
```

Parenthetical reference: (Virginia Highway Dept. 49)

For any congressional document, identify the house of Congress (Senate or House of Representatives) before the title and the number and session of Congress after the title:

```
United States. Cong. House. Armed Services Committee. Funding for the

    Military Academies. 108th Cong., 2nd sess. Washington: GPO, 2009.

    Print.
```

Parenthetical reference: (U.S. Armed Services Committee 41)

GPO is the abbreviation for the United States Government Printing Office.

For an entry from the *Congressional Record,* give only date and pages:

`Cong. Rec. 10 Mar. 2006: 2178-92. Print.`

Parenthetical reference: `(Cong. Rec. 2184)`

23. Document with Corporate or Foundation Authorship—MLA

`Hermitage Foundation.` *Global Warming Scenarios for the Year 2030.*
`Washington: Natl. Res. Council, 2009. Print.`

Parenthetical reference: `(Hermitage Foundation 123)`

24. Map or Other Visual Aid—MLA

Deaths Caused by Breast Cancer, by County. `Map.` *Scientific American*
`Oct. 1995: 32D. Print.`

Parenthetical reference: `(Deaths Caused)`

If the creator of the visual is listed, list that name first. Identify the type of visual (*Map, Graph, Table, Diagram*) immediately following its title.

25. Miscellaneous Items (Unpublished Report, Dissertation, and so on)—MLA
Provide information in this order:

`Author (if known). "Title" (in quotes). Sponsoring organization or`
`publisher, date. Page or page range. Medium of publication.`

For any work that has group authorship (corporation, committee, task force), cite the name of the group or agency in place of the author's name.

What to include in an
MLA citation for an
electronic source

MLA Works Cited Entries for Electronic Sources. Electronic sources include Internet sites, reference databases, CD-ROMs, computer software, email, and blogs. Any citation for an electronic source should allow readers to identify the original source (printed or electronic) and trace a clear path for retrieving the material. Provide all available information in the following order:

1. Name of author, editor, or producer of the work or site. If no author is given, begin with item 2. For works with multiple or anonymous authors, follow the guidelines for print sources.

2. Title of the work. For online postings such as email discussion lists or newsgroups, give the title of the posting. Italicize the title unless it is part of a larger work; in that case, enclose the title in quotation marks and italicize the larger work's title.

3. Title of the Web site (in italics), if this differs from item 2.

4. Version or edition of the site, if relevant.

5. Publisher or sponsor of the site (often listed at the bottom of the Web page). If this information is not given, use *N.p.* (for *no publisher*).

6. Publication date (day, month, and year, if available). If no date is given, use *n.d.*

7. Medium of publication that you accessed. For all online sources, this would be *Web.*

8. Date you accessed the source (day, month, and year).

> Kent, Maureen. "The Glass Ceiling." *Businessmonthlyonline.com.* n.d.
>
> Web. 4 Oct. 2009.

If the work you have accessed electronically exists in a print or other version, you can include the publication information for that medium if you decide readers would find it useful. Begin with (1) the citation format for the other medium, followed by (2) the title of the database or Web site (in italics) from which you retrieved the content, (3) the medium of publication (Web), and (4) your access date (day, month, and year).

> Cayer, Kevin. "The Silent Depression" *Cashflow Magazine. Moneyline,* 1
>
> June 2009. Web. 5 April. 2010.

Include the Web address only if the site likely cannot be found through any other information, or if your instructor requires. This would be the citations's final item, enclosed in angle brackets (< >) and followed by a period. Provide the full electronic address, including the access-mode identifier (*http, ftp,* etc.). When a Web address continues from one line to the next, break it only after a slash or a period; do not insert a hyphen.

> "Filing Your Taxes Online." *IRS.gov.* Internal Revenue Service. June
>
> 2009. Web. Oct. 2009 <http://www.irs/gov/factsheets/
>
> online-filing.htm>.

26. Online Abstract—MLA

> Lane, Amanda D., et al. "The Promise of Microcircuits." *Journal of*
>
> *Nanotechnology* 12.2 (2006): n.pag. Abstract. Web. 11 May 2009.

Parenthetical reference: (Lane et al.)

The *n. pag.* designates no page numbers. For more on citing an abstract, see page 439.

27. Print Article Posted Online—MLA

Jeffers, Anna D. "NAFTA's Effects on the U.S. Trade Deficit." *Sultana*

Business Quarterly 3.4 (2004): 65-74. Web. 5 Apr. 2008.

Parenthetical reference: (Jeffers 66)

28. Reference Database—MLA

Sahl, J. D. "Power Lines, Viruses, and Childhood Leukemia." *Cancer*

Causes Control 6.1 (Jan. 1995): 83-85. *MEDLINE.* Web. 7 Nov. 2001.

Parenthetical reference: (Sahl 83)

For entries with a print equivalent, begin with print publication information, then the database title (italicized, as in *MEDLINE*), the *Web* designation to indicate the medium, the service provider, and the date of access. The access date is important because frequent updatings of databases can produce different versions of the material.

For entries with no print equivalent, give the title and date of the work in quotation marks, followed by the electronic source information:

Argent, Roger R. "An Analysis of International Exchange Rates for

2009." *Accu-Data.* Dow Jones News Retrieval. Web. 10 Jan. 2010.

Parenthetical reference: (Argent)

If the author is not known, begin with the work's title. If the Web document has page numbers, include them in your entry and in your parenthetical reference.

29. Computer Software—MLA

Virtual Collaboration. Software. New York: Pearson, 2010.

Parenthetical reference: (*Virtual*)

Begin with the author's name, if known.

30. CD-ROM—MLA

Canalte, Henry A. "Violent Crime Statistics: Good News and Bad News."

Law Enforcement Feb. 1995: 8. *ABI/INFORM.* CD-ROM. ProQuest. Sept.

2010.

Parenthetical reference: (Canalte 8)

If the material is also available in print, begin with the information about the printed source, followed by the electronic source information: name of database (italicized), *CD-ROM* designation, vendor name, and electronic publication date. If the material has no print equivalent, list its author (if known) and its title (in quotation marks), followed by the electronic source information.

For CD-ROM reference works and other material that is not routinely updated, give the work title followed by the place, electronic publisher, date, and the *CD-ROM* designation:

> *Time Almanac.* Washington: Compact, 2008. CD-ROM.

> *Parenthetical reference:* (Time Almanac 74)

Begin with the author's name, if known.

31. Email Discussion Group—MLA

> Kosten, A. "Major Update of the WWWVL Migration and Ethnic Relations."
>
>   7 Apr. 1998. *ERCOMER News.* E-mail.

Begin with the author's name (if known), followed by the title of the work (in quotation marks), date of message, title of discussion group (italicized), and medium. Do not include the date of your access.

32. Newsgroup—MLA

> Dorsey, Michael. "Environmentalism or Racism?" 25 Mar. 2002. Online
>
>   posting. 1 Apr. 2003 <news: alt.org.sierra-club>.

33. Personal Email—MLA

> Wallin, John Luther. "Frog Reveries." Message to the author. 12 Oct.
>
>   2009. E-mail.

Cite personal email as you would printed correspondence. If the document has a subject line or title, enclose it in quotation marks. For publicly posted email (say, a newsgroup or discussion list), include the address and the date of access.

34. Home Page for a Course—MLA

> Dumont, R. A. Home page. *An Online Course in Technical Writing.* Fall
>
>   2009. Dept. of English, UMASS Dartmouth. 6 Jan. 2010. <http://
>
>   www.umassd.edu/englishdepartment.html>.

> *Parenthetical reference:* (Dumont)

Begin with the instructor's name, followed by "Home page" (without quotation marks or italics), course title (in italics), course dates, academic department, school, and your date of access.

35. Blogs, Wikis, Podcasts, and Other Real-Time Communications—MLA

Synchronous communication occurs in "real-time" forums and on instant messaging, text messaging, and chat spaces. The message typed in by the sender appears instantly on the recipient's screen. Blogs, wikis, and podcasts, in contrast, are asynchronous. However, both can be cited as follows:

> Frank, James. "Online Debate on Global Warming." 3 Apr. 2009.
>
> *EarthWatch*. Web. 10 May 2009.
>
> *Parenthetical reference:* (Frank)

Begin with the name of the communicator and topic title (in quotation marks), followed by the posting date, name of forum blog, wiki, or podcast (in italics), medium, and access date.

36. General Reference to a Web Site—MLA

In referring to an entire site instead of a specific item, include the following information, as available:

> Name of author, editor, or compiler; title of the site (in italics);
>
> site sponsor; date of publication or latest update; medium (Web);
>
> and your date of access.

APA DOCUMENTATION STYLE

One popular alternative to MLA style is detailed in the *Publication Manual of the American Psychological Association*, 6th ed. (2009). Because it emphasizes the publication date, APA style (or any similar author-date style) is preferred in the sciences and social sciences, where information quickly becomes outdated.

As in MLA style, APA style requires that you cite a source in text (parenthetical reference) as well as at the end of the report (where it is called a References list rather than a Works Cited list).

APA Parenthetical References

How APA and MLA parenthetical references differ

APA's parenthetical references differ from MLA's as follows: the citation includes the publication date; a comma separates each item in the reference; and *p.* or *pp.* precedes the page number (which is optional in the APA system) or range, respectively. Here are specific guidelines:

- If your discussion names the author, do not repeat the name in your parenthetical reference; simply give the date and page number or range. When two authors of a work are named in your text, their names are connected by *and*, but in a parenthetical reference, their names are connected by an ampersand (&).

> Lederman (1995) cites recent data provided by 796 colleges indicating that violent crime on campus is increasing (p. 31).

Author named in the text

- If you cite two or more works in a single reference, list the authors in alphabetical order and separate the citations with semicolons:

> (Gomez, 2002; Jones, 2004; Leduc, 1998)

Two or more works in a single reference

- If you cite a work with three to five authors, try to name them in your text, to avoid an excessively long parenthetical reference. In any subsequent references to this work, name only the first author, followed by *et al.* (Latin abbreviation for "and others").

> Franks, Oblesky, Ryan, Jablar, and Perkins (2004) studied the role of electromagnetic fields in tumor formation.

A work with three to five authors

- If you cite two or more works by the same author published in the same year, arrange the works alphabetically by title, and add a lowercase letter (a, b, c) to the year to differentiate them:

> (Lamont, 2005a, p. 135) (Lamont, 2005b, pp. 67–68)

Two or more works by the same author in the same year

- When a subsequent reference to a source follows closely after the initial reference, the date need not be included.

APA Reference Entries

Like the MLA Works Cited list, the APA References list includes each source you have cited in your paper; it appears on a separate page at the end of the document. Arrange all entries alphabetically by the author's surname (when the author's name is unknown, alphabetize by the first word or numeral, as if the numeral were spelled out). Begin each entry flush with the left margin and indent second and subsequent lines 1/2 inch (or five spaces). Double-space within and between entries. In one notable difference from MLA style, APA style calls for only "retrievable" sources to appear in the reference list. Therefore, cite personal interviews, letters, and email messages in text only.

How to format the References list

How to cite nonretrievable sources

Following are examples of complete citations as they would appear in the References list. Shown immediately below each entry is its corresponding parenthetical reference as it would appear in the text. Note the capitalization, abbreviation, spacing, and punctuation in the sample entries.

How to cite individual items

Table A.2 provides an overview of the types of citations discussed in this section.

APA Entries for Books. Any citation for a book should contain all applicable information in the following order: author, date, title, editor or translator, edition, volume number, and facts about publication—city, state (abbreviated), and publisher.

What to include in an APA citation for a book

TABLE A.2 INDEX TO APA REFERENCES ENTRIES

BOOKS

1. Book, single author
2. Book, two to five authors
3. Book, six or more authors
4. Book, anonymous author
5. Multiple books, same author
6. Book, one to five editors
7. Book, indirect source
8. Anthology selection or book chapter

PERIODICALS

9. Article, magazine
10. Article, journal with new pagination for each issue
11. Article, journal with continuous pagination
12. Article, newspaper

OTHER SOURCES

13. Encyclopedia, dictionary, alphabetical reference
14. Report
15. Conference presentation
16. Interview, personally conducted

17. Interview, published
18. Personal correspondence
19. Brochure or pamphlet
20. Unpublished lecture
21. Government document
22. Miscellaneous items (unpublished manuscript, dissertation, and so on)

ELECTRONIC SOURCES

23. Online abstract
24. Print article posted online
25. Book or article available only online
26. CD-ROM abstract
27. Online encyclopedia, dictionary, or handbook
28. Personal email
29. Blog posting
30. Newsgroup, discussion list, or online forum
31. Wiki

GRAY LITERATURE

32. Press release
33. Technical or research report

1. Book, Single Author—APA

Reardon, K. K. (1995). *They don't get it, do they? Communication in the workplace—closing the gap between women and men.* Boston: Little, Brown.

Parenthetical reference: (Reardon, 1995, pp. 3-4)

Use only initials for an author's first and middle names. Capitalize only the first words of a book's title and subtitle and any proper names. Identify a later edition in parentheses between the title and the period. Omit the state abbreviation if the city is unambiguous.

2. Book, Two to Five Authors—APA

Aronson, L., Katz, R., & Moustafa, C. (2010). *Toxic waste disposal methods.* New Haven, CT: Yale University Press.

Parenthetical reference: (Aronson, Katz, & Moustafa, 2008)

Use an ampersand (&) before the name of the final author listed in an entry. As an alternative to a full parenthetical reference, name the authors in your text and include date (and page numbers, if appropriate) in parentheses. Give the publisher's name in full ("Yale University Press") but omit *Publisher, Company,* or *Inc.* Use the two-letter U.S. Postal Service abbreviations for states.

3. Book, Six or More Authors—APA

```
Fogle, S. T., et al. (2009). Hyperspace technology. Boston: Little,
    Brown.
```

Parenthetical reference: (Fogle et al., 1998, p. 34)

Et al. is the Latin abbreviation for *et alia,* meaning "and others."

4. Book, Anonymous Author—APA

```
Structured programming. (2010). Boston: Meredith Press.
```

Parenthetical reference: (*Structured Programming,* 2008, p. 67)

In your list of references, place an anonymous work alphabetically by the first key word in its title (ignoring *The, A,* or *An*). In your parenthetical reference, capitalize all key words in a book, article, or journal title.

5. Multiple Books, Same Author—APA

```
Chang, J. W. (2009a). Biophysics. Boston: Little, Brown.

Chang, J. W. (2009b). MindQuest. Chicago: Pressler.
```

Parenthetical reference: (Chang, 2009a) (Chang, 2009b)

Two or more works by the same author published in different years are distinguished by their dates alone, without the added letter.

6. Book, One to Five Editors—APA

```
Morris, A. J., & Pardin-Walker, L. B. (Eds.). (2009). Handbook of new
    information technology. New York: HarperCollins.
```

Parenthetical reference: (Morris & Pardin-Walker, 2009, p. 79)

For more than five editors, name only the first, followed by *et al.*

7. Book, Indirect Source—APA

```
Stubbs, J. (2002). White-collar productivity. Miami, FL: Harris.
```

Parenthetical reference: (cited in Stubbs, 2002, p. 47)

When your source has cited another source, list only this second source, but name the original source in your text: "Kline's study (cited in Stubbs, 2002, p. 47) supports this conclusion."

8. Anthology Selection or Book Chapter—APA

Bowman, J. (1994). Electronic conferencing. In A. Williams (Ed.),

Communication and technology: Today and tomorrow (pp. 123-142).

Denton, TX: Association for Business Communication.

Parenthetical reference: (Bowman, 1994, p. 126)

The page numbers in the complete reference are for the entire selection cited from the anthology.

What to include in an APA citation for a periodical

APA Entries for Periodicals. A citation for an article should give this information (as available) in this order: author, date, article title (without quotation marks), publication, volume and (when necessary) issue number, and page numbers for the entire article, not just the portion cited.

9. Article, Magazine—APA

DesMarteau K. (1994, October). Study links sewing machine use to

Alzheimer's disease. *Bobbin, 36,* 36-38.

Parenthetical reference: (DesMarteau, 1994, p. 36)

If no author is given, provide all other information, placing the title in the author position. Capitalize only the first words in an article's title and subtitle. Capitalize all key words in a periodical title. Italicize the periodical title and volume number.

10. Article, Journal with New Pagination for Each Issue—APA

Thackman-White, J. R. (2010). Computer-assisted research. *American*

Library Journal, 51(1), 3-9.

Parenthetical reference: (Thackman-White, 2010, pp. 4-5)

Because each issue for a given year has page numbers that begin at "1," readers need the issue number (in this instance, 1). Here 51 is the volume number, which is italicized.

11. Article, Journal with Continuous Pagination—APA

Barnstead, M. H. (2009). The writing crisis. *Journal of Writing Theory,*

12, 415-433.

Parenthetical reference: (Barnstead, 2009, pp. 415-416)

In this example, 12 is the volume number. When page numbers continue from issue to issue for the full year, readers won't need the issue number because no other issue in that year repeats the same page numbers. (You can include the issue number if you think it will help readers retrieve the article more easily.)

12. Article, Newspaper—APA

> Baranski, V. H. (2010, January 15). Errors in medical diagnosis. *The Boston Times*, pp. B3,6.
>
> *Parenthetical reference:* (Baranski, 2010)

In addition to the year of publication, include the month and date. If the newspaper's name begins with *The,* include it in your citation. Include *p.* or *pp.* before page numbers. For an article on nonconsecutive pages, list each page, separated by a comma. If the entire article appeared on one page, no page number is necessary in the citation.

APA Entries for Other Sources. Miscellaneous sources range from unsigned encyclopedia entries to conference presentations to government documents. A full citation should give this information (as available): author, publication date, title of work, city, publisher (or volume and issue number), and page numbers (if applicable).

What to include in an APA citation for a miscellaneous source

13. Encyclopedia, Dictionary, Alphabetical Reference—APA

> Communication. (2008). In *The business reference book.* Upper Saddle River, NJ: Prentice Hall, p. 201.
>
> *Parenthetical reference:* (Communication, 2008)

For an entry that is signed, begin with the author's name and publication date.

14. Report—APA

> Electrical Power Research Institute. (1994). *Epidemiologic studies of electric utility employees* (Rep. No. RP2964.5). Palo Alto, CA: Author.
>
> *Parenthetical reference:* (Electrical Power Research Institute [EPRI], 1994, p. 12)

If authors are named, list them first, followed by the publication date. When citing a group author, as in example 14, include the group's abbreviated name in your first parenthetical reference, and use only that abbreviation in any subsequent reference. When the agency (or organization) and publisher are the same, list "Author" in the publisher's slot.

15. Conference Presentation—APA

> Smith, A. A. (2007). Multicultural stereotypes in Elizabethan prose
>   fiction. In A. Hodkins (Ed.), *First British Symposium on*
>   *Multicultural Studies* (pp. 106-121). London: Harrison Press.
>
> *Parenthetical reference:* (Smith, 2007, p. 109)

The date of the presentation is in parentheses. The name of the symposium is a proper name, so it is capitalized. For an unpublished presentation, include the presenter's name, year and month, title of the presentation (italicized), and all available information about the conference or meeting: "Symposium held at . . ." Do not italicize this last information.

16. Interview, Personally Conducted—APA

This material is considered a nonrecoverable source, so it is cited only in the text, as a parenthetical reference:

> *Parenthetical reference:* (G. Nasson, personal communication, April 2, 2010)

If you name the interviewee in your text, do not repeat the name in your citation.

17. Interview, Published—APA

> Jable, C. K. (2009, June 7). The future of graphics [Interview with
>   James Lescault]. In K. Prell (Ed.), *Executive views of automation*
>   (pp. 216-231). Miami: Haber Press.
>
> *Parenthetical reference:* (Jable, 2009, p. 218)

Begin with the name of the interviewer, followed by the interview date and title (if available), the designation (in brackets), and the publication information.

18. Personal Correspondence—APA

This material is considered nonrecoverable data, so it is cited only in the text, as a parenthetical reference:

> *Parenthetical reference:* (L. Rogers, personal communication, May 15, 2010)

If you name the correspondent in your text, do not repeat the name in your citation.

19. Brochure or Pamphlet—APA

This material follows the citation format for book entries (pages 445–450).

20. Unpublished Lecture—APA

> Dumont, R. A. (2010, January 15). *Androgyny and the rhetorical tradition.*
>   Lecture presented at the University of Massachusetts at Dartmouth.
>
> *Parenthetical reference:* (Dumont, 2010)

If you name the lecturer in your text, do not repeat the name in your citation.

21. Government Document—APA

If the author is unknown, present the information in this order: name of the issuing agency, publication date, document title, place, and publisher.

> Virginia Highway Department. (2009). *Standards for bridge maintenance.*
>
> Richmond, VA: Author.

Parenthetical reference: (Virginia Highway Department, 2009, p. 49)

When the issuing agency is both author and publisher, write *Author* in the publisher's slot. For any congressional document, identify the house of Congress (Senate or House of Representatives) before the date.

> United States Congress. House. Armed Services Committee. (2009).
>
> *Funding for the military academies.* Washington, DC: U.S.
>
> Government Printing Office.

Parenthetical reference: (U.S. Congress, 2009, p. 41)

22. Miscellaneous Items (Unpublished Manuscript, Dissertation, and so on)—APA

Provide information in this order:

> Author (if known). (Date of preparation). *Title of work* (italicized).
>
> Description (Unpublished manuscript, unpublished raw data, or the
>
> like).

For any work that has group authorship (corporation, committee, and so on), cite the name of the group or agency in place of the author's name.

APA Entries for Electronic Sources.

In June 2007, the APA published the *APA Style Guide to Electronic References.* The APA's general advice for citing electronic sources is to "include the same elements, in the same order, as you would for a [print] source, and add as much electronic retrieval information as needed for others to locate the sources you cited" (p. 1). When you cite sources in the References section of your document, identify the original source (printed or electronic) and give readers a path for retrieving the material. Provide all available information in the following order:

What to include in an APA citation for an electronic source

1. Author, editor, creator, or sponsoring organization.
2. Date the item was published or was created electronically. For magazines and newspapers, include the month and day as well as the year. If the date of an electronic publication is not available, use *n.d.* in place of the date.

3. Publication information of the original printed version (as in previous entries), if such a version exists. Follow this by designating the electronic medium—[CD-ROM]—or the type of work—[Abstract], [Brochure], or the like—unless this designation is named in the title of the work (as in "Inpatient brochure").

4. Retrieval information. It is not always necessary to include the information "Retrieved from (database name)." Include your retrieval date only if the content might be altered at some point, as for a wiki posting or a Web article that is undated or subject to updating or revision.

5. Database names. It is not necessary to list database names (unless the database is obscure or the material is hard to find), as long as you include the Web address (or DOI, to be discussed).

6. Web addresses and DOIs. Provide the full and accurate electronic address. For Internet sources, provide the complete Web address. For CD-ROM and database sources, give the document's retrieval number. Do not underline, italicize, use angle brackets, or add a period at the end of a Web address. When a Web address continues from one line to the next, break it before a slash or other punctuation (except for http://, which should not be broken). The APA now recommends using the DOI (Digital Object Identifier), when available, in place of a Web address in references to electronic texts. DOI numbers are found on some recent scholarly journals, especially in the sciences and social sciences. Here is a sample reference for a journal article with a DOI assigned:

Schmidt, D., et al. (2009). Advances in psychotropic medication. *Boston
  Journal of Psychotherapy, 81*(3), 398-413. doi: 10.1037/0555-
  9467.79.3.483

23. Online Abstract—APA

Stevens, R. L. (2010). Cell phones and cancer rates. *Oncology Journal,
  57*(2), 41-43. [Abstract]. Retrieved from the Dialog database.
  (MEDLINE Item: AY 24598).

Parenthetical reference: (Stevens, 2010)

Ordinarily an APA entry ends with a period. Entries that end with a Web address (or a DOI), however, omit the period at the end of the electronic address. If you are citing the entire article retrieved from a full-text database, delete [Abstract] from your citation.

24. Print Article Posted Online—APA

Alley, R. A. (2009, January). Ergonomic influences on worker
  satisfaction. *Industrial Psychology, 5*(12), 672-678. Retrieved
  from http://www.psycharchives/index/indpsy/2009_1.html

Parenthetical reference: (Alley, 2009)

If you were confident that the document's electronic and print versions were identical, you could omit the Web address and insert "[Electronic version]" between the end of the article title and the period.

25. Book or Article Available Only Online—APA

Kelly, W. (2009). *Early graveyards of New England.* Retrieved from
    http://www.onlinebooks.com/search/itemID=65321

Parenthetical reference: (Kelly, 2009)

This source exists only in electronic format.

26. CD-ROM Abstract—APA

Cavanaugh, H. (1995). An EMF study: Good news and bad news [CD-ROM].
    Electrical World, 209(2), 8. Abstract retrieved from ProQuest
    File: ABI/INFORM database (62-1498).

Parenthetical reference: (Cavanaugh, 1995)

In this entry, 8 is the page number of this one-page article.

27. Online Encyclopedia, Dictionary, or Handbook—APA

Ecoterrorism. (2009). *Ecological encyclopedia.* Washington, DC: Redwood.
    Retrieved May 1, 2010, from http://www.eco.floridastate.edu/
    index.html

Parenthetical reference: ("Ecoterrorism," 2009)

Include the retrieval date for reference works that are routinely updated. If the work on CD-ROM has a print equivalent, the APA currently prefers that it be cited in its printed form.

28. Personal Email—APA

Parenthetical reference: Fred Flynn (personal communication, May 10, 2008)
provided these statistics.

Instead of being included in the list of references, personal email (considered a nonretrievable source) is cited fully in the text.

29. Blog Posting—APA

Owens, P. (2010, June 1). How to stabilize a large travel trailer.
    Message posted to http://rvblogs.com/comm/bilge

Parenthetical reference: (Owens, 2010)

30. Newsgroup, Discussion List, or Online Forum—APA

LaBarge, V. S. (2009, October 20). A cure for computer viruses. Message
posted to http://www.srb/forums/frwl/webZ/m2237.html

Parenthetical reference: (LaBarge, 2009)

Although email should not be included in the list of references, postings from blogs, newsgroups, and online forums, considered more retrievable, should be included.

31. Wiki—APA

Skull-base tumors. (n.d.). Retrieved June 10, 2009, from the Oncology
wiki: http://oncology.wikia.com/wiki/Skull_base_tumors

Parenthetical reference: ("Skull-Base," n.d.)

Notice the "n.d." ("no date") designation for this collaborative Web page that can be written or edited by anyone with access.

What to include in an APA citation for gray literature

APA Entries for Gray Literature. The APA has new guidelines for citing so-called gray literature—material such as annual reports, fact sheets, consumer brochures, press releases, and technical reports (each type is so named in the title, in brackets, or elsewhere in the citation). In the *APA Style Guide to Electronic References*, gray literature is defined as "scientific information that falls outside the peer review process but is written by scholars or summarizes a body of scholarly work. Government departments, corporations and trade groups . . . and other . . . organizations produce gray literature" (p. 18). Much of this is written for the general public. In the sample citation in entry 32, the type of item is identified in brackets; in entry 33, it is part of the titling information.

32. Press Release—APA

American Natural Foods Association. (2009, January 20). *Newest food
additive poses special threat to children, according to the
upcoming issue of* Eating for Health [Press release]. Retrieved
from http://www.anfha.org/releases/additives0620.html

Parenthetical reference: (American Natural Foods Association, 2009)

33. Technical or Research Report—APA

Gunderson, H., et al. (2007). *Declining birthrates in rural areas:
Results from the 2005 National Census Bureau Survey* (Report No. 7864

NCB 2005-171). Retrieved from the National Center for Population

Statistics: http://ncps.gov/pubs2007/pubs2007/2007171.pdf

Parenthetical reference: (Gunderson, 2007)

Notice that the report number, if available, is given after the title.

CSE DOCUMENTATION STYLE

In the numbered version of CSE style, a citation in the text appears as a superscript number immediately following the source to which it refers:

> A recent study[1] indicates an elevated leukemia risk among children exposed to certain types of electromagnetic fields. Related studies[2-3] tend to confirm the EMF/cancer hypothesis.

Numbered citations in the text

When referring to two or more sources in a single note (as in [2-3] above) separate the numbers by a hyphen if they are in sequence, and by commas but no space if they are not in sequence: ([2,6,9]).

The full citation for each source then appears in the numerical listing of References at the end of the document. CSE's References section lists each source in the order in which it was first cited. In preparing the list, which should be double-spaced, begin each entry on a new line. Type the number flush with the left margin, followed by a period and a space. Align subsequent lines directly under the first word of the first line, as in the following example:

CSE References list

References

1. Baron, KL, et al. The electromagnetic spectrum. New York: Pearson; 2007. 476p.

2. Klingman, JM. Nematode infestation in boreal subtropical environments. J Entymol 2006;54:475–8.

Table A.3 provides an overview of the types of citations discussed in this section.

TABLE A.3 INDEX TO CSE REFERENCES ENTRIES

BOOKS	PERIODICALS
1. Book, single author	6. Article, magazine
2. Book, multiple authors	7. Article, journal with new pagination each issue
3. Book, anonymous author	8. Article, journal with continuous pagination
4. Book, one or more editors	9. Article, newspaper
5. Anthology selection or book chapter	10. Article, online source

Following are examples of complete citations as they would appear in the References section for your document. For more guidelines and examples, consult the *Scientific Style and Format: The CSE Manual for Authors, Editors, and Publishers,* 7th ed. or go to these Web sites: <www.councilscienceeditors.org/publications/style.cfm> and <www. lib.ohio-state.edu/guides/csegd.html>.

CSE Entries for Books

Any citation for a book should contain all available information in the following order: number assigned to the entry, author or editor, work title (and edition), facts about publication (place, publisher, date), and number of pages. Note the capitalization, abbreviation, spacing, and punctuation in the sample entries.

1. Book, Single Author—CSE

1. Kerzin-Fontana JB. Technology management: a handbook. 3rd ed.
   Delmar, NY: American Management Assn; 2007. 356p.

2. Book, Multiple Authors—CSE

1. Aronson L, Katz R, Moustafa C. Toxic waste disposal methods. New
   Haven: Yale Univ Pr; 2010. 316p.

3. Book, Anonymous Author—CSE

1. [Anonymous]. Structured programming. Boston: Meredith Pr; 2010. 267p.

4. Book, One or More Editors—CSE

1. Morris AJ, Pardin-Walker LB, editors. Handbook of new information
   technology. New York: Harper; 2009. 345p.

5. Anthology Selection or Book Chapter—CSE

1. Bowman JP. Electronic conferencing. In: Williams A, editor:
   Communication and technology: today and tomorrow. Denton, TX:
   Assn for Business Communication;1994. p 123-42.

CSE Entries for Periodicals

Any citation for an article should contain all available information in the following order: number assigned to the entry, author, article title, periodical title, date (year, month), volume and issue number, and inclusive page numbers for the article. Note the capitalization, abbreviation, spacing, and punctuation in the sample entries.

6. Article, Magazine—CSE

```
1. DesMarteau K. Study links sewing machine use to Alzheimer's disease.
     Bobbin 1994 Oct:36-8.
```

7. Article, Journal with New Pagination Each Issue—CSE

```
1. Thackman-White JR. Computer-assisted research. Am Library J
     2010;51(1):3-9.
```

8. Article, Journal with Continuous Pagination—CSE

```
1. Barnstead MH. The writing crisis. J of Writing Theory 2009;12:415-33.
```

9. Article, Newspaper—CSE

```
1. Baranski VH. Errors in medical diagnosis. Boston Times 2010 Jan
     15;Sect B: 3(col 2).
```

10. Article, Online Source—CSE

```
1. Alley RA. Ergonomic influences on worker satisfaction. Industrial
     Psychology [serial online] 2009 Jan;5(12). Available from:
     ftp.pub/journals/industrialpsychology/2009 via the INTERNET.
     Accessed 2010 Feb 10.
```

Citation for an article published online follows a similar format, with these differences: write "[article online]" between article title and publication date; after "Available from," give the Web address followed by a period and your access information.

RECOGNIZING COPYRIGHT ISSUES

Copyright is the legal system that gives authors and owners rights over their original works of authorship. These works can include books, musical recordings, photographs, drawings, letters, memos, email, Web pages, and any other expressions of ideas that are, as the law puts it, "fixed in a tangible medium." Copyright holders have the exclusive right to reproduce, distribute, perform, display, prepare derivative works, and publish their copyrighted material. Copyright holders also have the right to grant a license (essentially, to give permission) for others to use the material. In the United States, works created after 1978 are automatically copyrighted as soon as the material is fixed; that is, the moment the idea is recorded, written down, turned into an electronic document, or otherwise.

Definition of copyright

The purpose of copyright is to balance the reward for the intellectual labor of the author with the importance of making information freely available to the public. If all information were covered by copyright protection forever and ever, there would be no source of public information that authors and artists could use to create new ideas. But if all information were completely free of copyright protection, creators might not have any incentive to write songs or books, for example. This is why in the United States copyright is not forever, just for a limited time. This is also why there are some conditions under which you do not need to request copyright permission.

Works in the Public Domain

Many images, sounds, books, and other materials fall into what is called the *public domain*. In these cases, you do not need to request permission for use. Public domain works include works that were published in the United States ninety-five years before the current year. Most government documents are also public domain, and most commonplace information, such as height and weight charts or metric conversion tables, are also public domain. Many authors and artists publish work and expressly state that the work is in the public domain. Look on the Web site or document for more information. (If you are unsure about the work's status, you may want to request permission.)

Fair Use

Fair use is a legal doctrine that allows the use of some copyrighted material, under some circumstances, without permission. Congress established fair use as a way to balance creators' rights with public access. Fair use states that under certain conditions, it is legal to use copyrighted works without permission so long as the source is clearly identified. Courts tend to ask four questions about whether a use is considered fair:

- is the material educational or commercial? (educational use is favored)
- has the material been previously published? (use of published works is favored)
- how much of the material is being used? (less is favored)
- how will your use of the material affect the market value of the original? (if your use does not have an impact on the value of the original, this is favored)

Classroom and student use is almost always considered fair. Most use of small snippets of text, cited in a student or academic paper, is also considered fair use. Even commercial documents, such as annual reports, routinely cite information from publications such as the newspaper or research papers. These uses are all considered fair. However, if you are a consultant or employee of a for-profit organization and you wish to use a large amount of material or visuals such as photographs or graphics, fair use may not apply. In these cases, it is best to seek permission.

The Difference Between Plagiarism and Copyright Infringement

If you receive permission to use someone else's material or if your use qualifies as fair use, you are probably covered when it comes to copyright. Most of the writing you will do for this class and in college generally will be situations where your use of outside material is considered educational and thus fair. But you still must document your source by providing an appropriate in-text citation as well as a reference; otherwise, you run the risk of plagiarism. Always provide a citation or caption, even if you didn't need copyright permission. Whether you use a direct quotation or a paraphrase, always include the source.

In our digital age, there is a tension between the openness of the Internet, which allows people to access music, text, and images easily on the one hand, and the restrictions on such items that copyright calls for on the other. It is easy to cut and paste material online but also easy to forget that this material is probably covered by copyright protection.

Copyright in a digital age

B) A Brief Handbook

The last page of this book displays editing and revision symbols and corresponding page references. When your instructor marks a symbol on your paper, turn to the appropriate section here or in Chapters 6 and 7 for explanations, examples, and exercises. Chapter 6, which covers matters of structure, includes the following topics keyed to the editing and revision symbols:

- TS: the topic sentence (page 92)
- UN: paragraph unity (page 93)
- COH: paragraph coherence (page 94)

Chapter 7, which discusses matters of style, includes the following additional topics, also keyed to the editing and revision symbols:

- REF: avoiding ambiguous pronoun references (page 104)
- MOD: avoiding ambiguous modifiers (page 105)
- AV: using active voice whenever possible (page 105)
- PV: using passive voice selectively (page 106)
- NOM: avoiding nominalizations (page 107)
- ST MOD: unstacking modifying nouns (page 108)
- JARG: avoiding unnecessary jargon (page 109)
- W: avoiding wordiness (page 109)
- RED and REP: eliminating redundancy and repetition (page 111)
- COMB: combining related ideas (page 112)
- VAR: varying sentence construction and length (page 112)
- PAR: using parallel structure (page 113)
- TONE: adjusting your tone (page 114)
- SEXIST and BIAS: avoiding sexist and biased language (page 115).

GRAMMAR

The following common grammatical errors are easy to repair.

Sentence Fragments

frag

Watch the **Video** on Sentence Fragments at mytechcommlab

A sentence fragment is a grammatically incomplete sentence. A grammatically complete sentence consists of at least one subject-verb combination and expresses a complete thought. It might include more than one subject-verb combination, and it might include other words or phrases as well.

> This book summarizes recent criminal psychology research.
> The smudge tool creates soft effects.
> My dog, Zorro, ate my paper.

Complete sentences

Even though the following example contains a subject-verb combination, it doesn't express a complete thought:

> Although the report was not yet complete.

Sentence fragment

Watch out for *although* and other words like it, including *because, if, as, while, since, when,* and *unless.* These are called subordinating conjunctions. Any of these words combined with a subject-verb combination produces a subordinate clause (a clause that expresses an incomplete idea). Subordinating conjunctions leave readers waiting for something to complete the thought. The thought can be completed only if another subject-verb combination that does express a complete idea is added:

> Although the report was not yet complete, I began editing.

Additional subject-verb completes the thought

This next group of words is a fragment because it contains no verb:

> DesignPro, a brand-new desktop publishing program.

Fragment with no verb

Simply add a verb to turn the fragment into a complete sentence:

> DesignPro, a brand-new desktop publishing program, will be available soon.
> or
> DesignPro is a brand-new desktop publishing program.

Addition of verb corrects fragment

Avoid sentences that seem to contain a subject-verb combination but actually do not. Gerunds (verb forms ending in *-ing* that act like nouns, such as *being* in the first sentence given) and participles (verb forms ending in *-ing* that act like adjectives, such as *barking* in the second sentence given) look like verbs but actually are not:

Gerund and participle fragments

> Dale being a document design expert
>
> The barking dog

These fragments can be turned into complete sentences by substituting a verb for the gerund, or adding a verb:

Verb substitution or new verb corrects fragment

> Dale is a document design expert.
>
> The barking dog finally stopped.

Run-On Sentences

ro

A run-on sentence contains too many grammatically complete sentences joined together as one:

Run-on sentence

> For emergencies, we dial 911 for other questions, we dial 088.

Watch the Video on Run-On Sentences at mytechcommlab

This sentence can be repaired in various ways. One possibility is to divide it into two sentences:

Division into two sentences corrects run-on

> For emergencies, we dial 911. For other questions, we dial 088.

Another possibility is to use a semicolon to join the two parts of the sentence. This option indicates a break that is not quite as strong as the period, and therefore signals to the reader that the two items are closely related:

Added semicolon corrects run-on

> For emergencies, we dial 911; for other questions, we dial 088.

Another possibility is to add a comma followed by a coordinating conjunction (*for, and, nor, but, or, yet, so*):

Coordinating conjunction corrects run-on

> For emergencies, we dial 911, but for other questions, we dial 088.

Comma Splices

cs

In a comma splice, two complete ideas (independent clauses) that should be *separated* by a period or a semicolon are incorrectly *joined* by a comma:

Comma splice

> Sarah did a great job, she was promoted.

There are a number of options for correcting comma splices. One option is to divide the splice into two separate sentences:

> | Sarah did a great job. She was promoted.

Watch the Video on Comma Splices at **mytechcommlab**

Division into two sentences corrects comma splice

Another option is to use a semicolon to show a relationship between the two items:

> | Sarah did a great job; she was promoted.

Semicolon corrects comma splice

A third option is to use a semicolon with a conjunctive adverb (an adverb, ending in -*ly*, that shows a relationship between the items, such as *consequently*):

> | Sarah did a great job; consequently, she was promoted.

Semicolon with conjunctive adverb corrects comma splice

A fourth option is to use a coordinating conjunction. There are seven such conjunctions: *for, and, nor, but, or, yet, so*—you can remember them using the acronym "fanboys." Coordinating conjunctions create an equal relationship between the items:

> | Sarah did a great job and was promoted.

Coordinating conjunction corrects comma splice

Finally, as on page 463, you can use a subordinating conjunction (a conjunction that creates an unequal relationship between the items):

> | Because Sarah did a great job, she was promoted.

Subordinating conjunction corrects comma splice

Faulty Agreement—Subject and Verb

agr sv

The subject of a sentence must agree in number with the verb. But when subject and verb are separated by other words, we sometimes lose track of the subject-verb relationship:

Watch the Video on Subject-Verb Agreement at **mytechcommlab**

> | The lion's share of diesels are sold in Europe.

Faulty subject-verb agreement

To correct the error, make the verb agree with its subject (*share*), not with a word that comes between the subject and the verb (in this case, the plural noun *diesels*):

> | The lion's share of diesels is sold in Europe.

Correct subject-verb agreement

Some cases are trickier than others. For example, treat compound subjects connected by *and* as plural:

> | Terry and Julie enjoy collaborating on writing projects.

Compound subject takes plural verb

In addition, with compound subjects connected by *or* or *nor*, the verb is singular if both subjects are singular and plural if both subjects are plural. If one subject is singular and one is plural, the verb agrees with the one closer to the verb. In the following example, the verb agrees with the closer subject, the plural *students*:

Verb agrees with closer subject in compound subject

> | Neither the professor nor the students were able to see what was going on.

Also, treat most indefinite pronouns (*anybody, each, everybody*, etc.) as singular subjects:

Indefinite pronoun agrees with singular verb

> | Almost everybody who registered for the class was there on the first day.

Additionally, treat collective subjects (*team, family, group, committee*, etc.) as singular unless the meaning is clearly plural. Both of the following sentences are correct. In the first sentence, the *group* is understood as a singular subject (the group is a single entity) and agrees with the singular verb *respects*, whereas in the second sentence, the *board* is understood as plural (as indicated by the plural word *authors*) and agrees with the plural verb *are*:

Collective subjects agree with singular or plural verbs depending on meaning

> | The group respects its leader.
> | The editorial board are all published authors.

Faulty Agreement—Pronoun and Referent

agr p

Watch the Video on Pronoun-Referent Agreement at mytechcommlab

A pronoun must refer to a specific noun (its *referent* or *antecedent*), with which it must agree in gender and number. Faulty pronoun-referent agreement is easy to spot when the gender and number clearly don't match (e.g., "He should proceed at their own pace" should obviously read "He should proceed at his own pace"). However, when an indefinite pronoun such as *each, everyone, anybody, someone*, or *none* is the referent, the pronoun is always singular, as in the following examples:

Indefinite referents agree with singular pronouns

> | Everybody should proceed at his or her own pace.
> | None of the candidates described her career plans in detail.

Faulty Coordination and Subordination

coord   *sub*

Give equal emphasis to ideas of equal importance by joining them with one of the coordinating conjunctions: *for, and, nor, but, or, yet*, and *so* (you can memorize these by using the acronym "fanboys"). Likewise, show an unequal relationship between ideas (one idea dependent upon the other) by using a subordinating conjunction: *because, whereas, if, although, until*, and so on.

Coordination may be faulty when the ideas connected by a coordinating conjunction are not of equal importance or are not sensibly connected:

| I was late for work and wrecked my car.

Faulty coordination

To correct the problem, use a subordinating conjunction instead. Or express cause and effect or opinion in some other way, as in the following two examples:

| Because I was late for work, I backed out of my driveway too
| quickly into oncoming traffic, wrecking my car.

Corrected versions

or

| Late for work, I backed out of my driveway too quickly into oncoming
| traffic, wrecking my car.

Avoid subordinating ideas that should be of equal importance or that don't represent a genuine cause and effect relationship:

| Although John gets up early, he is never late for work.

Faulty subordination

To correct the problem and show a balanced relationship between the ideas, use a coordinating conjunction instead:

| John gets up early and is never late for work.

Corrected version

Avoid both excessive coordination and excessive subordination in complex sentences. Following are two versions of the same sentence, the first with excessive coordination and the second with excessive subordination:

| The climax in jogging comes after a few miles and I can no longer feel
| stride after stride and it seems as if I am floating and jogging becomes
| almost a reflex and my arms and legs continue to move and my mind
| no longer has control over my actions.

Excessive coordination

| The climax in jogging comes when after a few miles I can no longer feel
| stride after stride, yet it seems as if I am floating, because jogging
| becomes almost a reflex since my arms and legs continue to move
| while my mind no longer has control over my actions.

Excessive subordination

To repair either instance, blend coordination and subordination, deciding exactly which ideas should be balanced and which of the subordinated ideas is most important, as in the following revision. Here, the writer has decided to emphasize *jogging almost by reflex* as the most important idea (using the subordinating conjunction *when*) and to coordinate the four equally important sensations involved (*no longer able to feel every stride, nearly floating, my arms and legs still moving,* and *my mind no longer controlling my actions*) using commas and the coordinating conjunction *and.*

Balance of coordination and subordination

| The climax in jogging comes after a few miles, when I am jogging almost by reflex, no longer able to feel every stride, nearly floating, my arms and legs still moving, and my mind no longer controlling my actions.

Faulty Pronoun Case

Watch the Video on Pronoun Case at **mytechcommlab**

A pronoun's case (nominative, objective, or possessive) is determined by its role in the sentence: as subject, object, or indicator of possession.

If the pronoun serves as the subject of a sentence (*I, we, you, she, he, it, they, who*), or follows a version of the linking verb *to be,* its case is *nominative:*

Nominative pronoun case

| She completed her graduate program in record time.
| Who broke the chair?
| The chemist who perfected this distillation process is he.

If the pronoun serves as the object of a verb or a preposition (*me, us, you, her, him, it, them, whom*), its case is *objective:*

Objective pronoun case

| The employees gave her a parting gift.
| To whom do you wish to complain?

If a pronoun indicates possession (*my, mine, our, ours, your, yours, his, her, hers, its, their, whose*), its case is *possessive:*

Possessive pronoun case

| The brown briefcase is mine.
| Whose opinion do you value most?

The following sentences are incorrect and are followed by the corrected versions in parenthesis.

Faulty pronoun case

| Whom is responsible to who? (Who is responsible to whom?)
| The debate was between Marsha and I. (The debate was between Marsha and me.)

PUNCTUATION

Punctuation marks are like road signs and traffic signals. They govern reading speed and provide clues for navigation through a network of ideas. The three marks of end punctuation—period, question mark, and exclamation point—work like a red traffic light by signaling a complete stop.

Period

A period ends a declarative sentence.

| I see that you've all completed the essay.

Period ends
declarative
statement

It is also used as the final mark in some abbreviations, such as "Dr." and "Inc." and for certain numerical purposes ($18.43 and 26.2%).

Question Mark

A question mark follows a direct question:

| Have you all completed the essay?

?/

Question mark ends
direct question

A question mark should not be used to end an indirect question:

| Professor Grim asked if all students had completed the essay?
| Professor Grim asked if all students had completed the essay.

Incorrect

Period ends indirect
question

Exclamation Point

Use an exclamation point only when expression of strong feeling is appropriate:

| I can't believe you finished the essay so fast!

!/

Exclamation point
provides emphasis

Semicolon

Like a blinking red traffic light at an intersection, a semicolon signals a brief but definite stop. Semicolons have several uses.

A semicolon can be used to separate independent clauses (logically complete ideas) whose contents are closely related and are not already connected by a comma and a coordinating conjunction (*and, or, but*, etc.):

;/

◉ **Watch** the **Video**
on the Semicolon
at **mytechcommlab**

| The project was finally completed; we had done a good
| week's work.

Semicolon separates
independent clauses

To Accompany Conjunctive Adverbs. A semicolon must accompany a conjunctive adverb such as *besides, otherwise, still, however, furthermore, moreover, consequently, therefore, on the other hand, in contrast,* or *in fact*:

| The job is filled; however, we will keep your résumé on file.
| Your background is impressive; in fact, it is the best among our
| applicants.

Semicolon
accompanies
conjunctive adverbs

To Separate Items in a Series.

When items in a series contain internal commas, semicolons provide clear separation between items.

Semicolon separates
items in a series

> I am applying for summer jobs in Santa Fe, New Mexico; Albany, New York; Montgomery, Alabama; and Moscow, Idaho.

Colon

Like a flare in the road, a colon signals you to stop and then proceed, paying attention to the situation ahead. Colons have several uses.

To Signal a Follow-up Explanation.

Use a colon when a complete introductory statement requires a follow-up explanation:

Colon signals a
follow-up explanation

> She is an ideal colleague: honest, reliable, and competent.

Do not use a colon if the introductory statement is incomplete:

Incorrect

> My plans include: finishing college, traveling for two years, and settling down in Santa Fe.

To Replace a Semicolon.

A colon can replace a semicolon between two related, complete statements when the second one explains or amplifies the first:

Colon replaces a
semicolon

> Pam's reason for accepting the lowest-paying job offer was simple: she had always wanted to live in the Northwest.

To Introduce a Quotation.

Colons can introduce quotations:

Colon introduces a
quotation

> The supervisor's message was clear enough: "You're fired."

To Follow Salutations.

Colons follow salutations in formal correspondence (e.g., Dear Ms. Jones:).

Comma

The comma is the most frequently used—and abused—punctuation mark. It works like a blinking yellow light, for which you slow down briefly without stopping. Never use a comma to signal a *break* between independent ideas, only a brief slow down. Use commas only in the following situations.

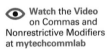 Watch the Video
on Commas and
Nonrestrictive Modifiers
at mytechcommlab

To Pause Between Complete Ideas.

In a compound sentence in which a coordinating conjunction (*and, or, nor, for, but*) connects equal (independent) statements, a comma usually precedes the conjunction.

Comma to pause
between complete
ideas

> This is an excellent course, but the work is difficult.

To Pause Between an Incomplete and a Complete Idea.

A comma is usually placed between a complete and an incomplete statement in a complex sentence when the incomplete statement comes first.

> | Because he is a fat cat, Jack diets often.

Comma between an incomplete and complete idea

When the order is reversed (complete statement followed by an incomplete one), the comma is usually omitted:

> | Jack diets often because he is a fat cat.

No comma needed

To Separate Items (Words, Phrases, or Clauses) in a Series.

Use commas after items in a series, including the next-to-last item:

> Helen, Joe, Marsha, and John are joining us on the term project.
> The new employee complained that the hours were long, the pay was low, the work was boring, and the supervisor was paranoid.

Comma separates items in a series

Use no commas if *or* or *and* appears between all items in a series:

> | She is willing to study in San Francisco or Seattle or even in Anchorage.

No commas needed if *or* or *and* appears between all items

To Set Off Introductory Phrases.

Introductory phrases include infinitive phrases (*to* plus a simple form of the verb), prepositional phrases (beginning with *at, of, in, on,* etc.), participial phrases (beginning with an *-ing* or *-ed* form of a verb), and interjections (emotional words that have no connection with the rest of the sentence). These phrases are set off from the remainder of the sentence by a comma:

> To be or not to be, that is the question. (infinitive phrase)
> In the event of an emergency, use the fire exit. (prepositional phrase)
> Being an old cat, Jack was slow at catching mice. (participial phrase)
> Oh, is that the verdict? (interjection)

Commas to set off introductory phrases

To Set Off Nonrestrictive Phrases and Clauses.

A *restrictive* phrase or clause modifies or defines the subject in such a way that deleting the modifier would change the meaning of the sentence. In the following sentence, "who have work experience" *restricts* the subject by limiting the category from all students to just those with work experience. Because this phrase is essential to the sentence's meaning, it is *not* set off by commas:

Restrictive phrase (no comma)

> | All students who have work experience will receive preference.

A *nonrestrictive* phrase or clause could be deleted without changing the sentence's meaning ("Our new manager is highly competent") and *is* therefore set off by commas:

Nonrestrictive phrase (use comma)

> Our new manager, who has only six weeks' experience, is highly competent.

To Set Off Parenthetical Elements. Elements that interrupt the flow of a sentence (such as *of course, as a result, as I recall,* and *however*) are considered parenthetical and are enclosed by commas. These items may denote emphasis, afterthought, or clarification.

Commas to set off parenthetical elements

> This deluxe model, of course, is more expensive. (emphasis)
>
> Your essay, by the way, was excellent. (afterthought)
>
> The loss of my job was, in a way, a blessing. (clarification)

A direct address also interrupts a sentence and is set off by commas:

Commas to set off direct address

> Listen, my children, and you shall hear my story.

A parenthetical element at the beginning or the end of a sentence is also set off by a comma:

Commas to set off parenthetical elements at beginning and end

> Naturally, we will expect a full guarantee.
>
> You've done a good job, I think.

To Set Off Quoted Material. Quoted items within a sentence are set off by commas:

Comma to set off quoted material

> The customer said, "I'll take it," as soon as he laid eyes on our new model.

To Set Off Appositives. An *appositive*, a word or words explaining a noun and placed immediately after it, is set off by commas when the appositive is nonrestrictive:

Comma to set off appositives

> Martha Jones, our new president, is overhauling all personnel policies.
>
> Alpha waves, the most prominent of the brain waves, are typically recorded in a waking subject whose eyes are closed.

Other Uses. Commas are used to set off the day of the month from the year in a date (May 10, 1989), to set off numbers in three-digit intervals (6,463,657), to separate city and state in an address (Albany, Iowa), to set off parts of an address in a sentence (J. B. Smith, 18 Sea Street, Albany, Iowa, 51642), to set off day and year in a sentence (June 15, 2009, is my graduation date), and to set off degrees and titles from proper names (Roger P. Cayer, M.D. or Gordon Browne Jr.).

Apostrophe

Apostrophes indicate the possessive, a contraction, and the plural of numbers, letters, and figures.

ap/

Watch the Video
on the Apostrophe
at **mytechcommlab**

To Indicate the Possessive. At the end of a singular word, or of a plural word that does not end in -*s*, add an apostrophe plus -*s* to indicate the possessive. Single-syllable nouns that end in -*s* take the apostrophe before an added -*s*:

> The people's candidate won.
> I borrowed Chris's book.

Apostrophe to
indicate possessives

For words that already end in -*s* and have more than one syllable, add an -*s* after the add apostrophe:

> Aristophanes's death

Do not use an apostrophe to indicate the possessive form of either singular or plural pronouns:

> The book was hers.
> Ours is the best school in the county.

At the end of a plural word that ends in -*s*, add an apostrophe only.

> the cows' water supply
> the Jacksons' wine cellar

At the end of a compound noun, add an apostrophe plus -*s*:

> my father-in-law's false teeth

At the end of the last word in nouns of joint possession, add an apostrophe plus -*s* if both own one item:

> Joe and Sam's lakefront cottage

Add an apostrophe plus -*s* to both nouns if each owns specific items:

> Joe's and Sam's passports

cont

To Indicate a Contraction. An apostrophe shows that you have omitted one or more letters in a phrase that is usually a combination of a pronoun and a verb:

Apostrophes to show
contractions

> I'm
>
> they're
>
> you'd

Be careful with faulty contractions: For example, *they're* (short for "they are" and often confused with the possessive *their* and the adverb *there*); *it's* (short for "it is" and often confused with the possessive *its*); *who's* (short for "who is" and often confused with the possessive *whose*); and *you're* (short for "you are" and often confused with the possessive *your*). See Table B.1 (pages 480–482) for further examples.

To Indicate the Plurals of Numbers, Letters, and Figures. For example:

Apostrophes to
pluralize numbers,
letters, and figures

> The *6's* on this new printer look like smudged *G's*, *9's* are illegible, and the *%'s* are unclear.

 " " /

Quotation Marks

Quotation marks have a variety of uses:

To Set Off the Exact Words Borrowed from Another Speaker or Writer.
The period or comma at the end is placed within the quotation marks:

Quotation marks to
set off a speaker's
exact words

> "Hurry up," Jack whispered.
>
> Jack told Felicia, "I'm depressed."

A colon or semicolon is always placed outside quotation marks:

> Our student handbook clearly defines "core requirements"; however, it does not list all the courses that fulfill the requirements.

When a question mark or exclamation point is part of a quotation, it belongs within the quotation marks, replacing the comma or period.

> "Help!" he screamed.
>
> Marsha asked John, "Can't we agree about anything?"

But if the question mark or exclamation point pertains to the attitude of the person quoting instead of the person being quoted, it is placed outside the quotation mark:

> Why did Boris wink and whisper, "It's a big secret"?

To Indicate Titles. Use quotation marks around titles of articles, paintings, book chapters, and poems (but titles of books, journals, or newspapers should be underlined or italicized):

> The enclosed article, "The Job Market for College Graduates," should provide some helpful insights.

Quotation marks to indicate titles

To Indicate Irony. Finally, use quotation marks (with restraint) to indicate irony.

> She is some "friend"!

Quotation marks to indicate irony

Ellipses

. . . /

Three dots . . . indicate that you have omitted material from a quotation. If the omitted words come at the end of the original sentence, a fourth dot indicates the period.

> According to Beulah Montgomery, paper memorandums ". . . are now being . . . replaced with email correspondence in most workplace situations. . . ."

Ellipses to indicate omitted material from a quotation

Brackets

[ ] /

Brackets are used within quotations to set off material that was not in the original quotation but is needed for clarification:

> "She [Amy] was the outstanding candidate for the scholarship."
> "It was in early spring [April 2, to be exact] that the tornado hit."

Brackets to indicate material added to quotations

Use *sic* (Latin for "thus," or "so") in brackets when quoting an error from the original source:

> The assistant's comment was clear: "He don't [sic] want any."

Brackets to indicate an error in a quotation

Italics

ital

Use italics or underlining for titles of books, periodicals, films, newspapers, and plays; for the names of ships; and for foreign words or technical terms. Also, you may use italics *sparingly* for special emphasis.

> The *Oxford English Dictionary* is a handy reference tool.
> My only advice is *caveat emptor*.
> *Bacillus anthracis* is a highly virulent organism.
> Do *not* inhale these fumes under any circumstances!

Various uses of italics

Parentheses

Material between parentheses, like all other parenthetical material discussed previously can be deleted without harming the logical and grammatical structure of the sentence. Use parentheses to enclose material that defines or explains the statement that precedes it:

Parentheses to define or explain preceding material

> An anaerobic (airless) environment must be maintained for the cultivation of this organism.
>
> The cost of running our college has increased by 15 percent in one year (see Appendix A for full cost breakdown).

Dashes

Dashes can be effective to set off parenthetical material if, like parentheses, they are not overused. Parentheses deemphasize the enclosed material, whereas dashes emphasize it:

Dashes to set off and emphasize material

> Have a good vacation—but watch out for sandfleas.
>
> Mary—a true friend—spent hours helping me rehearse.

On most word processing programs, a dash is created by two hyphens, which the software will typically convert to a dash.

MECHANICS

The mechanical aspects of writing a document include abbreviation, hyphenation, capitalization, use of numbers, and spelling. (Keep in mind that not all of these rules are hard and fast; some may depend on style guides used in your field.)

Abbreviation

The following should *always* be abbreviated:

Always abbreviate

- Titles such as *Ms.*, *Mr.*, *Dr.*, and *Jr.*, when they are used before or after a proper name.
- Specific time designations (400 B.C.E., 5:15 A.M.).

The following should *never* be abbreviated:

Never abbreviate

- Military, religious, academic, or political titles (*Reverend, President*).
- Nonspecific time designations ("Sarah arrived early in the morning"—not "early in the A.M.").

Avoid abbreviations whose meanings might not be clear to all readers. Units of measurement can be abbreviated if they appear frequently in your document. However, a unit of measurement should be spelled out the first time it is used. Avoid abbreviations in visual aids unless saving space is absolutely necessary.

Hyphenation

-/

Hyphens divide words at line breaks, and join two or more words used as a single adjective if they precede the noun (but not if they follow it):

> Com-puter (at a line break)
> An all-too-human error (but "The error was all too human")

Correct use
of hyphens

Other commonly hyphenated words include the following:

- Most words that begin with the prefix *self-* (*self-reliance*, *self-discipline*—see your dictionary for exceptions).

Other uses
of hyphens

- Combinations that might be ambiguous (*re-creation* versus *recreation*).

- Words that begin with *ex* when *ex* means "past" (*ex-faculty member* but *excommunicate*).

- All fractions, along with ratios that are used as adjectives and that precede the noun, and compound numbers from twenty-one through ninety-nine (*a two-thirds majority*, *thirty-eight windows*).

Capitalization

cap

Use capitalization in the following situations:

- The first words of all sentences ("This is a good idea.")

Uses of capitalization

- Titles of people if the title precedes the person's name, but not after (Senator Barbara Boxer but Barbara Boxer, U.S. senator)

Watch the Video
on Capitalization
at mytechcommlab

- Titles of books, films, magazines, newspapers, operas, and other longer works. In addition to capitalizing the first word, also capitalize all other words within the title (*A Long Day's Journey into Night*) except articles, short prepositions, and coordinating conjunctions (*and, but, for, or, nor, yet*).

- Parts of a longer work (Chapter 25, Opus 23)

- Languages (French, Urdu)

- Days of the week (Saturday)

- Months (November)

- Holidays (Thanksgiving)

- Names of organizations or groups (World Health Organization)
- Races and nationalities (Asian American, Australian)
- Historical events (War of 1812)
- Important documents (Declaration of Independence)
- Names of structures or vehicles (Empire State Building, the *Queen Mary*)
- Adjectives derived from proper nouns (Chaucerian English).
- Words such as *street, road, corporation, university,* and *college* only when they accompany a proper noun (High Street, Rand Corporation, Stanford University).
- The words *north, south, east,* and *west* when they denote specific regions (*the South, the Northwest*) but not when they are simply directions (*turn east at the light*).

Do not capitalize the seasons (*spring, winter*) or general groups (*the younger generation, the leisure class*).

num   Numbers and Numerals

Numbers expressed in one or two words can be written out or written as numerals. Use numerals to express larger numbers, decimals, fractions, precise technical figures, or any other exact measurements:

Uses of numerals

> 543
>
> 2,800,357
>
> 3.25
>
> 15 pounds of pressure
>
> 50 kilowatts
>
> 4,000 rpm

Use numerals for dates, census figures, addresses, page numbers, exact units of measurement, percentages, times with A.M. or P.M. designations, and monetary and mileage figures.

Additional uses
of numerals

> page 14
>
> 1:15 P.M.
>
> 18.4 pounds
>
> 9 feet
>
> 12 gallons
>
> $15

Do not begin a sentence with a numeral. If the figure needs more than two words, revise your word order:

> Six hundred students applied for the 102 available jobs.
> The 102 available jobs attracted 600 applicants.

Uses of numbers in sentences

Do not use numerals to express approximate figures, time not designated as A.M. or P.M., or streets named by numbers less than 100:

> About seven hundred fifty
> Four fifteen
> 108 East Forty-Second Street

When not to use numerals

In contracts and other documents in which precision is vital, a number can be stated both in numerals and in words:

> The tenant agrees to pay a rental fee of eight hundred and seventy-five dollars ($875.00) monthly.

Spelling

sp

Always use the spell-check function in your word-processing software. However, don't rely on it exclusively. Take the time to use a dictionary for all writing assignments. If you are a poor speller, ask someone else to proofread every document before you present the final version.

 Watch the **Video** on Spelling and Grammar Checkers at **mytechcommlab**

USAGE

ww

Be aware of the pairs of words (and sometimes groups of three words) that are often confused. Refer to Table B.1 for a list of the most commonly confused words.

TRANSITIONS

trans

You can choose from three techniques to achieve smooth transitions within and between paragraphs.

Use Transitional Expressions

Use words such as *again, furthermore, in addition, meanwhile, however, also, although, for example, specifically, in particular, as a result, in other words, certainly, accordingly, because,* and *therefore*. Such words serve as bridges between ideas.

Transitional expressions

(*Text continues on page 482.*)

TABLE B.1   Commonly confused words

Similar Words	Used Correctly in a Sentence
Accept means "to receive willingly."	She *accepted* his business proposal.
Except means "otherwise than."	They all agreed, *except* Bob.
Affect means "to have an influence on."	Meditation *affects* concentration in a positive way.
Affect can also mean "to pretend."	Boris likes to *affect* a French accent.
Effect used as a noun means "a result."	Meditation has a positive *effect* on concentration.
Effect used as a verb means "to make happen" or "to bring about."	Meditation can *effect* an improvement in concentration.
Already means "before this time."	Our new laptops are *already* sold out.
All ready means "prepared."	We are *all ready* for the summer tourist season.
Among refers to three or more.	The prize was divided *among* the four winners.
Between refers to two.	The prize was divided *between* the two winners.
Cite means "to document."	You must always *cite* your sources in research.
Sight means "vision."	Margarita seems to have the gift of second *sight.*
Site means "a location."	Have the surveyors inspected the *site* yet?
Continual means "repeated at intervals."	Our lower field floods *continually* during the rainy season.
Continuous means "without interruption."	His headache has been *continuous* for three days.
Council means "a body of elected people."	I plan to run for student *council.*
Counsel means "to offer advice."	Because you have experience, I suggest you *counsel* Jim on the project as it moves along.
Differ from refers to unlike things.	This plan *differs* greatly from our previous one.
Differ with means "to disagree."	Mary *differs with* John about the plan.

TABLE B.1 *(Continued)*

Similar Words	Used Correctly in a Sentence
Disinterested means "unbiased" or "impartial."	Good science calls for *disinterested* analysis of research findings.
Uninterested means "not caring."	Boris is *uninterested* in science.
Eminent means "famous" or "distinguished."	Dr. Ostroff, the *eminent* physicist, is lecturing today.
Imminent means "about to happen."	A nuclear meltdown seemed *imminent.*
Farther refers to physical distance (a measurable quantity).	The station is 20 miles *farther.*
Further refers to extent (not measurable).	*Further* discussion of this issue is vital.
Fewer refers to things that can be counted.	*Fewer* than fifty students responded to our survey.
Less refers to things that can't be counted.	This survey had *less* of a response than our previous one.
Imply means "to insinuate."	This report *implies* that a crime occurred.
Infer means "to reason from evidence."	From this report, we can *infer* that a crime occurred.
It's stands for "it is."	*It's* a good time for a department meeting.
Its stands for "belonging to it."	The cost of the project has exceeded *its* budget.
Lay means "to set something down."	Please *lay* the blueprints on the desk.
Lie means "to recline." It takes no direct object.	This patient needs to *lie* on his right side all night.
(Note that the past tense of *lie* is *lay.*)	The patient *lay* on his right side all night.
Precede means "to come before."	Audience analysis should *precede* a written report.
Proceed means "to go forward."	If you must wake the cobra, *proceed* carefully.
Principle is always a noun that means "basic rule or standard."	Ethical *principles* should govern all our communications.
Principal, used as a noun, means "the major person(s)."	All *principals* in this purchase must sign the contract.

(Continued)

TABLE B.1   Commonly confused words   (*Continued*)

Similar Words	Used Correctly in a Sentence
Principal, used as an adjective, means "leading."	Martha was the *principal* negotiator for this contract.
Stationary means "not moving."	The desk is *stationary*.
Stationery means "writing supplies."	The supply cabinet needs *stationery*.
Their means "belonging to them."	They all want to have *their* cake and eat it too.
There means "at that location."	The new copy machine is over *there*.
They're means "they are."	*They're* not the only ones who disagree.

(*Transitions, continued from page 479.*)

Repeat Key Words and Phrases

To help link ideas, repeat key words or phrases or rephrase them in different ways, as in this next paragraph (emphasis added):

Repeated key words and phrases

> Whales are among the most *intelligent* of all mammals. Scientists rank whale *intelligence* with that of higher primates because of *whales' sophisticated* group behavior. These *bright creatures* have been seen teaching and disciplining *their* young, helping *their* wounded comrades, engaging in elaborate courtship rituals, and playing in definite *gamelike patterns*. *They* are able to coordinate such *complex cognitive activities* through *their* highly effective communication system of sonar clicks and pings. Such remarkable social organization apparently stems from the *humanlike* devotion that *whales* seem to display toward one another.

The key word *intelligent* in the preceding topic statement reappears as *intelligence* in the second sentence. Synonyms describing intelligent behavior (*sophisticated, bright, humanlike*) reinforce and advance the main idea throughout.

Use Forecasting Statements

Forecasting statements tell your readers where you are going next:

Forecasting statements

> The next step is to further examine the costs of this plan.
>
> Of course, we can also consider other options.
>
> This plan should be reconsidered for several reasons.

If you encounter a situation in which you think you need a better transition but none of these methods seems appropriate, you may need to delete or move some information.

LISTS

Listed items can be presented in one of two ways: running in as part of the sentence (embedded lists) or displayed with each item on a new line (vertical lists).

Embedded Lists

An embedded list integrates a series of items into a sentence. To number an embedded list, use parentheses around the numerals and either commas or semicolons between the items, as in the following example:

> In order to complete express check-in for your outpatient surgery, you must (1) go to the registration office, (2) sign in and obtain your registration number, (3) receive and wear your red armband, and (4) give your check-in slip to the volunteer, who will escort you to your room.

Embedded list

Vertical Lists

Embedded lists are appropriate for listing only a few short items. Vertical lists are preferable for multiple items. If the items belong in a particular sequence, use numerals or letters; if the sequence of items is unimportant, use bullets.

There are a number of ways to introduce vertical lists. You can introduce a vertical list with a sentence that closes with "the following" or "as follows" and ends with a colon:

> All applicants for the design internship must submit the following:
> - Personal statement
> - Résumé
> - Three letters of reference
> - Portfolio

Vertical list using *following* and a colon

You can also introduce a vertical list with a sentence that closes with a noun and ends with a colon:

> All applicants for the design internship must submit four items:
> 1. Personal statement
> 2. Résumé
> 3. Three letters of reference
> 4. Portfolio

Vertical list using a noun and a colon

Finally, you can introduce a vertical list with a sentence that is grammatically incomplete without the list items:

Vertical list using grammatical incompleteness

To register as a new student:

1. Take the placement test at the Campus Test Center.
2. Attend a new student orientation.
3. Register for classes by Web or telephone.
4. Pay tuition and fees by the due date.

Do not use a colon with an introductory sentence that ends with a verb, a preposition, or an infinitive, as in the following incorrect examples:

Incorrect because the introductory sentence ends with a verb

All applicants for the design internship must submit:

• A personal statement
• A résumé
• Three letters of reference
• A portfolio

Incorrect because the introductory sentence ends with a preposition

All applicants for the design internship need to:

• Submit a personal statement and résumé
• Forward three letters of reference
• Provide a portfolio

Incorrect because the introductory sentence ends with an infinitive

All applicants for the design internship need to submit:

• A personal statement
• A résumé
• Three letters of reference
• A portfolio

If the sentence that introduces the list is followed by another sentence, use periods after both sentences. Do not use a colon to introduce the list:

Vertical list without a colon

The next step is to configure the following fields. Consult Chapter 3 for more information on each field.

• Serial port
• Baud rate
• Data bits
• Stop bits

Note that some of the preceding examples use a period after each list item and some do not. As a general rule, use a period after each list item if any of the items contains a complete sentence. Do not use a period if none of the list items contains a complete sentence. Also note that items included in a list should be grammatically parallel. For more on parallelism, see page 113.

WORKS CITED

Carliner, Saul. "Demonstrating Effectiveness and Value: A Process for Evaluating Technical Communication Products and Services." *Technical Communication* 44.3 (1997): 252–65. Print.

Coe, Marlana. *Human Factors for Technical Communicators.* New York: Wiley, 1996. Print.

Consumer Product Safety Commission. *Fact Sheet No. 65.* Washington, DC: GPO, 1989. Print.

Corbett, Edward P. J. *Classical Rhetoric for the Modern Student.* 3rd ed. New York: Oxford, 1990. Print.

Crosby, Olivia. *Employment Interviewing.* Washington, DC: U.S. Department of Labor, 2000. Print.

Daugherty, Shannon. "The Usability Evaluation: A Discount Approach to Usability Testing." *INTERCOM* Dec. 1997: 16–20. Print.

Fisher, Anne. "Truth and Consequences." *Fortune* 29 May 2000: 292. Print.

Gartaganis, Arthur. "Lasers." *Occupational Outlook Quarterly* (Winter 1984): 22–26. Print.

Gibaldi, Joseph, and Walter S. Achtert. *MLA Handbook for Writers of Research Papers.* 3rd ed. New York: Modern Language Assn., 1988. Print.

Girill, T. R. "Technical Communication and Law." *Technical Communication* 32.3 (1985): 37. Print.

Golen, Steven, et al. "How to Teach Ethics in a Basic Business Communications Class." *Journal of Business Communication* 22.1 (1985): 75–84. Print.

Greenberg, Ilan. "Selling News Short." *Brill's Content* Mar. 2000: 64–65. Print.

Hart, Geoff. "Accentuate the Negative: Obtaining Effective Reviews through Focused Questions." *Technical Communication* 44.1 (1997): 52–57. Print.

Hein, Robert G. "Culture and Communication." *Technical Communication* 38.1 (1991): 125–26. Print.

Hoft, Nancy L. *International Technical Communication: How to Export Information About High Technology.* New York: Wiley, 1995. Print.

Japikse, Catharina, "Lasagna in the Making." *EPA Journal* 20.3 (1990): 27. Print.

Kipnis, David, and Stuart Schmidt. "The Language of Persuasion." *Psychology Today* Apr. 1985: 40–46. Rpt. in *Understanding Persuasion.* 3rd ed. Ed. Raymond S. Ross. Englewood Cliffs: Prentice, 1990. Print.

Lavin, Michael R. *Business Information: How to Find it, How to Use It.* 2nd ed. Phoenix, AZ: Oryx, 1992. Print.

MacKenzie, Nancy. Unpublished review of John M. Lannon's *Technical Writing.* 5th ed. Boston: Little, 1991.

"Misconduct Scandal Shakes German Science." *Professional Ethics Report* [American Assoc. for the Advancement of Science] 3 (Summer 1997): 2. Print.

Office of Technology Assessment. *Harmful Non-Indigenous Species in the United States.* Washington, DC: GPO, 1993. Print.

"Performance Appraisal—Discrimination." *The Employee Problem Solver*. Ramsey, NJ: Alexander Hamilton Institute, 2000. Print.

Ross, Raymond S. *Understanding Persuasion*. 3rd ed. Englewood Cliffs: Prentice, 1990. Print.

Rubin, J. *Handbook of Usability Testing: How to Plan, Design, and Conduct Effective Tests*. New York:Wiley, 1994. Print.

Spencer, SueAnn. "Use Self-Help to Improve Document Usability." *Technical Communication* 43.1 (1996): 73–77. Print.

Stanton, Mike. "Fiber Optics." *Occupational Outlook Quarterly* (Winter 1984): 27–30. Print.

Vaughan, David K. "Abstracts and Summaries: Some Clarifying Distinctions." *Technical Writing Teacher* 18:2 (1991): 132–41. Print.

Victor, David A. *International Business Communication*. New York: Harper, 1992. Print.

Weymouth, L. C. "Establishing Quality Standards and Trade Regulations for Technical Writing in World Trade." *Technical Communication* 37.2 (1990): 143–47. Print.

Wojahn, Patricia G. "Computer-Mediated Communication: The Great Equalizer between Men and Women?" *Technical Communication* 41.4 (1994): 747–51. Print.

PHOTO CREDITS

INDEX

A Guide to the
CHECKLISTS

EDITING AND REVISION SYMBOLS

Symbol	Problem	page	Symbol	Problem	page
ab	wrong abbreviation	476	st mod	stacked modifying nouns	108
agr p	error in pronoun agreement	466	sub	faulty subordination	466
agr sv	error in subject-verb agreement	465	tone	inappropriate tone	114
av	active voice needed	105	trans	transition needed	479
bias	biased language	115	ts	faulty topic sentence	92
ca	wrong pronoun case	468	un	paragraph lacks unity	93
cap	capital letter needed	477	var	sentence variety needed	112
coh	paragraph lacks coherence	94	w	wordiness	109
comb	combine sentences	112	ww	wrong word	479
coord	faulty coordination	466	pct	faulty punctuation	468
cs	comma splice	464	. /	period	469
frag	sentence fragment	463	? /	question mark	469
jarg	needless jargon	109	! /	exclamation point	469
mod	misplaced modifier	105	; /	semicolon	469
nom	nominalization	107	: /	colon	470
num	faulty numbering	478	, /	comma	470
par	faulty parallelism	113	ap/	apostrophe	473
pv	passive voice needed	106	cont	contraction	474
red	redundant phrase	111	" " /	quotation marks	474
ref	faulty pronoun reference	104	. . . /	ellipses	475
rep	needless repetition	111	[ ] /	brackets	475
ro	run-on sentence	464	ital	italics	475
sexist	sexist usage	115	( ) /	parentheses	476
sp	misspelled word	479	– – /	dash	476
			– /	hyphen	477